Course on
Computer Concepts

COURSE ON COMPUTER CONCEPTS

STRICTLY AS PER NEW DOEACC SYLLABUS

RAMESH BANGIA
B.Sc., Dip. Comp. Sc. (IIT D)
Formerly: Incharge Computer Centre,
Hindustan Copper Limited, New Delhi
Ex. Managing Editor: Software Today

FIREWALL MEDIA
(An Imprint of Laxmi Publications Pvt. Ltd.)
BANGALORE • CHENNAI • COCHIN • GUWAHATI • HYDERABAD
JALANDHAR • KOLKATA • LUCKNOW • MUMBAI • RANCHI
NEW DELHI • BOSTON, USA

Published by :

FIREWALL MEDIA

(An Imprint of Laxmi Publications Pvt. Ltd.)
113, Golden House, Daryaganj,
New Delhi-110002

Phone : 011-43 53 25 00
Fax : 011-43 53 25 28

www.laxmipublications.com
info@laxmipublications.com

New Edition

OFFICES

✆ **Bangalore**	080-26 75 69 30	✆ **Chennai**	044-24 34 47 26
✆ **Cochin**	0484-237 70 04, 405 13 03	✆ **Guwahati**	0361-251 36 69, 254 38 81
✆ **Hyderabad**	040-24 65 23 33	✆ **Jalandhar**	0181-222 12 72
✆ **Kolkata**	033-22 27 43 84	✆ **Lucknow**	0522-220 99 16
✆ **Mumbai**	022-24 91 54 15, 24 92 78 69	✆ **Ranchi**	0651-220 44 64

FCO-3107-175-COURSE ON COMP CONCEPT-BAN C—

Typeset at : Kalyani Computer Services, New Delhi.

Printed at : Repro Knowledgecast Limited, Thane

Contents

Preface

The new syllabus of DOE's various levels of courses, popularly called O-level, A-level, B-level and C-level is out. This syllabus has been designed keeping in mind the various developments taking place around the world in the field of computers. While keeping in mind the level of students studying the various levels, the degree of difficulties of the syllabus have been very well designed. I hope that after the new syllabus the courses would be as popular as they were before.

There had been a long struggle between Training Institutes and Government Organizations, since these organizations would not recognize the degree/diploma given by them. Students passing out from these institutions were not given jobs based upon the said diplomas/degrees. Ultimately, the Government formed a society under the Department of Electronics, called DOEACC, which conducts tests and gives grades to the students irrespective of the institutes where they have studied. It is also possible to give the test without having any proper institutional studies. This is more or less on the terms of SAT and GRE conducted by USA. The only difference is that this is not online. There are fixed dates for the exams.

The course for this has been designed for students to appear in the exams at various levels. These levels are O-level, A-level, B-level, C-level. The most popular among these is the O-level, since it is the entry level. Once you have cleared the O-level, you are eligible for a government job. Each course has been divided into various modules. Various books are available for various modules. This book is also made for you to prepare for the O-level course.

This book has been written totally in accordance with the syllabus. Each chapter has been embedded with the screen shots for you to know what to expect on the screen, while running the application. Each chapter contains examples which can be attempted to supplement the reading. At the end of the chapter, there is a thorough revision of the text read. Not to mention of the questions provided in the beginning, both in the form of objective and subjective. The book also contains Sample papers which are based on the samples provided by DOEACC society. These would help you in preparing for the exams.

Author

SYLLABUS

COURSE ON COMPUTER CONCEPTS (CCC)

Syllabus Outline

S.No.	*Topic*	*Theory*	*Tutorials*	*Practical*
1.	Introduction to Computer	1	1	2
2.	Introduction to Windows	2	–	6
3.	Basic DOS Commands	2	–	4
4.	Elements of Word Processing	4	2	10
5.	Spreadsheet	4	2	10
6.	Computer Communication and Internet	4	–	5
7.	WWW and Web browsers	2	–	3
8.	E-mail	2	–	2
9.	Making Small Presentations	4	–	8
	Grand Total	25	5	50

DETAILED SYLLABUS

1. **Introduction to Computer**

What is computer: Characteristics of Computers, Basic Applications of Computer. Components of Computer System: Central Processing Unit (CPU), VDU, Keyboard and Mouse, Other Input/output Devices, Computer Memory, Concepts of Hardware and Software.

Classification of Computers.

Representation of Data/Information concepts of data processing: Definition of Information and Data, Basic Data Types, Storage of Data/Information as Files.

2. **Introduction to Windows**

What is an operating system and basics of Windows.

The User Interface: Using Mouse and Moving Icons on the screen, The My Computer Icon, The Recycle Bin, Status Bar, Start and Menu & Menu Selection, Running an Application, Windows Explorer Viewing of Files, Folders and Directories, Creating and Renaming of files and folders, Opening and closing of different Windows.

Windows Setting: Control Panels, Wall paper and Screen Savers, Setting the Date and Sound, Concept of menu using Help.

Advanced Windows: Using Right Button of the Mouse, Creating Shortcuts, Basics of Windows Setup, Notepad, Windows Accessories.

3. **Basic DOS Commands**

Comparision of DOS and Windows.

Switching between DOS and Windows.

Basic DOS Commands: File/Directory Manipulations, Copying of Files and Disks, Delete/Undelete, Formatting a Floppy.

4. **Elements of Word Processing**

Word Processing Basics: An Introduction to Word Processing, Opening Word Processing Package, The menu bar, Using the Help, Using the Icons below menu bar.

Opening Documents and Closing Documents: Opening Documents, Save and Save As, Page Setup, Printing of Documents, Display/Hiding of Paragraph Marks and Inter Word Space.

Moving Around in a Document: Scolling the Document, Scrolling by line/paragraph, Fast Scrolling and Moving Pages.

Using a Document/Help Wizard

Text Creation and Manipulation: Paragraph and Tab Setting, Text Selection, Cut, Copy, and Paste, Font and Size selection, Bold, Italics, and Underline, Alignment of Text: Center, Left, Right, and Justify.

Formatting the Text: Changing font, Size and Colour, Paragraph indenting, Bullets and Numbering, Use of Tab and Tab setting, Changing case

Handling Multiple Documents: Openng and closing of Multiple documents, Cut, Copy and Paste across the documents, Saving of Clipboards.

Table Manipulation: Concept of table: Rows, Columns, and Cells, Draw table, Changing cell Width and Height, Alignment of Text in Cell, Copying of Cell, Delete/ Insertion of Row and Coloumns, Borders for Table.

Printing: Printing, Print Preview, Print a Selected Page.

5. **Spreadsheet**

Elements of Electronics Spreadsheet: Application/usuage of Electronic Spreadsheet, Opening of Spreadsheet, The menu bar, Creation of cells and addressing of cells, Cell inputting.

Manipulation of cells: Enter text numbers and dates, Creation of tables, Cell Height and Widths, Copying of Cells.

Providing Formulas: Using basic functions/formalism a cell, Sum function, Average, Percentage, Other basic functions.

Spreadsheet for Small accountings: Maintaining invoices/budgets, Totalling of various transactions, Maintaining daily and monthly sales reports.

6. Computer Communication and Internet

Basic of Computer Networks: LAN, WAN.

Internet: Concept of Internet, Application of Internet.

Service on Internet: WWW and web-sites, Electronic mails, Communication on Internet.

7. WWW and Web Browsers

Web Browsing software: Internet Explorer, Netscape Communicator.

Surfing the Internet: Giving the URL address, Search, Moving around in a web-site, Printing or saving portion of web pages, Down loading.

Chatting on Internet.

8. E-mail

Basic of electronic mail: What is an Electronic mail, E-mail addressing, Mailbox: Inbox and outbox.

Using E-mails: Viewing an E-mail, Sending an E-mail, Saving mails, Sending same mail to various users.

Document handling: Sending soft copy as attachment, Enclose to e-mail, Sending a Portion of document as e-mail.

9. Making Small Presentations

Basics: Difference between presentation and document, Using PowerPoint, Opening a PowerPoint Presentation, Using Wizard for creating a presentation.

Creation of Presentation: Title, Text Creation, Fonts and Sizes, Bullets and indenting, Moving to Next Slide.

Prepration of Slides: Selection of type of Slides, Importing text from word documents, Moving to next Slide, The Slide Manager.

Providing aesthetics: Slide Designs, Background and Text colours, Making your own slide format, Footnotes and slide numbering.

Slide Manipulation and Slide Show.

Presenting of the Slides: Using the Slide Show, Printing the Slides and Handouts, Slide sorter, Title sorter.

Chapter 1 Introduction to Computers

1.1 WHAT IS COMPUTER?

The word computer has been derived from two words, mainly, Compute and Calculator. A computer is a device used for performing calculations automatically. Most of us use computers either at work or home. We can use computers for creating office documents or formating presentations and at home we can use it for checking our e-mails, playing games, or browse Internet for local news updates.

1.1.1 Characteristics of Computers

A computer is made of different parts which when looked at from any user angle will give a different definition. We should just remember that a computer:

1. Cannot think
2. It has vast capabilities of calculations like addition, subtraction, etc. and
3. It is totally under the control of the user.

So, we can say that a computer is a machine, totally at the command of the user, which can perform operations at a much higher speed than a human being.

There is nothing magical about a computer. It is actually a friendly machine which is totally at your command. Do you remember the story Aladdin and the Magic Lamp? Just like the Genie of the magic lamp, a computer will obey your command. If you make a mistake in giving commands to the computer, it will carry out these commands giving wrong results.

1.1.2 Basic Applications of Computer

There are lots of uses of computers. In fact, in our everyday life it is used in almost every step. Some of the places where it is used are listed below. I have listed them alphabetically.

Airlines booking: Now you can book your ticket for a flight leaving New York while sitting in Meerut. All the airlines are interconnected through computers. The same goes for Railways but it is restricted to individual countries only.

Banks: Computers in Banks have made it possible that you can get your account information while sitting at home or on your mobile phone. For this your bank must be an e-bank, which most of them are. ATMs are another computer applications of banks.

Business: For most of the companies, all the work relating to accounts is now done on computers, for accuracy and speed. You can even have your correspondence on it.

Cartoons: There are various programs available in computers which allow you to create animations. By learning about them you can become an expert animator. You may even make a movie of your own.

Cinema: Now a days most of the film editing is done by computers. You can add and delete film clips at a snap using computers. In fact, some movies are totally made using computers. Films like Toy Story are made using computers.

Defence: America has used the computers in defence for the fullest with pin pointing the position of enemy targets. Most of the missiles these days are computer controlled.

DTP: It has revolutionized how composing for printing used to be done. Now every book for printing is composed on computer since it is very easy to edit and read on screen.

Education: Computers can help in teaching too. In fact this book on computers was created using computers. Most of the schools now use computers for accounting, students record management, papers preparation and even results compilation.

Home: At home it has become an additional entertainment media. You can use it for playing games, watching movies, listening to songs, writing letters, creating your own database of friends, etc., the options are unlimited.

Library: Maintaining the records in library manually used to be a very cumbersome method. Computers have dramatically changed the way the cataloging is done in libraries.

Medicine: Lots of research in medicine is done using computers. Doctors now a days can see the complete inside of the human beings using the computers.

Space Technology: All the movements of the satellites are controlled using computers.

Weather: Using computers and satellites you can predict the weather for the next few days. In fact, the biggest computer in India is with the Meteorological Department of India, at New Delhi.

1.2 COMPONENTS OF COMPUTER SYSTEM

Though the first fully operational electronic computer was introduced to the world in 1946, however the historian assumes the starting of a computer age from 1951, when first commercial computer UNIVAC was introduced. The remarkable thing about the computer age is that so much has happened in so much short time. We have leapfrogged four generations of technology in about 50 years - a span of time whose events are within the memories of many people today. The first three computer generations are pinned to three technological developments:

1. vacuum tube
2. transistor and
3. integrated circuit

Each has drastically changed the nature and size of computers. We define the timing of each generation according to the beginning of commercial delivery of the hardware technology. Defining subsequent generations has become more complicated because the entire industry has become more complicated.

1.2.1 Central Processing Unit (CPU)

It is actually the main brain of the computer system. It is here that the whole processing takes place. It consists of 4 main units:

Primary Storage
Arithmetic Logic Unit
Control Unit
Output Unit

Let us read about them one by one.

1.2.1.1 Primary Storage Unit

This is main storage area, which is also called the main memory area. Its main functions are listed below:

1. Holding the data in its memory till it is required to be processed.
2. Holding the result of the processed data.
3. Holding program instructions which are required for processing.

1.2.1.2 Arithmetic Logic Unit

This is used for the most of the logical processing, for example, for calculations or comparisons. The arithmetic operations like, +, –, *, and / are performed here. The logical operations like, <, >, =, <=, >=, and <> are also performed here. In most of the arithmetical operations the result is in numerical form while in the case of logical operations the result can be YES/NO or TRUE/FALSE.

1.2.1.3 Control Unit

This unit controls the flow and manipulation of data and information. It also controls the flow of data from input devices to memory and from memory to output devices.

1.2.1.4 Output Unit

The output unit consists of the output devices attached to the computer. These devices take machine-coded output results from the processor and convert them into a form that can be understood by the user.

1.2.2 VDU, Keyboard and Mouse

1.2.2.1 Video Display Units

There would be no What You See Is What You Get (WYSIWYG) on PCs, if there were no monitors or displays on which to see what you get. The PC must produce outputs that can be handled by the senses of humans and so far, technology is limited to sight and sound. Given a choice, most of us still prefer sight over sound. You can accomplish a lot on a PC without sound, but not much would get done without the ability to see what you are working on.

The two general categories of PC visual presentation are the monitor and the display. A monitor has a CRT (cathode ray tube) and looks something like a traditional television set (without the controls, of course). On the other hand, a display is a flat-panel device that can be attached to a portable PC or hung on the wall. A monitor is largely desk or table-bound, but a display can get up and move about. A flat-panel display is really an adaptation of the monitor, but because it uses different technology, they are treated as two different components.

The PC Monitor: With personal computer technology advancing as fast as it is, it is hard to believe that any part of a PC could be considered an investment. However, the PC monitor is the only part of the personal computer that actually holds its value and has some durability. A good quality monitor will last for years through several generations of the PC systems.

Video Cards: In general, the video card processes the graphics data produced by software running on the PC and prepares it for use by the monitor for converting it from digital data to an analog signal. The video card also sends out the data needed by the monitor to refresh the image or renew it as it changes.

Video cards, graphics cards and accelerator cards are all names for the adapter card inside the PC that is responsible for generating the signals that tell the monitor what to display. The relationship between the video card and the monitor should be carefully matched. These two devices must be compatible in terms of the signal used to communicate to the monitor, the type of connector used to connect them together, the video display standards they support and their speed.

Dumb Terminal: It has been named as such since it is really dumb. It has no memory or processing unit, just a keyboard and the monitor. It takes everything else from the computer with which it is attached.

Smart Terminal: If you add microprocessor to dumb terminal, then it becomes a smart terminal. But, it still relies upon the main computer for programming and other jobs.

1.2.2.2 Keyboard

One look at it and you would be reminded of the old typewriter keypad. Well yes, the placing of alpha keys is exactly the same. This is called the QWERTY type of keyboard. This has been done specially keeping in mind the migration of people from typewriter to keyboard. It is the most important part of the computer. I am yet to see a computer without it. It is there in each computer. There are some software available in the market which teach you how to master the keyboard, but the old asdf method of typing would be sufficient. If one does not have speed for typing, it is ok but, the placement of keys is very important before you sit down on a computer.

Let us see how the various keys are placed on the keyboard.

Keyboard Keys: Most keyboard layouts are still a variation of the key layout of a typewriter, at least for the alphabetic, numerical and special character keys. Keyboards are available for various languages other than English too, but, for our purposes we would stick to the English one. There are mostly **101 keys** on the keyboard. The important keys are as follows:

Alpha Keys: Alphabet keys are marked from [A] to [Z]. As in typewriter, you can use [SHIFT] to make them capital, i.e., ABCDE, etc. So if you press a b c d e .... etc., with [SHIFT] key already pressed, you will get A B C D E .... etc. Similar results can be obtained by putting CAPS LOCK key ON. For typing capital A, you press [SHIFT] key and then while keeping [SHIFT] key pressed, press the "a" key. Otherwise for typing a, you don't need to press the [SHIFT] key, just press the a key.

Numeric Keys: The numeric keys (with the characters 0 to 9) are located on the computer's keyboard at two places. You can see them in the top row above the alpha keys (as in a typewriter). A second set of these keys is provided on the right-hand side of the keyboard. The numeric keys in the top row can be used straightaway to type in numeric characters. By simultaneously holding down the Shift key (as in a typewriter), you can also type in special upper characters like ! % $ *, etc. However, to type numeric characters by using the keys on the right side, you will need to press the Num Lock key ON.

Function Keys: These keys are marked [F1] to [F12]. These keys are used for specific purposes as defined in the computer (a computer program is a set of instructions given to a computer to perform a specific task) which you may be using. For example, in BASIC programming (BASIC is a computer language used for writing programs) [F3] will load the program, [F1] will list the program after loading and [F2] will run the program.

Arrow Keys: On 101 keys keyboard these are placed at two places. The first is called the cursor pad which works independently. The other is the numeric-cum-cursor pad. It is similar to the one on the 84 key keyboard. When the Num Lock key is not in the ON position, pressing the key of the numeric keypad moves the cursor in the direction shown on each key. Otherwise, this portion is used to enter numbers.

1.2.2.3 Mouse

These days even the mouse has become very important part of computer. It has become integral part of computer since Windows has become the operating system for computers. It is in fact a pointing device. With this you can point at any place on the monitor and start the typing after clicking from that point. All Windows-based programs use mouse, making working with computers easier as you are not required to type commands.

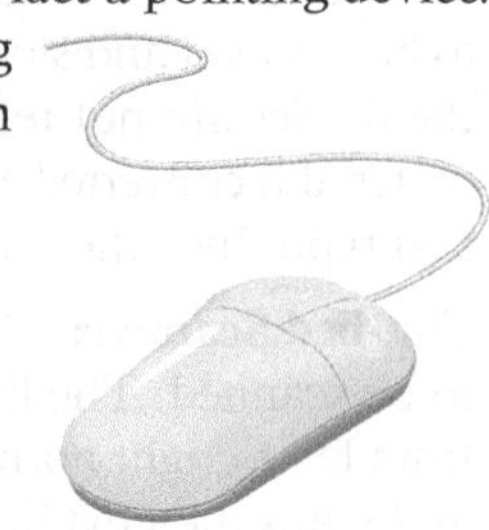

Types of Mouse

There are three basic types of Mouse

1. Mechanical Mouse
2. Optomechanical Mouse
3. Optical Mouse

Mechanical Mouse: A mechanical mouse has a rubber or metal ball on its underside that can roll in all directions. Mechanical sensors within the mouse detect the direction of the rolling ball and make a movement of the screen pointer accordingly.

Optomechanical Mouse: Optomechanical mouse is also similar to a mechanical mouse except that it uses optical sensors to detect the movement of the ball on the Mouse Pad.

Optical Mouse: Optical mouse uses a laser beam to detect the movement of mouse on specially designed Mouse Pad. We must move the mouse along a special mat with a grid so that optical mechanism has a frame of reference. This type of mouse has no mechanical moving parts. Optical mouse responds more quickly and precisely than any other mouse. These are more expensive than the other two.

1.2.3 Other Input/Output Devices

We would take up Input devices first and then the Output devices.

1.2.3.1 Input Devices

Joysticks (or Paddle): You must have seen a joystick with a video game at various video game parlours. Well the same joystick can be attached to the computer too. For playing game obviously. It consists of a small, vertical lever (called the stick) mounted on a base that is used to steer the screen cursor around. Some joysticks are mounted on a keyboard, others function as stand- alone units. The joystick can be moved left or right, forward or backward, springs are often used to return the joystick to its home center position.

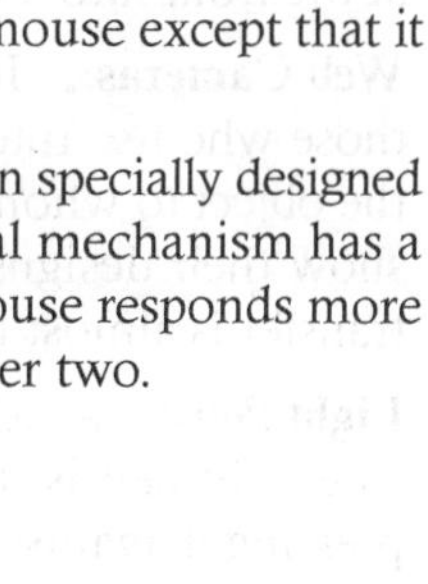

Scanners: Whereas a keyboard, mouse or trackball requires manual input of data, scanners allow input of printed data. A scanner reads text, photographs and graphics from paper which are then converted into bit patterns for processing, storage or output. Scanner is a device that examines a spatial pattern one part after another and generates analog or digital signals corresponding to the pattern. Scanners are often used in mark sensing, pattern recognition or character recognition.

Practically a scanner uses light for examining the spatial patterns. In a scanner, as the image is scanned, it is converted into light and dark picture elements, or pixels, similar to newspaper photo. Colour scanners can assign a specific colour to a pixel. The pixel are then stored as bit patterns. This technique makes the images usable by word processing, desktop publishing, and graphic packages.

There are two types of scanners, Hand-held scanner and Flat-bed scanner

Hand-Held Scanner: These devices read data on price tags, shipping labels, inventory part number, book ISBNs, and the like. Hand-held scanner, sometimes called wand scanners, use either contact or laser technology. It has a set of light emitting diodes. It is placed over the material to be scanned and slowly dragged from the top to the bottom. The light emitted by the diodes are not reflected by black lines and are reflected by whole areas. The material is converted and stored in a bitmap. Typical applications are to store images and reproduce them in publications.

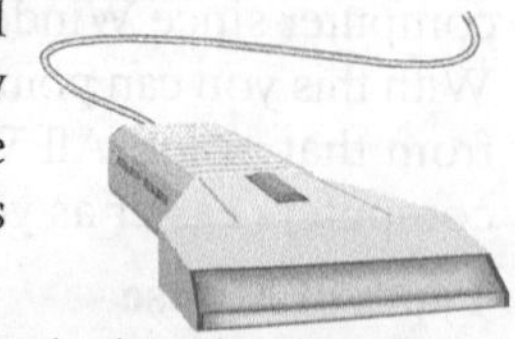

Flat-bed Scanner: It consists of a box with glass plate on top, which is used for placing the document to be scanned. The light beam is situated below the glass plate and is moved from left to right horizontally. After scanning one line the beam moves up little and scans the next line. The scanner can also store colour images.

Digital Camera: A digital camera can store many more pictures than an ordinary camera. Pictures taken using a digital camera are stored inside its memory and can be transferred to a computer by connecting the camera to it. A digital camera takes pictures by converting the light passing through the lens at the front into a digital image.

Web Cameras: It is fast becoming an integral part of the computer specially for those who use Internet quite often. With this you can take an instant picture of the object to whom you focus it. It is very useful specially for those who have to show their designs, products, etc., on the computer to the clients. The picture transfer is almost instant.

Light Pens: A light pen is a small pen-shaped wand, which contains light sensors. The light pen is used to choose objects or commands on the screen either by pressing it against the surface of the screen or by pressing a small switch on its side. This sends a signal to the computer, which then works out the light pen's exact location on the screen. The advantage of a light pen is that pen is that unlike a touch screen it doesn't need a special screen on screen coating. Used like an ordinary writing pen, this electronic pen is used to enter data by writing on the screen. The data you write is displayed on the monitor.

Trackball: Trackball is a pointing device that works like an upside-down mouse. You rest your thumb on the exposed ball and your fingers on the buttons. To move the cursor around the screen, you roll the ball with your thumb. Because you do not move the whole device, a trackball requires less space than a mouse. It is particularly used in notebook and laptop computers.

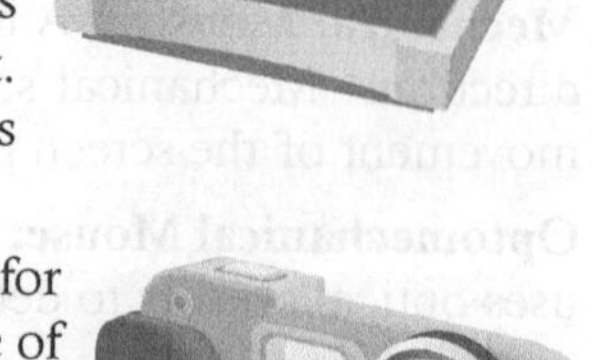

Touch Screens: Similar in use to the light pen is the touch-screen, which enables users to input instructions by merely touching on-screen prompts. The edges of the monitor of a touch-screen emit horizontal and vertical beams of light that criss-cross the screen. When a finger touches the screen, the interrupted light beams can pinpoint the location selected on the screen. Such screens are especially helpful when people are unfamiliar with computers. Information systems in shopping malls, airports, and amusement parks are now being developed using touch-sensitive screens as the only input hardware.

Touch Pad: A small, touch-sensitive pad is used as a pointing device on some portable computers. By moving a finger or other object along the pad, we can move the pointer on the display screen. The touch pad is related to the touch screen, but activated by different means. The touch pad uses pressure sensitive materials to record data at the point where the pad is touched. Many appliances around the home, such as microwave ovens, use touch pads for programming time or temperature.

Digitizer: A digitizer, or graphics tablet, is similar to a light pen; however, instead of drawing on the screen, a separate tablet is used on which a special stylus is moved. Input tablets or digitizer tablet are typically found in CAD terminals or engineering workstations, etc. Digitizers are also called Digitizing Tablets, Graphics Tablets, Touch Tablets or simply Tablets.

1.2.3.2 Output Devices

Printers: Once considered an expensive luxury for any PC, especially for home or small office systems, a printer is now virtually a necessity on any PC system. Technology has advanced to the point that good quality, color printers are available for less than Rs.8,000 and it is common for PC sale bundles to include one. When software was still fairly unsophisticated and applications that produced output worth saving were few, the printer was a true luxury. Electronic spreadsheet and word processing applications allowed the user to prepare budgets, reports, letters and other documents prepared for the sole purpose of being physically shared. Even in today's networked environments, where documents can be shared and collaborated on electronically, the need to produce a printed paper copy of a document is still a necessity for a significant portion of documents produced on the PC. The printer has definitely become a necessity for today's PC user.

The printers can be divided into two distinct categories:

1. Impact Printers
2. Non-impact Printers

Impact Printers: A printer in which printing is the result of mechanically striking the printing medium. An impact printer makes contact with the paper to produce an image. The impact may be produced by a print hammer character, like that of a typewriter key striking a ribbon against the paper or by a print hammer hitting paper and ribbon against a character. An impact printer must be used if printing a multiple copy report so that the duplicate copies will receive the imprint. Impact printers are of following types:

Dot-Matrix Printer: In it the individual characters are formed by a matrix of wires or styluses. Dot-matrix printers are also called serial printers. The images are formed by a print head that is composed of a series of little print hammers that look like the heads of pins. The print head usually has nine pins or 24 pines. The bottom 2 pins are used to form the descenders of lower case letters, viz., p, q, g and y. Many expensive dot-matrix printers do not provide descenders, but print quality is improved when they are used.

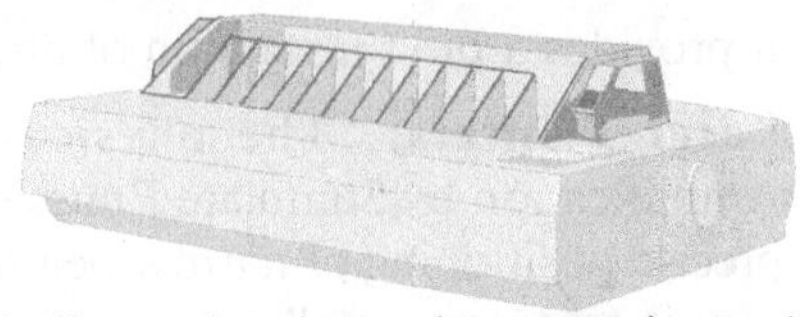

Features common to most dot-matrix printers include boldface, underline, subscript and superscript and compressed print (narrowed letters). Optional features include proportional spacing (using more or less space, depending on the width of the character) and italics. Dot matrix printers are very versatile since the character set can be changed by software or firmware such as a PROM for different styles, alphabets or graphic symbols. Dot-matrix printers are comparatively inexpensive and one of the fastest types of character-at-a-time printers available. The speed ranges from 50 cps to 400 cps (character per second).

Their abilities to use different type fonts, different line densities and different types of paper are also important.

Daisywheel Printers: A serial impact printer in which the printing element is a plastic hub that has a large number of flexible radial spokes, each spoke having one or more different raised printing characters, the wheel is rotated as it is moved horizontally step by step under computer control, and stops when a desired character is in a desired print position so a hammer can drive that character against an inked ribbon.

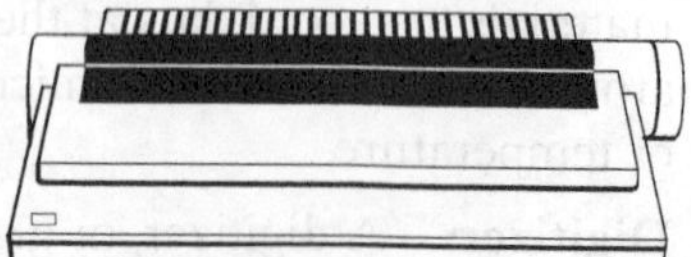

Daisy Wheel Printers are slower than dot-matrix printers, but they produce a high-resolution output. This high-resolution output is often called letter quality printing because it is suitable for business letters and memos. You can print in as may type fonts or foreign languages on a daisywheel printer as there are print wheels to fit your particular model of machine.

It is also called as a smart printer because of its bi-directional printing and built-in microprocessor control features.

Line Printers: It prints an entire line in a single operation without necessarily printing one character at a time. These are generally electro-mechanical devices which print complete lines of print, up to 160 characters in width, at speeds about 300 to 2000 lines per minute. Line printers are used primarily in the mini/mainframe processing environment.

Examples of line-at-a-time impact printers are:

1. Chain Printers
2. Band Printers and
3. Drum Printers

Non-Impact Printers: Printers that do not strike characters against ribbon or paper when they print, are non-impact printers. Example of non-impact printers include

1. Ink-jet printers
2. Laser printers

These printers makes much less noise than impact printers.

If you are using a non-impact printer, do not try to print on multiple-part carbon forms: because no impact is being made on the paper, you will end up with no copies.

Ink-jet Printers: It uses a technique of projecting droplets of ink at paper to form the required image. Ink-jet printer create an image directly on paper by spraying ink through as many as 64 tiny nozzles.

It provides a print resolution of around 360 dots per inch.

Laser Printers: The physical properties of LASERs (Light Amplification by Stimulate Emission of Radiation) allows for the very precise positioning of narrow beam of light, transferring a high energy source to a very small area. This property is used to control printing, i.e., laser printers, to read information from bar codes and to read and write information in optical storage devices.

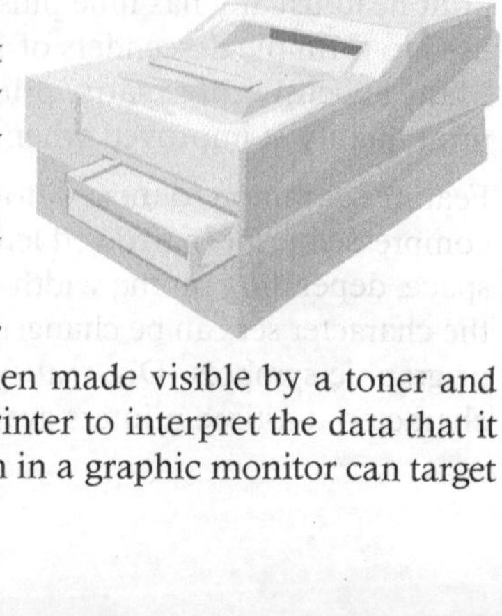

Laser printer is a non-impact printer that creates, by means of a laser beam directed on a photosensitive surface, a latent image which is then made visible by a toner and transferred and fixed on paper. A separate computer is built into the printer to interpret the data that it receives from the computer and to control the laser. Just as electron gun in a graphic monitor can target

any pixel, the laser in a laser printer can aim at any point on a drum creating an electrical charge. The resolution of laser printers is 600 DPI(Dots Per Inch) both horizontally and vertically; some high-end models have resolution of 1200 DPI.

1.2.4 Computer Memory

So far at every stage we have said that computer cannot think on its own and cannot remember anything unless we store in hard disk with save. While working all the information is stored in what is called the memory of the computer till we press the button to save it. Till that point all the information and results are stored in memory. So usually a big memory means a faster and more useful computer.

A PC's memory is made up of electronic components in which the PC temporarily stores data and instructions. Technically, any device that stores data or instructions on the PC can be called memory, including the hard disk, floppy disks, ROM, CMOS, RAM and cache. However, what is commonly referred to as memory on the PC is its primary storage, which is also known as system memory, temporary storage or RAM. With the exception of ROM, the other forms of storage (hard disk, floppy disk, CD-ROM and the like) are known as secondary storage.

ROM

It's logical then that data stored on read-only memory (ROM) cannot be changed, as its name implies. ROM also has the added feature of being nonvolatile, which means that it can keep its contents even without a power source. This makes it ideal for storing the PC's startup instructions and system BIOS (Basic Input/Output System). While virtually all ROM chips are packed in a DIP (dual inline packaging) form, there are three types of ROM used in a PC:

PROM (programmable read-only memory): This type of ROM chip is programmed using a special type of programming device called a RPOM burner (a.k.a. PROM programmer), which permanently stores machine language (binary instructions) code on the PROM chip. A PROM chip is also referred to as OTP (One Time Programmable) memory.

EPROM (erasable programmable read-only memory): This type of ROM, pronunced "e-prom," is erasable and can be reprogrammed. Unlike a PROM chip that cannot be reused and can only be thrown out when it becomes obsolete, an EPROM chip can be reprogrammed and reused. An EPROM has a quartz window on the face of the chip that exposes the chip's interior circuits. When ultraviolet (UV) light is shined through this window, it causes a chemical reaction that erases the EPROM. In order to reprogram an EPROM, it must be removed from the computer, erased with UV light and then reprogrammed on a PROM programmer.

EEPROM (electronically erasable programmable read-only memory): Most newer PCs now include an EEPROM (pronounced"e-e-prom") that can be reprogrammed like an EPROM, but unlike the EPROM doesn't need to be removed from the CP to be reprogrammed. An EEPROM can be reprogrammed, a process called flashing, using specialized software that runs on your PC. An EEPROM is also referred to as flash ROM. Flashing lets you upgrade your computer's BIOS easily without removing and replacing the ROM chip. One thing that all DIP chips suffer from including removable and replaceable PROMs and EPROMs is a condition called chip creep. DIP chips are inserted into what are called through-hole sockets and can and do squirm out of their sockets. Should a ROM chip creep out of its socket, it can cause startup problems. If you have an older motherboard that includes removable DIP ROM or memory chips, you should check them occasionally for creep.

CMOS

Because of the initial cost of Complementary Metal Oxide Semiconductor (CMOS) technology, memory,

transistors and large parts of most microprocessors were once reserved for storing the startup configuration of the PC. With technology advances and lower costs, however, CMOS technology is now used throughout the PC. CMOS memory requires only about one-millionth of an amp to hold any data stored on it. Using only a lithium battery, CMOS memory is able to store the startup configuration of a PC for many years. The term CMOS is still synonymous with the PC's startup configuration data.

RAM

RAM or random access memory, is used in the PC for its primary memory. RAM is where all active programs and data are stored so that they are readily available and easily accessed by the CPU and other components of the CPU. When you execute a program on your PC, a copy of the program is copied into RAM from whatever secondary storage it is on, usually the hard disk. Once it is in RAM, the instructions that make up the program are passed one at a time to the CPU for execution. Any data the program accepts or reads from a disk is also stored in RAM. There are several reasons that RAM is used in a PC but perhaps the most important is that RAM can transfer data to and from the CPU much faster than all secondary storage devices. Without RAM, all programs instructions and data would be read from the disk drive, slowing the computer to a crawl. With RAM speeds as fast, if not faster, than the speed of the CPU, the entire PC operates much more efficiently. RAM is a group of integrated circuits (ICs or chips) that contain small electronic components (called capacitors) that store binary 1s and 0s. A variety of memory chips can be used for RAM, but some are better suited to storing large amounts of data, fit better in the space available in the PC and are less expensive. However, not all memory applications in the PC need to store a large amount of data, so most PCs use three different layers of memory: primary memory, level 1 (l1) cache and level 2 (l2) cache. RAM in its common usage refers to the primary memory layer of the PC's memory.

1.2.5 Concepts of Hardware and Software

There are two ways of looking at it. First is this that Hardware is something which we can see with our eyes and touch whereas Software is something which we don't see and works in the background and definitely we can't touch it. A very practical example of this can be given in the form of a VCR. In this case the VCR where the video cassette is put is the hardware whereas the video cassette which has the film in it can be called as Software. Without each other they have no value. You cannot run video cassette without a VCR and VCR is nothing but a machine in itself if it has no movie to run.

Similarly in computers Hardware and Software go neck-in-neck. They are totally dependent upon each other. This is why when you buy a software, it has the hardware requirements mentioned on it since without that much of hardware, it will not work. But, software is a very vast field. Lots and lots of software are available, which one would suit your requirements, you have to use according to your needs.

1.3 CLASSIFICATION OF COMPUTERS

Computers can be classified into two categories:

1. Classification according to the logic used
2. Classification according to the size.

1.3.1 Classification According to the Logic Used

Analog Computer: Analog computers are in which numerical magnitudes are represented by physical quantities, such as electric current, voltage or resistance, mechanical movements etc. Analog computers accepts data and then process it to produce analog data.

Analog computer are machines designed to perform arithmetical functions upon numbers where the numbers are represented by physical quantity. For example, in mechanical analog computers the numbers are often represented by physical dimensions of the members forming the various functional units, for instance by the angular rotation of the shaft or gear wheels.

In electrical analog machines voltages are used to represent the input variables.

Essentially an analog computer must be able to accept inputs which vary with respect to time, and directly apply these inputs to various devices within the computer which perform the computing operations of addition, subtraction, multiplication, division and integration. The output from the system may be in the form of a graph produced by a plotting pen or a trace on a cathode-ray tube. The computing units of analog computers are able to respond immediately to the changes which they detect in the input variable and the connection of these various units in a particular fashion can cause an analog computer to perform very complex arithmetical functions at high speed while the actual process under study is in operation. The ability to operate in real time mode means that analog computers has many application in the scientific and industrial fields in simulating various physical systems or automatically controlling industrial processes. They are widely used for research into design problems. Analog computers are used in manufacturing units where temperatures, pressure or flow of liquids are to be monitored continuously. It is also used at service station where gasoline pump contains an analog processor that connects fuel flow measurements into quantity and price values.

Digital Computers: A digital computer operates on data in the form of digits, rather than the physical quantities used in analog computers. That is, its input must be discrete rather than continuous and may consist of combinations of numbers, characters and special symbols, written in appropriate programming language. Computers generate digital signals representing bit patterns, whereas standard telephone lines were designed to handle analog signals in the form of voices and other sound patterns to use telephone for data communication digital signals need to be converted to an analog format.

Originally digital computers were mechanical devices employing cogs, gears and levers, they now depend upon electronic technique enabling them to deal automatically with a wide range of problems at a very high speeds. Some of the earlier digital computing devices were developed from punched card machines and the program was set up by means of connections on a plugboard, machines of this category are generally referred to as calculators, rather than computers.

Modern digital computers are usually based on the binary notation, numbers and letters being coded into group of digits consisting only of 1 or 0. Each of these digits is represented in an electronic circuit or magnetic store by a component in an on or off state. For example, passing current or not passing current, magnetized or not magnetized. Data in this form is processed in the CPU of the computer by gates (switches) which obey the instructions of the program.

The individual operations performed by a digital computer are very simple arithmetic or logical processes involving the manipulation of the bits in words or characters of information. The great power of any digital computer rets in the ability to store large volumes of data and to perform these various functions at extremely high speed. Arithmetic and logical circuits for processing data in binary form are constructed from simple basic units designed to perform the operations of Boolean algebra AND, OR, NOT etc. These simple units are used as building blocks in constructing the complex logic and control circuits required.

General purpose digital computers: It is also known as all purpose digital computer. Theoretically it can be used for any type of application. e.g., computers that are used for payroll, graphs, analysis etc.

Special purpose digital computers: A digital computer designed to solve problems of a restricted type. That is, special-purpose digital computer is designed to be especially efficient in a certain class of applications. For example, computers installed in washing machines.

1.3.2 Classification According to Size

Computers come in sizes from tiny to monstrous, in both appearance and power. The size of a computer that a person or an organization needs depends on the computing environments. Clearly, the National Weather service provided by Meteorological Department of India keeping watch on the weather fronts of many continents has requirements different from those of a two wheeler dealer's service department that is trying to keep track of its parts inventory. And the requirements of both of them are different from the needs of a salesperson using a small laptop computer to record client orders on a sales trip.

In general the classification of computers can be characterized by cost, size, storage capacity, number of users and processing speed. In many cases, there is a considerable amount of overlapping of these characteristics. So broadly, computers can be classified as

- Super computers
- Mainframe computers
- Mini computers
- Workstations
- Micro computers or Personal computers

Supercomputers, the biggest of all, have greater computing capacities than mainframe computers. Mainframe computers have greater computing capacities than minicomputers and Minicomputers have greater computing capacities than microcomputers. Rapid advances in computer technology have blurred what used to be distinguishing characteristics (physical size, cost, memory capacity and so on).

1.3.2.1 Large Computer Systems

These are sometime called the mainframe computers too.

Super computers: The speed of a computer is limited by two things:

1. The switching time
2. The time taken by an electric pulse to go from one part of the computer to another.

The Switching time may be thought of as the time a transistor takes to go from a conducting state to nonconducting state or vice versa. Since the switching time is now only of one thousand millionth of a second, the time an electric pulse takes to travel from one part of the computer to another is becoming a more serious limitation. Nothing can travel faster than the speed of light and light can only travel one foot in a thousand millionth of a second. Thus it is not feasible to increase the speed of sequential computer (e.g. PCs, mainframe etc.) made with a single processor beyond a limit. The only alternative for achieving higher speed of computing is to use many processors to work in parallel. Also it is very important that everything is made as small as possible and the memory does not require too much space.

One of the problems with packing a very large numbers of silicon chips into a small space is that they use power and this means a lot of heat is generated in this space. An elaborate cooling system is a very important part of a supercomputer.

Mainframe Computers: Next step down from supercomputers, in terms of speed and storage capacity are mainframes. Mainframes are large, relatively expensive machines that offer extensive problem-solving capabilities. It can have memory capacities measured in gigabytes and more. The largest mainframes can

process well over 100 MIPS. Their operating systems usually handle multiple applications within a timesharing environment. This provides many users with the ability to perform different processing tasks Data storage is primarily on hard disks, with tapes used as backup. Mainframe is a large computer, in particular one to which other computers can be connected so that they can share facilities the mainframe provides. e.g; a System/370 computing system to which personal computers are attached so that they can upload and download programs and data.

The term mainframe usually refers to hardware only : main storage, execution circuitry and peripheral units. Mainframe word-length may be 48, 60 or 64 bits. It has got a system memory (i.e; RAM) of 64 to 256 MB, hard disk of capacity 1 -10 GB or more and processing speed of 30 - 100 Millions of Instructions per seconds. A substantial amount of peripherals can be attached to mainframe computer.

Mainframe computers are designed to handle tremendous amount of input, output and storage. Mainframe computers often act as host computers i.e., computers that serve as central receiving and switching computers in regional or national computer networks. Mainframe acts as a database server, that is, the database is controlled by mainframe computer that can handle the input and output needs of all terminals connected to it.

Mini Computers: The next step down from mainframe computers, in terms of speed and storage capacity are minicomputers. It is an intermediate - size computer that can perform the same kind of applications as a mainframe but has less storage capacity, processing power and speed than a mainframe.

It is functionally intermediate between a microcomputer and a mainframe. Minicomputers are floor-standing or desktop devices, frequently connected to a mainframe to perform subsidiary operations. They are priced for purchase by smaller businesses and are sufficiently compact to be located in a typical office environment. When Digital Equipment Corporation (DEC) began shipping its PDP series computer in the early 1960s the press dubbed these machines, minicomputers, because of their small size compared to other computers of the day.

Some minicomputers are uniprocessor systems whereas some are multiprocessor systems. The processing speed lies in the range 10 -30 MIPS. Memory capacity lies in the range of 8 - 256 MB and can easily range into gigabytes of temporary storage. Minicomputers have operating systems with multitasking and network capabilities enabling them to serve more than one user. It serves as a centralized storehouse for cluster of workstations or as a network server. For example, a team of architects working on different subsystems within the same building could be directly linked to the office minicomputer that maintains everyone's files and documentation. A mini computer can support more than 100 terminals. Generally, the processing speeds and related capabilities of minicomputers exceed those of microcomputers and more peripheral devices can be attached to them. Minicomputer also tend to have more sophisticated operating systems than microcomputers and can usually be programmed in a wider variety of programming languages.

1.3.2.2 Small Computer Systems

The following computers are generally grouped into this.

Supermini: The term supermini has been coined to describe minis at the top of the size-price scale. It is a large minicomputer. Physically it is a 32-bit minicomputer which supports more simultaneous users (one hundred or more) and more peripheral devices and large memories than previous minicomputer.

Workstations: Between minicomputers and microcomputer in terms of processing power is a class of computers known as workstations. A workstation looks like a personal computer and is typically used by only one person, much as is a personal computer. Although workstations are still more powerful than the average personal computer, the difference is the capabilities of these types of machines.

Microcomputers and Personal Computers: The microcomputer is a scaled-down version of the mainframe. Microcomputer is a digital computer whose processing unit consists of one or more microprocessors, one or more input/output units and sufficient memory to execute instructions. The essential components of a microcomputer are often contained within a single enclosure. Microcomputers are usually desktop or portable devices with a display, a keyboard and tape disk and diskette storage, they are designed primarily for stand-alone operation but can be used as workstations in terminal emulation mode. Every microcomputer is capable of performing jobs once handled by only the largest computers. A typical microcomputer memory unit stores upto 64 MB of data. Processing speeds of microcomputer are measured in megahertz instead of MIPS. A microcomputer running at 90 MHz is faster than one running at 33 MHz and works at approximately 90 MIPS.

The terms microcomputer and personal computer are interchangeable however, PC-which stands for personal computer-has a more specific meaning. In 1981, IBM called its first microcomputer the IBM PC. Within a few years, many companies were copying the IBM design creating "clones" or "compatibles" that aimed at functioning just like the original. For this reason, the term PC has come to mean the family of computers that includes IBMs and compatibles.

Personal computer is a type of microcomputer primarily intended for stand-alone use by an individual. It is a desktop, floor - standing or portable microcomputer that usually consists of a system unit, a display monitor, a keyboard, one or more diskette drives, internal hard disk storage, and an optional printer. PCs are designed primarily to give independent computing power to a single user and are inexpensively priced for purchase by individuals or small businesses. A few of the major personal computer manufacturers are APPLE, IBM, Compaq, Dell, AST and Hewlett-Packard.

Supermicros: The upper-end machines used by workers such as engineers, financial traders and graphics designers are small enough to fit on a desk top but approach the power of a mainframe.

1.4 REPRESENTATION OF DATA/INFORMATION CONCEPTS OF DATA PROCESSING

Computer systems can store tremendous amounts of data, which can be located or retrieved efficiently. A typical mainframe computer system will have many billions of characters stored and available for instant recall. High end PCs have access to about a billion characters of data. Most of this data is stored in Hard Disks which is fixed in the computer or the data can be fed in with the help of various storage devices like floppy disks, CD-ROMs, etc.

The storage capacity of disks depends on the number of tracks per inch of the surface and the bits per inch of track. Larger disks have more tracks and hence they have greater storage capacity. The total number of bytes that can be stored on a disk pack can be calculated as:

Number of cyclinders x Tracks per cyclinder x Sectors per track x Bytes per sector

The total number of bytes that can be stored on a disk can be calculated as:

Number of sector x Sectors per cyclinder x Number of cyclinders x Number of heads

For example, a hard disk drive having 14 heads, 723 cyclinders and 51 sectors and each sector can store 0.5 KB has a storage capacity of 258 MB.

14 x 723 x 51 x 0.5 = 258,111.00 KB = 258 MB approx.

1.4.1 Processing of Data

There are two type of processing. They are:

1.4.1.1 Batch Processing

It is a method in which data are gathered and batched through either an on line or off line data gathering process and processed periodically without user intervention.

1.4.1.2 Transaction Processing

It is an on-line method in which data are processed immediately, and files are updated as a transaction takes place. This allows the user to communicate with the computer during processing, through interactive programs which supply the results of processing so that they can be used when needed to control an operation or modify a process. This procedure is called real time processing. It is used in airlines offices to book and prepare a ticket.

1.4.2 Definition of Information and Data

Data is technically, raw facts and figures which are processed into information. However, in common usage, both data and information are used synonymously the amount of data kept in the computer versus the amount of information is a tradeoff. Data can be processed into different forms of information, but it takes time to sort and sum transactions. Data is "processed". Software is "run". Information can be in any form whether on paper or in electronic form. In electronic form, data refers to data fields, records, files and databases, word processing documents, graphic images and digitally-encoded voice and video. Data items in data files and databases in contrast with text, graphics, voice and video files.

1.4.3 Basic Data Types

A data type defines the set of values the variable can store, as well as the set of operations that can be performed on the data. For example, integer, character, float, etc., we cannot perform division on characters. So, for each data type variable there are set of permissible operations in computer. The main *five primary data* types are shown in the following table.

Data Type (Keyword)	*Meaning*
int	Integer
char	Character or String
float	Floating-point
double	Used with int and float data types for larger numbers
void	Accept any type of data based on cast operator it returns the value

1.4.4 Storage of Data/Information as Files

Memory is not the only place where you store the data or program, since it is volatile. So you need to have storage devices which can store your data and programs permanently. For this we use so called storage units. These can be used for storing the data and then, maybe, transferring it to another computer or storage media.

1.4.4.1 Hard Disk Drives

Hard disks have been there since the time of mainframe systems of 3rd generation computers. The only difference is that the disks at that time were removable and were of very small capacity. However, the

basic technology used in the earliest hard disks has not changed all that much over the years, although the size and capacity of the drives has.

1.4.4.2 Floppy Disk Drives

Although manufacturers have been trying for years to replace the floppy disk, with a device that holds more data, the 3.5 inch floppy disk drive is still very common on most PCs sold today.

The floppy disk has survived well beyond what anyone expected. It has changed in size over the years and is available in drives that fit inside the system case as well as outside. The floppy disk has come in a variety of sizes over its lifetime, but for about the past ten years the most popular size has been the 3.5 inch diskette.

1.4.4.3 Optical Disks

Optical disks differ from magnetic disk storage by the way data is stored and read from the storage media. A laser beam is used to write and read data on these reflective disks, so they are also known as laser disks. In this technology a laser hits a layer of metallic material spread over the surface of a disk. When data is being entered heat from the laser produces tiny spots on the disk surface. To read the data, the laser scans the disk, and a lens picks up different light reflections from the various spots.

Optical disks are becoming a very inviting option for users. They are less sensitive to environmental fluctuations, and they provide more direct-access storage at a cost than is much less per megabyte of storage than the magnetic disk alternative.

Optical disk technology is still emerging and has yet to stabilize; however at present there are three different types of optical disks in common use:

read-only

recordable, and

erasable

1.4.4.4 CD-ROMs and DVDs

The CD-ROM and its comparatively huge storage capacity (over 600 floppy disks) has been very attractive to software and multimedia producers and soon virtually all software, including databases, books, encyclopedias and other materials not available to the PC in the past suddenly became available and accessible for the PC.

A CD-ROM drive is as common on PCs today as floppy drives were only a few years ago. In fact, some manufacturers now replace the floppy disk drive with a single CD-ROM on their latest PC models. The CD-ROM is by far the most common method of software distribution and data storage due to their combination of high capacity and easy, inexpensive manufacturing. A PC without a CD-ROM drive simply is not able to install the vast majority of PC software available on the market today. Some CD-ROM software even requires that your PC's drive meet a specific minimum requirement. For example, if you have an older CD-ROM drive, such as a 4X, in your system, it may need to be replaced before it can run some newer CD-ROM titles that require at least a 12X drive.

CD-ROM Technology: The CD-ROM uses compact disc (CD) technology, the same technology used to record the music on your favorite audio CDs. The physical media used for recording data, programs, music and multimedia on a CD-ROM is the same as that used to record music. In fact, the physical disc is the same for both.

Video CD (VCD): The video CD (VCD) is used to store compressed video information using a standard

also defined in the White Book. VCDs use MPEG (Motion Picture Experts Group) compression to store 74 minutes of full-motion video in the same space used by CD-DA audio. To play a video CD requires a CD-ROM drive or video CD player that is video CD-compatible. The compression algorithm used for VCD does not produce a high quality video; this format will likely give way to the DVD.

CD-Recordable: Each of the CD types covered to this point have been CD-ROMs or read-only discs, which means that except for during their manufacturing processes, data cannot be stored to them and they cannot be modified, other than to be destroyed. To take advantage of its large storage space, methods have been developed, along with special CD media that allow data to be written to a CD. A CD Recordable (CD-R) disc is manufactured essentially the same as a CD-ROM disc, with some slight variations. In place of the substrate is a layer of organic dye, over which is placed a reflective gold-colored metallic coating. Over this is the protective lacquer layer, just like a CD-ROM.

1.4.5 Mass Storage Devices

So far what we have read is what was relevent only a few years ago, The latest in this line are the various mass storage devices which have been deviced only recently. These are mentioned here.

1.4.5.1 USB Thumb Drive

USB flash drives are NAND-type flash memory data storage devices integrated with a USB (universal serial bus) interface. They are typically small, lightweight, removable and rewritable. As of November 2008, memory capacities for USB Flash Drives currently are sold from 32 megabytes up to 256 gigabytes. Capacity is limited only by current flash memory densities, although cost per megabyte may increase rapidly at higher capacities due to the expensive components. (USB Memory card readers are also available, whereby rather than being built-in, the memory is a removable Flash memory card housed in what is otherwise a regular USB flash drive, as described below.)

USB flash drives offer potential advantages over other portable storage devices, particularly the floppy disk. They are more compact, generally faster, hold more data, and are more reliable (due to both their lack of moving parts, and their more durable design) than floppy disks. These types of drives use the USB mass storage standard, supported natively by modern operating systems such as Linux, Mac OS X, Unix, and Windows.

A flash drive consists of a small printed circuit board encased in a plastic or metal casing, making the drive sturdy enough to be carried about in a pocket, as a key fob, or on a lanyard. Only the USB connector protrudes from this protection, and is usually covered by a removable cap. Most flash drives use a standard type-A USB connection allowing them to be connected directly to a port on a personal computer.

To access the data stored in a flash drive, the drive must be connected to a computer, either by plugging it into a USB host controller built into the computer, or into a USB hub. Flash drives are active only when plugged into a USB connection and draw all necessary power from the supply provided by that connection.

However, some flash drives, especially high-speed drives utilizing the USB 2.0 standard, may require more power than the limited amount provided by a bus-powered USB hub, such as those built into some computer keyboards or monitors. These drives will not work unless plugged directly into a host controller (i.e., the ports found on the computer itself) or a self-powered hub.

LET US REVISE

1. The processor, more formally known as the central processing unit (CPU), has the electronic circuitry that manipulates input data into the information people want.
2. CPU coordinates and controls the activities of input, output and storage devices, and performs all the arithmetic and logical processes to be applied to data.
3. Computer memory also known as primary storage, is closely associated with the central processing unit.
4. A PC's memory is made up of electronic components in which the PC temporarily stores data and instructions.
5. Data stored on read-only memory (ROM) cannot be changed.
6. RAM is a group of integrated circuits that contain small electronic components that store binary 1s and 0s.
7. Accessing data from a hard disk drive takes from 8 to 16 milliseconds.
8. A storage device is used to store the data in the computer.
9. CD-ROMs are now used as media for computers.
10. CDs can be used as recording media too.
11. A computer is made of different parts.
12. Computer is a machine, totally at the command of the user.
13. The first three computer generations were based on : vacuum tube, transistor and integrated circuit.
14. The computer is physically divided into 3 main parts: Monitor, Central Processing Unit and Keyboard.
15. CPU consists of 4 main units: Primay Storage, Arithmetic Logic Unit, Control Unit and Output Unit.
16. The main functions of the Primary storage are: Holding the data in its memory till it is required to be processed; Holding the result of the processed data and Holding program instructions which are required for processing.
17. Arithmetic Logic Unit is used to process Arithmetic and Logic problems.
18. Input device is used to input data into computer.
19. Output device is used to get result from the computer.
20. Keyboard has 101 keys.
21. Alpha keys are there for typing alphabets A to Z.
22. Numeric keys are there for typing numerals 0 to 9.
23. Mouse is basically a pointing device.
24. Joystick is used for playing games.
25. There are two types of optical recognition input devices: Optical Character Recognition (OCR) and Optical Mark Reading (OMR).
26. A scanner reads text, photographs and graphics from paper which are then converted into bit patterns for processing, storage or output.
27. A digital camera can store many more pictures than an ordinary camera.
28. Trackball is a pointing device that works like an upside-down mouse.
29. Monitor is like a TV and is used to display output.
30. The printers can be divided into two distinct categories: Impact Printers and Non-impact Printers.

31. Dot matrix printers use hammers to print characters.
32. Line printer prints an entire line in a single operation without necessarily printing one character at a time.

MULTIPLE CHOICE QUESTIONS

1. RAM stands for:
   (a) Random Allowed Memory (b) Ready Access Memory (c) Random Access Memory
2. CPU contains Primary Storage, Arithmetic Logic Unit and
   (a) Control Unit (b) Data Unit (c) Alpha Unit
3. System software controls:
   (a) Hard disk (b) Internal computer system (c) Floppy disk
4. Data stored in ROM cannot be changed:
   (a) Yes (b) No
5. CDs are of which shape:
   (a) round (b) square (c) rectangular
6. Hard disks have:
   (a) cubicles (b) platters (c) keys
7. For seeing the output, you use:
   (a) Monitor (b) Keyboard (c) Mouse
8. Keyboard has ________ number of keys.
   (a) 100 (b) 88 (c) 101
9. With CD you can:
   (a) Read (b) Write (c) Both
10. A scanner scans
    (a) Pictures (b) Text (c) Both
11. With digital camera, you can store:
    (a) text (b) pictures
12. Trackball has a
    (a) ball (b) track (c) football
13. Dot matrix printers uses ______ for printing
    (a) hammers (b) slugs (c) mouse

TRUE/FALSE QUESTIONS

1. Computer memory also known as primary storage, is closely associated with the central processing unit.
2. Data stored on read-only memory (ROM) can be changed.

3. RAM is a group of integrated circuits that contain small electronic components that store binary 1s and 0s.
4. Accessing data from a hard disk drive takes from 8 to 16 milliseconds.
5. CD-ROMs are now used as media for computers.
6. CDs cannot be used as recording media too.
7. Computer is a machine, totally at the command of the user.
8. CPU consists of 4 main units: Primay Storage, Arithmetic Logic Unit, Control Unit and Output Unit.
9. Input device is used to input data into computer.
10. Output device is used to get result from the computer.
11. Keyboard has 101 keys.
12. Mouse is basically a pointing device.
13. Joystick is not used for playing games.
14. A digital camera can store many more pictures than an ordinary camera.
15. Monitor is like a TV and is used to display output.
16. The printers can be divided into two distinct categories: Impact Printers and Non-impact Printers.
17. Dot matrix printers use slugs to print characters.
18. Line printer prints an entire line in a single operation without necessarily printing one character at a time.

MATCHING COLUMNS

Match the matter in Column A with the matter in Column B.

Column A	Column B
A. SIC	1. Read Only Memory
B. Registers	2. Compact Disk-Read Only Memory
C. RAM	3. CD Recordable
D. ROM	4. Simplified Instructional Computer
E. CPU	5. Arithmetic Logic Unit
F. CD-ROM	6. Programable Read Only Memory
G. CD-R	7. Erasable Programable Read Only Memory
H. ALU	8. To store information temporarily
I. PROM	9. Central Processing Unit
J. EPROM	10. Random Acess Memory

FILL IN THE BLANKS WITH APPROPRIATE WORDS

a. Read	b. System	c. Memory	d. Programmable
e. Windows	f. Erasable	g. Access	h. Semiconductor
i. Processing	j. Logic		

1. Complementary Metal Oxide __________ (CMOS).
2. Arithmetic ________ Unit (ALU).
3. Random ________ Memory.
4. ________ RAM (WRAM).
5. Windows is a __________ software.
6. ________ Only Memory (ROM).
7. CD Read Only __________ (CD ROM).
8. ________ Read Only Memory (PROM).
9. Central __________ Unit.
10. ________ Erasable Programable Read Only Memory (EEPROM).

DESCRIPTIVE TYPE QUESTIONS

1. Describe the various functions of CPU.
2. What does CPU consist of?
3. What is Internal memory?
4. Describe the various types of memory in computers.
5. What do you understand by Logical Memory Configuration?
6. What is a hard disk?
7. Describe the various types of CDs available.
8. How a CD is read?
9. Describe the following terms:

Arithmetic Logic Unit	Central Processing Unit
Data Formats	Addressing Modes
Instruction Set	Application Software
System Software	Speed of computers
Storage capacity of computers	High Memory Area
Upper Memory Area	RAM
ROM	CD-R
DVDs	Floppy Disks

ANSWERS TO OBJECTIVE QUESTIONS

Multiple Choice Questions

1. c	2. a	3. b	4. b
5. a	6. b	7. a	8. c
9. c	10. c	11. c	12. a
13. a			

True False Questions

1. T	2. F	3. T	4. T
5. T	6. F	7. T	8. T
9. T	10. T	11. T	12. T
13. F	14. T	15. T	16. T
17. F	18. T		

Matching Columns

A. 4	B. 8	C. 10	D. 1
E. 9	F. 2	G. 3	H. 5
I. 6	J. 7		

Fill in the Blanks with Appropriate Words

1. h	2. j	3. g	4. e
5. b	6. a	7. c	8. d
9. i	10. f		

Chapter 2

Introduction to GUI based Operating Systems

2.1 INTRODUCTION AND OBJECTIVES

An operating system (OS) is a set of computer programs that manages the hardware and software resources of a computer. It processes raw data which is given to the computer as input. It then allocates and manages the tasks of the internal system resources of the computer. It is the operating system which performs basic tasks such as controlling and allocating memory, prioritizing system requests, controlling input and output devices, facilitating networking and managing file systems.

Most operating systems come with an application that provides an interface to the operating system managed resources. These applications have had command line interpreters as a basic user interface, but more recently have been implemented as a Graphical User Interface (GUI) for ease of operation.

> ***Definiton: Operating Systems themselves have no user interfaces; the user of an operating system is an application, not a person.***

The operating system forms a platform for other system software and for application software. Windows, Linux, and Mac operating systems are some of the most popular Operating Systems.

2.1.1 Objectives

The objective of this chapter is to learn about the operating system, specially from the following angles:

- What is operating system
- Which are the various types of operating systems
- Popular operating systems
- Linux operating system
- Windows operating system

2.1.2 Types of Operating Systems

Operating system can be classified into various categories, with respect to the type of processing it supports. Following are the main types of Operating System:

2.1.2.1 Batch Operating System

Batch processing requires that a program, its related data and relevant control commands should be submitted together, in the form of a Job. Batch operating system allows no interaction between the users and the executing programs. Thus the programs that have long execution times (like payrolls, forecasting, statistical analysis and large scientific number-crunching programs) and require little operator interaction during execution, were well served by Batch Processing. However, due to long turn-around delays and infeasibility of online debugging, the Batch Processing was not at all suitable for software development. The typical features of a batch operating system are:

1. **Scheduling**. The scheduling of jobs was normally in the order of their arrival, i.e., First Come First Served (FCFS). This criteria provides a fair deal to the jobs, but suffers from long average turn-around time and average waiting time, since some short jobs may have to wait for unduly long periods to get executed, if some long jobs are already queued ahead of the short jobs. To overcome this limitation, another criteria known as Shortest Job Next, was evolved, which offered preference to pending shorter jobs over the long jobs. This offered much better average turn around time and average waiting time of the pending jobs.
2. **Memory Management**. Memory used to be divided into two permanent partitions—one permanently occupied by the resident portion of the operating system and the other dynamically used to load the transient programs for execution. When a transient program terminates, it vacates the memory partition occupied by it and the same is assigned to other waiting transient program.
3. **I/O Management**. Since, only one program is used to be under execution at a time, there was no contention for the allocation of I/O Devices. So, a simple program-controlled I/O approach was good enough to access the I/O Devices.
4. **File Management**. Since, these used to be only one program accessing the files at a time, there was no need of providing concurrency control.

   Thus, in a nutshell the Batch operating system was limited to a Loader and some simple Device Drivers.

2.1.2.2 Multi-programming Operating System

A multi-programming oprating system permits multiple programs to be loaded into the memory and execute the programs concurrently. A program in execution is called a "Process" or a "Task".

In short: ***The concurrent execution of programs has a significant potential for improving the utilization of system resources and thus enhancing the system throughout, as compared to batch and serial processing.***

This potential is exploited by multi-programming operating system, which multiplexes the computer resources amongst a multitude of concurrent programs. A program in execution is called a Process. When a running process requests one I/O, it goes to "Wait" state. Then another Ready process (i.e., one of the processes from the "Ready" queue) is scheduled to "Run". So, when a process goes for I/O, the CPU is not left idling. When the I/O requested by a Waiting process is completed, it is transferred from "Waiting" to "Ready" state and wait to be scheduled, as per the predecided scheduled criteria.

2.1.2.3 Time-sharing Interactive Operating System

The time-sharing interactive operating systems belong to the era of a large mainframe systems, that were made available to a large number of users for accessing concurrently in an interactive mode. Each user used to interact with the system through a separate Video Terminal. A programmer could enter its source code using sophisticated editors, compile the source code, link the object code and run the executable code interactively. At any stage, the user could interact with the execution of its program. Debugging could be performed online. This reduced the time needed for program development, drastically. The operating system served the interactive users, in a round-robin fashion, allowing a fixed time-slice for each user to have control of the CPU. Since, the operators were interacting through slow I/O devices, each user had a feel as if the CPU was available solely to itself. So, the computation capacity of the CPU is multiplexed evenly, amongst the interactive users.

In short: At any stage, the user could interact with the execution of its program. Debugging could be performed online.

So, time-sharing systems were large multi-programmed multi-user systems, designed for program development. One of the major requirements of such a system is good terminal response. It should give an illusion to each user as if the entire computer resources are available to itself, solely. It should provide an equitable share of common resources to each user. For example, when the system is overloaded, the program with higher processing requirements is made to wait longer.

Most time-sharing systems use time-sliced, non pre-emptive scheduling. It has FCFS Queue; and a program requiring service is put at the end of the queue. When the process reaches the front of the queue, it is despatched. If it is not completed within the time slice, it is pre-emptied at the end of the time-slice and put at the end of the queue. Now, it has to wait for the next time-slice, to resume its execution from the point where it left at the end of previous time-slice. A process continues to run in bursts like this, till it terminates.

The main features of a time-sharing interactive operating system are:

1. **Memory Management**. The memory management in time-sharing systems provides for isolation and protection of co-resident programs. Since, the programs are being executed on behalf of different users, they do not involve much of inter-process communication.
2. **I/O Devices Management**. I/O Management must be sophisticated enough to cope with the requirements of multiple users, contending for multiple devices. However, due to relatively slow speed of terminals and users, processing of terminal-interrupts would not be so critical. As in most multi-user environments, allocation and de-allocation of devices must be handled in a manner so as to provide the system integrity, while attempting to optimize the system performance.
3. **File Management**. Since multiple users will be sharing access to multiple files, the file management must provide protection and access control.

2.1.2.4 Real Time Operating System

It refers to the environment of embedded systems, with a very rigid requirement to complete the processing of input data, in a pre-specified time. The input data, in such systems, is invariably received from real-world sensors. The outputs may be used to control some real-world processes.

For example, an Adir Defence system, receiving information about aircraft movements from radars and control weapons for the elimination of hostile aircraft. For such an application, it can be well appreciated that the processing of data inputs, within specified time limits, is absolutely critical.

So, the real time systems are used in environments, where a large number of events, mostly external to the computer system, must be accepted and processed to a highly time-bound manner (with specified deadlines).

Such applications include process control in indusry (like steel, petro-chemical plants, thermal plants and nuclear plants, etc.), military systems for processing of sensor information and weapon control, telephone switching equipment, flight control, real-time simulations, etc.

1. **Scheduling**. A primary objective of a real-time system is to provide quick response to external events, so as to meet the specified deadlines of processing. Such systems have to be multi-tasking (may not be multi-user). The scheduling is normally priority-based pre-emptive, in which the processes handling the priority process become ready to run, it pre-empts a lower priority running process. User convenience and resource optimization are of secondary concern. Such systems

may be expected to handle thousands of interrupts per second, with a stringent requirement of not missing even a single event.

2. **Memory Management**. The memory management is relatively less demanding, since the process population is more or less static and memory is so designed that most of the processes will always be memory resident, in order to provide a quick response. In fact, the programs are normally ROM resident. But, the processes have closer interaction. This requires features that enable sharing of memory, amongst processes and at the same time provide protection from each other.
3. **I/O Devices Management**. Time critical device management is one of the major requirements of real time systems. The external events and data have to be accepted and processed, in a highly time-bound manner. This is implemented using interrupt mechanism. The system calls allow the users to connect the devices and access Interrupt Service Routines (ISRs) directly, so as to achieve a good response time.
4. **File Management**. The file management is not very critical, since most of the real-time databases will be memory-resident. Some embedded systems may have program and static data on ROM and may not need any online secondary devices at run-time. The dynamic databases are maintained in ROM. If at all any files are to be accessed, as in the case of large real-time systems, the primary objective is fast access.

2.1.2.5 Category of Real Time Operating Systems

1. **Hard Real Time Operating System**. In Hard Real Time Systems, all critical tasks have to be completed stricly within the specified time limits. Not meeting the deadlines can be catastrophic; like an embedded system controlling the operation of a refinery. In such systems, all code and data must be in RAM/ROM. All kernel delays must be bounded. So, the Operating System should not have any unnecessary frills. Interrupt mechanism must be optimized, so as to respond to the real world inputs, with minimal delays.
2. **Soft Real Time Operating System**. This is less restrictive type of real time system. If the input data is not processed within specifed time intervals, the results may not be catastrophic, but the output may lose its utility. For example, in a system monitoring flight path of an aircraft, the delayed information will have no utility. In such systems, tasks are divided into two categories—Real Time Tasks and Non-Real Time Tasks. The Real-Time Tasks are accorded priority over the other tasks. Any output from such systems would be useful, only if it is produced within a specified time after receiving the corresponding inputs. So, the kernel delays must be bounded. The soft real time systems are not suitable for industrial and defence use, since the delays are not uncertain.

2.1.2.5 Combination Operating System

Different types of operating systems are optimized or geared up to serve the needs of specific environments. However, sometimes an environment may be a hybrid of such environments, for example the same computer may be used as software development platform and as a target machine in a real-time environment. For this reason, the commercial operating systems like UNIX, VMS, etc., are designed to provide a large set of services, catering to the need of various environments. If batch and interactive jobs are being run simultaneously, lower priority is assigned to batch jobs. In fact, the batch jobs may be used as filter, executed only when system resources are idling. The processes, handling real-time interrupts to receive real-world events and inputs, will be assigned higher priority. Such systems would normally employ time-sliced, priority-based pre-emptive scheduling. A combination operating system will be one which

caters for the needs of a wide spectrum of target environments. For obvious reasons, such operating systems will not be optimized for a specific environment.

In short: ***If batch and interactive jobs are being run simultaneously, lower priority is assigned to batch jobs.***

2.1.2.6 Distributed Operating System

A distributed operating system caters for a distributed environment, wherein a collection of autonomous computer systems, capable of communicating and cooperating with each other through network, are connected to each other through a Local Area Network/Wide Area Network. A distributed operating system governs the operation of such a distributed system and provides a virtual machine abstraction to its users. Key objective of distributed operating system is transparency, i.e., the resource distribution must be hidden from the users and the application programs, unless they need to determine this information, in which case the information is provided through system services, provided the user has authorization for the same. The distributed operating system provides means for system-side sharing of resources like computational capacity, I/O and files, etc.

In short: ***A distributed operating system governs the operation of such a distributed system and provides a virtual machine abstraction to its users.***

Thus, it should also cater for the following services:

1. **Global sharing of resources**
2. **Distribution of computations:** Computation can be partitioned into a number of Sub Computations that can run concurrently, then a distributed system may allow us to distribute the computation among the various sites - to run that computation concurrently.
3. **Enabling processes to access remote resources**: If a number of different sites are connected to one another, then a user at one site may be able to use the resource available at another. For example — a user at site A may be using a laser printer available only at site B. Meanwhile a user at B may access a file that resides at A.
4. **Enabling processes to communicate with remote processes**: There are many instances in which programs need to exchange data with one another on one system. When many sites are connected to one another by a communication network, the processors at different sites have the opportunity to exchange information. Users may initiate file transfer or communicate with one another via electronic mail.
5. **Reliability**: If one site fails in a distributed system, the remaining sites can potentially continue operating.

2.2 IMPORTANCE OF OPERATING SYSTEMS

We all know the importance of operating system in a computer system. It is there to run the computer and that too without any fault. For this we look at the various needs, goals, services and characteristics of the operating system.

2.2.1 Needs of Operating Systems

Initially the computers were introduced as bare machines. The programs in them were developed by manually translating sequence of instructions into binary or some other code where base is usually an integer power of 2. Then the instructions and data were entered into computer by means of console switches or through a hexadecimal keyboard. Then address of first instruction was loaded into program as a counter to start execution of the program.

Results were obtained by examining the contents of the relevant registers and memory locations. Input/output devices were controlled by the executing program itself. There was no concept of any supporting system software at all. User had to do mostly all of sub-controlling jobs manually or through program. The need was of a user who knew each and everything about machine. A general/naive user was not at all able to work on computer.

At that time the following needs gave birth to the system software and development of operating system.

1. **For fast and automatic working:** As the manual entry and working in absence of system software result into the slow speed of processing so a need of such a software was felt which could do most of the intermediate job automatically so that user has to be least bothered about machines working, resulting into fast and automatic working of the machine. The operating system automates the sequencing of operations involved in program execution.
2. **For better utilization of system resources:** The bare machine approach was not very efficient. With this approach, running of computer system may require frequent manual loading of programs and data. This results in low utilization of system resources. To overcome this problem operating systems with multiuser environment were developed. In absence of operating system even with the help of editors, debuggers and loaders, the program development process was very slow.
3. To realize the resource utilization potential of batch processing, a mounted batch of jobs must be executed automatically, without slow human intervention and their results into the development of operating system.
4. To provide a human interface which could present a communication mode for both of them, the operating system was developed.
5. To match the speed of fast processors and comparatively slow I/O devices the need of operating system was felt.

2.2.2 Goals of Operating Systems

Any operating system should meet the following major goals:

1. Optimize the use of computer resources so as to maximize its throughput.

$$\text{Throughput} = \frac{\text{The number of jobs completed}}{\text{The total time required to complete the jobs}}$$

2. Create a user-friendly computing environment for accessing the computer resources.

To fulfill these two goals, operating system started from command mode and travelled upto graphical user interfaces, i.e., the operating system progressed and became more and more friendly. To facilitate the use of hardware resources researchers developed different types of operating systems which also consider the user and time requirements. Various types of operating systems were developed over 45 years and they were discussed earlier.

2.2.3 Services of Operating System

An operating system provides an environment for the execution of user programs. Operating System provides certain services to the programs and to the users of those programs for the accessing of system resources.

Some of the common services are:

2.2.3.1 Program Execution

The main purpose of operating system is to provide an efficient and convenient environment for the execution of programs. So, an operating system must provide various functions for loading of a program into RAM and execute it. Each executing program must terminate, either normally or abnormally.

2.2.3.2 I/O Operations

A running program would need I/O operations for reading-in of input data and for outputting of results. This I/O may be from/to a file or from/to an I/O device. For each device, some special functions may be necessary (such as rewind a tape, clear screen, etc). All these operations are managed by an operating system.

2.2.3.3 File Manipulations

Each executing program would need to create, delete and manipulate files, which is managed by the operating system.

2.2.3.4 Communications

Operating system manages inter-process communication between the processes, executing on the same computer or running on different computers in a distributed/multi-processor environment. An operating system would provide mechanisms for the inter-process communications like mailboxes, shared memory, etc.

2.2.3.5 Error Detection and Recovery

Errors may occur during execution of a program; like divide by zero, memory access violation, etc. The operating system should provide for detection of such errors (or exceptions) and handle recovery (called Exception Handling).

2.2.3.6 Resource Allocation

When multiple users are logged onto the system or multiple jobs are running concurrently, resources would need to be shared amongst them. The operating system would decide on the allocation of resources; like the CPU scheduling algorithm will determine the control of CPU amongst the concurrent processes. Similarly, there will be routines for the allocation and de-allocation of other resources like memory, I/O devices, files, etc.

2.2.3.7 Accounting

It relates to the accounting of resources used by each user in a multi-user environment. Resource usage statistics may be useful in planning the futuristic requirements of an enterprise.

2.2.3.8 System Protection

This is also a service provided to ensure that the users and user processes are protected from each other. For example, when a process is having an exclusive access to a device allocated to it, no other process would be granted access to that device during that period. Also, no process would be permitted to access

a memory location in a segment not assigned to that process. This service ensures that a process can execute safety.

2.3 POPULAR OPERATING SYSTEMS

Most operating systems come with an application that provides an interface to the OS managed resources. These applications have had command line interpreters as a basic user interface, but more recently have been implemented as a Graphical User Interface (GUI) for ease of operation. Operating Systems themselves have no user interfaces; the user of an OS is an application, not a person. The operating system forms a platform for other system software and for application software. Windows, Linux, and Mac OS are some of the most popular OS's.

In this chapter, we will read about Linux whereas Windows will be tackled in the next chapter.

2.4 OVERVIEW OF LINUX

Linux is used in two ways: specifically to refer to the kernel itself—the heart of any version of Linux—and more generally to refer to any collection that runs on the kernel, usually referred to as a distribution. The kernel's job is to provide the basic environment in which applications can run, including the basic interfaces with hardware and the systems for managing tasks and currently running programs. In the specific sense, there is only one current version of Linux at any one time the current revision of the kernel. Torvalds keeps the kernel as the domain in the world of Linux development, leaving all the applications and services that sit on top of the kernel to any of the thousands of other Linux developers in the world.

In the general meaning of the term Linux, referring to cohesive collections of applications that run on top of the Linux kernel, there are numerous versions of Linux. Each distribution has its own unique characteristics, including different installation methods, different collections of features and different upgrade paths. But since all distributions are fundamentally Linux, in almost every case an application that works with a current version of one distribution will work with a current version of another distribution. The interesting thing about this dichotomous use of the term "Linux" is that it exactly parallels the same confused usage of the term "operating system".

For consumers, an operating system has come to mean a large collection of applications centered around a kernel. This is what Windows 95, 98, Me, NT and 2000 are. This is what the Macintosh OS is. In a purist, technical sense, an operating system is a much smaller core kernel that provides those basic system functions needed to develop any application. In both ways, Linux is an operating system.

Important:* *One of the features of the Linux kernel that sets it apart from other consumer operating systems designed to run on desktop PCs is that it is both multitasking and multiuser.

2.5 BASIC LINUX ELEMENTS

Various Linux elements are given below:

File System

File, files and files. In LINUX everything is s file. Whether it is a file or directory. Even all hardware devices, such as input output devices, storage devices, etc., are all treated as files. The LINUX file system is organized in a hierarchy which starts with the root directory, as is done in the DOS. The root is

represented by a forward slash (/). Under the root directory are several system directories and the home directory.

Kernel

It is the core of LINUX system and is loaded into the memory as soon as the system starts. This in fact, manages main memory, files and peripheral devices. Maintaining the time and date, launching applications and allocating system resources are also its functions.

Shell

It is different from the DOS Shell. It is a program which interprets commands given by the user. The command can be either typed in through the command line or contained in a file called 'shell script'. Commands in 'shell script' files are interpreted by the shell.

Various features of the Shell are:

Interactive Processing: Shell issues the prompts to user to give a command, by which user can communicate with the Linux system.

Input/Output Redirection: Linux is restricted to accept the data from standard I/O lines. When a user issues a command through keyboard, the shell is responsible to redirect the data into standard input file. Kernal places the output of these commands into standard output file. Shell also redirects the output data to printer or screen from standard output file.

Piping Facility: Another Linux utility is called as pipe utility by which simple functions can be connected together and form the more complex functions. By using this facility the output of one command is to be sent as input of another command.

Background Processing: Shell gives the control to the Kernal for execution of jobs such that Kernal executes the non-interactive and time consuming jobs in the background.

Selection criteria with special characters: Shell provides special characters called as "meta characters" to the user. By using these meta characters user can specify a pattern or selection criteria to select one or more files.

Shell Variables: Shell allows the user to control the environment, by setting of these variables.

Shell Script: Shell script is a set of commands and treated as a Linux program file. This feature allows the user to use the shell as a programming language.

2.6 POPULAR COMMANDS OF LINUX

Some of the Linux commands and filters are:

Mkdir

Creates one or more directories.

`mkdir [-p] [-m mode] [-parents] [-mode=mode] directory ...`

where the variables are:

-m/— mode mode: Sets the mode for the created directory using the same symbolic notation as the chmod command. If this is not specified, the default mode is assigned to the directory.

-p/—parents: Ensures that the parents of the specified directory exist and creates any missing parent directories needed.

CD

Changes the current directory. If you type cd without specifying an argument, this command changes to the current user's home directory.

```
cd [directory | path name]
```

where the variables are:

directory: is the name of the directory.

path name: path name of the directory

mdir

Displays the contents of a directory on an MS-DOS file system such as a floppy disk. If specific files are indicated, then only those files are listed. Similar to the DOS DIR command.

```
mdir [-w] msdosdirectory
    mdir [-a] [-f] [-w] msdosfile [msdosfile ...]
```

where the variables are:

-a: Lists hidden files as well as regular files.

-f: Displays files without listing total free space at the end of the listing

-w: Displays files in wide output.

ls

Displays a listing of files and directories. If no file or directory is specified, then the current directory's contents are displayed. By default, contents are sorted alphabetically.

```
ls [-acdlrRsStuX] [—all] [—time=ctime] [—time=status] [—directory] [—format-long] [—format=verbose] [—reverse] [— recursive] [—size] [—sort-size] [—sort=time] [—time=atime] [—time-access] [—time-use] [—sort=extension] [file |directory ...]
```

where the variables are:

-a/—all: Lists all files in the directory, including those that start with ".".

-c/—time=ctime,—time=status: Sorts entries by the change time of the files.

-d/—directory: Lists directory names only, without showing directory contents. By default, directory contents are listed.

-l/—format-long/—format=verbose: Lists files in long format, including file type, permissions, owner and size.

-r/—reverse: Displays files in reverse order.

-R/—recursive: Lists the content of all subdirectories recursively.

-s/—size: Displays the size of files, in kilobytes.

-S/—sort=size: Sorts entries by the file starting with the largest file.

-t/—sort=time: Sorts entries by timestamp starting with the newest files.

-u/—time=atime/—time=access/—time=use: Sorts entries by the last access time.

-X/—sort=extension: Sorts files by the file extension in alphabetical order.

who

Displays a list of the uses currently logged into the system. If you type who without an option, you will see the user's name, the terminal they are using, and the time they logged on.

```
who [option]
```

If you use -H or -heading as options, you will get column headings. -help will give you the list of available options.

whoami

Displays the username of the user currently logged in to this terminal session or it identifies the user who invoked the command.

```
whoami
```

cat

Combines one or more files and displays them on the standard output. If no files are given, then the standard input is written to the standard output.

```
cat [-benstvAET] [-number] [-number-nonblank] [squeese-blank] [-show-nonprinting] [-show-ends] [-show-tabs] [-show-all] [file...]
```

where the variables are:

-A/—show-all: Displays a $ at the end of each line, tab characters as ^I and control characters preceded by a^. This is the same as the combination of –v, -T and –E.

-b/—number-nonblank: Causes all non-blank lines to appear numbered. Numbering starts at 1.

-e: Displays a $ at the end of each line and control characters preceded by a ^. This is the same as the combination of –v and –E.

-E/—show-ends: Displays a $ at the end of each line.

—n/—number: Causes al lines to appear numbered. Numbering starts at 1.

-s/—squeeze-blank: Replaces sequences of multiple blank lines with single blank lines when displayed.

-t: Displays tab characters as ^I and control characters preceded by a^. This is the same as the combination of –v and -T.

-T/—show-tabs: Displays tab characters as ^I.

-v/—show-nonprinting: Displays control character preceded by a^.

more

Displays one or more files screen-by-screen and allows for searching and jumping to an arbitrary location in the file.

```
more [-dlfs] [-number] [+number] [file ...]
```

where the variables are:

-number: Sets the number of lines per screen.

+number: Specifies the line to start on when displaying.

-d: Prompts the user at the end of each screen.

-f: Causes long lines not to be folded and to be counted as a single line.

-l: Prevents Ctrl+L from being treated as a form feed.

-s: Squeezes multiple blank lines into a single blank line.

For details of the commands that can be used when viewing files, consult the more man page.

tail

Print the last ten lines of each file to the standard output. You can specify more than one filename in a space-separated list or by using a shell pattern. The command prints the name of each file before the text. If you remove the filename, the command accepts input from the standard input.

```
tail [option] [filename]
```

where the options can be:

-retry: Keep trying to open the file.

-c, -bytes=n: Output the last n bytes

-f, -follow: Ouput appended data the file grows

-help: Shows the available options

-n, -lines=n: Output the last n lines instead of the last 10 lines

-pid=pid: Terminates after pid terminates

-q, -quiet, -silent: Suppress the display to filenames

-s, -sleep-interval=n, Sleep n seconds after iterations

-v, -verbose Always show filenames

-version Show the version number

head

Displays the first part of one or more files. By default, unless otherwise specified, the first 10 lines of each file are displayed. If no filenames are provided, then needs data from the standard input and displays the first section of the data, following the same rules as for files.

```
head [-c number[bkm] [-n number] [-qv] [—bytes number[bkm]] [—lines number]
[—quiet] [—silent] [file ...]
```

where the variables are:

-c/—bytes number: Displays the specified number of bytes from the start of each file. Optionally, the number can be followed by b for 512-byte blocks, k for kilobytes and m for megabytes.

-n/—lines number: Displays the specified number of lines from the start of each file.

-q/—quiet/—silent: Prevents printing of filename headers when multiple files are being processed.

concept of mv

Renames and moves files. When a directory is the last argument, move all other specified files into that directory.

```
mv [-bfiu] [—backup] [—force] [—interactive] [—update] [source destinations
```

```
| source ... directory]
```

where the variables are:

-b/—backup: Makes a backup of files that are about to be overwritten by the move without prompting.

-f/—force: removes existing files that are about to be overwritten by the move without prompting.

-i/—interactive: Prompts before overwriting any existing files.

-u/—update: Does not overwrite an existing file if it has the same or newer modification time.

chmod

Changes the access permissions of one or more files or directories.

```
chmod [-Rcfv] [—recursive] [—changes] [—silent] [—quiet] [—verbose] mode
file ...
```

where the variables are:

-c/—changes: Displays the names of only those files whose permissions are being changed.

-f/—silent/—quiet: Suppresses display or error messages when a file's permissions cannot be changed.

-R/—recursive: Recursively changes the permissions of all files in all subdirectories of any directory that has its permissions changed.

-v/—verbose: Displays the results of all permission changes.

Modes can be specified in two ways: symbolically and numerically. When done symbolically, modes take the form [ugoa] [[+-=] [rwxXstugo ...]. The first element ([ugoa]) represents the users whose permissions are being affected (u=user who owns the file or directory, g=all members of the group that owns the file or directory, o=anyone who is not the owner or in the owner group, a=all users). The + symbol means that the specified modes should be added to already specified permissions, the – symbol means the specified modes should be removed from existing permissions and the = symbol means that the specified modes should replace existing permissions. There are many different permissions that can be specified in the third element of the mode, including r for read permissions, w for write permissions and x for execute permissions.

Full details of symbolic and numeric modes appear in the chmod man page.

grep

Searches files for lines matching a specified pattern and displays the lines.

```
grep [-bCcEFGiLinux] [-number] [-e pattern] [-f file] [-basic-regexp] [—
byte-offset] [—exended-regexp] [—fixed-strings] [—byte-offset] [—context]
[—count] [—regex[=pattern] [—file=file] [—ignore=case] [—files-without-
match] [—files-with-match] [—line-number] [—revert-match] [—word-regexp]
[—line—regexp] [pattern] file [file ...]
```

where the variables are:

-number: Displays matching lines with the specified number of lines of leading and trailing context.

-b/—byte-offset: Prints the byte offset of the match before each line.

-c/—count: Instead of displaying matching lines, simply outputs a count of the total number of lines matching the expressions (when combined with –v, displays the total count of non-matching lines).

-C/—context: Displays matching lines with two lines of leading and trailing context (this is the same as -2).

-e pattern/—regexp=pattern: Uses the specified pattern rather than one provided as an argument.

-E/—extended-regexp: Treats the pattern as an extended regular expression (similar to egrep).

-f file/—file=file: Uses the pattern found in the specified file rather than one supplied as an argument.

-F/—fixed-strings: Treats the pattern as a list of new line separated strings, one of which must match. This is the same as fgrep.

-G/—basic-regexp: Treats the pattern as a basic regular expression.

-i/—ignore=case: Ignores case in both the pattern and the files being searched.

-l/—files-with-matches: Instead of displaying each matched line, simply displays the name of each file that contains at least one match for the pattern.

-L/—files-with-match: Instead of displaying each matched line, simply displays the name of each file that contains no matches for the patterns.

-n/—line-number: Prefixes each output line with its line number in the file.

-v/—revert-match: Displays non-matching lines instead of matching lines.

-w/—word-regexp: Displays only those lines with matches for the pattern that are complete words.

-x/—line-regexp: Displays only those lines with matches for the pattern that are complete lines.

The syntax of regular expressions used by grep can be found in the grep man page.

wc

Prints the number of bytes (characters), words and lines in one or more documents. When multiple filenames are provided, each file will be counted and displayed separately and then a cumulative total will be displayed. If no files are specified, then the standard input is counted.

```
wc [-clw] [—byte]s [—chars] [—lines] [—words] [file ...]
```

where the variables are:

-c/—bytes/—chars: Displays only the number of bytes.

-l/—lines: Displays only the number of lines.

-w/—words: Displays only the number of words.

The results are displayed in this order: characters, words, lines. The values are separated by spaces.

comm

The comm command in Linux is a utility that is used to compare two files. It shows common lines in one column and differing lines in separate columns for left and right files. This functionally is similar to diff.

One notable difference between comm and diff is that comm will not try to indicate that a line has "changed" between the two files; lines are either shown in the "from file #1", "from file #2", or "in

both" columns. This feature can be especially useful if one wishes two lines to be considered different even if they only have subtle differences.

comm also has options to suppress any of the three columns which is useful for a scripting.

split

split is a Unix utility most commonly used to split a file into one or more smaller files.

The command-syntax is:

```
split (optional parameters) (input filename) (output filename)
```

The default behaviour of split is to generate output files of up to 1000 lines. The files are named by appending aa, ab, ac, etc. to output filename. If output filename is not given, the default filename of x is used, for example, xaa, xab, etc. When a hyphen (-) is used instead of input filename, data is derived from standard input.

To join the files back together again use the cat command

```
cat xaa xab xac > filename
```

or

```
cat xa[a-c] > filename
```

Additional program options permit a maximum character count (instead of a line count), a maximum line length, how many incrementing characters are there in generated filenames, and whether to use letters or digits.

sort

Sorts the lines contained in one or more text files and displays the results. If no files are indicated, data is taken from the standard input and sorted. The resulting sorted data is displayed to the standard output.

```
sort [-cu] [-t separator] [-o file] [-T temdier] [-bdfMnr] [+POS1 [-POS2]] [-k POS1[,POS2]] [file ...]
```

where the variables are:

-b: Ignores leading blanks in lines when trying to find sort keys.

-c: Checks whether the input data is sorted and prints an error message if it isn't. No sorting actually takes place.

-d: Ignores all characters except letters, digits and blanks in the sorting process.

-f: Converts lowercase letters to uppercase letters during the sorting process.

-k POS1[,PS2]: Specifies the field to use as the sorting key. The field will start at POS1 and run up until POS2 or the end of the line. Fields and character positions are specified starting at zero.

-M: Sorts months. That is, any strings that starts with zero or more blank followed by three letters are converted to uppercase and sorted as if they were abbreviated month names.

-n: Compares strings numerically, which assumes that strings start with zero or more blanks followed by an optional sign and then number.

-o file: Outputs the results to the specified file instead of the standard output.

+POS1 [-POS2]: Specifies the field to use as the sorting key. The field will start at POS1 and run up

until POS2 or the end of the line. Fields and character positions are specified starting at zero.

-r: Reverse the sort order.

-t separator: Indicates that the specified separator should serve as the field separator for finding sort keys on each line.

-u: When two lines compare as equal, only output the first.

diff

In Linux, diff is a file comparison utility that outputs the differences between two files. The program displays the changes made per line for text files. Modern implementations also support binary files. The output is called a diff or more commonly a patch since the output can be applied with the program patch. The output of similar file comparison utilities are also called a "diff". Like the use of the word "grep" for describing the act of searching, the word diff is used in jargon as a verb for calculating any difference.

kill

Sends a kill signal to one or more running processes.

```
kill [-s signal| -p] pid ...
kill -l
```

where the variables are:

-l: Displays a list of signal names.

-p: Prints the process ID of a specified process rather than sending it a signal.

-s signal: Sends the specified signal to the specified processes.

-pid: Specifies either the ID of a process or its name. When specifying processes by name, all processes with the specified name will receive the signal.

write

Write is the Linux facility to forward the contents of a file to a user. This command allows to send a message to another user, currently on the system.

```
writer user [tty] [<file name>]
```

Communication continues from one terminal to another, unit <ctrl + D> is pressed. <EOT> or <EOF> on the other user's screen indicating the end of transmission or end of the file.

wall

Wall has similar function as the write command. However, the main difference is that wall delivers the message to all the users logged on the system. Once the user is given the message from standard input, command reads the message from standard input (keyboard) and proceeds to write it simultaneously on every user's terminal.

merge

This command combines the features of mail and news, which are listed next.

mail

Sends and receives e-mails. The user will be prompted for the test of the message unless it is provided through the standard input. Also, other information such as the subject can be provided as a flat when sending messages or the program can prompt for the information. If no options or arguments are specified, the current user's mailbox is opened for reading.

```
mail [-s subject] [-c address …] [-b address ….] address
    mail -f [mailbox]
    mail - u [user]
```

where the variables are:

ib address ...: Indicates a list of addresses that should receive blind carbon copies of outgoing messages.

-c address ...: Indicates a list of addresses that should receive a carbon copy of outgoing messages.

-f [mailbox]: Reads mail from your inbox or the mailbox specified.

-s subject: Specifies the subject line of outgoing messages.

-u user: Opens the specified user's inbox for reading.

The mechanics of using mail to read messages is discussed in the mail man page.

news

Write and wall commands are used to give the message to all users who are currently logged onto the system. By using news command, the messages or news can be sent to all users even if they are not logged in.

```
news [option]
```

2.7 FILE HANDLING IN LINUX

There are two important features of Linux files, Naming conventions and File information.

2.7.1 Naming Conventions

Following is what you have to keep in mind while naming the files.

- You can create file names of upto 255 characters in length.
- Linux file names are case sensitive, e.g., subject.DOC,. SUBJECT.doc, subject.doc are three different files.
- Avoid using the illegal characters in the file name.

Character	Function
#	Inserts a comment; bash ignores the rest of the line.
&	Inserts a named variable.
* ? [ ] ~ !	Constructs shell patterns.
< >	Redirects input and output.
`	Inserts the output of the specified command.

; Begins new command on the same line.

( ) Groups commands for execution in a subshell. The grouped commands execute before other commands.

{ } Groups commands so that they execute before other commands.

- You can use only the letter a–z, A–Z, the numbers 0–9, and underscore (_).
- Avoid using the <space bar>, <Tab> and <Backspace> in filenames for practical reasons.
- Linux does not require the use of suffers called as extensions. Extension is the part of file name mostly of three characters after the period.
- Filenames begining with a period are called hidden files.

2.7.2 File Information

Each Linux file has the following information:

Information	Meaning
Location	Where is the file stored on the disk?
File type	What is the type of file?
Permissions	Who can access the file-owner, group members, or other users?
Number of Linux	How many names of the existing file?
Owner name	Name of the owner of the file.
Grouphone	Group's name of file.
Size	Size of files in bytes
Modification	Date and time of file when was last modified.
Filename	Name of the file.

Command to be given for the information about the file.

file

Determines and displays the type of files.

```
file [-zL] [-f file] file ...
```

where the variables are:

-f file: Reads the list of files to be checked from the specified file. These will be checked before checking files provided as arguments.

-L: Causes symbolic links to be followed.

-z: Attempts to look at the type of files inside compressed files.

2.7.3 File Structure

Linux uses the method of hierarchical file structure. The files which it uses are ordinary, directory, character and block device files. It is as said earlier, an upside-down tree structure with the root directory on the top. It can be followed by three types of directories:

System directory: These directories make the Linux system. All system directories have same files and system programs used to specify the features of Linux system.

Home directory: When user logs in system opens the home directory for user to create the number of files. System gives the same name to home directory as the user's log in name called as working directory of user.

User directory: User's home directory containing a number of directories created by user is called as users directory.

Standard Directory Structure

Directory	Purpose
/	The root directory. Stores essential start-up files and serves as the top-level directory for the entire directory structure. It is different from with/root.
/bin	Stratup programs and commands used in signle-user mode.
/boot	Files used to start the system.
/dev	Special files representing system devices and device drivers.
/etc	System-level configuration files and scripts.
/home	The user's home directories
/lib	Shared library files.
/mnt	The mount point for temporary file systems.
/opt	The installation directory for commercial software.
/proc	The virtual file system for kernal and process information.
/root	The home directory for the user. It is different from the root directory (/).
/sbin	Essential system utilities that are used for booting the system.
/tmp	The storage space for temporary files.
/usr	The storage space for files that need to be made available system wise, including user utilities and programs (/usr/bin); documentation (/usr/doc); libraries used by user-installed programs (/usr/lib); software installed by users (/usr/local); man pages (/usr/man); non-essential system administration utilities (/usr/sbin); and other shared items, such as fonts and icons (/usr/share).
/var	Data files of variable length, including spool directories for mail and printing.

Directory Names and Symbols

Example	Description
.	The current or working directory
..	The parent directory
-	The home directory of the current user
/	The root directory (not/root)
../directory	Refers to another directory of the same parent
/home/class/subject/chapter	The absolute path name.

2.7.4 Listing, Displaying and Printing Files

Various commands which are used for listing files are: dir, is, and pwd. For displaying are: od, cat, more, comm, diff, tail, split, and less. For printing we use the commands lpr, and lpq. Details of the commands are as follows:

dir

Displays a listing of the files in a specified directory, in alphabetical order unless otherwise specified. By default, displays the contents of the current directory unless another directory is specified.

```
dir [-acCGlnrRStuU[ [-all] [—no-group] [—numeric-uid-gid] [—reverse] [—
recursive] [file ...]
```

where the variables are:

-a/—all: Shows all entries, including those whose names start with *.*.

-c: Sorts by the creation time of the file and when displaying complete file information (with the –l flag), displays the creation time.

-C: Displays entries in column.

-G/—no-group: Prevents display of group information.

-l: displays files with long listing format.

-n/—nimeric-uid-gid: Lists user IDs and group IDs (UIDs and GIDs) instead of names.

-r/—reverse: Reverses order of entries when sorting.

-R/—recursive: Recursively lists contents of subdirectories.

-S: Sorts files by size.

-t: Sorts by the modification time of the file and when displaying complete file information (with the –l flag), displays the modification time.

-u: sorts by the last access time of the file and when displaying complete file information (with the –l flag), displays the last access time.

-U: Displays entries in their directory order rather than sorted.

ls

(Refers to the command reference given earlier)

pwd

Displays the name of the current directory.

```
pwd
```

Displays the full path name of the current directory. If you have forgotten which directory is current, type pwd and press Enter to see the directory's path name. pwd accepts no input. It has no options and displays a single line of output.

od

Writes filename to the standard output in octal and other formats. When no filename is specified, the utility accepts input from the standard input.

```
od [option] [filename]
```

Various options which can be used are:

Option	To do
–A	Use radix as the file offset. For radix, you can use d for decimal, o for octal, x for hexadecimal, or n for none.
–help	Show the available options.
–j n	Skip n bytes at the start of each file.
–N n	Do not process more than n bytes per file.
–s [n]	Output strings of n graphics characters.
-t type	Use the specified type of output format. The output formats are listed below.
–v, –output	Suppress use of asterisks to mark line suppression.
–w n, –width [=n]	Write n bytes per output line.

Output Types

Name	Description
a	Named character
c	ASCII character or backslash Escape
d [n]	Signed decimal with n bytes per integer
f [n]	Floating point with n bytes per integer
o [n]	Octal with n bytes per integer
u [n]	Unsigned decimal with n bytes per integer
x [n]	Hexadecimal with n bytes per integer.

The following commands are covered earlier.

cat, more, comm, diff, tail, split

less

Displays the specified filename on-screen and enables you to page through it easily. You can specify more than one filename in space-separated list or by using a shell pattern. If you omit the filename, the utility accepts input from the standard input.

```
less [option] [filename]
```

Various options which can be used are:

Option	To do
–?, –help	Displays available options.
+ command	Start less with command.
–a	Begin searches after the screen's last line.
–h n	Scroll back no more than n lines.
–l, –ignore-case	Ignore case in searches.
-1, -IGN, E-CASE	Ignore case in searches even when the search expression contains uppercase letters.
–j n	Jump to line number n. The first line of the screen is line 1.

–n, –line-numbers Suppress the line numbers.

–N, –LINE NUMBERS Display the line numbers.

–u, –undeline-special Display back spaces and carriage returns as control characters.

–V, –version Displays the version number of less.

–w, –hilite-unread Highlight the first new line after scrolling.

–W, –HILITE-UNREAD Highlight the first new line after any forward movement.

–x n, –tabs=n Set tab stops every n spaces. The default is 8.

–y n, –max-f=n, w-scroll=n Scroll forward no more than n lines.

lpr

Prints filename. Sends a file to the line printer.

```
lpr [option] filename
```

Various options which can be used are:

Option	To do
–# n	Prints n copies.
–C string	Print the specified string as the job classification on the burst page.
–h	Suppress the printing of the burst page.

lpq

Prints one or more files to the specified printer spool. If no files are indicated, then the standard input is sent to the printer spool. If no printer is specified, data will be sent to the default printer.

```
lpt [[-Pprinter] [-#number] [-C class] [-j job] [-I [numcols]] [-hlmrs]
[file ...]
```

where the variables are:

-#number:	Specifies the number of copies to print of each file. The default is one copy.
-C class:	Prints the specified class name instead of the host name on the header page.
-h:	Suppresses the printing of a header page.
-I [numcols]:	Indicates that output should be indented by the number of blanks specified or by 8 characters if no number is indicated
-j job:	Prints the specified job name instead of the filename on the header page.
-l:	Allows control characters to be printed while suppressing page breaks.
-m:	Sends an e-mail to the user when the print job is finished.
-Pprinter:	Prints to the specified printer.
-r:	Removes files after printing them.
-s:	Creates a symbolic link to the file being printed rather than copying the file to the spool directory. This is useful when printing extremely large files.

2.8 IDENTIFYING THE CURRENT WORKING DIRECTORY

For this you can use the *pwd* command mentioned earlier.

2.9 INSTALLATION OF LINUX

Before installing any software, you must check whether your computer hardware is going to support it or not. So before we read about the actual installing, we must know what all is needed both in terms of Hardware and Software for installing Linux.

2.9.1 Hardware Requirements

For an ideal Linux based PC your computer must have the following:

- An IBM Compatible PC with minimum 80386. 80486 is better.
- Any processor from Intel, Sparc, Alpha or AMD
- Minimum 128 MB RAM
- Minimum 2 GB free hard disk space
- Input devices such as keyboard, mouse, etc.
- Controller cards such as SCSI, IDE, etc.
- A Network card such as ISA, PCI or USB etc.
- Sound card compatible to LINUX

2.9.2 Software Requirements

- A partitioning program such as fdisk or disk druid supplied by Red Hat.
- Linux Software package.

2.9.3 Steps before Installation

First you must create an installation disk.

2.9.4 Creating an Installation Disk

For this do the following:

1. Copy the file **boot.img** from the Red Hat CD-ROM disk to a floppy disk. This file can be found in the /images directory of the CD. The file can be created using either the DOS rewrite command (in a DOS/Windows system) or the Linux dd command (in an existing LINUX or UNIX system). For example, to create an installation diskette using the dd command, do the following:
   (a) Insert and mount the CD-ROM and then insert a blank floppy into the floppy drive of your computer.
   (b) Now give the following command

   ```
   # dd if = mnt/cdrom/images/boot.img of = /dev/fd0 bs = 1440k
   ```

   and then press Enter

   The above command will copy form the input file ("if) mnt/cdrom/boot.img onto the output file ("of") /dev/fd0. It is assumed that floppy drive is accessible from /dev/fd0. To create an installation diskette using the rewrite program, give the following command. (it is assumed that CD-ROM is accessible as drive D):

```
D:>cd images dousutils\rawrite enter
```

For the source file enter "D:\boot.img" and for destination enter "A:".

The bootable installation disk is now ready and you can use it to install your LINUX system.

Red Hat LINUX can also be installed by booting using any of the following methods using :

- a floppy diskette
- CD-ROM
- hard drive partition to hold the installation software
- DOS command line
- a network using HTTP or FTP protocols.
- an NFS (Network File System) mounted hard drive.

2. This is the most important step, partitioning. For this you must have some knowledge of the hardware. For this you have to look into the following:
   - Disk space, required now and maybe in future
   - Requirement of any other operating system
   - Installation of applications software, now and in future
   - Data back up needs
   - Number of users
3. Refer to the step above, where if you have opted for one or more operating system besides Linux, then that step becomes compulsory. All you have to do is to select a boot loader. It is a software that is responsible for booting LINUX along with any other operating system. It can be either LILO (LINUX Loader) or GRUB (Grand Unified Boot loader). Here you must know whether the version of operating system is compatible with the current version of Linux.
4. Now insert the floppy disk (the installation diskette you have created if you are using floppy to boot your system) into a floppy drive and power-on your system. After a few moments, the Red Hat installation program screen will appear.
5. Follow the steps as directed on the screen.

2.10 HARD DISK PARTITIONING

Here is an optimum partition of a hard disk.

/swap directory	About double the main directory size. For example, a system having 128 MB memory should get 256 MB swap space.
/directory (root)	About 60% of the available space. That is about 1200 MB in a 2 GB hard disk.
/bin directory	About 20% of the available space. This is about 400 MB in a 2 GB hard disk.
/user directory	Remaining space

The size of /user should be the largest one. This is because all the users' directories and files, installed application softwares, web pages, log files etc. will be stored here only. You can have a perfectly running LINUX system on a single partitioned hard disk also. Partitioning the hard disk however, has the following advantages:

(a) Reduces the time required to perform file system checks.

(b) Mounting of one or more of your partitions as read only.

(c) Protects filesystem. If a filesystem gets destroyed due to some reason, you will probably lose only the files on a single partition. All other partitions will remain unaffected.

(d) Allows you to have multiple operating systems.

2.11 BOOTING A LINUX SYSTEM

The booting process may differ from system to system and depending upon the type of hardware platforms being used. Generally, it involves checking of the basic subsystems of your computer, such as amount and validity of RAM, CPU time and speed, presence of floppy, CD-ROM or hard drive, keyboard and other attributes and peripherals. The booting process will fail, if there is hardware failure or if there is mismatch in the configuration. Next, comes the software part which is there in the BIOS of the bootable disk or CD, whichever may be mentioned in the bootable process of the BIOS. Then it will look for the boot code in the Master Boot Record (MBR) of the first hard disk. This area of the disk (MBR) contains the boot sector which loads the boot loader (viz. LILO, GRUB or BootMagic).

Once the operating system of Linux is loaded, Kernel takes over and performs the following operations:

- Initializes the RAM disk image.
- Performs timing tests
- Parse for any boot time kernel arguments.
- Recognise, sets-up and initialises the CPU.
- Sets up kernel memory and process handling.
- Opens a console for displaying kernel boot messages.
- Initializes configured system devices.
- Starts memory handling
- Sets up and mounts the file system
- Starts the init command

The entire sequence of events that take place when the LINUX kernel is loaded can be found in the file usr/src/linux/init/main.c. If all goes well, you will see a "login" prompt. You can now login using your username and password.

LET US REVISE

1. Linux is an operating system.
2. It is available free.
3. Linux runs on PC machines with minimum of 386 processor.
4. Linux is a complete operating system with Graphical User Interface, X windows system, TCP/IP, Emacs editor and other components usually found in an operating system.
5. Kernal, Shell and File structures are three major components of Linux.
6. Kernal is a master program that runs programs and controls the resources of the computer system.

7. Shell provides an interface to the user. Three types of Linux shell are: Boure Again Shell, TC-Shell and Public Domain Shell.
8. Linux has Hierarchical File structure.
9. Linux is a command line Interpreter.
10. Prompt designates the beginning of the command line.
11. Keyboard and screen are treated as standard input and standard output respectively.
12. dir command lists the files in the current directory.
13. cd changes the current directory
14. is lists the files in the current directory.
15. pwd displays the full path name of the current directory.
16. mkdir creates the specified directory.
17. rmdir removes the directory.
18. cat displays the specified file name on screen.
19. more displays filename on screen page wise.
20. tail prints the last ten lines of the each file on the screen.
21. head displays the first ten lines of filename on screen.
22. chmod changes the permissions of the file name.
23. symbolic and numeric are the two types of modes to set the permissions of the file.
24. mv renames or moves one source file to a destination file.
25. rm removes the specified file.
26. wc displays line, word and character counts for the specified file.
27. sort command sorts the specified file line by line in character order.
28. cmp compares the two specified files.
29. diff locates the differences between two files.
30. com prints the lines in each file as well as those common to both.
31. who displays a list of users currently logged in.
32. whoami identifies the user who invoked the command.
33. ps displays information about processes executing on the system.
34. kill terminates the execution of a background process.
35. write is used to send a message to a user on the system.
36. wall is used to send a message to all users on the system.
37. news is used to send a message to all users who logged or not logged in.
38. mail is used to send the message to all users on the network.
39. grep is a utility to search and select Linux filters.
40. !, #, $, &, &&, ( ), / , ;, " ", { }, | | are the special characters of shell.
41. *, ?, < >, are wild card characters.
42. ' ', " ", \ are quotation characters, used to prevent bash from processing special characters.
43. >, <, >>, << are redirectional symbols.
44. '1' is the pipe character.
45. 2 > 2 >> & 1, >& are redirecting symbols for standard errors.

46. 1 & are the piping symbol for standard errors.
47. File descriptions for standard input, standard output and standard errors are 0, 1, 2 respectively.
48. A sequence of Linux commands to perform a specific task is called as shell script.
49. Shell script can be run by sh or . commands.
50. Command given by user is called as job performed by system.

MULTIPLE CHOICE QUESTIONS

1. Cost of Linux operating system is:
   (a) $100 (b) $480 (c) Its FREE
2. Windows version of Linux is:
   (a) L Windows (b) X Windows (c) M Windows
3. Linux can be loaded on PC:
   (a) Yes (b) No
4. There is no software based on Linux:
   (a) True (b) False
5. Database available on Linux is known as:
   (a) mSQL (b) lSQL (c) Not available
6. Popular distributor of Linux is:
   (a) Red Hat (b) Blue Hat (c) Green Hat
7. Linux can be installed from :
   (a) floppy disk (b) CD ROM (c) both
8. Linux components have :
   (a) kernel (b) shell (c) both
9. Hard disk is partitioned to have :
   (a) another operating system (b) more hard disk space (c) less hard disk space
10. There are two types of pathnames, Absolute and :
    (a) Relational (b) Relative (c) Reasonable
11. In Linux directory is also a :
    (a) shell (b) hard disk (c) file
12. Linux file system uses :
    (a) backslash (b) forward slash (c) both

TRUE/FALSE QUESTIONS

1. Linux can be downloaded free from Internet.
2. Linux is similar to Unix.
3. Linux has no versions.
4. Linux does not support multitasking operating system.
5. Linux can be developed as an applications server.

6. A wide variety of programming and scripting languages and tools are available for Linux .
7. X Windows is a highly flexible and configurable GUI environment that runs on Linux as well as on most Unix systems.
8. There are no software available for Linux operating systems.
9. Kernel is the core of the Linux system.
10. Shell is not there in Linux.
11. In Linux everything is a file.
12. Linux uses a backward slash in its file system.
13. You can give either a Relative pathname or an Absolute pathname to the Linux files.
14. Hard disk has to be partitioned if you have to have more than one operating system.
15. Red Hat Software is the most popular version of Linux.
16. It is not possible to get Linux up and running on a 386-based computer with only 4MB of RAM.
17. A sound card will enhance your working under Linux.
18. Linux, which offers a wealth of powerful and flexible Web server as well as fully functional relational database systems.
19. Linux in a small office environment is as the actual desktop operating system.
20. X Windows is a complete graphics interface for Unix and by extension, for Linux.

MATCHING COLUMNS

Match the matter in Column A with the matter in Column B.

Column A	Column B
A. Red hat Linux	1. Operating system
B. Pathnames: Relative and	2. X Windows
C. Partition hard disk to have	3. Forward slash
D. Kernel	4. file
E. Cost of linux software	5. 128 MB
F. Linux is an	6. mSQL
G. Everything in Linux is a	7. It is free
H. Linux uses	8. Absolute
I. Windows version of Linux	9. A version of Linux
J. RAM requirement for Linux installation	10. CD ROM
K. Linux database	11. Another operating system
L. Linux can be installed from	12. A Linux component

FILL IN THE BLANKS WITH APPROPRIATE WORDS

a. mSQL	b. Forward	c. X Windows	d. Networking
e. Relative	f. floppy disk	g. Shell	h. Partitioned

i. Absolute j. Red k. CD-ROM l. 128

m. files n. Operating o. Kernel

1. Linux can be installed from _______ and _______.
2. _______ is a Linux database.
3. Popular linux version is _______ hat linux.
4. Windows version of Linux is known as _____ .
5. A hard disk has to be _________ to have second operating system.
6. RAM requirement for Linux installation is _____ MB.
7. Linux files can have _______ and _______ pathnames.
8. Linux uses _____ slash.
9. Linux is an _______ system.
10. In Linux even directories are ______.
11. _____ and _____ are part of Linux components.
12. Linux supports _________.

DESCRIPTIVE TYPE QUESTIONS

1. What is Linux?
2. How was Linux developed?
3. How can you use Linux as an operating system?
4. Is Linux a multiuser operating system?
5. Describe the various applications of Linux system.
6. How can Linux be obtained?
7. What are the feautes of Linux?
8. What is meant by Linux distribution?
9. Write a short note on Red Hat Linux distributor.
10. What are the minimum requirements for Linux working on PC?
11. How does Linux support the file system?
12. Write a short note on Linux as database server.
13. What is X Windows?
14. How does it differ from Microsoft Windows?
15. Describe the various components of Linux.
16. Which are the main directories of Linux?
17. How would you install Linux?
18. What are the hardware requirements for installing Linux?
19. What are the software requirements for installing Linux?
20. What steps you have to follow before installing Linux?

ANSWERS TO OBJECTIVE QUESTIONS

Multiple Choice Questions

1. c	2. b	3. a	4. b
5. a	6. a	7. c	8. c
9. a	10. b	11. c	12. b

True False Questions

1. T	2. T	3. F	4. F
5. T	6. T	7. T	8. F
9. T	10. F	11. T	12. F
13. T	14. T	15. T	16. F
17. T	18. T	19. T	20. T

Matching Columns

A. 9	B. 8	C. 11	D. 12
E. 7	F. 1	G. 4	H. 3
I. 2	J. 5	K. 6	L. 10

Fill in the Blanks with Appropriate Words

1. f, k	2. a	3. j	4. c
5. h	6. l	7. e, i	8. b
9. n	10. m	11. g, o	12. d

Chapter

3 Introduction to Windows

3.1 INTRODUCTION TO WINDOWS

Windows is nothing but graphics-based operating environment from Microsoft. It provides a desktop environment similar to the Macintosh, in which each active application is displayed in a resizable, moveable window on the screen. Initially Windows ran on DOS platform, but now-a-days it runs on its own platform.

Windows 1.x, Windows 286 (2.x) and Windows 386 were first attempts. Windows 3.0 had its own enhanced user interface and ability to manage extended memory, upto 16MB with built-in DOS extender.

Windows 3.1 (1992) was faster and supported multimedia, true type fonts, drag and drop, among other features. It was the last of the Windows versions based to work on DOS platform. From this point onward Microsoft introduced Windows 95 which was independent of DOS and had its booting capabilities.

Windows for Workgroups for was introduced in 1993. It was the first version of Windows which truly supported networking. This was later enhanced to Windows NT, which was introduced in 1993.

3.2 FEATURES OF WINDOWS XP

The new version of Windows XP has 2 editions mainly, Home and Professional. So even the new features are also given for both separately, starting with Home Edition.

3.2.1 Improved/New Features in Home Edition

Fast User Switching: Sharing a PC? You can access your own account without having to close each other's applications or restart the computer.

New, Simplified Visual Design: The clean, simple design of Windows XP puts the features you use most often up front and center, so you can get to them quickly.

Windows Media Player for Windows XP

A single, easy-to-use place to play DVDs, organize music, burn CDs and more.

Windows Messenger: Communicate with your friends and family in real time. See who is online and choose to communicate through text messaging, voice or video, with excellent performance and better quality than ever.

Windows Movie Maker: Capute, edit, organize and share home movies on your computer, whether you made them with a digital or analog video camera.

My Pictures: Organize, preview digital photos and even order prints via a Web service.

Internet Explorer 6: Includes new and better features to simplify Web browsing tasks, increase reliability and help keep your personal information private.

Remote Assistance: Allow a friend or support professional who is also running Windows XP to remotely control your computer to demonstrate a process or help solve a problem.

System Restore: If something goes wrong with your computer, you can revert the system back to a previous working state.

Network Setup Wizard: The easy way to set up your own home network so all the computers in your house can share printers, devices, files and an Internet connection.

3.2.2 Improved/New Features in Professional Edition

Business-level Reliability: Windows XP delivers a new level of stability so you can focus on your work, experience less downtime and handle multiple tasks.

Advanced Perfomance: Windows XP manages system resources efficiently, keeping the system running 45% faster than Windows 98.

Remote Desktop: Access all of your data and applications remotely from another computer running Windows 95 or later.

New Task-based Visual Design: gets you to your most commonly used tasks quickly.

Wireless 802.1x Networking Support: Provides support for secured access, as well as performance improvements for wireless networks.

Winodws Messenger: Communicate and collaborate in real time. See the online status of your contacts and communicate through text, voice or video with better performance and higher quality.

Encrypting File System: High level protection from hackers and data theft by transparently encrypting files with a randomly generated key.

Fast Resume from Hibernation or Standby: Save battery power when you are on the road. Your laptop enters Hibernate or Standby modes faster and also resumes from Hibernate or Standby faster.

Help and Support Center with Remote Assistance: A comprehensive set of help and support documentation. Remote Assistance, a feature that permits a friend or IT professional running Windows XP to remotely control your computer to help you solve a problem.

3.3 THE USER INTERFACE

As you might have noticed that there are various icons on the desktop. These are nothing but the graphical representations of the applications, programs, documents, etc. I will explain later in the chapter, how

these icons can be created. By clicking with mouse onto an icon, once or twice, as you may set in the Windows setup, you can run the program or application.

On the desktop, there are few icons which are a must for all the desktops being used by Windows and there are few which are optional and are created by the users according to their likings. Among the permanent ones are: My Computer, Recycle Bin, My Documents, Network Neighborhood, etc.

3.3.1 Task Bar

Task bar is the bottom key line on the desktop. Starting with the right most corner, we see the following:

Date and Time	It shows you the date and time of the system.
Task Scheduler	It shows the tasks which you have scheduled for running at different times.
Quick Launch Toolbar	Various icons here are the ones used for launching different programs. You have an option to put these icons here for the programs which you often use.
Running Tasks	When you have a program running in your system, its name will be reflected here on this taskbar to show that this program is open.

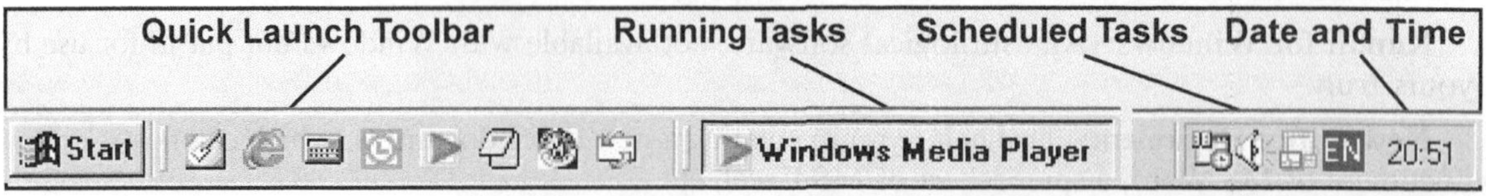

You can change the various options of the taskbar using the option dialog box from Start button, Settings, Taskbar and Start menu. This dialog box is shown here. It has 2 panels: Taskbar options and Start Menu Programs. Select the panel and make the changes you would like to make.

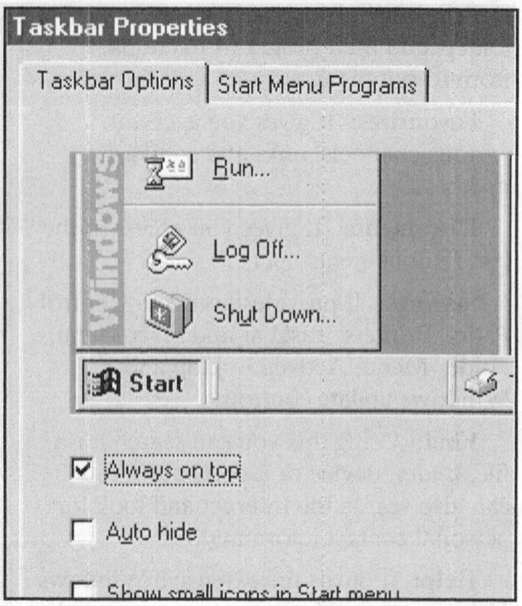

3.3.2 Icons

Icon is a graphic presentation of a window element. Icons are of four types which are as follows:

3.3.2.1 Disk Drive Icons

These type of Icons represent the Drives of the computer. For example: Drive3½ Floppy A:, Hard Disk drive, CD Drive, etc.

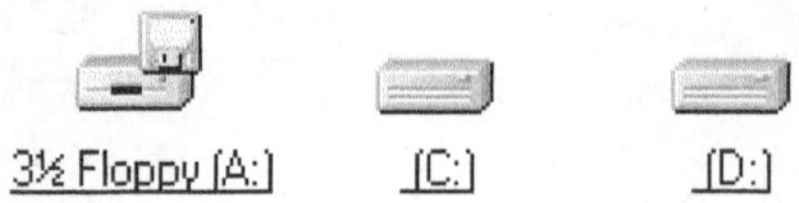

3.3.2.2 Application Icons

Application Icons mean the software package which are used to run various programs. For Example: MS-Office, MS-Word, MS-Excel, MS- Access, PageMaker, CorelDraw etc.

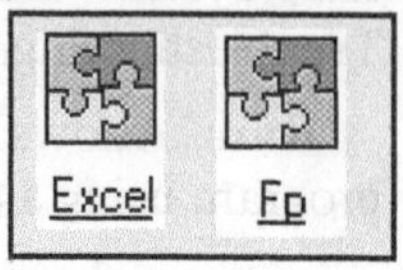

3.3.2.3 Shortcut Icons

Shortcut Icons are created by using the option from Desktop/New/Shortcut.

3.3.2.4 Document Icons

You can create a graphical representation of any document.

3.3.3 Start Menu

There are lot of things which can be done from the Start button. For others you have to use either My Computer or Windows Explorer. At the bottom most left corner of the desktop is the Start button. By pressing it you can launch the following options (your computer may have different options, but quite a number of them are same):

Windows Update: Microsoft from time to time announces the update of the software. Using this option you can upgrade your Windows version after connecting to the Microsoft website.

WinZip: A very useful program for compressing the files.

TRUCHHIPLAYSTATION: Another one of my programs.

Kundli for Windows: An astrological software, not available with Windows but put in for use by yours truly.

New Office Document: This helps you in creating a new office document, which can be a document of MS Word, a spreadsheet of MS Excel, etc.

Open Office Document: Similar to above, you can open an existing document.

Programs: It opens a list of various folders and their programs to choose from to run them.

Favourites: It gives you access to various channels, links and software updates.

Documents: It gives you access to the last 15 documents opened.

Settings: It provides access to Control Panel, Printers, Taskbar and Start Menu, Folder Menu, Active Desktop and Windows update controls.

Find: Using this you can search for a file, folder, device or a computer. You can also search the Internet and look for personal contact information.

Help: It opens the extensive Windows Help system and gives you access to the Troubleshooting.

Run: Allows you to run a particular program using a dialog box.

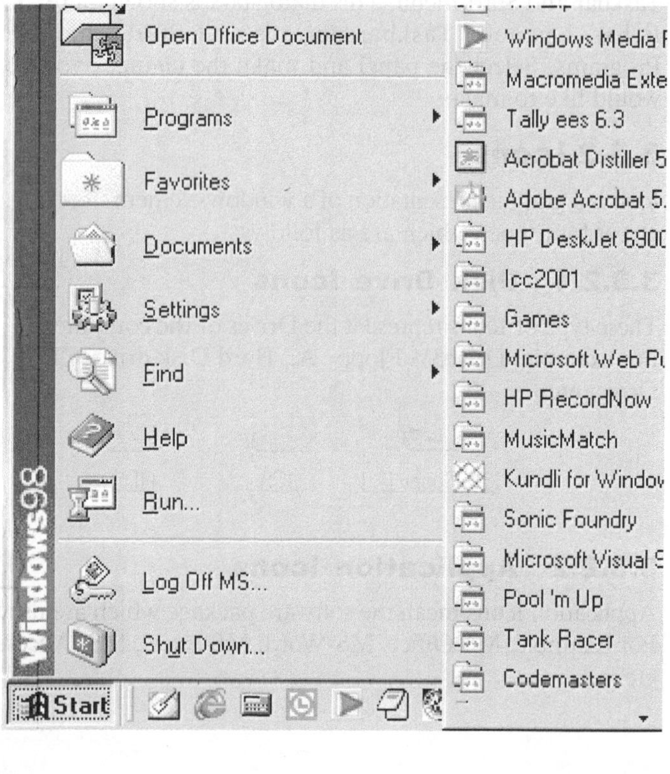

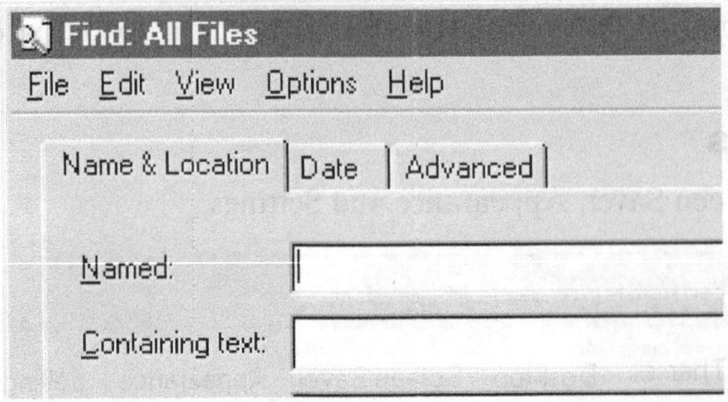

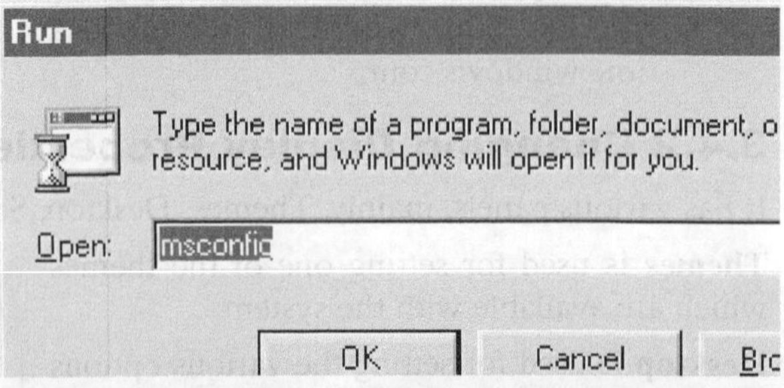

Log Off: It logs off the system quickly so that you can log back on with a different user profile or so that another user can log on.

Shut Down: It prepares the computer to shut down or to be restarted.

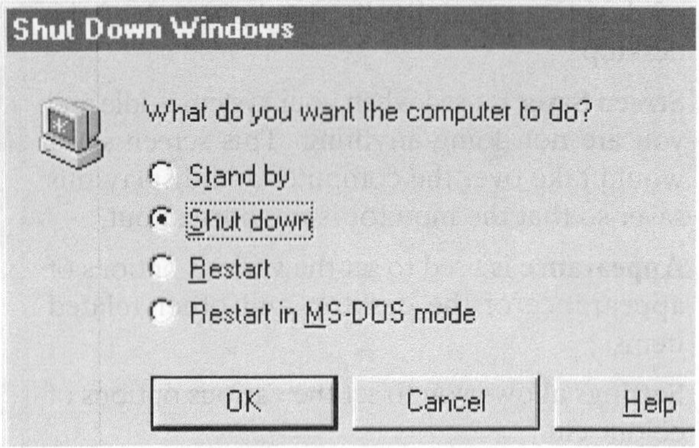

3.3.4 Running an Application

An application can be run under Windows by various methods. They are:

3.3.4.1 By Icon

Clicking at the icon of the application at the desktop.

3.3.4.2 From Windows Explorer

Click at the file/icon of the application in Windows Explorer.

3.3.4.3 From Start Menu

Click at Program and then the program name from its sub-menu. For example, for running Paintbrush, you will have to go to Programs, Accessories and then Paint.

3.4 OPERATING SYSTEM SIMPLE SETTING

Following options can be used for undertaking the various steps:

3.4.1 Changing System Date and Time

1. Click the Start button and select Control Panel.
2. Click the Date, Time, Langaugues and Regional Languages icon.
3. Change at Date and Time icon.
4. Date and Time dialog box appear.
5. To adjust the clock, highlight the portion to be changed in the text box and click the up and down arrows until the time you want is displayed.
6. Click the Time Zone tab to change the time zone, selecting the one you want from the drop-down list.

7. Internet Time would allow you to automatically change the time according to the site time.windows.com.

3.4.2 Changing Display Properties

It has various panels, mainly, Themes, Desktop, Screen Saver, Appearance and Settings.

Themes is used for setting one of the themes which are available with the system.

Desktop is used for setting the various options of desktop specially the background of the desktop.

Screen Saver is used when your system is idle and you are not doing anything. This screen saver would take over the computer and display this saver so that the monitor is not burned out.

Appearance is used to set the various options of appearance of the desktop and other related items.

Settings allows you to set the various options of colour etc.

3.4.3 To Add or Remove a Windows Component

Using the option of Add/Remove programs from the Control Panel, you can Add or Remove programs from the hard disk. The program files should never be deleted from the directory itself using delete command. This leaves the program infomation in Windows Registery and does not remove all the files. This lists out all the programs loaded into the hard disk, their size and the date of last used. If you want to update it, click at Program and then on Change/Remove button.

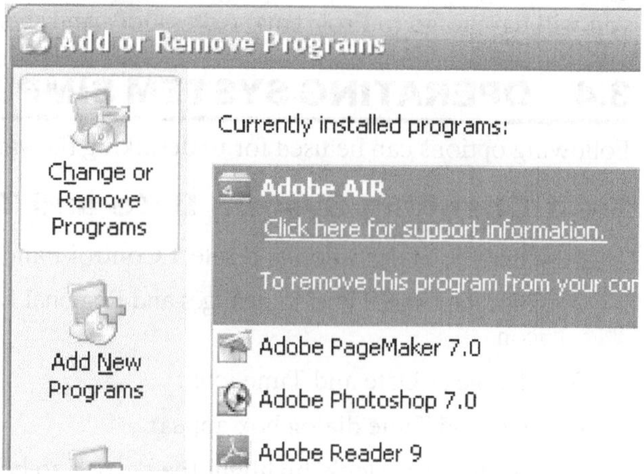

3.4.4 Changing Mouse Properties

Since most of the activities in Microsoft Office are done using the mouse, it is very important to have the complete knowledge of working of mouse while using the constituents of Microsoft Office.

To click: Position the pointer on a menu, a button, or an icon and click the left mouse once.

To double-click: Position the pointer on an item and click the left mouse button twice in quick succession.

To select: Position the pointer on the first item to select; Click and hold down the mouse button; Move the mouse pointer across the items to select; Release the mouse button.

To drag: Position the pointer on an item; Click and hold down the left mouse button; Move the mouse; Release the mouse button.

To scroll: Drag the scroll button in the scroll bar up or down; Or, Click a scroll arrow at either end of the scroll bar.

To choose from a menu: Click the menu name; Click an item on the menu; Or, if the item is followed by an arrow, position the mouse pointer on the item to open the submenu and then click an item on the submenu.

To move a window: Position the pointer on the window's title bar and press and hold the mouse button as you drag the window.

To resize a window: Position the pointer on the window's corner and, when you see the diagonal pointer, drag to resize the window.

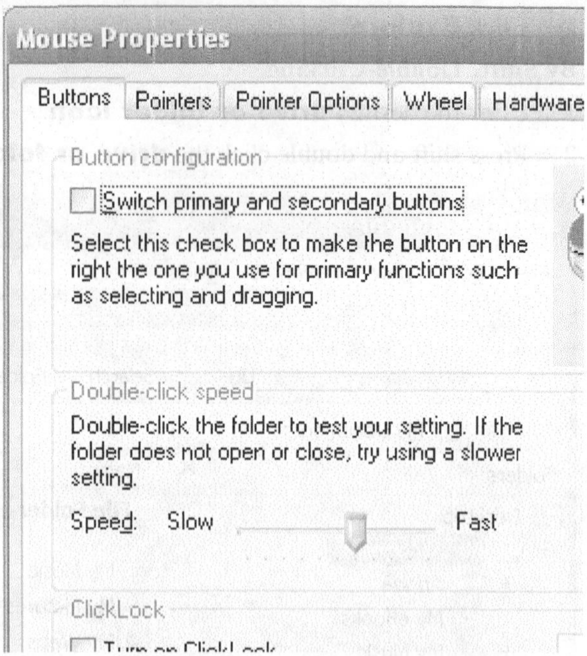

To minimize a window: Click the Minimize button.

To restore a minimized window: Click the button for the window on the taskbar.

To maximize a window: Click the Maximize button.

To switch windows: Click any visible part of the window; Or, Click the button for the window on the taskbar.

To close a window: Click the Close button on the window; Or, Right click the button for the window on the taskbar and choose Close from the shortcut menu.

It is not that you have to use the left button of the mouse only. You can use the right button on the mouse too. For this you will have to make the changes.

To make changes to the mouse and mouse pointers you need to work in the Mouse Control Panel. To open Mouse properties dialog box, click Start, click Control Panel, and then double-click Mouse. The mouse properties dialog box, appears.

From the mouse dialog box, you can change the speed of the mouse, shape of the pointer, etc.

3.4.5 Adding and Removing Printers

For this you have to work with the dialog box called Printers and Faxes from the Control Panel.

This gives rise to a dialog box, as shown on the next page. Here the installed printers would be shown.

Add a Printer: This would give rise to a Wizard, which would lead you to add a printer in an easy way.

You can change the settings of a printer by clicking at it.

3.5 FILE AND DIRECTORY MANAGEMENT

When you open Windows Explorer, it shows the hierarchy of folders in the All Folders pane (left pane) and the contents of the selected folder in the Contents pane (right pane).

You can run Explorer multiple times and drag items between each Explorer window.

From Desktop

Using Start Button

1. Click **Start Button**.
2. Point to **Programs** ➢ **Accessories**.
3. Click **Windows Explorer**.

By Right Clicking

1. Right click the desired **drive or folder icon**.
2. Click **Explore**.

By Shift, Double-Clicking

1. Click the desired **drive or folder icon**.
2. Press shift and double click the **drive or folder icon**.

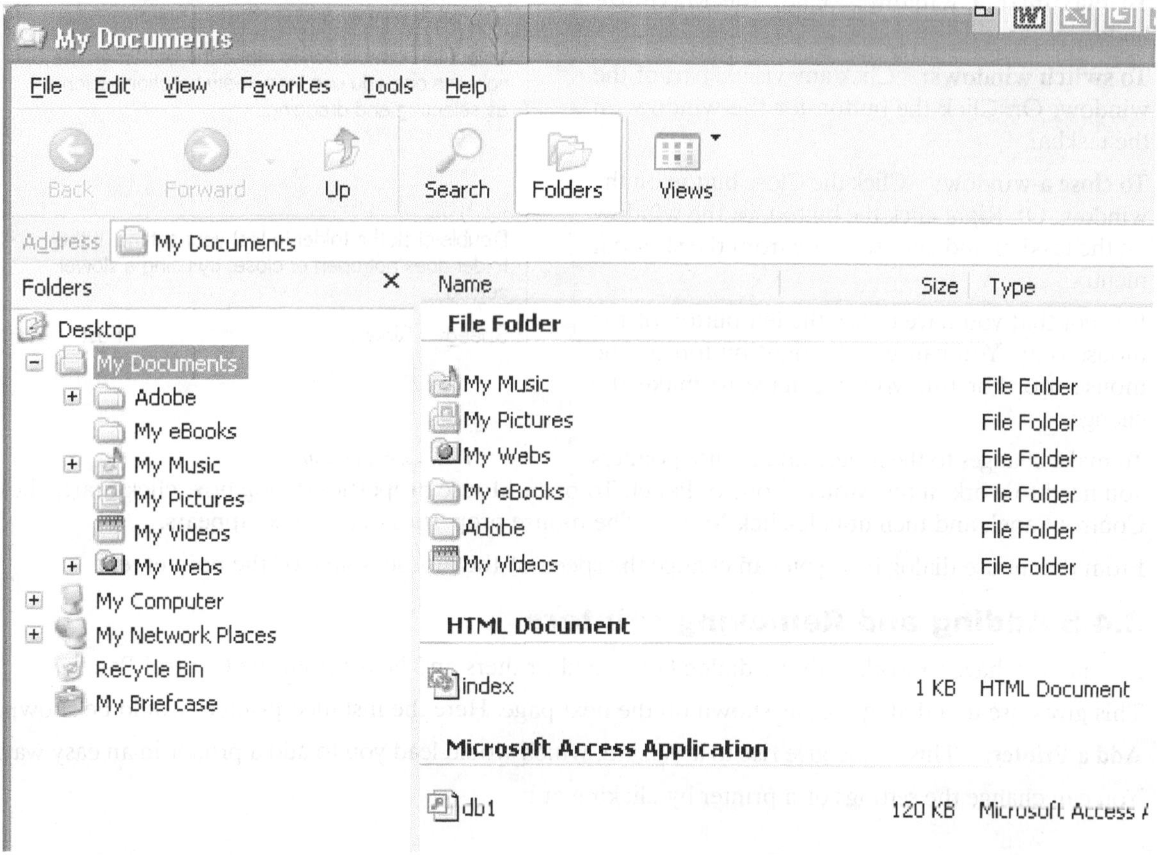

Size Explorer All Folders and Contents Panes

1. Point to Pointer till it becomes a **split bar**.
2. Drag **split bar outline** to left or right.

Use Explorer to Browse Folders and Open Files

Explorer shows the hierarchy of folders in the All Folders pane (left pane) and the contents of the selected folder in the contents pane (right pane). The current folder name appears in the **Go to a different folder** list box on the toolbar.

Open Any Folder

1. Click **Folder icon** in All Folders pane.

   Or

2. Click **Folder icon** in contents pane.

Go to a Different Folder

1. Show toolbar.
2. Select desired folder in the list.

Open Parent Folder

1. Show Toolbar.
2. Click Up One Level button.

Expand Folder Levels

From All Folders Pane

1. Click **[+]** to the left of folder to show folder it contains.

Collapse Folder Levels

1. Click **[–]** to the left of folder to hide folders it contains.

Open a File

1. Click **File icon** in the Contents pane.

Arrange Files and Folders in Sort Order

Arrange files on the desktop, in a folder window, the Explorer Contents pane, the Find result list, and a common dialog box. Sort options will depend on the type of folder or workspace.

By Right Clicking

1. Right click empty area on **desktop**.

   Or on **Folder workspace**

   Or on **Explorer contents pane**

   Or on **Find result list**

2. Point to **Arrange Icons**.
3. Select desired options:

   Folder or desktop: by *Name*, by *Type*, by *Size*, by *Date*.

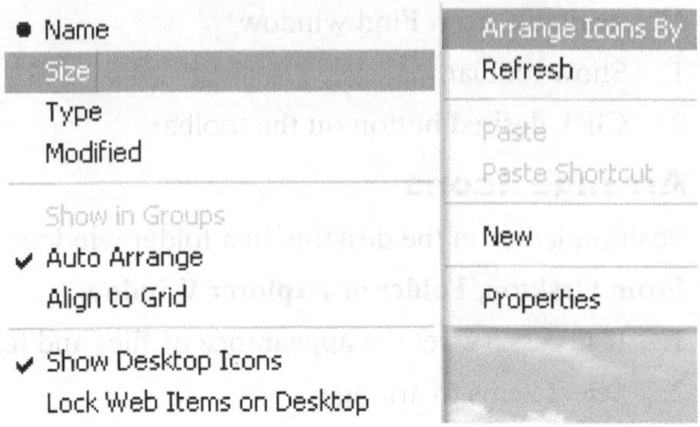

My Computer folder: by *Drive Letter*, by *Type*, by *Size*, by *Free Space*

Network Neighborhood folder: by *Name*, by *Size*, by *Date*

Common dialog box: by *Name*, by *Type*, by *Size*, by *Date*

Using Menu

Not available from the desktop or a common dialog box.

1. Click **View**.
2. Point to **Arrange icons**.
3. Select desired options:

   Folder: by Name, by *Type*, by *Size*, by *Date.*

   My Computer folder: by *Drive Letter*, by *Type*, by *Size*, by *Free Space*

   Network Neighborhood folder: by *Name*, by *Size*, by *Date*

   Find result list: by *Name,* by *Folder*, by *Type*, by *Size*, by *Date*

Using Column Headings

1. Set appearance of files and folders to Details.
2. Click to sort by **column heading**.

Set Appearance of Files and Folders

Set the appearance of files or folders in a folder window, the Explorer contents pane, a common browse dialog box.

Using Menu

Not available from a common browse dialog box.

1. Click **View**.

Select one of the following :

Large Icons;

Small Icons;

List;

Details

Using Toolbar

Not available from Find window

1. Show toolbar.
2. Click desired button on the toolbar.

Arrange Icons

Position icons on the desktop, in a folder window, and the Explorer Contents pane.

From Desktop, Folder or Explorer Window

1. If necessary, set the appearance of files and folders to Large or Small Icons.
2. Select items to arrange.

3. Drag **selected outline** to the desired position.
4. Deselect the Auto Arrange option if icons do not remain where placed.

Line Up Icons

Align icons evenly (in relation to one another) on the desktop, in a folder window, the Explorer Contents pane, and the Find result list.

Set appearance of icons to Large or Small.

By Right Clicking

1. Right click empty area on **desktop**.

   Or on **Folder workspace**

   Or on **Explorer contents pane**

   Or on **Find result list**
2. Click **Line Up icons**.

Using Menu

1. Set appearance of files and folders to Large or Small icons.
2. Click **View, Line up icons**.

Set Auto Arrangement of Icons

Select to arrange icons automatically when appearance of icons is set to Large or Small.

By Right Clicking

1. Right click empty area on **desktop**.

   Or on **Folder workspace**

   Or on **Explorer contents pane**

   Or on **Find result list**
2. Point to **Arrange icons**.
3. Click **Auto Arrange**.

Using Menu

Not available from the desktop or a common dialog box.

1. Click **View**
2. Point to **Arrange icons**.
3. Click **Auto Arrange** to select or deselect.

Use Common Dialog Boxes

Common dialog boxes help locate, select, save and open files. In a common dialog box, the list of items shows the contents of the current folder—the folder name in the Look in list box.

From any Common Dialog Box

The common dialog box is used to browse while creating a shortcut or when selecting browse from the run dialog box.

Open Any Folder

1. Select desired folder in the **Look in...**

Open a Folder Appearing in List of Items

1. Click the desired **folder icon** in list of items.

Open Parent Folder

1. Click **Up One Level** button.

Limit File Names Displayed in the List of Items

1. Type filespec in **File name**.
2. Press **Enter**.

View Specific File types in List of Items

1. Click **file icon**.

   Or

2. Click **file icon** in the list of files.
3. Click **open**.

Create New Folder in Current Folder

1. Click **Create New Folder** button.

Set Appearance of Icons

1. Click **List button**

   Or

2. Click **Details button**.

Common Dialog Box—Right Click Options

1. Right click **File or Folder icon**. A shortcut menu appears.
2. Click appropriate shortcut menu item.

Common Dialog Box—Right Drag Options

1. Right drag **File or Folder icon** on destination item.
2. Click appropriate **menu item**.

Set File and Folder Attributes

From the desktop, a folder window, the Explorer Contents pane, a common browse dialog box, and the Find result list.

Change the attributes of a file or folder only if you understand the effect of the change.

1. Right click desired **File or Folder icon**.
2. Click **Properties**.
3. Select or deselect attribute options:
4. Click

   Read Only

Archive

Hidden

5. Click **Ok**.

Cut or Copy Data in Document to Clipboard

Existing Clipboard data is replaced.

From a Windows Application

1. Select data to cut or copy.
2. Click **Edit**

   Or
3. Right click **Selection**.
4. Click **Cut** to move selection to Clipboard.

   Or
5. Click **Copy** to selection to Clipboard.

From an MS-DOS Application

1. Select **text** to copy. (cut is not allowed)
2. Click application's **Control Symbol**.
3. Point to **Edit**.
4. Click **Copy**.

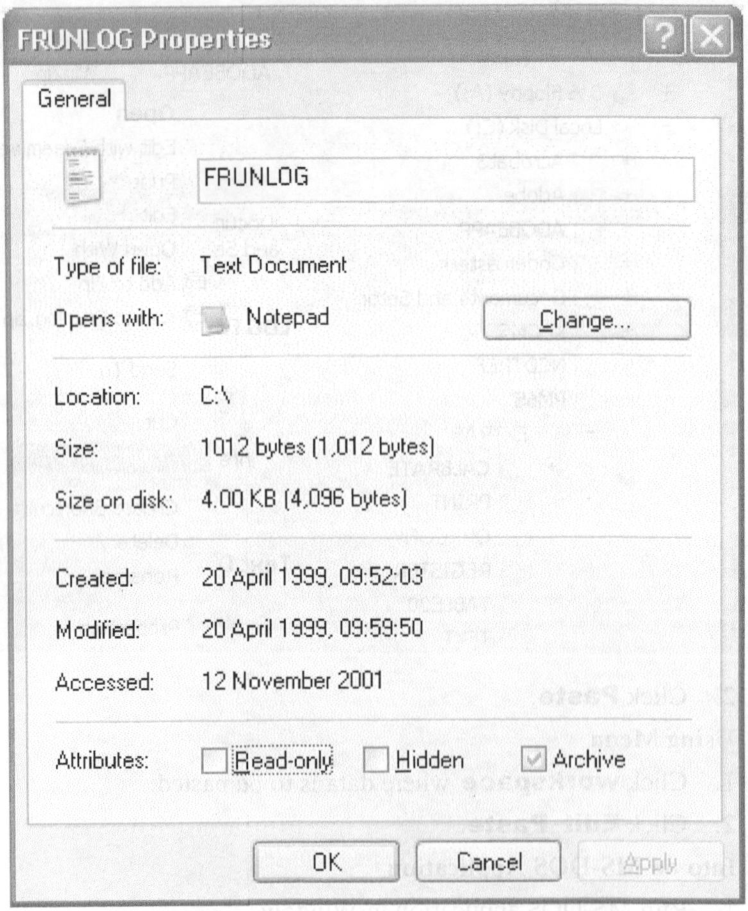

Copy Screen Image to Clipboard

Entire Screen

1. Press **Print Screen**.

Active Window

1. If image is an MS-DOS application, run MS-DOS application in a window.
2. Select window to copy.
3. Press **Alt+Print Screen**.

Paste Data from Clipboard into Document

Into a Windows Application

1. Run or select **application that will receive data**.

By Right Clicking

1. Right click on **workspace** where to place data.

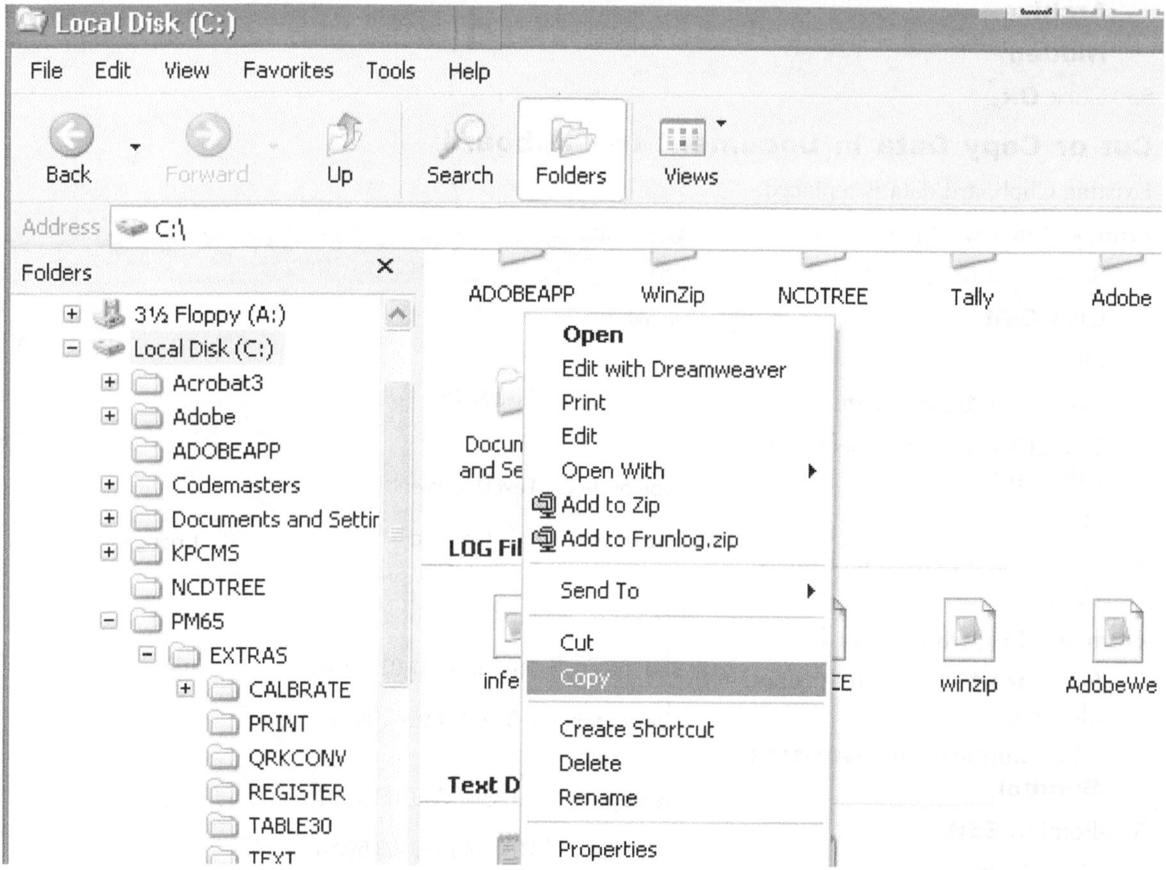

2. Click **Paste**.

Using Menu

1. Click **workspace** where data is to be pasted.
2. Click **Edit**, **Paste**.

Into an MS-DOS Application

1. Run MS-DOS application in Window.
2. Position cursor in **workspace** where text will be pasted.
3. Click application's **control symbol**.
4. Point to **Edit**.
5. Click **Paste**.

Paste Data into Document as an OLE Object

Make sure that data has been copied to clipboard from an OLE object application such as Paint.

From Application to receive Object

1. Click on **workspace** where to place data.

2. Click **Edit**, **Paste Special**.
3. Select **Paste** to paste data as an embedded object

   Or
4. Select **Paste Link** to paste as linked object.
5. If Paste Link options are grayed, the application did not recognize the object; in such a case use Insert Existing File as Linked OLE Object in document.
6. Select format of object in **As: in list box.**

Display object as an icon

1. Select **Display as Icon**.
2. Click **Ok**.

3.6 TYPE OF FILES

A folder is like a directory where all the relative files are kept. For example, all your files pertaining to a book would be in one folder. If you look at the picture shown earlier of Windows Explorer, it contains the various folders and files. Each folder has the files related to that folder.

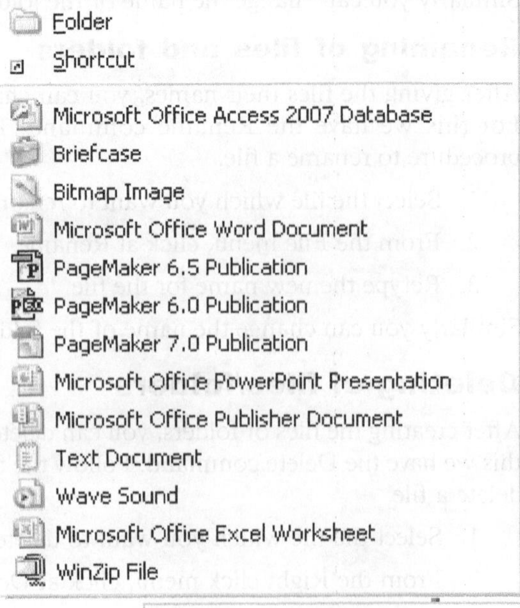

Creating a Folder

For creation of a new folder, you will have to go to either My Computer or Windows Explorer. Let me explain how it is done in Windows Explorer.

For that follow the following steps.

1. Start Windows Explorer from Start Button > Programs > Accessories.
2. Right click the mouse to get the menu.
3. Click at New and then Folder to get a new blank folder on the screen.
4. By clicking at its name you can type the name you want for the folder.
5. After typing press Enter to have the folder.

Cut, Copy and Paste files/folders

Copying of a File

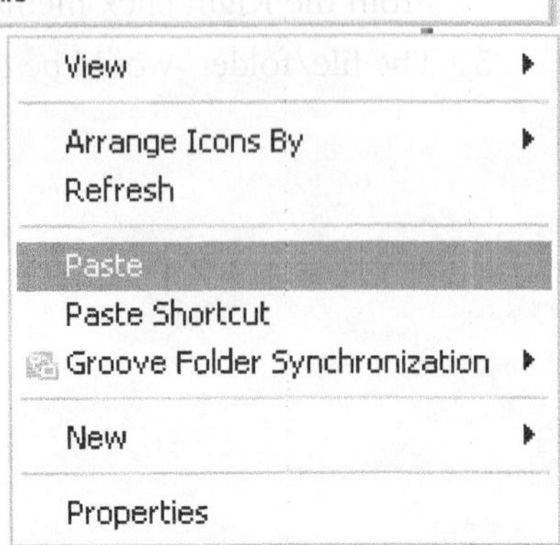

For copying also you can use either My Computer or Windows Explorer.

For that follow the following steps.

1. Start Windows Explorer as above.
2. Right click the mouse to get the menu.

3. Click at Copy and then the Folder where you want this file to be copied.
4. Reclick the right mouse.
5. Select Paste this time
6. The copied file will be pasted here.
7. The original will remain at its original place.

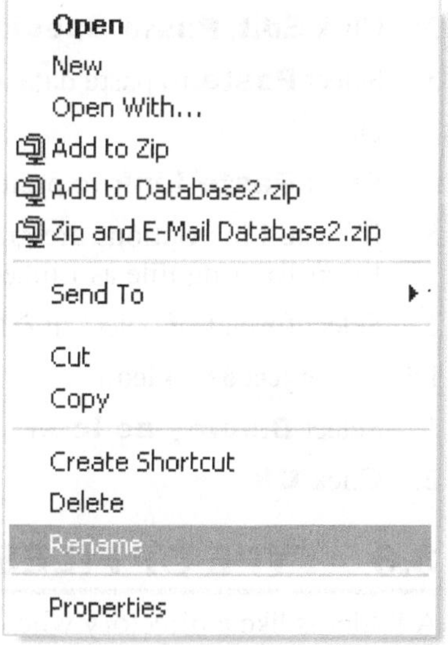

Moving of files/folders

After giving the files their names, you can change them if you like. For this we have the Rename command. Follow the following procedure to rename a file.

1. Select the file which you want to rename by single clicking it.
2. From the File menu, click at Rename.
3. Retype the new name for the file.

Similarly you can change the name of the folder.

Renaming of files and folders

After giving the files their names, you can change them if you like. For this we have the Rename command. Follow the following procedure to rename a file.

1. Select the file which you want to rename by single clicking it.
2. From the File menu, click at Rename.
3. Retype the new name for the file.

Similarly you can change the name of the folder.

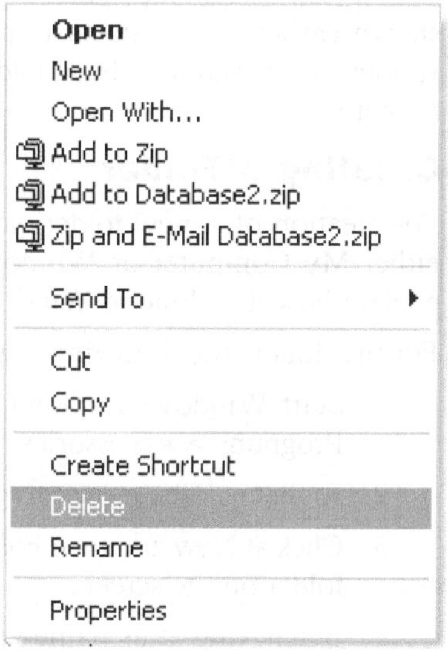

Deleting of files/folders

After creating the files or folders, you can delete them if you like. For this we have the Delete command. Follow the following procedure to delete a file.

1. Select the file which you want to delete by single clicking it.
2. From the Right click menu, click at Delete.
3. The file/folder would be deleted, only after confirming from you.

LET US REVISE

1. By using Windows Explorer you can: Create a folder, Copy a file/folder; Rename a file/folder or delete the file/folder.
2. A Windows dialog box has the following units: Title bar, Menu bar, Scroll bar and Status bar.
3. Accessories are additional programs which are there alongwith the main program called Windows.
4. Accessories can be accessed from Start Menu and Programs.
5. When you run Disk Cleanup, it checks for files that can be safely deleted and then presents a list of such files.
6. Disk defragmenter does the job of housekeeping and puts the files on one side and the blank space in the hard disk on the other side.
7. Drive Space allows you to see how of the space has been utilized in the hard disk.
8. Maintainance wizard allows you to set the time and dates for running various utility programs.
9. Scan disk scans the various partitions of the hard disk.
10. Scheduled tasks allow you to see what jobs have been scheduled.
11. System information gives the complete information about the system.
12. Character map allows you to see and use the various fonts available in the system.
13. Imaging allows you to see various graphics.
14. Paint is a useful graphics program which allows you to create graphics too.
15. Word pad is a small word processing program.
16. Calculator has 2 varities, standard and scientific.

MULTIPLE CHOICE QUESTIONS

1. Among the 2 types of calculators, one is standard and the other one is?
   (a) Ordinary (b) Scientific (c) Physical
2. Which accessory would you use to schedule your tasks?
   (a) Disk Cleanup (b) Disk Defragmenter (c) Task Scheduler
3. For fragmenting you hard disk which accessory you would use:
   (a) Disk Fragmenter (b) Tools (c) Fragmenter
4. For creating drawings, you would use:
   (a) Drawing (b) Paint (c) Painter
5. For viewing Video CDs you would use:
   (a) CD Player (b) Windows Media Player (c) Video
6. For sound recorder, what is necessary?
   (a) Speaker (b) Microphone (c) Mouse
7. For Phone dialer, what extra equipment you need to have in your computer?
   (a) Mouse (b) Printer (c) Modem

8. For seeing how the various fonts look, you would use:
   (a) Font (b) See (c) Character Map
9. A small word processing program available in Accessories is called:
   (a) Word (b) Processing (c) Word Pad
10. Solatire is a :
   (a) System tool (b) Game (c) Internet tool

TRUE/FALSE QUESTIONS

1. Task Scheduler is used for defragmenting disk.
2. Scientific calculator is a part of Windows Accessories.
3. You can put computer on Stand by mode from the Shut Down button.
4. Small graphical items on desktop are known as icons.
5. For drawings in Windows, Paint can be used.

MATCHING COLUMNS

Match the matter in Column A with the matter in Column B.

Column A	Column B
A. Paint	1. For scheduling the maintaince jobs
B. Recycle Bin	2. Standard and Scientific
C. Solatire	3. Controlling the volume of speakers
D. CD Player	4. To see the various font formats
E. Volume control	5. For seeing items in bigger size
F. Phone dialer	6. For running an application
G. Character Map	7. For finding file and folders
H. Maintainance Wizard	8. For creating small drawings
I. Magnifier	9. For dialing from the PC
J. Find	10. For playing an audio CD
K. Run	11. Game
L. Calculator	12. For collecting the deleted files

FILL IN THE BLANKS WITH APPROPRIATE WORDS

a. Recycle Bin	b. Restore	c. Icon	d. Find
e. Accesories	f. Direct Cable Connector		g. Entertainment
h. Run	i. Minimize	j. Title bar	k. Disk Defragmenter
l. Desktop			

1. An application can be started by using ________ in the Start button.
2. Calculator is part of ____________.
3. By clicking the ________ button you can restore the application window to its original format.
4. The deleted files and folders go to ___________.
5. The accessory which allows you to defragment the hard disk is called _________.
6. The initial windows screen is called _______.
7. Graphical representation of applications is called ________.
8. The accessory which allows you to connect various computers is called ____________.
9. The button which is used to reduce the application window is called _________.
10. Games are there is accessories _________ subgroup.
11. For locating files and folders, you would use ______ utility.
12. The bar which displays the name of the document or application at the topmost in any application is called _________.

DESCRIPTIVE TYPE QUESTIONS

1. How can you run an application in Windows?
2. What do you understand by:
   Minimizing the Windows   Maximizing the Windows
   Restoring the Windows   Closing the Windows
3. What is the function of Windows Explorer?
4. How would you do the following using Windows Explorer?
   Rename a file   Copy a file   Create a folder
   Delete a file   Move a file
5. Describe the various components of a Windows dialog box.
6. What is the purpose of Disk clean up?
7. For what purpose do you use Disk Defragmenter?
8. How would you control the volume of the CDPlayer?
9. If you have a Video CD, how would you run it on your computer?
10. How would you see the shape of various fonts under Windows?
11. If you have to dial from your computer, what would you use?
12. If you have to create a drawing, which program would you use?
13. To clean up your hard disk, which program would you use?

ANSWERS TO OBJECTIVE QUESTIONS

Multiple Choice Questions

1. b	2. c	3. a	4. b
5. b	6. b	7. c	8. c
9. c	10. b		

True False Questions

1. T	2. T	3. T	4. T
5. T			

Matching Columns

A. 8	B. 12	C. 11	D. 10
E. 3	F. 9	G. 4	H. 1
I. 5	J. 7	K. 6	L. 2

Fill in the Blanks with Appropriate Words

1. h	2. e	3. b	4. a
5. k	6. l	7. c	8. f
9. i	10. g	11. d	12. j

Chapter 4

Elements of Word Processing

4.1 WORD PROCESSING BASICS

Word processor is a computer program for processing of words, very similar to a food processor (*mixie*) which processes food. Most of the word processors would start from a blank screen assumed to be a blank page with a blinking starting point known as **Cursor**. For all practical purposes it is like a typewriter, but it is much more than that.

You can type the text (even enter graphics) in the word processor, save it under a name to recall it again and again. Spell check it for errors, format it to look good, and then if needed print it too.

This makes it much easier for writing the text since you can make as many mistakes as you like since you can correct them by just pressing a key. This way you save a lot of paper and make the document look more neat and clean.

4.1.1 An Introduction to Word Processing

Before we go any further and study word processing, let us understand few basic terms of word processing:

Text	It is the matter which you type.
Document	It is whole text matter which you create, like a letter, or a chapter, etc.
Fonts	In typewriting you have just one type of handwriting. In word processing you can have your text written in many writings, these are called Fonts. Each font has its own way to writing the alphabets (A to Z) and even numerals (0 to 9).
Cursor	It is as said before, the blinking point which tells you where to start typing or what your current position is.
Arrow keys	These keys are on the arrow pads of your keyboard and are shown as: Up-arrow (↑), Down-arrow (↓), Left-arrow (←) and Right-arrow (→).
Space bar	It plays a very important role in word processing. The space between the words is given by this.
Tabs	These are used to set the text into tabular form.
Backspace	This is another important keyboard key which is used to delete the wrongly typed character in your text. You can even use the Del key for this.

4.1.1.1 Things which can be done by Word Processing

Let us now see what are the things which can be done by Word Processing and cannot be done on the typewriter.

Alignment	You can set your text in any alignment, e.g., Left, Right or Centre. You can even do box setting, i.e., aligned from both sides.

Deleting Mistakes	You can delete word, line, paragraph in a stroke and the rest of the matter will get adjusted automatically.
Line Spacing	You can set line spacing according to your liking from one to nine.
MailMerging	A very important feature of any word processing. This helps you in sending the same text to the different people, all in original format.
Moving the Cursor	You can move your cursor from word to word or from paragraph to paragraph, if needed.
Naming a Document	As mentioned earlier, you can name a document and recall it anytime from hard disk for editing, updating, correcting and even printing.
Overwriting Mistakes	You can overwrite your mistakes on the screen itself. No more messing of eraser and spoiling of paper.
Page Breaks	You can set a page break at any place within the text so that while printing it will jump to next page.
Page Numbers	You can set page numbers according to your liking.
Search and Replace	You can search for a particular word in the whole document and replace it with another one. You can even replace all the occurrence of the same word.
Spell Checking	Probably the most important part of any word processing. Each word processor comes with a dictionary built inside it. You can check your text with it see whether any word has been wrongly typed.

4.1.2 Opening Word Processing Package

Most of the big time software producers have a word processing program of their own. But, it depends on the operating system which you are using. If you are working under DOS, then there is nothing to beat WordStar. It has been a very popular word processing software till more and more users started working under Windows. Then, the preference shifted to Word for Windows. So here we will discuss Word for Windows.

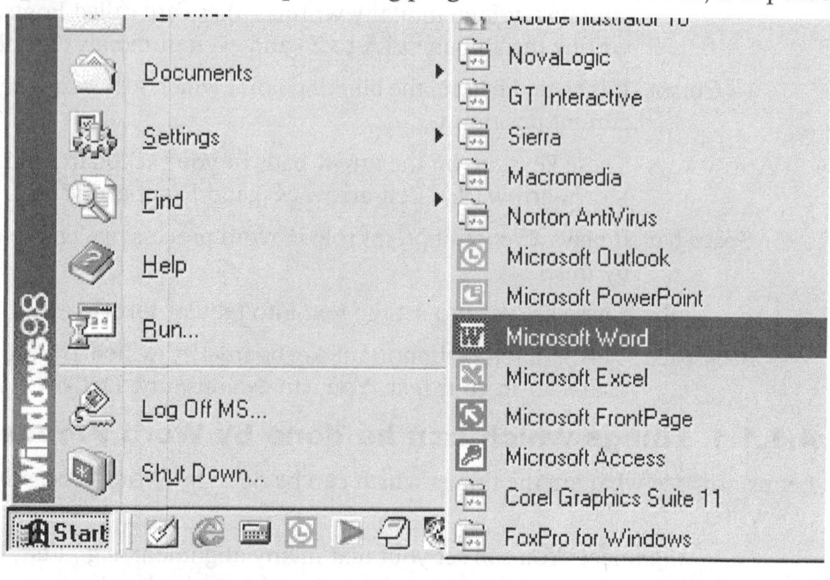

4.1.2.1 Starting Word

You can start Word by one of the following methods:

From Start Button: Click at Start button to access the various commands. Click on Programs to get the various programs. From here click at the program called Microsoft Word to run Word for Windows, as shown here.

From Icon of Word: You can choose to have an icon of Word on your desktop. This icon can be created by using the feature of Creating Shortcut.

4.1.2.2 Microsoft Word Screen

Once started Word gives rise to a blank slate for typing your text. This screen has various items on it. One must know them before actually starting typing and using the commands.

Close button	This would close Word for Windows session.
Drawing toolbar	One of the various toolbars which can be made available on the screen. This particular one is used for making drawings in the document.
Formatting bar	This bar is used to format the text. For example you can set font, font size, alignment, etc., using this bar.
Horizontal scroll bar	Sometimes the width of the text is such that it cannot be displayed on the whole screen. This bar is then used to see the text on the left or right.
Menu bar	Like in other programs Word for Windows also has various commands which can be accessed by clicking at the menu options under these menu heads.
Minimize button	While working, you can minimize your word document to reach desktop for working with another program, maybe.

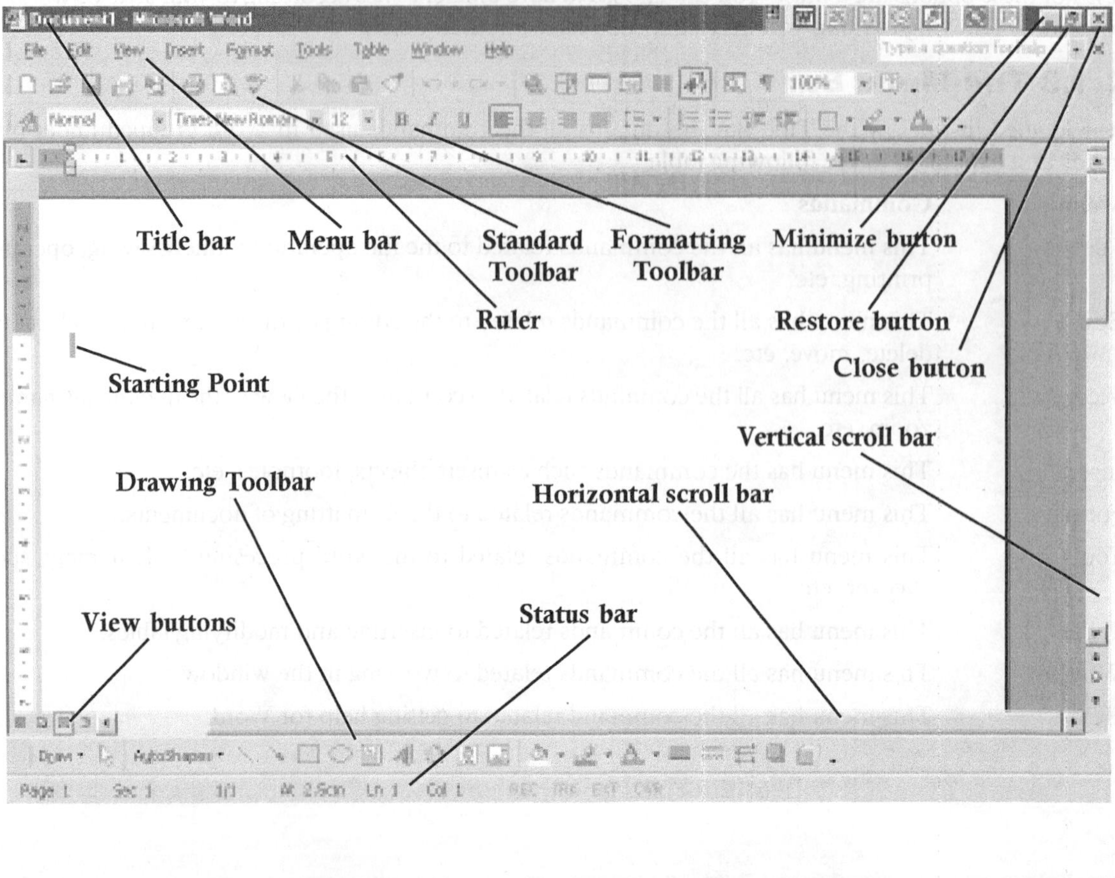

Restore button	You have the option of working between two different views of the document by toggling this switch.
Ruler	Using this ruler you can see how much of the line you have consumed by typing.
Standard toolbar	There are a number of toolbars which allow you to select various tools for working in Word for Windows. This one is the standard which has all the icons of various file options, etc.
Starting point	This is the starting point of your text on the document. This is the point from where you would start typing.
Status bar	This bar will always show you your current position as far as the text goes. It will tell you your current position with respect to page number, line number, etc.
Title bar	Another permanent feature of Word for Windows which shows you the name of the file on which you are working and at the end has the various buttons like Close, Restore and Minimize.
Vertical scroll bar	For a larger text in the document, you can scroll the vertical bar to see the text at various positions.
View buttons	Word for Windows allows you to work in various views of the document. Using these buttons you can go from one view to another.

It is not these options are a must. You can choose to have different ones according to your style of working. Instead of Drawing toolbar, you may choose to have another toolbar.

4.1.3 The Menu Bar

It is located just below the Title Bar. It contains all the commands used in Word grouped under nine heads and explained in the following table.

Menu	**Commands**
File	This menu has all the commands related to the file operation namely saving, opening, printing, etc.
Edit	This menu has all the commands related to the editing of the document namely, copy, delete, move, etc.
View	This menu has all the commnds related to conrolling the view of the documents names, zoom, etc.
Insert	This menu has the commands such as insert objects, footnotes, etc.
Format	This menu has all the commands related to the formatting of documents.
Tools	This menu has all the commands related to the word procesing tools namely, spell checker, etc.
Table	This menu has all the commands related to inserting and modifying tables.
Window	This menu has all the commands related to working in the window.
Help	This menu has all the command related to getting help for Word.

4.1.4 Using the Help

In Word, the Help comes in the form of an Office Assistant. It allows you to type your questions and get the appropriate answers.

To get the Help, do the following:

1. Click the Office Assistant button on the Standard toolbar or Click Help menu and choose Microsoft Word Help or press Help or press F1 key.
2. The Office Assistant window appears or double click on-screen Office Assistant.
3. Type your question in the What would you like to do? text box or click desired choice.
4. Click Search.
5. To get the content search help, click the Help menu and choose what is this option or press Shift + F1 keys together. The mouse pointer changes to a question mark. Click the element you want help on.
6. Complete the prompted instructions that follow to answer your questions in details.
7. When you are finished, Click Ok to close help options.

4.2 OPENING DOCUMENTS AND CLOSING DOCUMENTS

Most of these commands regarding opening, closing and saving of the document file, you will find them under File menu.

4.2.1 Opening Documents

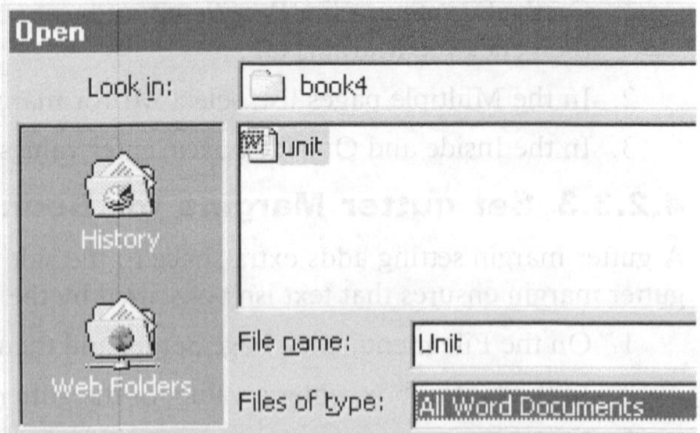

Opening of the file can be done by 2 methods if you are already working under Word.

From File menu: There is an Open command under the File menu. Click at it to open the Open dialog box as shown next.

From Open Icon: You can get the same Open dialog box by clicking at Open icon on the Standard toolbar. In both cases you will get the dialog box shown on the next page. From here you can click the file you want to open. If it is not there on the screen, try to locate it in different directories with the help of icons on the left or from the drop-down list of directories.

4.2.2 Save and Save As

Let us understand the difference between **Save** and **Save As**. You save your document file as you save any other file. **Save As** option allows you to save with another name, maybe another format at another drive/directory. It is not that the system will not allow you to save the file with the same name under **Save As** option. It will ask you whether you want to overwrite the file which exists. This is just a precautionary option so that you do not overwrite a file with the same name accidentally.

4.2.3 Page Setup

You can change the page layout of the document. Set the margins according to your likings. For all this you have the command called Pageset in File menu.

4.2.3.1 Change Page Margins

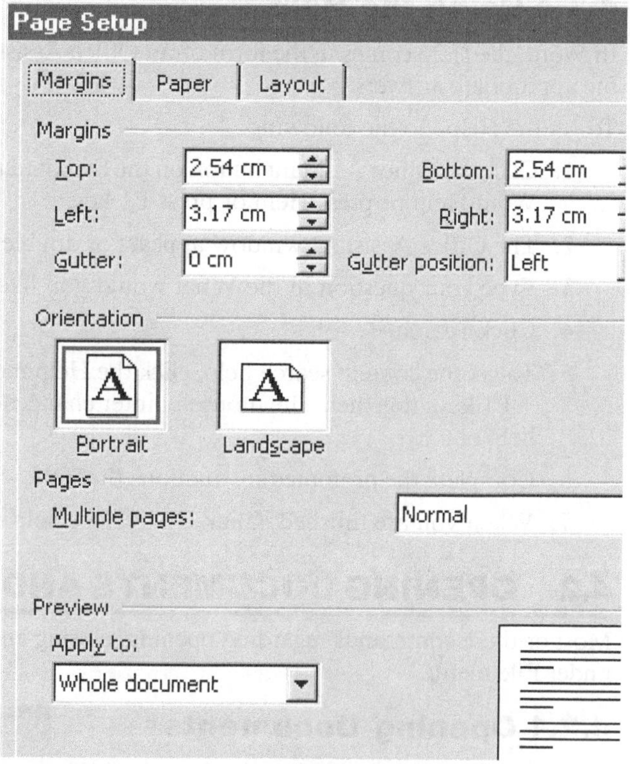

1. On the File menu, click Page Setup, and then click the Margins tab.
2. Under Margins, select the options you want.
3. To change the default margins, click Default after you select new margin settings. The new default settings are saved in the template on which the document is based.
4. Each new document based on that template automatically uses the new margin settings.

4.2.3.2 Set mirror margins for facing pages

Margins of the left page are a mirror image of those on the right page. That is, the inside margins are the same width, and the outside margins are the same width.

1. On the File menu, click Page Setup, and then click the Margins tab.
2. In the Multiple pages list, select Mirror margins.
3. In the Inside and Outside boxes, enter values for the mirror margins.

4.2.3.3 Set gutter Margins for Bound Documents

A gutter margin setting adds extra space to the side or top margin of a document you plan to bind. A gutter margin ensures that text isn't obscured by the binding.

1. On the File menu, click Page Setup, and then click the Margins tab.
2. In the Gutter box, enter a value for the gutter margin.
3. In the Gutter position box, click Left or Top.
4. To change the margins for part of a document, select the text, and then set the margins you want. In the Apply to box, click Selected text.
5. Microsoft Word automatically inserts section breaks before and after the text with the new margin settings. If your document is already divided into sections, you can click in a section or select multiple sections, and then change the margins.

4.2.3.4 Change the Orientation of Text

You can change the text orientation in drawing objects, such as text boxes (text box: A movable, resizable container for text or graphics. Use text boxes to position several blocks of text on a page or to give text a different orientation from other text in the document.), shapes, and callouts, or in table cells so that the text is displayed vertically or horizontally.

1. Click the drawing object or table cell that contains the text you want to change.

2. On the Format menu, click Text Direction.
3. Click the orientation you want.

4.2.3.5 Select a paper source

1. On the File menu, click Print.
2. Click Properties.
3. Click the Paper tab.
4. In the Paper source box, click the paper source you want.

4.2.3.6 Select paper size

1. On the File menu, click Page Setup, and then click the Paper tab.
2. Click a paper size.
3. To change the paper size for part of a document, select the pages and then change the paper size as usual. In the Apply to box, click Selected text. Microsoft Word automatically inserts section breaks before and after the pages with the new paper size. If your document is already divided into sections, you can click in a section or select multiple sections, and then change the paper size.

4.2.4 Printing of Documents

No document preparation process is complete without printing it. For this we have the **Print** option under the **File** menu. Once clicked it gives rise to a dialog box as shown below. The various options on the dialog box are as follows:

Printer: Select the printer to which you want to send the printing. From the drop-down list, you can select one of the many printers which you may have installed under Windows.

Properties: Clicking at it would lead to a dialog box having the properties of the selected printer. If some adjustments are to be made in the properties of the selected printer, they can be done here.

Print to file: Sometimes it is possible that you may like to print the document to the printer which is not installed in your computer. In this case you will select this option and create a print file for that particular printer and copy the file and then print on that printer where it is installed.

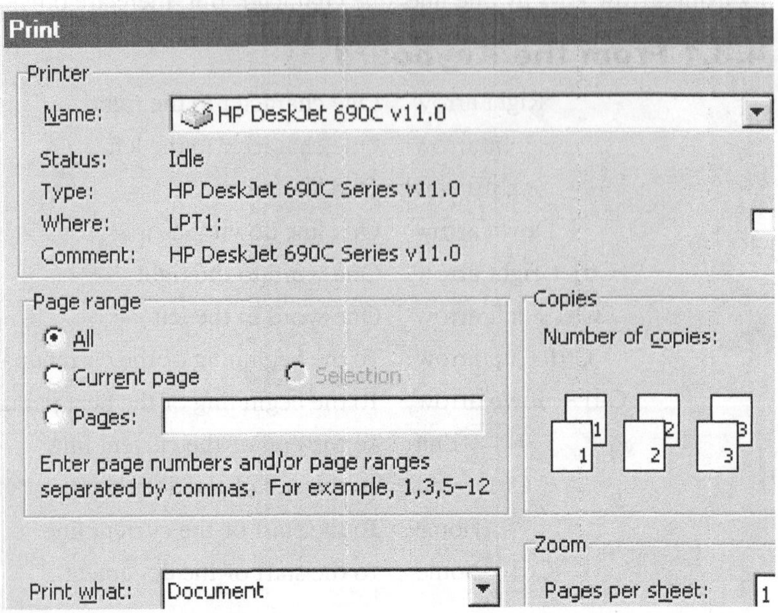

Print range: You may like to print few selective pages instead of printing the whole document. So either click **All**, for printing all pages of the document or **Pages**, for defining the pages you want to print. You can even print the current page, i.e., page on the screen.

Copies: Word 2000 allows you to print multiple copies of the pages in the document. You can mention here the number of copies you want. What's more you can have the copies collated for you, if you select the **collate** option.

Print what: Various options available here are Document, Document properties, Comments, Styles, AutoText entries, Key assignments. But, most of the time you would be printing with Document option.

Print: You have the option of printing all pages or all **odd pages** or all **even pages**.

Zoom: Pages per sheet allows you to print 1 to 16 pages of the document on one sheet. Scaling allows you to scale your document to the various sizes of the paper.

Options: This will lead to the print options, already described under **Options** and select the option of your choice.

Once you are sure that you have selected all the options required by you, just click Ok for document to start printing. However, do not forget to have the Printer ON before giving the final print command.

4.2.5 Display/Hiding of Paragraph Marks and Inter Word Space

When paragraph marks are hidden, you do not see them at the end of the paragraph. It is advisable to display paragraph marks to avoid accidental deletion of one of them because these marks hold paragraph formatting.

To display the paragraph, do the following:

1. Click the Tools menu and choose Options.
2. Click the View tab.
3. Choose Paragraph marks under Formatting marks.

4.3 MOVING AROUND IN A DOCUMENT

There are times when you would be needing to move around the text in the document. This can be done by using arrow keys by one line, one character. But, there are other methods too.

4.3.1 From the Keyboard

Right arrow	One character to the right
Left arrow	One character to the left
Up arrow	One line up
Down arrow	One line down
Ctrl + right arrow	One word to the right
Ctrl + left arrow	One word to the left
Ctrl + up arrow	To the beginning of the current paragraph
Ctrl + down arrow	To the beginning of the next paragraph
End	To the end of the current line
Ctrl + end	To the end of the document
Home	To the start of the current line
Ctrl + home	To the start of the document

Page up	Up one screen
Page down	Down one screen
Ctrl + page up	To the first character on the current screen
Ctrl + page down	To the last character on the current screen

4.3.2 Moving with Mouse

To position the cursor using the mouse, move the mouse pointer to where you want it and click.

1. Using the scrollbars, scroll until you reach the location you want the text to be inserted.
2. Click the location where you want to position the insertion point.

4.3.3 Scrolling the Document

Using the scroll bars on the right of the document and bottom of the document.

1. Click at the scroll bar to move the document from pages to pages.
2. While you move the scroll, you will see the page numbers in the block.

4.3.4 Scrolling by line/paragraph

Scrolling by line is easy. Just click at bottom arrow of the arrow key to move to the next line and similarly, use the up arrow to move up.

For moving from one paragraph to another, click at down arrow or up arrow alongwith the Crl key.

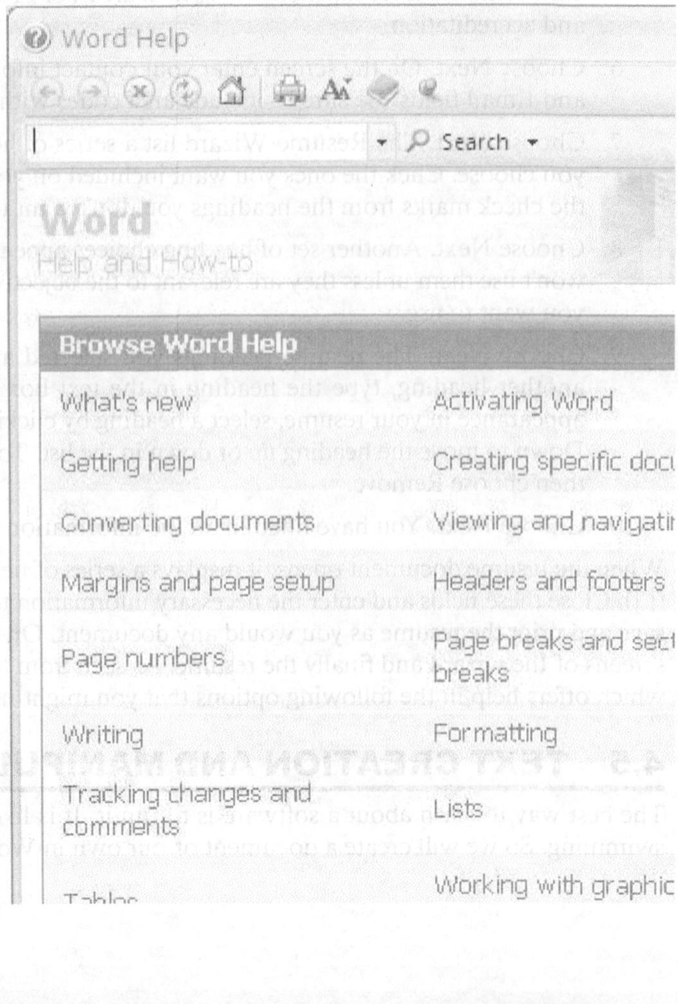

4.3.5 Fast Scrolling and Moving Pages

Fast moving is done by using the scroll bars, as mentioned above. While you can also use, the Ctrl + End combination to move to the end of the document.

4.4 USING A DOCUMENT/HELP WIZARD

Regarding Help Wizard, you can refer to the para 4.1.4. Wizards are there in any software to guide and create for you in a flash the document/output which you are trying to create using the software. These are there for like having fast food instead of having a good sit down dinner. Here everything is ready made and you have to

just fill in the data and the document is ready for you. I will start with Resume Wizard, which I am sure that at some stage of your life you must be needing it.

4.4.1 Resume Wizard

When you are looking for a job, the first thing you need is a resume of yours or better known as Bio-data in this part of the World. Word 2000 helps you in preparing a professional looking, neat and organized resume in no time. The following steps you have to take to create a resume using the Wizard.

1. Click the File menu and select New.
2. When the New dialog box appears, select the "Other Documents" tab.
3. Click the Resume Wizard icon to select it and then choose Ok. The Resume Wizard dialog box appears.
4. Choose Next. The wizard offers you 3 styles of resumes—Professional, Contemporary, or Elegant. A preview of each style appears beneath the option. Click the style you want to use.
5. Choose Next. The Resume Wizard lets you select the type of resume you are preparing. Use Entry-Level Resume if you are entering the job market or have limited experience, Chronological Resume to list your experiences in chronological order, Functional Resume to show your administrative level experience in several areas, or Professional Resume to highlight your education and accreditation.
6. Choose Next. On the screen enter your contact information in the Name, Address, Phone, Fax, and Email fields. Be sure to include area codes with the phone numbers.
7. Choose Next. The Resume Wizard list a series of headings that can appear on the resume style you choose. Click the ones you want included on your resume to check those boxes and remove the check marks from the headings you don't want to use.
8. Choose Next. Another set of heading choices appears. These can be included, but you probably won't use them unless they are relevant to the objective of the resume. Click to check the headings you want to use.
9. Choose Next. The resume headings you selected are listed on this screen. If you want to add another heading, type the heading in the text box and then choose Add. To set the order of appearance in your resume, select a heading by clicking on it and then choose Move Up or Move Down to move the heading up or down in the list. To remove a heading from the list, select it and then choose Remove.
10. Choose Next. You have filled in all the information needed for the resume, so choose Finish.

When the resume document opens, it displays a series of fields marked in gray and enclosed by brackets ([ ]). Close these fields and enter the necessary information to complete the resume document. Then you save and print the resume as you would any document. On the last few pages you have seen the various screens of the wizard and finally the resume. As seen from the above resume there is an Office Assistant which offers help in the following options that you might need in finishing your resume.

4.5 TEXT CREATION AND MANIPULATION

The best way to learn about a software is to run it. It is like jumping into the swimming pool to learn swimming. So we will create a document of our own in Word and learn the various commands side by

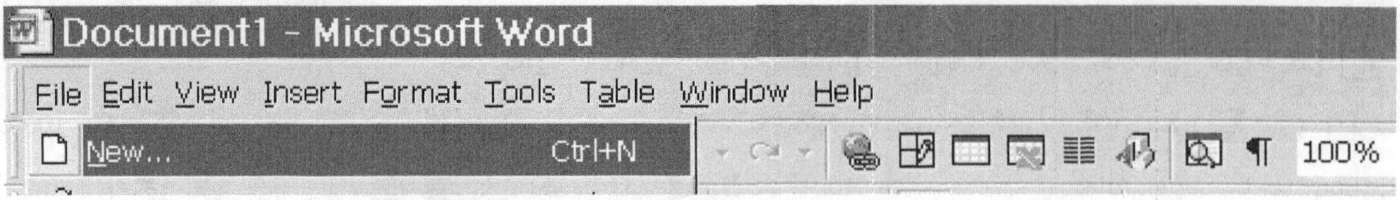

side. We have earlier learnt how to start Word. Now we have to start a new document in it. After you have opened Word click at **New** from the **File menu** as shown on the next page.

Supposing we have to create a document in the form of a letter written to the General Manager of Unit Trust of India complaining him of the non receipt of dividend warrant. This letter in original is shown below. The final product has to look like the one shown. Now that you have opened a new document, do not worry about any typing mistakes or any formatting, just type the text as it is of the document.

15th September, 2000

To,

The General Manager
Unit Trust of India
Gulab Bhawan
New Delhi - 110 002

Ref: Non-receipt of Dividend Warrant againt Folio no. 4000245497

Sir,

I am holder of the 100 units under the above folio number. For the last so many years I have been receiving the dividend againt it during the month of July itself. But, this year so far I have not received any intimtion. In fact, I have received dividend for my other units in July itself.

I hope that you would try to search for my dividend warrant and send the same to me at the earliest.

In case it is lost in post, please send me the replacement.

Hoping for an early action,

Thanking you,

Yours faithfully,

Shekhar Suman
T-391 Ahata Kidara
Delhi - 110 006

After typing, your screen will look like as shown next.

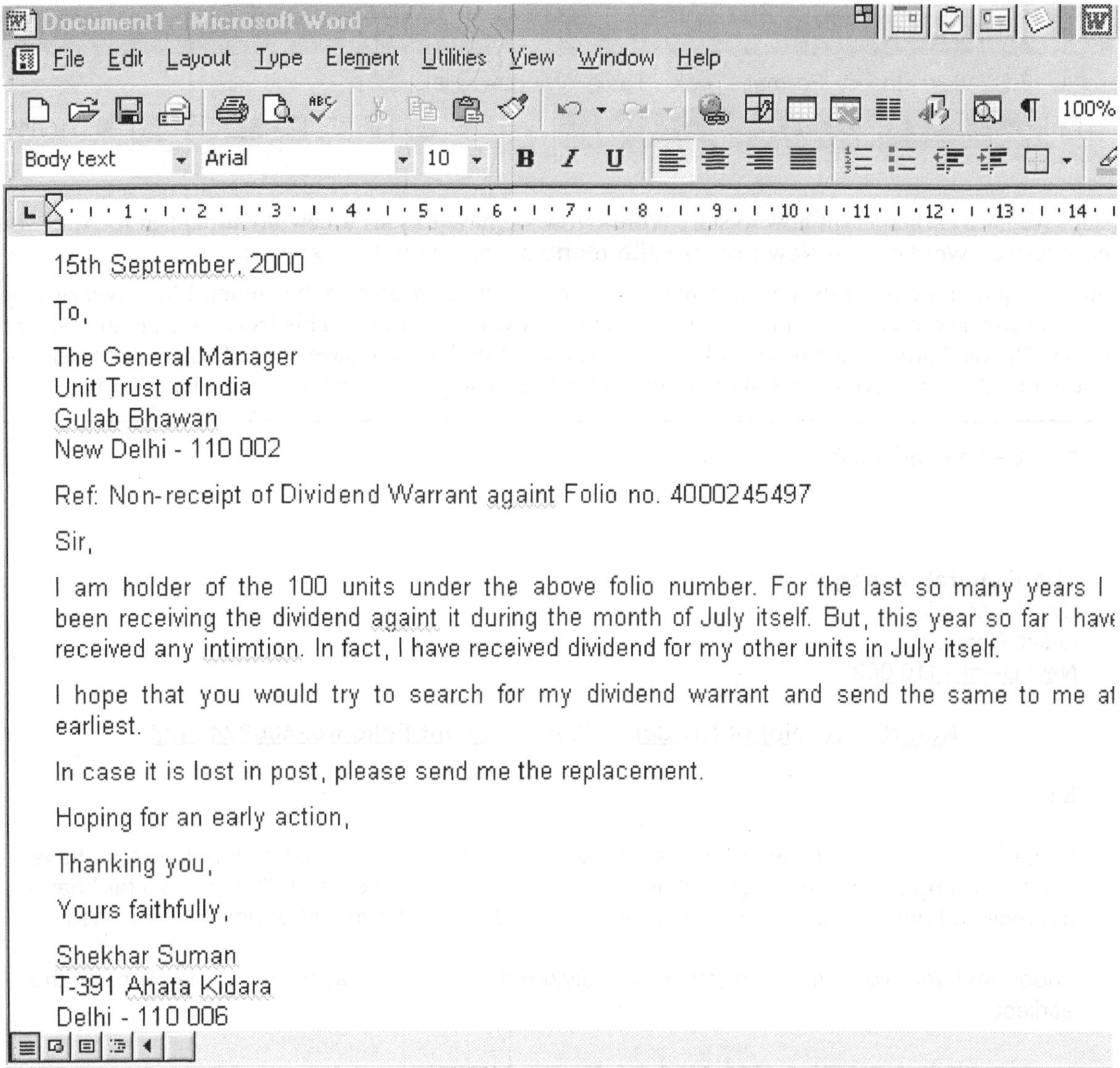
Document1 - Microsoft Word

15th September, 2000

To,

The General Manager
Unit Trust of India
Gulab Bhawan
New Delhi - 110 002

Ref: Non-receipt of Dividend Warrant againt Folio no. 4000245497

Sir,

I am holder of the 100 units under the above folio number. For the last so many years I been receiving the dividend againt it during the month of July itself. But, this year so far I have received any intimtion. In fact, I have received dividend for my other units in July itself.

I hope that you would try to search for my dividend warrant and send the same to me at earliest.

In case it is lost in post, please send me the replacement.

Hoping for an early action,

Thanking you,

Yours faithfully,

Shekhar Suman
T-391 Ahata Kidara
Delhi - 110 006

As you must have noticed there are few red and green wavy lines. The red lines, show that the word is incorrectly typed as per the dictionary available with the system and the word/words under whom the green line is, show that the words are grammatically wrong. This is the opinion of the software, you may beg to differ from it. Since most of the proper names like Shekhar Suman, are shown as wrong.

4.5.1 Paragraph and Tab Setting

Text in a document is typed in terms of paragraphs. A paragraph can have a number of lines. What we would learn now is how to leave some space between the paragraphs, lines of the paragraphs and their alignments.

For most of these we would be using the dialog box called Paragraph, which is available under Format menu and is shown on the next page. Various options which you can choose or change are given below:

4.5.1.1 General

This has the following options:

Alignment: As discussed above the various paragraph alignments are available here too for changing.

Outline Level: You can set here the various levels of text alignments.

4.5.1.2 Indentation

From here you can set the various options of paragraph spacing.

Left: Set here the margin from where the paragraph would be starting. If you set here 1", then the paragraph would start, leaving 1" space on the left.

Right: Similar to above, you can set here the space for the right margin.

Special: From here you can select whether you want to have the above margins applied to the first line or whole paragraph.

By: Within the above indentation/ margins you can even have further indentation by setting margins here.

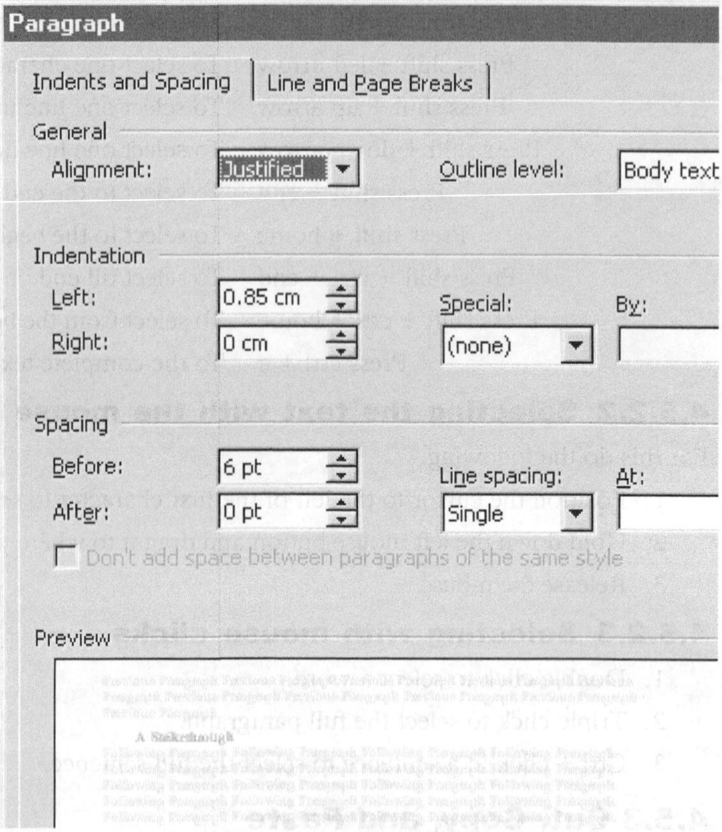

4.5.1.3 Spacing

Here you set the space which can be given after and before the paragraph.

Before: Set here the space which you want to give before the paragraph.

After: Set here the space which you want to give after the paragraph.

Line spacing: You have the option of selecting Single line, Double line, Exactly, etc. Select the type of space you want between the lines.

At: You can set here the width between the lines in terms of inches or other measure.

4.5.1.4 Preview

Whatever operation you perform above would be shown here in the form of preview in this window. So before applying a particular option you can see how it would look when applied.

4.5.2 Text Selection

For any text to be formatted, it has to be selected. There are various ways of selecting the text.

4.5.2.1 Selecting from keyboard

For selecting, place the cursor at the left of the word to be selected and then do the following:

Press shift + right arrow	To select one character to the right
Press shift + left arrow	To select one character to the left
Press shift + up arrow	To select one line up
Press shift + down arrow	To select one line down
Press shift + end	To select to the end of the line
Press shift + home	To select to the beginning of the line
Press shift + ctrl + end	To select till end of the document
Press shift + ctrl + home	To select from the beginning of the document
Press ctrl + a	To the complete text

4.5.2.2 Selecting the text with the mouse

For this do the following:

1. Position the cursor to the left of the first character to select.
2. Hold down the left mouse button and drag it to where you want to stop.
3. Release the mouse.

4.5.2.3 Selecting with mouse clicks

1. Double click to select a word.
2. Triple click to select the full paragraph.
3. Ctrl + click in a sentence to select the full sentence.

4.5.3 Cut, Copy, and Paste

Many editing functions are performed on selected text, such as cut, copy, move, and delete. There are various tools provided by Word to help you edit text:

4.5.3.1 Cut, Copy

Cutting and copying items places them on the Clipboard and you can paste these items anywhere in the document, wherever required. These items can be text, graphics, tables and any other object which is there in the word document. Cut and Copy can be performed using mouse and key strokes.

4.5.3.2 Paste

It is the command used to paste whatever is available on the Clipboard to paste it in the document. This is also done by the use of mouse and key strokes.

4.5.3.3 Move

It is an action associated with the mouse. However, if you cut and paste from one place to another, it can also be called move.

4.5.3.4 Insert Mode

It is the feature that adjusts spacing when you add new text to the document.

4.5.3.5 Overtype Mode

This option replaces the existing text with your new text.

4.5.3.6 Delete

It is an action you should reserve for text you want to permanently remove. Deleted text is not placed in the Clipboard. You can delete text with either mouse or key strokes.

4.5.3.7 Undo and Redo

Using these commands you can reverse the tasks performed earlier.

All these commands are available on the toolbars as icons too.

You can find them in the Edit menu too.

For either cutting or copying, you have to highlight the part of the text on which you want to perform this operation. All these commands have their keyboard strokes associated with them too.

They are:

Cut	Ctrl + X
Copy	Ctrl + C
Paste	Ctrl + V
Move	Ctrl + X and then Ctrl + V
Delete	Backspace or Delete
Undo	Ctrl + Z
Redo	Ctrl + Y

4.5.4 Font and Size Selection

By style in Word, we mean the appearance of the text. The various formats supported by Word are:

Bold
Italics
Underline

These are the main styles and we had earlier used them in our letter. But, if you go deep into the working of the software, you would see that these allow you to convert the character to:

Strikethrough
Double strikethrough
Superscript
Subscript
Shadow
Outline
Emboss
Engrave
Small Caps
All Caps
Hidden

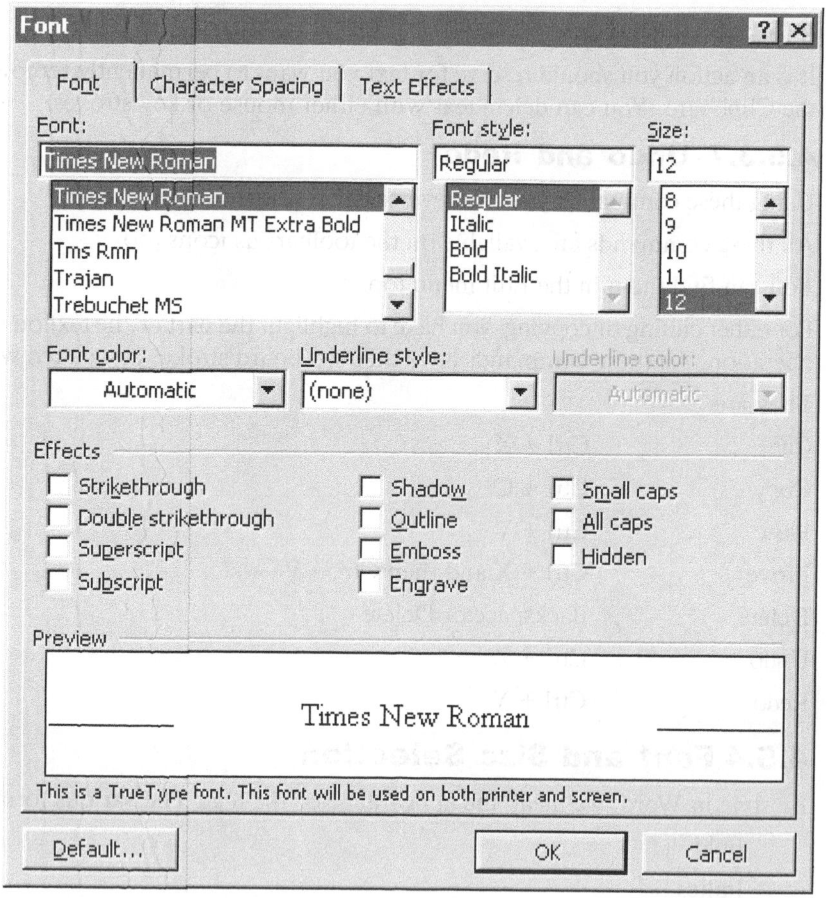

The first 3 are there on the Standard toolbar only. They can be used by just clicking at them. For example, if you have to make a word Bold, then select the word and click at B in the Standard toolbar, it will be made Bold. Similarly, you can make the characters italic and underlined.

Bold

Italics

Underline

The above example shows how they appear after changing the styles. For the other styles you have to do the following:

1. Select the text whose style you have to change.
2. Click at Format menu and select Font from it.
3. In the dialog box, select the option you want to use.
4. Your text would be changed accordingly.
5. Various options of the text are shown above.

4.5.4.1 Size of Text

The size of the text, pertains to the thickness of the text. As the size increases, the width of the character also increases. In fact, the proportionate height of the character also increases. You can change the size of the text from 2 places in Word.

From the Formatting Bar

1. Select the text whose size you want to change.
2. Click at font size in the formatting bar to have Word display various sizes.
3. Select the size which you want.

From the Font Dialog Box

1. Select the text whose size you want to change.
2. Click at Format and select Font.

3. From the Font dialog box, select the size you want to have.
4. Click Ok to have your text changed to the required size.

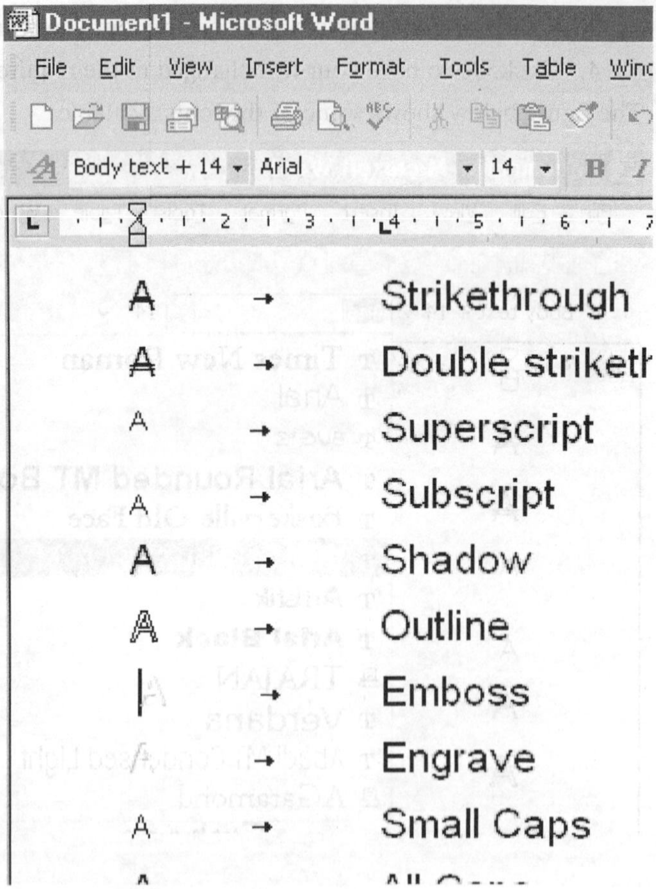

The following examples would show how the font size makes the difference:

A 12 point

A 20 point

A 40 point

4.5.4.2 Font of the Text

Fonts are nothing but the various styles which can be used to represent your text. Lots of fonts are available from fancy ones to ornamental types. Microsoft Word on its own does not have fonts, but, it takes the fonts available under the Windows. As usual there are 2 ways of selecting a font for the text.

From Formatting Toolbar

1. Select the text whose font you want to change.
2. Click at font in the formatting bar to have Word display various fonts.
3. Select the font which you want.

From the Font Dialog Box

1. Select the text whose font you want to change.
2. Click at Format and select Font.

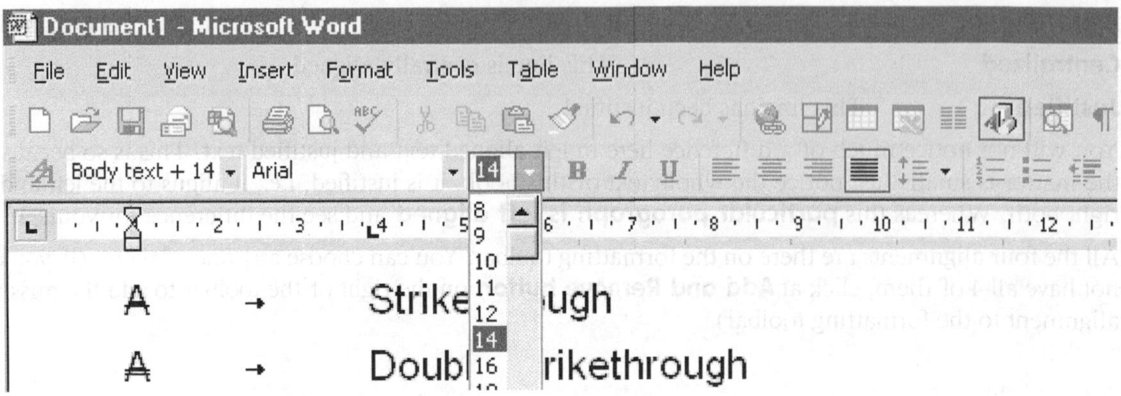

3. From the Font dialog box, select the font you want to have.
4. Click Ok to have your text changed to the required font.

The figure below shows some of the fonts available.

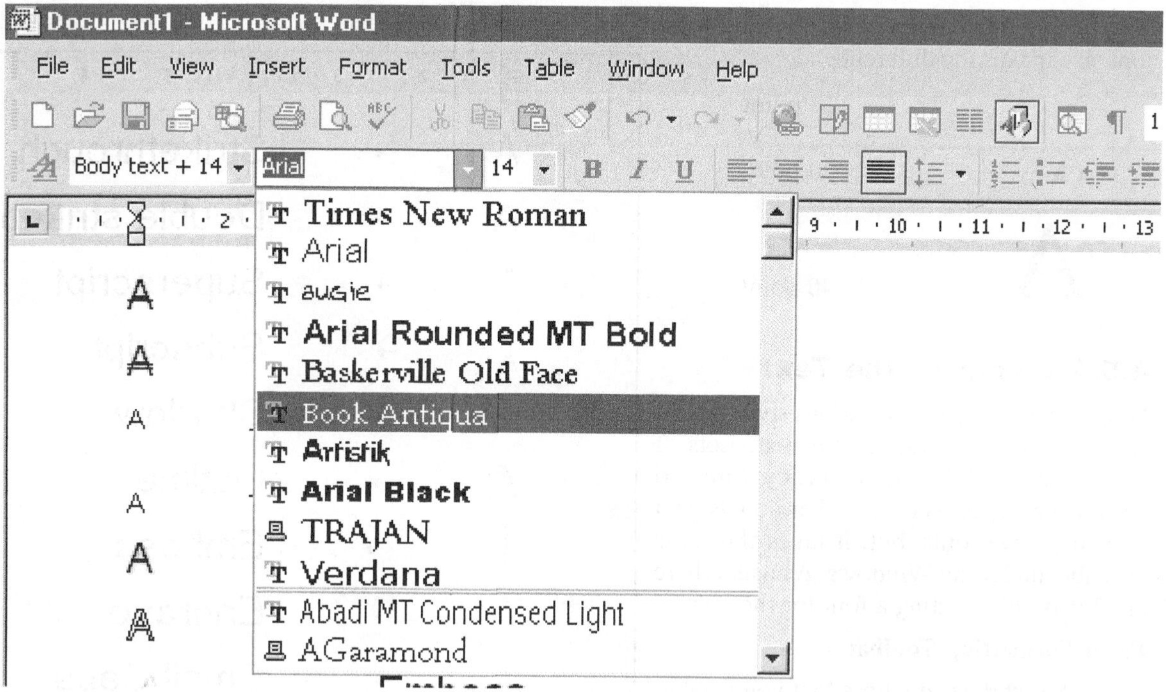

4.5.5 Bold, Italics, and Underline

See above para.

4.5.6 Alignment of Text: Center, Left, Right, and Justify

Word 2000 gives you the option of placing the text in four different alignments. These are:

Left aligned This line is left aligned.

Right aligned This line is right aligned.

Centralized This line is centrally aligned.

Justified This line has been justified.

You will not notice much of a difference here in left aligned text and justified text. This is so because the matter is small. Just notice the whole text of this book, it is justified, i.e., it aligns to the left and right both. Whereas this **particular paragraph is left aligned** and see the difference for yourself.

All the four alignments are there on the formatting toolbar. You can choose any one of them. (If you do not have all 4 of them, click at **Add and Remove button** on the right of the toolbar to add the missing alignment to the formatting toolbar).

4.6 FORMATTING THE TEXT

Text entered by typing in the document can be formatted using the various tools available in Word. Some of them are discussed here.

4.6.1 Changing Font, Size and Colour

Changing of Font and Size has been discussed earlier. Let us see how the colour is changed.

You can if you want change the colour of the text too. Since most of the printers now-a-days have the colour capabilities, you can print your letters in colours too. Microsoft Word supports the full colour features. You can have various colours for various portions of the text in your document.

For changing the colour of the text, do the following:

1. Select the text whose colour you want to change.
2. Click at A on the formatting toolbar.
3. A colour template would be shown to you.
4. Select the colour which you want.
5. Your text would be changed to that colour.
6. If you click at More Colors, another dialog box would give you more options of colours to choose from.
7. Both the dialog boxes are shown.

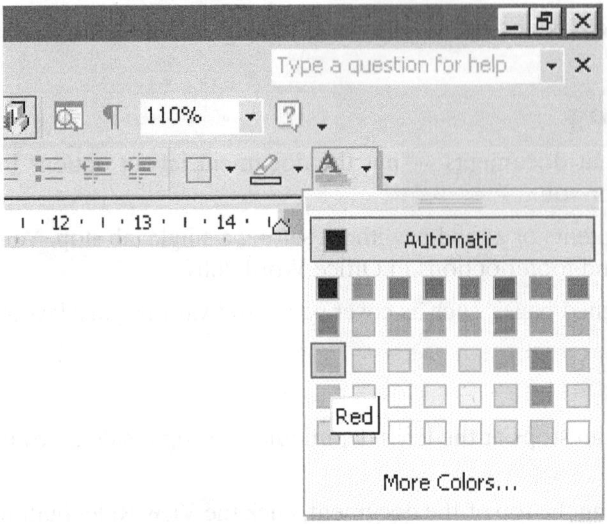

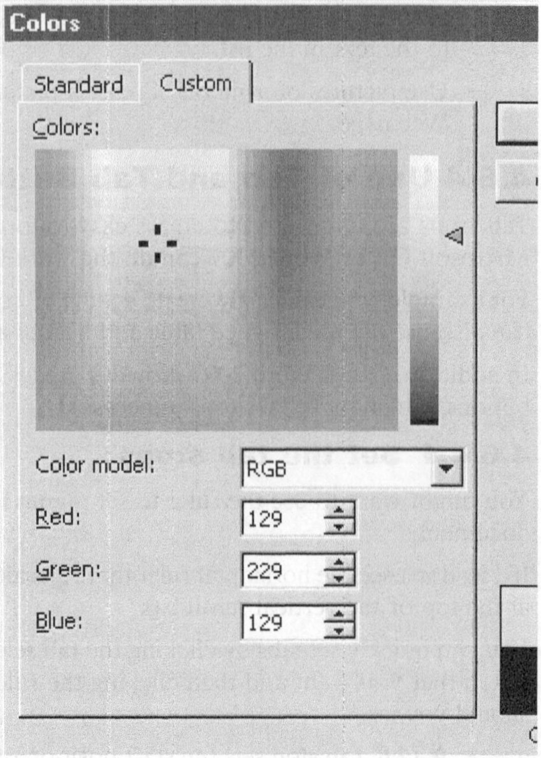

4.6.2 Paragraph Indenting

For this refer to the heading of Paragraph.

4.6.3 Bullets and Numbering

It is used to put numbers and bullets in the text. You can choose the bullet of your own and even in numbers you can choose the style.

4.6.3.1 Create a bulleted or numbered list

You can quickly add bullets or numbers to existing lines of text, or Word can automatically create lists as you type.

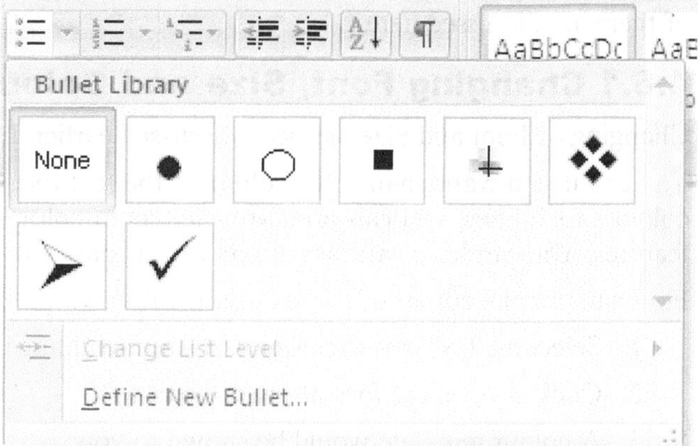

By default, if you start a paragraph with an asterisk or a number 1., Word recognizes that you are trying to start a bulleted or numbered list. If you don't want your text turned into a list, you can click the AutoCorrect Options button that appears.

4.6.3.2 Lists: One level or many levels

Make a list with just one level, or make a multilevel list to show lists within a list.

When you create a bulleted or numbered list, you can do any of the following:

- Use the convenient Bullet and Numbering libraries Use the default bullet and numbering formats for lists, customize the lists, or select other formats from the Bullet and Numbering libraries.
- Format bullets or numbers. Format bullets or numbers differently from the text in a list. For example, click a number and change the number color for the entire list, without making changes to the text in the list.
- Use pictures or symbols. Create a picture bulleted list to add visual interest to a document or a Web page.

4.6.4 Use of Tab and Tab Setting

Tab stops are often used to create easy-to-format documents — but the document layout options in Microsoft Office Word 2007 can do the work for you.

For example, you can easily create a table of contents or an index without setting a single tab stop. You can also use the predesigned table and header and footer options in Office Word 2007.

In addition, Office Word 2007 provides predesigned pages, such as cover pages and various page layout options, which make tab stops unnecessary.

4.6.4.1 Set the tab stops

You might want to use the ruler to set manual tab stops at the left side, middle, and right side of your document.

If you don't see the horizontal ruler that runs along the top of the document, click the View Ruler button at the top of the vertical scroll bar.

You can quickly set tabs by clicking the tab selector at the left end of the ruler until it displays the type of tab that you want and then clicking the ruler at the location you want. But which type of tab stop should you use?

- A Left Tab stop sets the start position of text that will then run to the right as you type.
- A Center Tab stop sets the position of the middle of the text. The text centers on this position as you type.

- A Right Tab stop sets the right end of the text. As you type, the text moves to the left.
- A Decimal Tab stop aligns numbers around a decimal point. Independent of the number of digits, the decimal point will be in the same position. (You can align numbers around a decimal character only; you cannot use the decimal tab to align numbers around a different character, such as a hyphen or an ampersand symbol.)
- A Bar Tab stop doesn't position text. It inserts a vertical bar at the tab position.

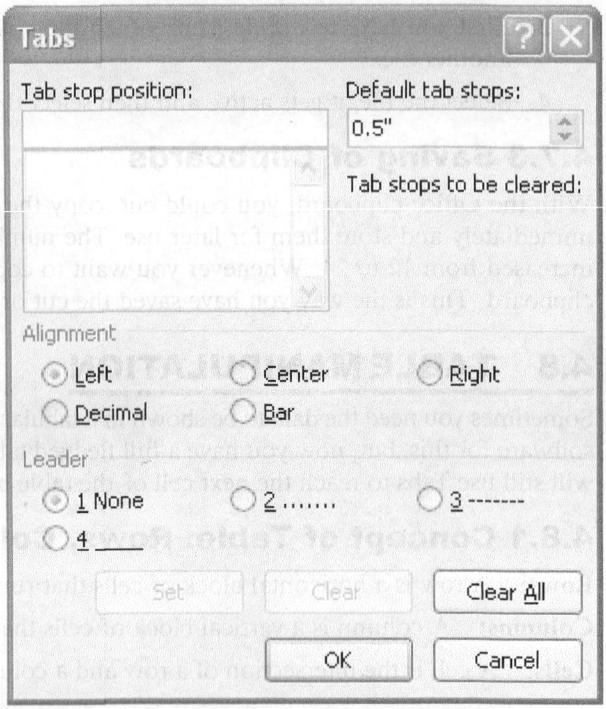

If you want your tab stops at precise positions that you can't get by clicking the ruler, or if you want to insert a specific character (leader) before the tab, you can use the Tabs dialog box. To display this dialog box, double-click any tab stop on the ruler.

4.6.5 Changing Case

Using this option you can change the case of the selected text. You can choose the option of having it all CAPS or in all lowercase. **Sentence case** will make only the first character Caps and the rest of the sentence in lower case. **Title case** will make all the title words start with a capital letter. **Toggle case** will make the Capital letter lower and lower letter as Capital, i.e., reverse the case. So choose the option which you want and click at the proper selection and see the result.

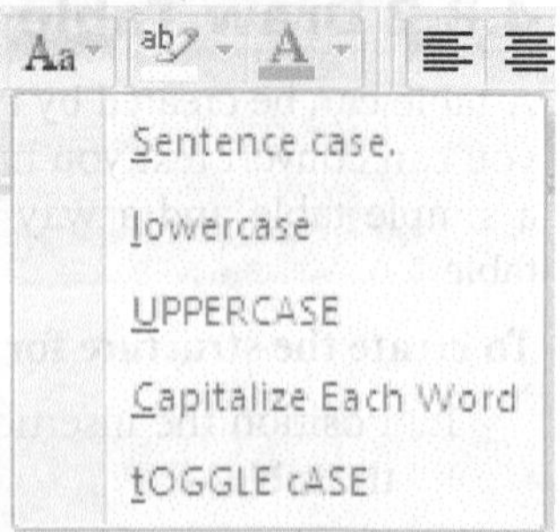

4.7 HANDLING MULTIPLE DOCUMENTS

Word allows you to have several documents open simultaneously. Each document window may contain different documents. You can work only in the active document window.

4.7.1 Opening and Closing of Multiple Documents

To open different doccument windows, do the following:

1. Click the File menu and choose Open. Or, click the Open buton on the Standard toolbar.
2. In the Open dialog box, choose the location of the file you want to open. Or. click the open drop down list and choose the desired option.

4.7.2 Cut, Copy and Paste Across the Documents

To do this, follow the following steps.

1. To display all document windows select Arrange, All option.
2. Both the files spit in the horizontal wise.

3. First you have to decide from which file you want to (cut or copy) means move the matter to another file.
4. Select the file, it gets active and then select the matter, right click the mouse and choose Cut.

4.7.3 Saving of Clipboards

With the Office clipboard, you could cut, copy the items from your document and either paste them immediately and store them for later use. The number of items you can collect on the Clipboard has increased from 12 to 24. Whenever you want to copy the items from the Clipboard you just open the clipboard. This is the way you have saved the cut or copy the items in the clipboard.

4.8 TABLE MANIPULATION

Sometimes you need the data to be shown in a tabular form. Tabs were used in the earlier word processing software for this, but, now you have a full fledged table menu in the new Microsoft Word. Though you will still use Tabs to reach the next cell of the table but the working of the whole tables is much easier.

4.8.1 Concept of Table: Rows, Columns, and Cells

Rows: A row is a horizontal block of cells that runs through the entire width of the table.

Columns: A column is a vertical block of cells that runs through the table.

Cells: A cell is the intersection of a row and a column.

4.8.2 Draw Table

A table can be created by two methods. You can create the table structure before you enter any text, or you can convert text you have already created to a table. There is an easy way to create the structure for a simple table and a way to create a more complex table.

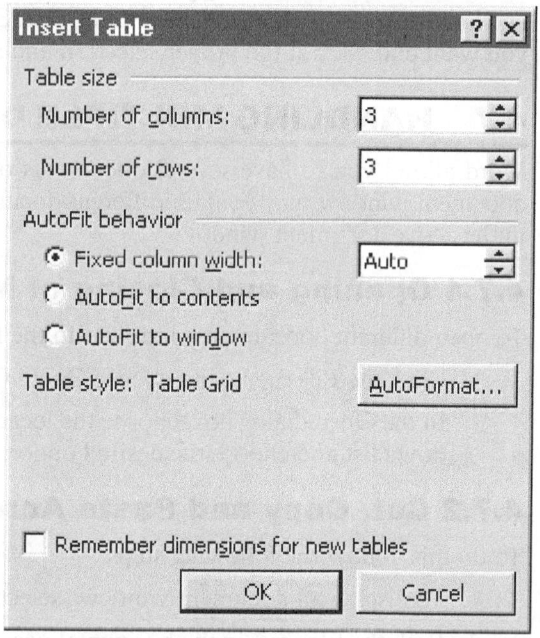

To create the structure for a simple table

1. Position the insertion point at the location for the table.
2. Click the Insert Table button on the Standard toolbar.
3. Drag across the number of columns and down, the number of rows you want

   An unformatted table appears

   or you can follow the following alternate method.

1. Position cursor at the location for the table.
2. From the Table menu, choose Insert and Table.
3. In the Insert Table dialog box, specify the columns and rows, in this case we have chosen a table of 3 x 3.
4. Click Ok.

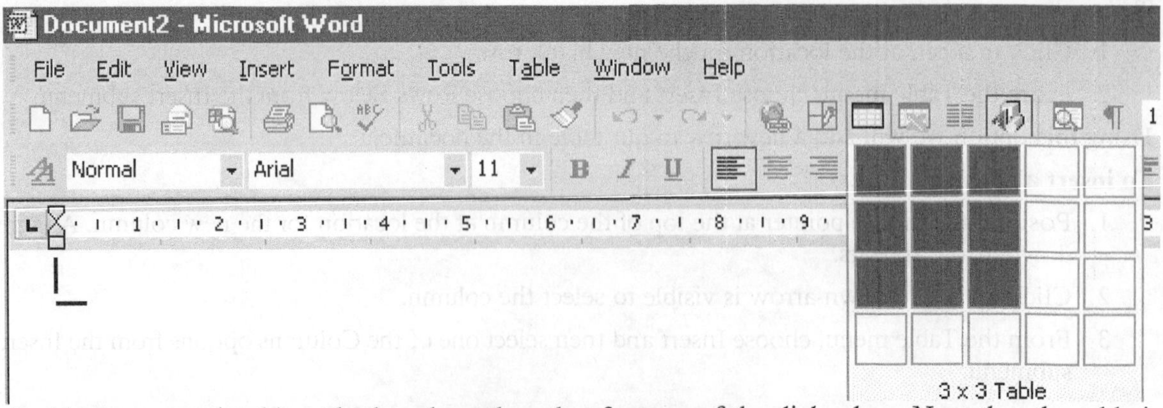

At this stage you should not bother about the other features of the dialog box. Now that the table is available you would like to enter the data into it.

4.8.3 Changing Cell Width and Height

1. Click in a cell with the mouse and type the data required to be typed. As you type, the cursor wraps within the cell and the entire row will become taller if it needs to accommodate multiple lines of text.
2. Press Tab to move to the cell to the right, and type text in the next cell.
3. Continue pressing tab after you finish each cell.
4. When you finish entering text in the last cell of the table, press Tab to create a new row, if required.

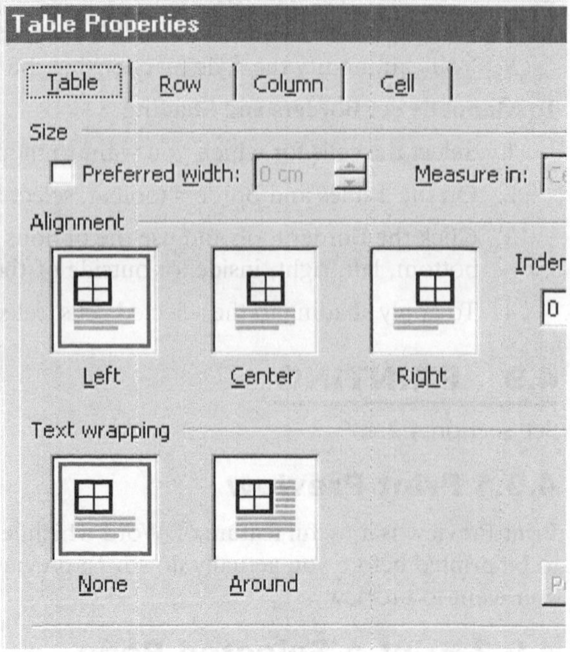

4.8.4 Alignment of Text in a Cell

1. Select the cells you want to align.
2. Click the Table Properties in the Table menu.
3. A dialog box will appear.
4. From here select the Table panel and the alignment wanted by you.

4.8.5 Copying of Cell

1. Select the cells you want to copy.
2. Right click to get the mini menu.
3. Click at Copy.
4. The data from the cell would be copied onto the Clipboard.

4.8.6 Delete/Insertion of Row and Coloumns

You can add rows and columns to any portion of your table on all the sides using the following options.

To insert a row

1. Click in a cell at the location for the new blank row.
2. From the Table menu, choose Insert and then choose Rows Below from the Insert submenu.

Using this option we will add a new row to our table in the document.

To insert a column

1. Position the mouse pointer at the top of the column at the location for the new column. A large down-arrow appears.
2. Click while the down-arrow is visible to select the column.
3. From the Table menu, choose Insert and then select one of the Columns options from the Insert submenu.

4.8.7 Borders for Table

By using Borders you can draw lines around the cells and fill them with shades using the command Shading.

To Automatically Format a Table with Template

1. Click anywhere in the table to select it.
2. From the Table Tools, choose Design tab.
3. In the Table Styles, choose the style you want for your table. You can click at right arrow to see more designs or click at More to see the dialog box of the built-in designs of the table.
4. Choose the one you want and it will be applied to your table.
5. You can modify the style by choosing the Modify Table Style option.

To Manually set Borders and Shading

1. Select the cells for which you want to modify the borders or add shading.
2. On the Tables and Borders toolbar, select line style and weight from the drop-down lists.
3. Click the Border tool, and use the options on the drop-down palette to apply borders to the top, bottom, left, right, inside, or outside of the selected cells.
4. To apply shading to the selected cells, select a shading option from the Shading drop-down list.

4.9 PRINTING

See section 4.2.4.

4.9.1 Print Preview

Print Preview is a useful feature of Word which lets you view your document exactly the way it is going to be printed before you actually do so. To preview the document you need to first open the document you want to preview.

4.9.2 Print a Selected Page

Printing a selected page is easy if you know the page number. Just give the page number in the Print dialog box and that page would be printed.

LET US REVISE

1. Word processing programs allow you to manipulate text consisting of words.
2. In a word processing program, you can change the various aspects of the text.
3. Among the various features of Word Processing are: Alignment, Deleting Mistakes, Line Spacing, MailMerging, Moving the Cursor, Naming a Document, Overwriting Mistakes, Page Breaks, Page Numbers, Search and Replace, Spell Checking.
4. Text is the matter which you type.
5. Document is whole text matter which you create, like a letter, or a chapter, etc.
6. Fonts are the various styles which you can use for your text.
7. Cursor is the blinking point which tells you where to start typing or what your current position is.
8. Space bar is used for giving space between the words.
9. Tabs are used to set the text into tabular form.
10. Backspace is used to delete the wrongly typed character in your text.
11. You can start Microsoft Word from the Start button and Programs.
12. You can also start Word from its icon.
13. Opening screen of Word is like a blank screen.
14. Click at New from the File menu to create a document.
15. You can save your Word document file with a name.
16. You can set the timings for Auto saving of files.
17. Closing of document is usually done after saving it.
18. To open an existing document, you use the Open command from File menu.
19. For formatting the text, you need to select it first.
20. You can select text with mouse too.
21. You can select text from keyboard too.
22. The various formats supported by Word are: Bold, Italics, Underline.
23. You can also make the text Strikethrough, Double strikethrough, Superscript, Subscript, Shadow, Outline, Emboss, Engrave, Small Caps, All Caps and Hidden.
24. You can change the size of the text from Formatting bar and Font dialog box.
25. You can change the font of the text too from Formatting bar and Font dialog box.
26. You can change the colour of the text too.
27. Alignment supported by Word are: Left, Right, Center and Justify.
28. Using Paragraph dialog box, you can change the line space and para space among other things.
29. You can put Headers on top of the pages of the document and Footers at the bottom.
30. You can set the page numbers according to your liking.
31. Spell checking is an important aspect of the word processing.
32. You can even add the words which are not there in the dictionary.
33. You can print all or few pages of the document on the printer.
34. You can do all the editing operations like Cut, Copy, Paste, Delete, etc., in Word.
35. You can also have graphics inserted into your Word documents.

36. Word has its own set Clip Arts which can be inserted in the documents.
37. You can have the text wrapped around the graphics in your document.
38. WordArt is an independent program which allows to create text in differnt formats.
39. You can set the various options of your page using Page Setup.
40. You can highlight your text using Bullets and Numering.
41. You can even have Borders around your text.
42. You can have various tabs in your documents to make the text tabular.
43. You can find particular word in Word and replace it with another.
44. You can have a table inserted into your document.
45. You can align your text in the table in any format which you may desire.
46. You can add Rows and Columns in your table.
47. MailMerge is an important feature of Word.
48. You can give page number to each page of the document.
49. You can have header and footer on each page.
50. You can insert a symbol from the hard disk in your document.
51. You can have border with shades around your text in Word.
52. You can have your text in multiple columns.
53. A Table of Contents can be created in Word.
54. You can create an index of the document.
55. You can place a bookmark in your text.
56. You can count the number of words in your text.

MULTIPLE CHOICE QUESTIONS

1. In word processing, you manipulate _______
   (a) numbers (b) text
2. You can set Left, Right and ______ alignment in word processing.
   (a) Center (b) Justify (c) Both
3. Can you spell check you text in word processing?
   (a) Yes (b) No
4. Can you locate a word in word processing?
   (a) No (b) Yes
5. Blinking point which shows your position in the text is called:
   (a) Cursor (b) Blinker (c) Position
6. Spacebar is used for :
   (a) giving space (b) deleting space
7. You can start Microsoft Word by using ________ button.
   (a) New (b) Start (c) Program
8. For creating a document, you use _____ command at File menu.
   (a) New (b) Open (c) Document

9. For saving a document, you need to have ________ for it.
   (a) Name (b) Surname
10. For opening an existing document, you need to give _____ command.
   (a) New (b) Open (c) Close
11. You can select the text by:
   (a) Keyboard (b) Mouse (c) Both
12. You click at B to make the text
   (a) Bold (b) Italics (c) Underline
13. Can you emboss you text?
   (a) Yes (b) No
14. You can change the size of the text from:
   (a) Formatting bar (b) Font dialog box (c) Both
15. You click at I to make the text
   (a) Bold (b) Italics (c) Underline
16. You can change the font of the text from
   (a) Formatting bar (b) Font dialog box (c) Box
17. Colour of the text can be changed:
   (a) Yes (b) No
18. You click at U to make the text
   (a) Bold (b) Italics (c) Underline
19. Word supports alignments like Left, Right, Center and ______
   (a) Justify (b) Up (c) Down
20. You can change the line and para spacing from ______ dialog box.
   (a) Font (b) Paragraph (c) Open
21. Header appears at the ______ of the page.
   (a) Top (b) Bottom (c) Center
22. Footer appears at the ________ of the page
   (a) Top (b) Bottom (c) Center
23. For printing a document you have to have _________ on.
   (a) Printer (b) Monitor (c) Scanner
24. Most of the editing tools are available under _____ menu.
   (a) File (b) Format (c) Edit
25. You can add picture in your document from the _______ menu.
   (a) File (b) Edit (c) Insert
26. Clip Art is
   (a) Text (b) Graphics (c) Both
27. Can Text be mingled with Graphics?
   (a) Yes (b) No
28. WordArt is a
   (a) Text (b) Graphic (c) Independent program

29. You can set margins by using the dialog box:
   (a) Font (b) Page Setup (c) Margins
30. Two main orientations are, Potrait and
   (a) Landscape (b) Photo (c) Lying
31. Can you shade your text?
   (a) Yes (b) No
32. Can you put border across your text in the document?
   (a) Yes (b) No
33. Decimal is tab?
   (a) Yes (b) No
34. In text you can find a word and replace it with another word using command ________.
   (a) Find (b) Replace (c) None
35. You can insert a table from ________ toolbar.
   (a) Formatting (b) Standard (c) Drawing
36. You can align data vertically in a table:
   (a) Yes (b) No
37. Can you insert more rows in a table?
   (a) Yes (b) No
38. Sending of same letter to different people is done by:
   (a) Send (b) Letter (c) Mailmerge
39. Headers are put:
   (a) at the top (b) at the bottom (c) in the middle
40. You can put page numbers :
   (a) at the top (b) at the bottom (c) both places
41. Footers are put:
   (a) at the top (b) at the bottom (c) in the middle
42. Table of contents has:
   (a) Page number (b) Marked entry (c) both
43. Borders can be shaded:
   (a) Yes (b) No
44. You can have line in between the columns:
   (a) Yes (b) No
45. Index has all marked enteries with page numbers:
   (a) Yes (b) No
46. Word count gives you :
   (a) Numuber of lines (b) Number of words (c) Both

TRUE/FALSE QUESTIONS

1. Word processing is to mix words.
2. You can spell check your typed text.

3. You cannot use various fonts available under Windows for your text.
4. Spacebar is used for giving space between words.
5. You use Open to start a new document.
6. You can save your documents with a name.
7. For formatting the text, you need not select it.
8. Keyboard cannot be used for selecting the text.
9. You cannot change the colour of your text.
10. You can change the size of your text.
11. You can change the line spacing from Paragraph option.
12. You cannot number your pages in Word.
13. You can check your grammer too in Word.
14. You can print some selective page too.
15. You can edit the text of your document.
16. You cannot insert graphics in your document.
17. You cannot align text in the table.
18. You can add more rows and columns in the table.
19. You cannot put borders across your text.
20. For mailmerging you have to create two files.
21. Table of Contents does not have page numbers.
22. Index usually appears in the beginning of the book.
23. There is no provision for Bookmark in Word.
24. Clip Art are graphics.

MATCHING COLUMNS

Match the matter in Column A with the matter in Column B.

Column A	Column B
A. Header	1. Merging of documents according to data
B. Table	2. Horizontal page
C. Clip Art	3. Used to identify rows
D. Portrait	4. It has rows and columns to refer text
E. Justify	5. Displays document before printing
F. Next page	6. Changing text to Bold
G. Data Source	7. Readymade documents
H. Page break	8. Readymade graphics
I. Save a document	9. Command to help you generate a document
J. Numbers	10. Start new section on new page
K. Print preview	11. Ctrl + S
L. Times New Roman	12. File having data

M. MailMerge	13. Displayed in top margin
N. Wizard	14. Bottom of the page
O. Use B for	15. An alignment
P. Template	16. Vertical page
Q. Footer	17. A font
R. Landscape	18. End of a page and beginning of new page

FILL IN THE BLANKS WITH APPROPRIATE WORDS

a. File	b. Centre	c. Tools	d. Backspace
e. Replace	f. Status	g. Save	h. Font
i. Green	j. Find	k. Insert	l. Standard

1. You can save your document using ______ command.
2. Using ________ command you can find a word.
3. The command used to replace one word with another is __________.
4. The bar which shows your current status in the document is called ___________.
5. You can delete one character using _________ key.
6. You can use _____ alignment to centralize your text.
7. Spell check is under ______ menu.
8. Grammatical errors are shown in _______.
9. All open, close icons are there on the _________ toolbar.
10. Text can be styled using _______.
11. You can enter page numbers from _____ menu.
12. You can start a new document using New command which is under ______ menu.

DESCRIPTIVE TYPE QUESTIONS

1. What is word processing?
2. What are the various features of word processing?
3. Define the following terms:

Text	Document
Fonts	Cursor
Arrow keys	Space bar
Tabs	Backspace

4. Describe the various methods of starting Microsoft Word.
5. Describe the various items on the screen of Word.
6. How would you create a new document?
7. Describe the process of saving a document.
8. How would you set the timing for AutoSave?

9. If you do not save before closing, what will happen?
10. Describe the process of opening an existing document.
11. Describe the various methods of selection of text.
12. Describe the process of making the text Bold, Italics and Underline.
13. Describe the various options of Font dialog box.
14. How would you change size & font of the text?
15. Describe the process of changing the colour of the text.
16. What is an alignment? Describe the various alignments supported by Word.
17. Describe the various options of Paragraph dialog box.
18. How would you allot page numbers to various pages in your document?
19. How is spell checking done?
20. What are various options of spell checking dialog box?
21. Describe the various options of Print dialog box.
22. Describe the various editing tools of Word.
23. Describe the various shortcuts attached to editing tools.
24. How would you insert graphics into your document?
25. What is a Clip Art? How would you add a clip art in your text.
26. Describe the process of wrapping text around the graphic.
27. What is WordArt? Describe the process of creating a WordArt text.
28. Describe the various options of Page Setup.
29. How are Bullets and Numering used?
30. Describe the various options of Borders and Shading.
31. Describe the various Tabs supported by Word and how they are used?
32. Describe the process of finding a word and replacing it with another.
33. How would you create a table in your document?
34. Describe the various options of table alignments.
35. How would you add rows and columns in a table?
36. Describe the complete process of MailMerge.
37. How would you enter a chart in your document?
38. How would you use Wizard to create your bio-data?
39. What are Headers and Footers and how are they put in the documents?
40. How would you insert a symbol in your document?
41. How would you put border across your text in the document?
42. What is columns command used for?
43. How would you create a Table of Contents?
44. Describe the process of creating the index.
45. What is bookmark used for?
46. How are the words in the document counted?

ANSWERS TO OBJECTIVE QUESTIONS

Multiple Choice Questions

1. b	2. c	3. a	4. b
5. a	6. a	7. b	8. a
9. a	10 b	11. c	12. a
13. a	14. c	15. a	16. c
17. a	18. a	19. a	20. b
21. a	22. b	23. a	24. c
25. c	26. b	27. a	28. c
29. b	30. a	31. a	32. a
33. a	34. b	35. a	36. a
37. a	38. c	39. a	40. c
41. b	42. a	43. a	44. a
45. a	46. c		

True False Questions

1. T	2. T	3. F	4. T
5. F	6. T	7. F	8. F
9. F	10. T	11. T	12. F
13. T	14. T	15. T	16. F
17. F	18. T	19. F	20. T
21. F	22. F	23. F	24. T

Matching Columns

A. 13	B. 4	C. 8	D. 16
E. 15	F. 10	G. 12	H. 18
I. 11	J. 3	K. 5	L. 17
M. 1	N. 9	O. 6	P. 7
Q. 14	R. 2		

Fill in the Blanks with Appropriate Words

1. g	2. j	3. e	4. f
5. d	6. b	7. c	8. i
9. l	10. h	11. k	12. a

Chapter 5 Spreadsheet

5.1 ELEMENTS OF ELECTRONIC SPREADSHEET

Excel for Windows is a spreadsheet program. A spreadsheet is a graphical representation of rows and columns. Data can be fed into these rows and columns and mathematical and other operations performed on it. An opening screen of Excel is shown here.

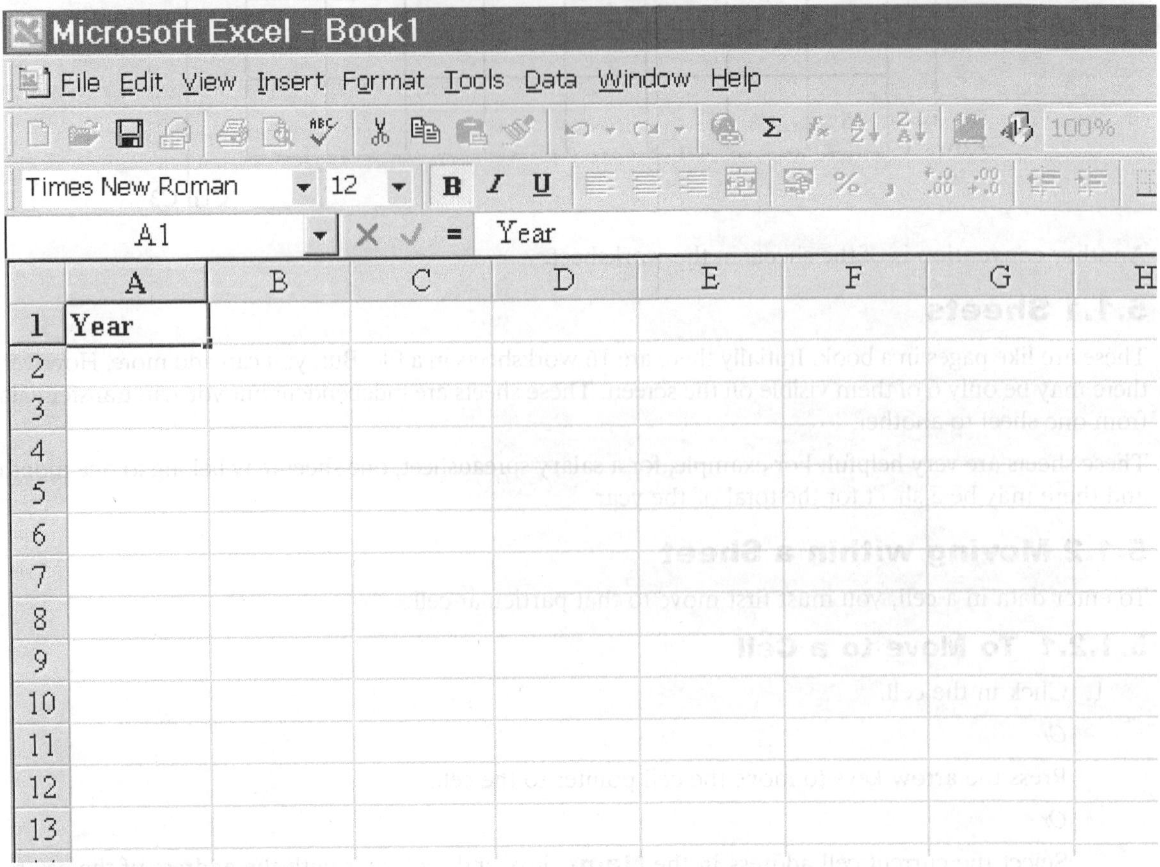

Naming Convention

It is not I have named rows from 1 onwards and columns A onwards on my own but they are so numbered by the software itself. These are the standard way of expressing these columns and rows.

If we have to name a large number of cells or columns, for that too we have the convention which asks us to call them with starting cell address and last cell address with colon in between. For example, see the addressed cells here.

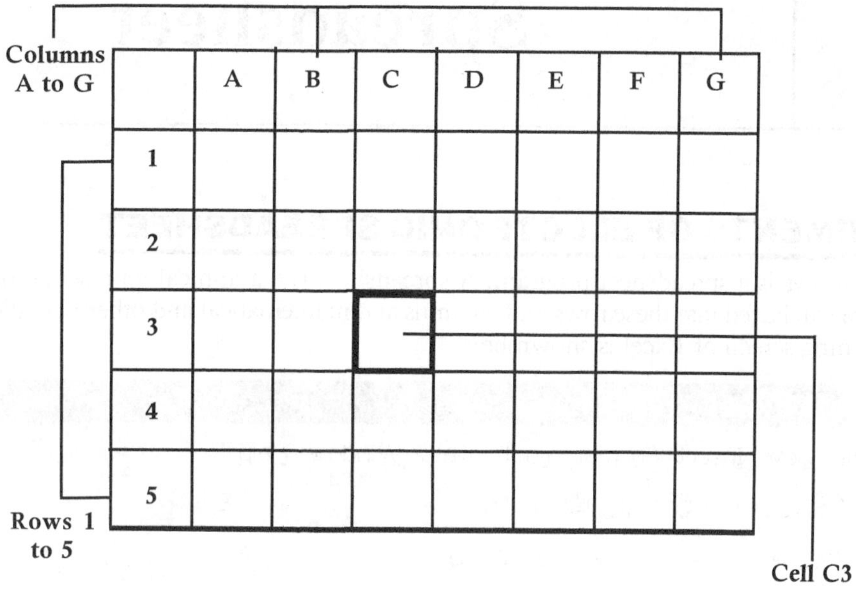

Another convention is of the sheets in the worksheet.

5.1.1 Sheets

These are like pages in a book. Initially there are 16 worksheets in a file. But, you can add more. However, there may be only 6 of them visible on the screen. These sheets are independent but you can transfer data from one sheet to another.

These sheets are very helpful. For example, for a salary spreadsheet, one sheet may belong to one month and there may be a sheet for the total of the year.

5.1.2 Moving within a Sheet

To enter data in a cell, you must first move to that particular cell.

5.1.2.1 To Move to a Cell

1. Click in the cell.

   Or

   Press the arrow keys to move the cell pointer to the cell.

   Or

   Select the current cell address in the **Name** box and replace it with the address of the cell to which you want to move.

Remember

1. The cell surrounded by the cell pointer is called the active cell.
2. You can use the scroll bars to scroll through the document without changing the active cell.
3. To move within the worksheet, you can use the keyboard shortcuts, given below:

5.1.2.2 Keyboard Shortcuts for Moving Around the Worksheet

Keyboard Shortcut	*Result*
Arrow key	Moves to the adjacent cell (Up, Down, Left or Right)
Ctrl+Arrow Key	Moves to the edge of the current data region (Up, Down, Left or Right)
Tab	Moves right one cell
Shift + Tab	Moves left one cell
Enter	Moves down one cell
Shift + Enter	Moves up one cell
Home	Moves to the first cell of the row
Ctrl + Home	Moves to cell A1
Ctrl + End	Moves to last cell of last row with data
Page Down	Moves down one screen
Page Up	Moves up one screen
Alt + Page Down	Moves one screen to the right
Alt + Page Up	Moves one screen to the left
Ctrl + Page Down	Moves to the next sheet in the workbook
Ctrl + Page Up	Moves to the previous sheet in the workbook

5.1.3 Entering Data

You can enter text, a number, or a formula into each cell in a worksheet. You enter text to create a label, such as a column heading. You can enter a number to provide information with which you can do calculations.

5.1.3.1 To Type Data in a Cell

1. Select the cell.
2. Type text, a number, or a formula. A flashing insertion point will appear at the end of whatever you type. You will notice that whatever you type will appear not only in the active cell but also in the Formula bar.
3. Press Enter key to move to the next cell. The cell below will become the new active cell.

Remember

1. You don't have to press Enter after you type the contents of a cell. You can simply press right arrow key to move to the next cell.
2. Excel right aligns the numbers in the cell but left aligns the text.

5.1.4 Editing the Data

The easiest way to change the text or number in a cell is to click the cell and then type right over the contents. But if you have a formula or extensive text in the cell, you might prefer to edit the existing contents to avoid retyping the whole entry.

5.1.4.1 To edit data in a cell

1. Click the cell and then type over its contents

   Or

   Double click the cell to position an insertion point with the cell contents.
2. Edit the contents as though you were editing text in Word.
3. Press Enter to enter the revised text in the cell.

This is if you have just one cell to edit. But, if you have more than one cell to edit, then you need to select the various cells.

5.1.5 Selecting Cells

You can select a number of consecutive cells called a range by one of the following methods:

1. Click and drag over the selection.
2. Click in one cell, and then hold down the Shift key and click in the opposite corner of the selection.
3. Click on the Select All button, the gray rectangle where the column and row heading meet, to select the entire worksheet.
4. Click in a column or row heading to select the whole column or row.

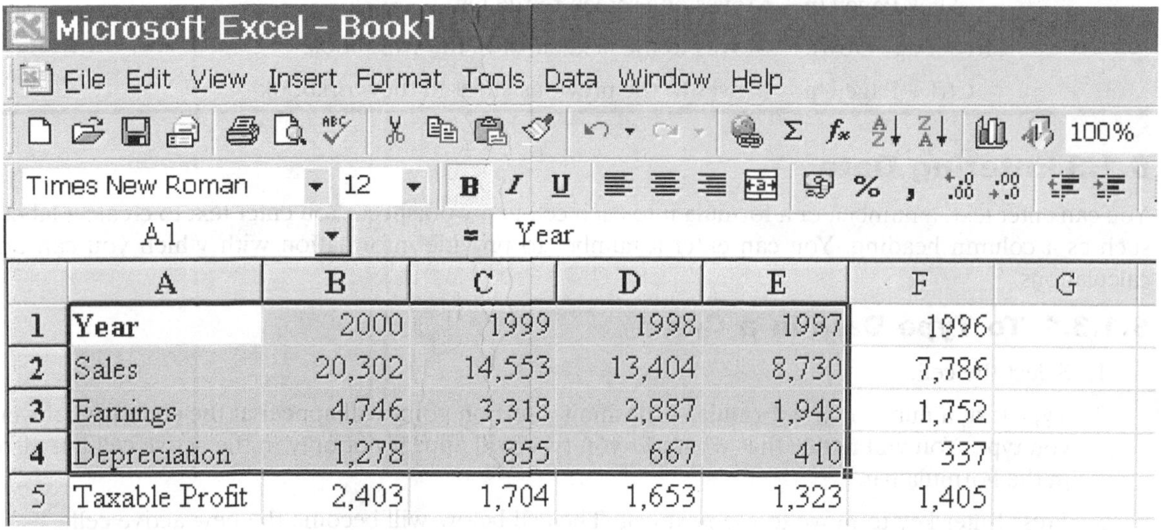

5.1.6 Moving Data

1. Select a range of cells. The cells will be highlighted.
2. Click on the Cut button. Moving dashes (called a marquee) will appear around your selection.
3. In this case the data does not disappear like text does in a word processor.
4. Click in the cell that will be upper left corner of the new location of the range. The cell will be selected.
5. Click on the Paste button. The data will be pasted in the new location.

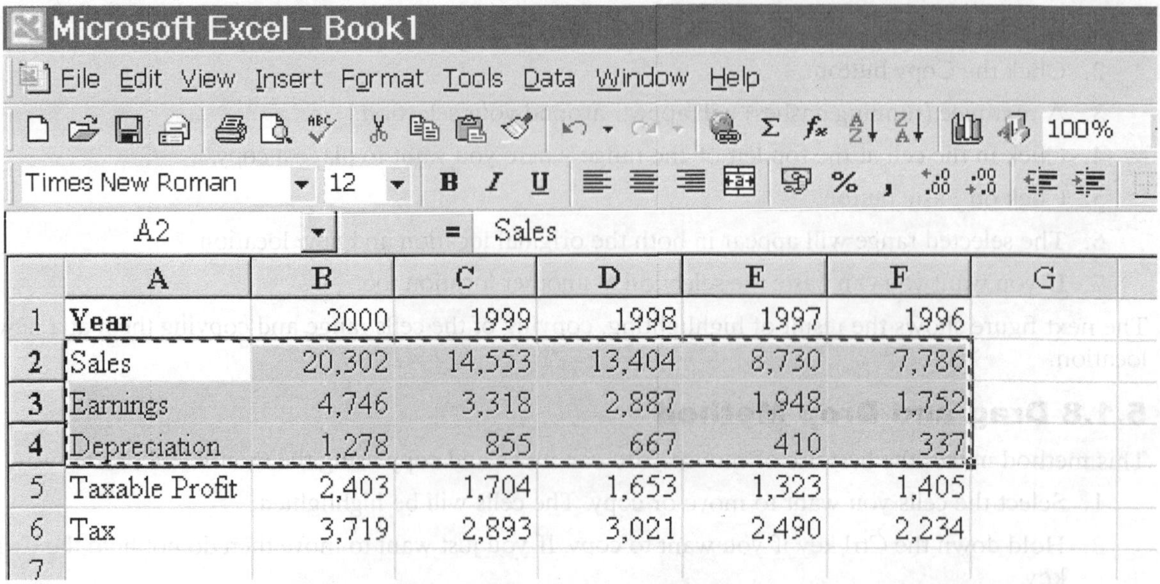

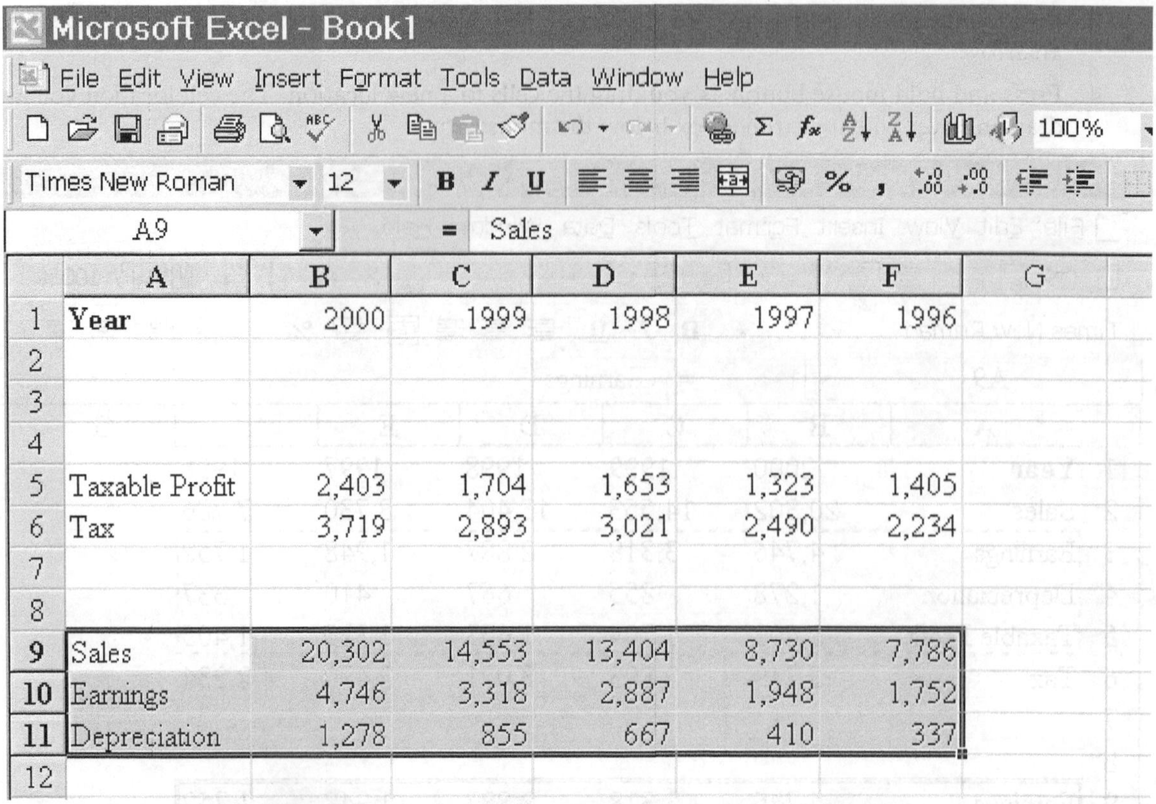

5.1.7 Copying Data

Copying puts selected data in a new location. Unlike moved data, copied data also remains in the original location.

1. Select a range of cell. The cells will be highlighted.
2. Click the Copy button.
3. A marquee (running dashes) will appear around your selection.
4. Click in the cell at the top left of the range where you want to place a copy.
5. Click on Paste button.
6. The selected range will appear in both the original location and new location.
7. If you want you can paste the selection at another location too.

The next figure shows the result of highlighting, copying of the cells range and copying them at a new location.

5.1.8 Drag and Drop Method

This method makes the best use of mouse. You can move and copy using the mouse in a shorter way.

1. Select the cells you want to move or copy. The cells will be highlighted.
2. Hold down the Ctrl key if you want to copy. If you just want to move then do not hold the Ctrl key.
3. Position the mouse pointer over the border of the selected area. The mouse pointer will become an arrow.
4. Press and hold mouse button as you drag the cells to a new location. The cell location you are dragging over will appear in a box below the mouse arrow.

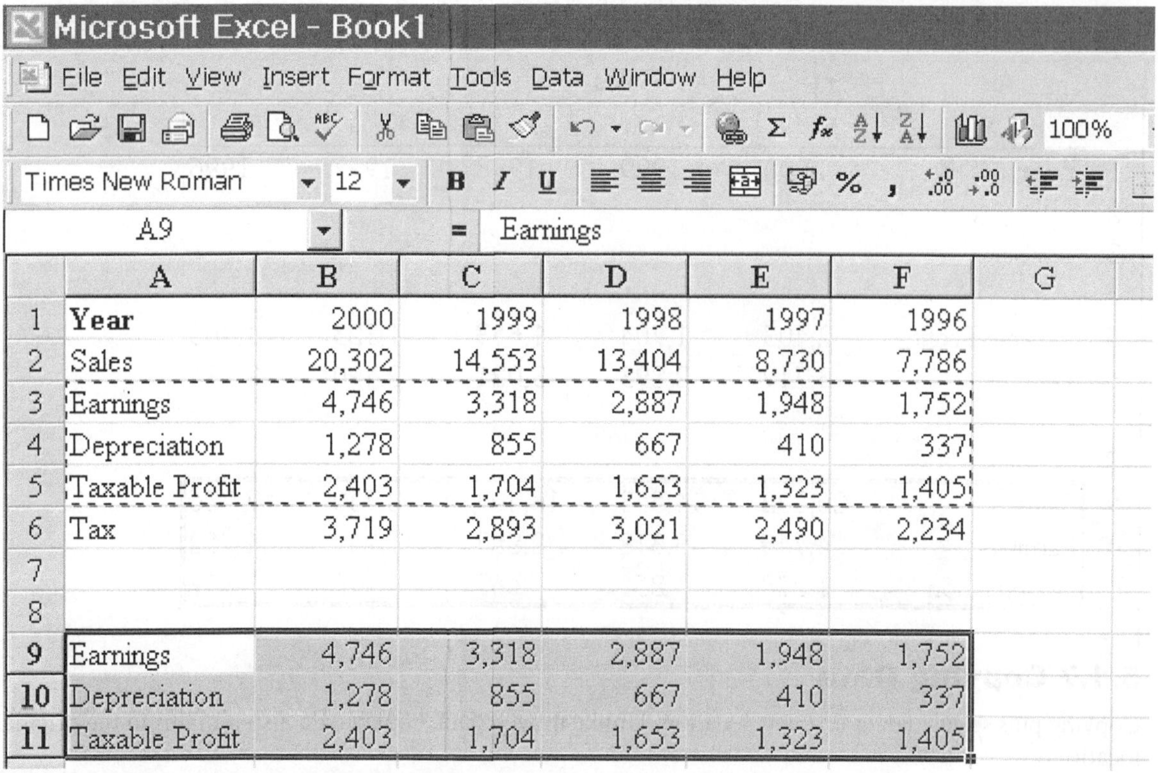

5. Release the mouse button.
6. The cells will be dropped in the new location. This is much quicker than using buttons or menus.

5.1.9 Inserting Rows and Columns

You can insert rows and columns at any time, and Excel adjusts all formulas to accommodate the new rows or columns. If you insert a row, it will appear **above** the selected cell; if you insert a column, it will appear to the **left** of the selected cell.

5.1.9.1 To insert a row or a column

1. Click any cell of the row or column in which you would like to insert the new blank row or column.
2. From the Insert menu, choose Rows to insert a row or choose Columns to insert a column, as shown next.

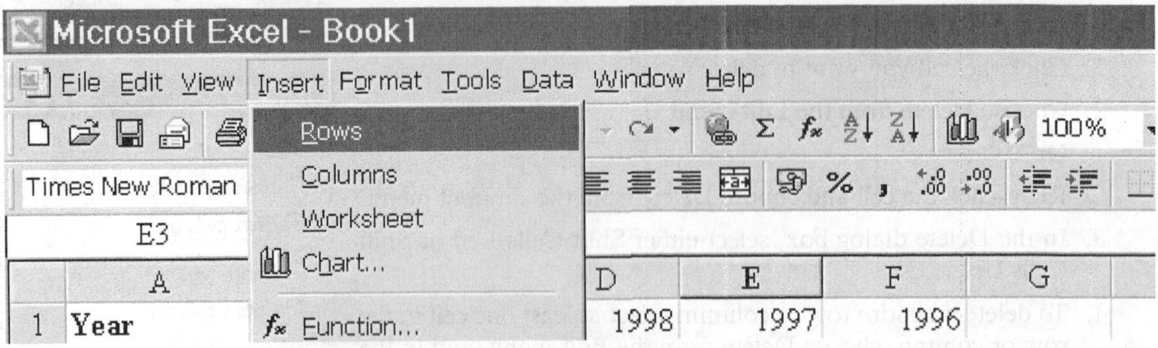

3. A new Row in this case will be inserted, as shown next.

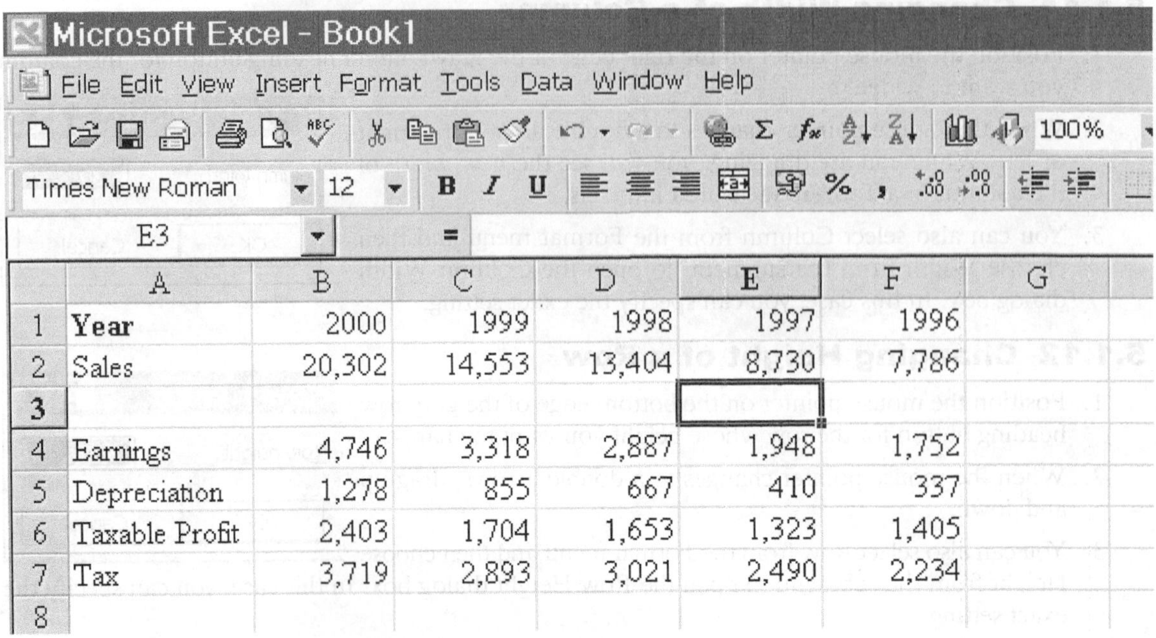

5.1.10 Inserting and Deleting Cells

When you tell Excel to insert or delete a cell within a range of data, Excel needs to know how to move the data that is in adjacent cells. You specify your preferences in the Insert or Delete dialog box.

5.1.10.1 To Insert a Cell

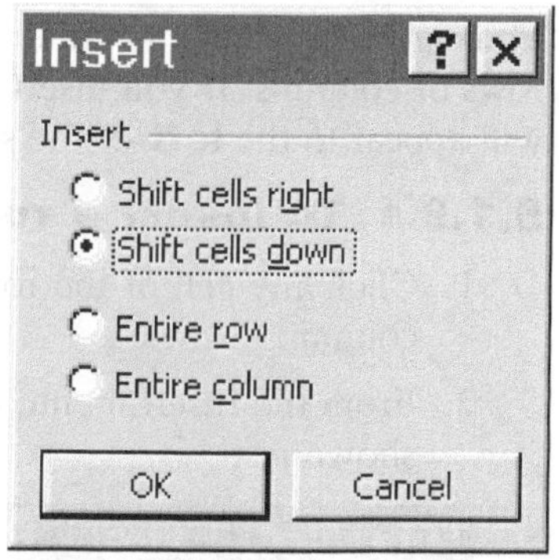

1. Click the destination for the new, blank cell.
2. Choose Cells from the Insert menu.

   Or

   Right-click the cell and choose Insert from the shortcut menu.
3. In the Insert dialog box, select either Shift Cells Right or Shift Cells Down.
4. The new cell appears.

5.1.10.2 To Delete a Cell

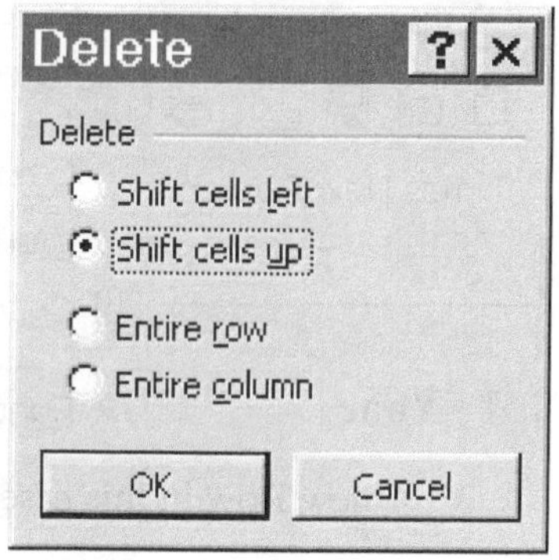

1. Click the cell you want to delete.
2. Choose Delete from the Edit menu.

   Or

   Right-click the cell and choose Delete from the shortcut menu.
3. In the Delete dialog box, select either Shift Cells Left or Shift Cells Up.
4. To delete an entire row or column, select at least one cell in the row or column, choose Delete from the Edit menu, and in the Delete dialog box, choose either Entire Row or Entire Column.

5.1.11 Changing Width of a Column

1. Position the mouse pointer on the right edge of the gray column heading button for the column you want to widen.

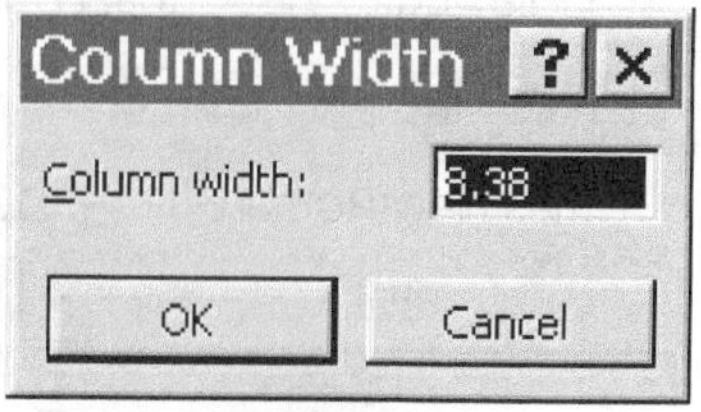

2. When the mouse pointer changes to a double arrow, drag right or left. While you are dragging, you will see the new width of the column in a ToolTip measured in pixels.
3. You can also select Column from the Format menu and then choose Width from the submenu to open the Column Width dialog box. In this case, you can specify the exact setting.

5.1.12 Changing Height of a Row

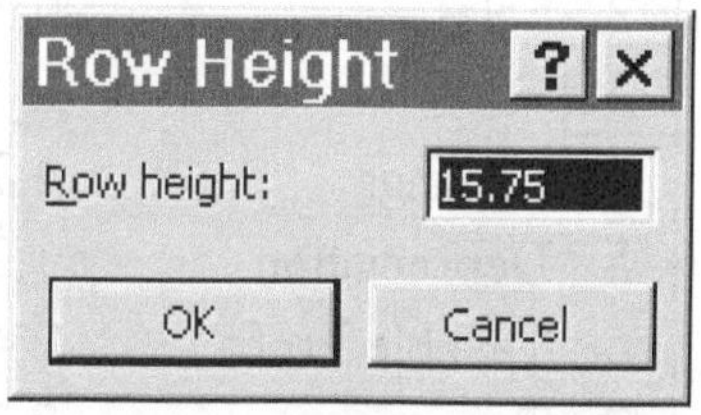

1. Position the mouse pointer on the bottom edge of the gray row heading button for the row whose height you want to change.
2. When the mouse pointer changes to a double arrows, drag up and down.
3. You can also select Row from the Format menu and then choose Height from the submenu to open the Row Height dialog box. In this case, you can specify the exact setting.

5.1.13 Formatting Text

You can use formatting to improve the appearance of your worksheet and to make it easier to locate the information you need.

To format selected text

1. Select the cell or cells containing the text to format.
2. Choose formatting options by clicking the text formatting buttons on the Formatting toolbar.

Or

1. Select the cell or cells containing the text to format.
2. From the Format menu, choose Cells, or right-click and choose Format Cells from the shortcut menu.
3. In the Format Cells dialog box, change the options on the Alignment and Font tabs.
4. Click Ok.

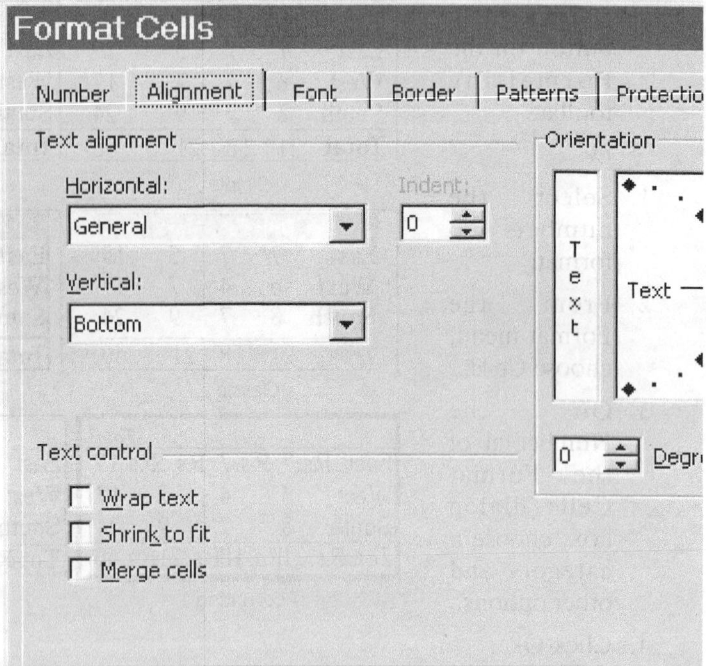

5.1.14 AutoFormat

The fastest and easiest way to make a worksheet presentable is to give an AutoFormat command. **AutoFormat** supplies a complete look for a range of data by changing the font, text alignment, number formatting, borders, patterns, colours, column widths, and row heights. Excel provides a selection of AutoFormats, each with a unique look.

5.1.14.1 To choose an AutoFormat

1. Click any cell in the range to format.

   Or

   Select the range to format.
2. From the Format menu, choose AutoFormat.
3. In the AutoFormat dialog box, select an AutoFormat from the display.
4. Click Ok.

5.1.15 Formatting Numbers

Excel makes available to you a variety of number formatting options, some from the Formatting toolbar and others from the Format Cells dialog box.

5.1.15.1 To format numbers

1. Select the numbers to format.

2. Click the appropriate number formatting button on the Formatting toolbar.

Or

1. Select the numbers to format.
2. From the Format menu, choose Cells.
3. On the Number tab of the Format Cells dialog box, choose a category and other options.
4. Click Ok.

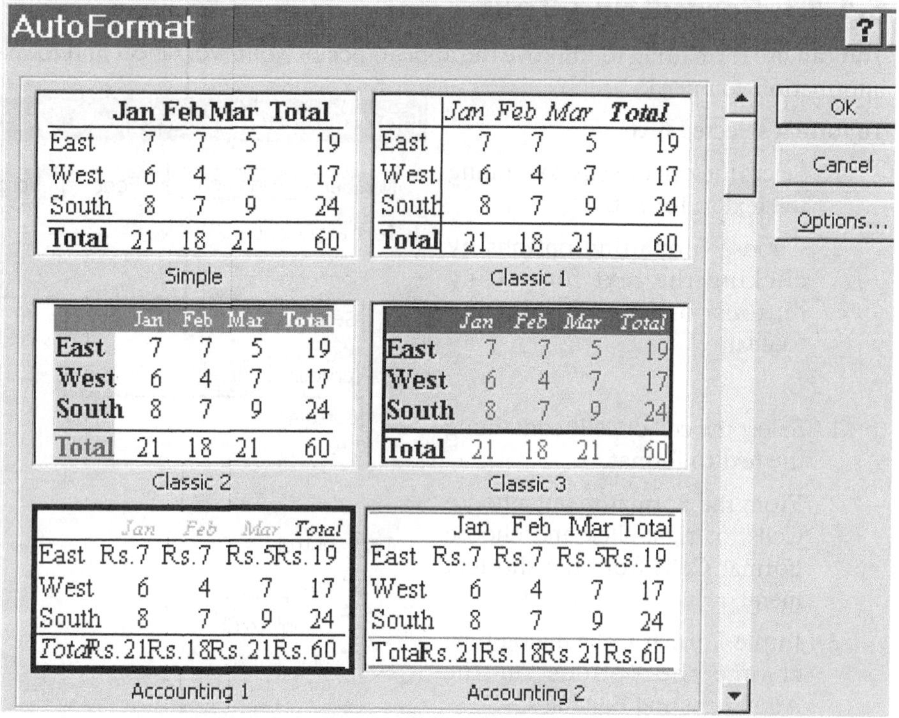

5.1.16 Adding Border to a Range

A border is a line at the edge of a cell. You can use borders to divide the information on the sheet into logical regions. Borders appear on the screen and will print when you print the sheet.

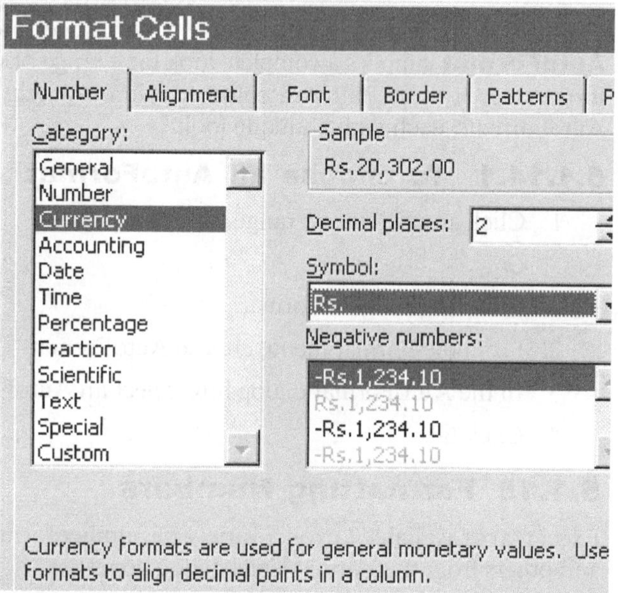

5.1.16.1 To add a border to a cell

1. Select the range to which you want to apply a border.
2. Click the arrow button next to the Borders button to see the full range of border you want for the range

Or

1. Select the range to which you want to apply a border.
2. From the Format menu, choose Cells, or right-click and choose Format Cells from the shortcut menu.
3. On the Border tab of the Format Cells dialog box, choose a border, a border style, and a colour.

4. Click Ok and the border is added to the range.

5.1.17 Formulae

They establish relationships between two or more cells. If you want to add the values in cells **C6** and **C7** and put the result in cell **C8**, move to the cell **C8** and type **=C6+C7** and press **Enter**. The result is displayed immediately in cell **C8**. Another way to achieve the same result is to move to cell **C8** and type **+**, point to cell **C6**, type **+**, then point to **C7**, and press **Enter**. The easiest way to achieve this operation is to point to **C8**, pick up the AutoSum button Σ on the toolbar.

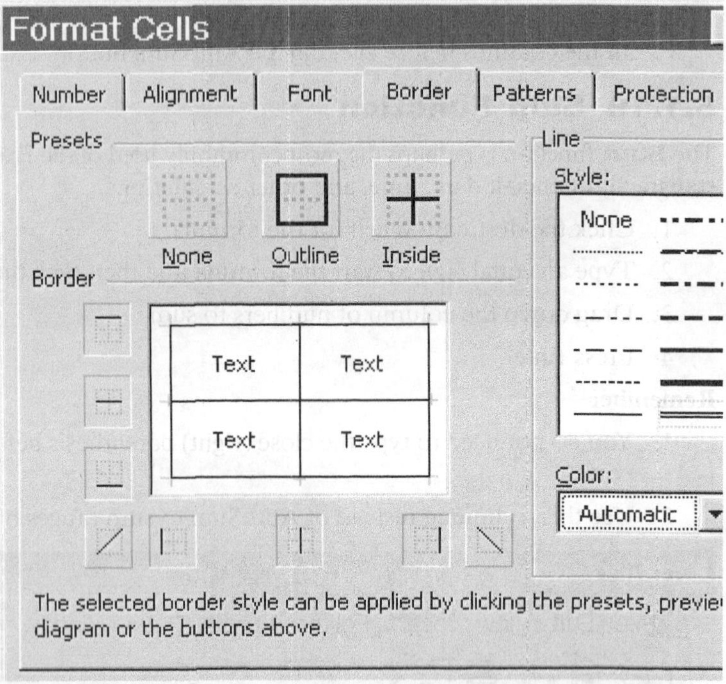

5.1.18 Summing of a Row or Column

1. Click in the empty cell below the last entry in the column or to the right of the last entry in the row.
2. Click the AutoSum button on the Standard toolbar.
3. Press Enter to enter the formula that has automatically appeared in the cell.

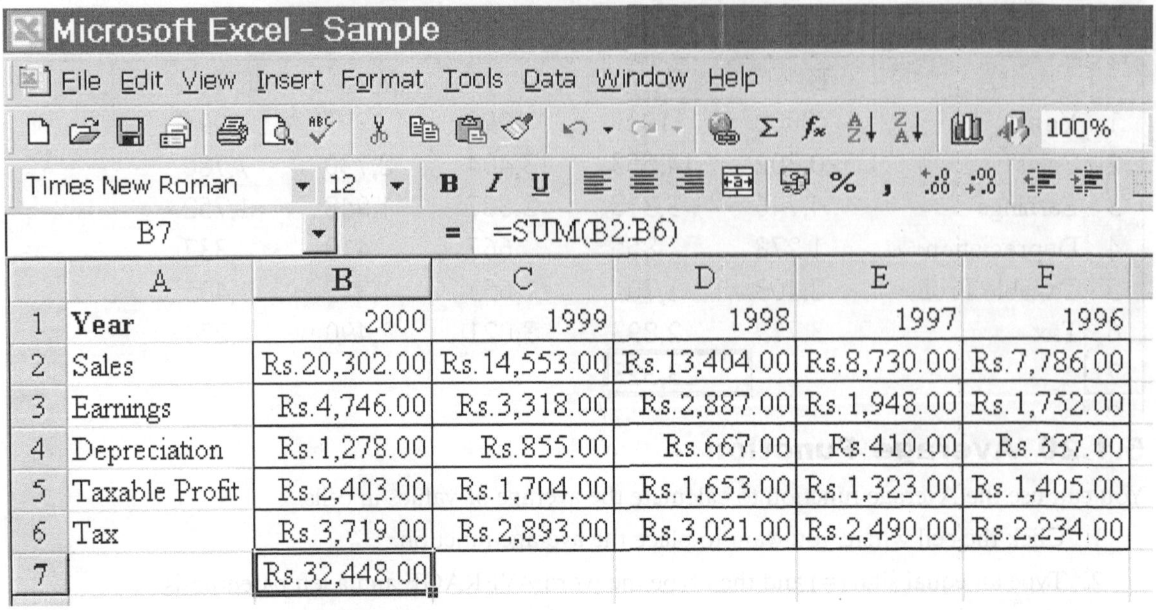

	A	B	C	D	E	F
1	Year	2000	1999	1998	1997	1996
2	Sales	Rs.20,302.00	Rs.14,553.00	Rs.13,404.00	Rs.8,730.00	Rs.7,786.00
3	Earnings	Rs.4,746.00	Rs.3,318.00	Rs.2,887.00	Rs.1,948.00	Rs.1,752.00
4	Depreciation	Rs.1,278.00	Rs.855.00	Rs.667.00	Rs.410.00	Rs.337.00
5	Taxable Profit	Rs.2,403.00	Rs.1,704.00	Rs.1,653.00	Rs.1,323.00	Rs.1,405.00
6	Tax	Rs.3,719.00	Rs.2,893.00	Rs.3,021.00	Rs.2,490.00	Rs.2,234.00
7		Rs.32,448.00				

Remember

1. Excel looks for the range of numbers to sum above the cell you have selected for the total. If it does not find a range of numbers or if it finds text, it looks to the left for a range of numbers.
2. Excel will not skip over an empty cell when it is looking for a range of cells to sum.
3. To quickly enter sums below multiple adjacent columns, select the empty cells at the bottoms of all the columns before clicking the AutoSum button. Excel will insert a sum in each selected cell.

5.1.19 Sum Function

The **Sum** function is perhaps the most commonly used of the Excel functions that carry out mathematical, statistical, financial, date, time, and other calculations.

1. Click the destination cell for the formula.
2. Type an equal sign to start the formula and then type the word SUM and a left parenthesis.
3. Drag down the column of numbers to sum.
4. Press Enter.

Remember

1. You do not need to type the close (right) parenthesis before you press Enter—Excel will do it for you.
2. Use this technique instead of AutoSum to sum ranges of cells that contain blanks.

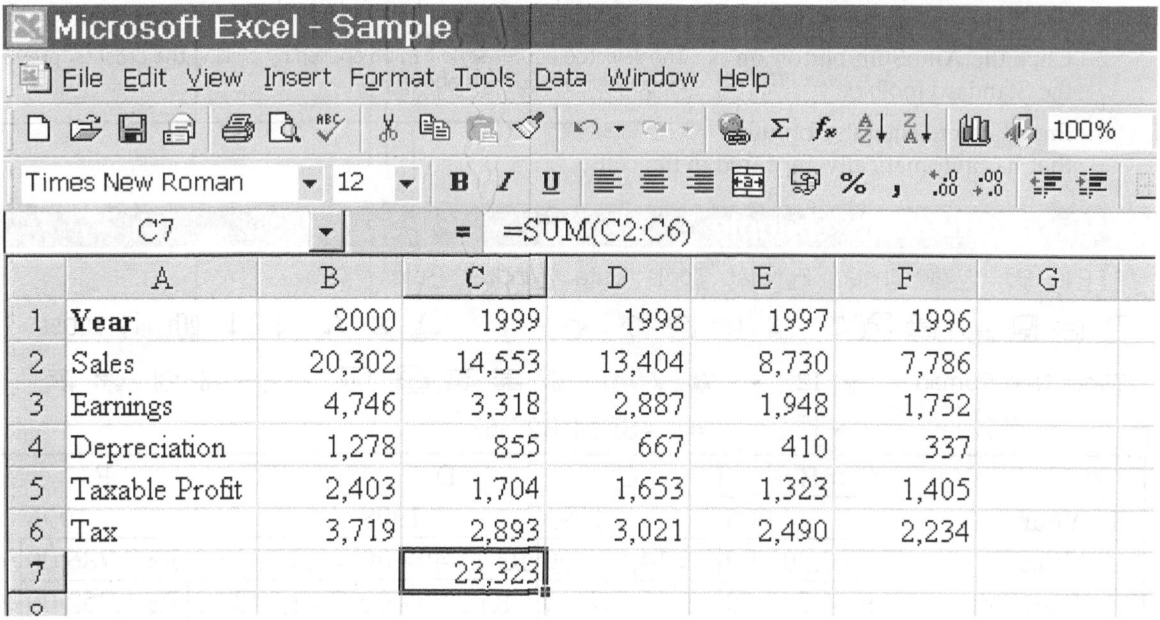

	A	B	C	D	E	F	G
1	**Year**	2000	1999	1998	1997	1996	
2	Sales	20,302	14,553	13,404	8,730	7,786	
3	Earnings	4,746	3,318	2,887	1,948	1,752	
4	Depreciation	1,278	855	667	410	337	
5	Taxable Profit	2,403	1,704	1,653	1,323	1,405	
6	Tax	3,719	2,893	3,021	2,490	2,234	
7			23,323				

5.1.20 Average Function

You can use the Average function to calculate the average of values in cells.

1. Click the cell where you want to place the average function.
2. Type an equal sign (=) and then type the word AVERAGE and a left parenthesis.

3. Drag across the cells whose values you want to average.
4. Press Enter.

Remember

1. Blank cells in the range are not counted in the average.

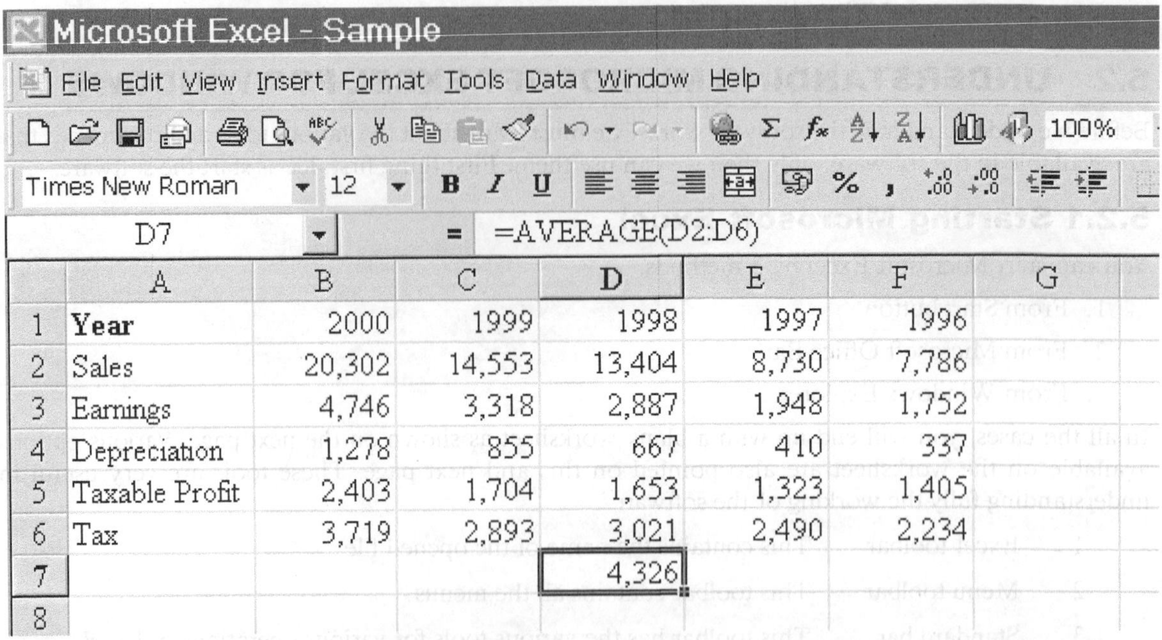

5.1.21 Using Function Wizard

Sum and Average are just two of the most commonly used functions whereas there are lots of them in Excel. You can use them to get the desired results in a flash. To get them click the **Paste Function** button on the Standard toolbar as you are building the formula. The Paste Function wizard takes you through the steps of building a formula.

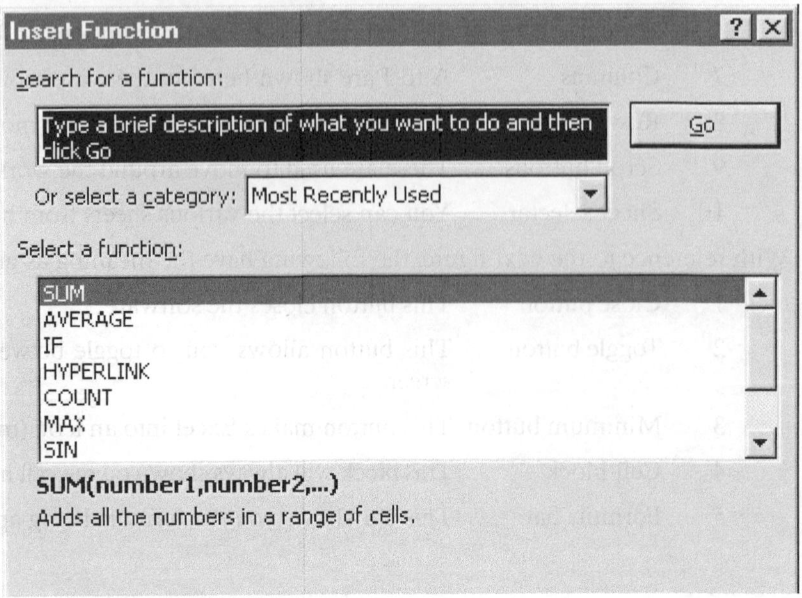

1. Click the destination cell for the formula.
2. Click the Paste Function button on the Standard toolbar.
3. In the Paste Function dialog box, select the category and then the function.

4. Click Ok.
5. Use the Paste Function Wizard to guide you in completing the formula.
6. Click Ok when you have finished.
7. The following screen has been created using the same function AVERAGE over the selected cells as used in the AVERAGE function.

5.2 UNDERSTANDING MICROSOFT EXCEL FOR WINDOWS

Before we understand how the software works, we must learn about the various tools and commands that are available in the software, only then we can use them. First thing first, let us start the software.

5.2.1 Starting Microsoft Excel

You can start Microsoft Excel by 3 methods.

1. From Start button
2. From Microsoft Office Bar
3. From Windows Explorer

In all the cases, you will end up with a blank worksheet as shown on the next page. Various options available on the worksheet are also pointed on this and next page. These tools are very useful in understanding fully the working of the software.

1	Excel toolbar	This contains the name of the opened file
2	Menu toolbar	This toolbar contains all the menus
3	Standard bar	This toolbar has the various tools for various operations in Excel
4	Font bar	It shows the font of the current cell
5	Selected Cell	It show the current cell
6	Formatting bar	This toolbar has the various options of formatting
7	Columns	A to J are shown here but there are more
8	Rows	1 to 19 are shown here but there are more
9	Scroll buttons	These are used to move around the worksheet
10	Sheet selecter	You can select the various sheets from here

With reference to the next figure, the following have the meaning as given.

1	Close button	This button closes the software
2	Toggle button	This button allows you to toggle between maximum and minimum of screen
3	Minimum button	This button makes Excel into an icon (minimum)
4	Cell block	This block will always show you the cell number on which you are working
5	Formula bar	This bar shows you the formula being applied

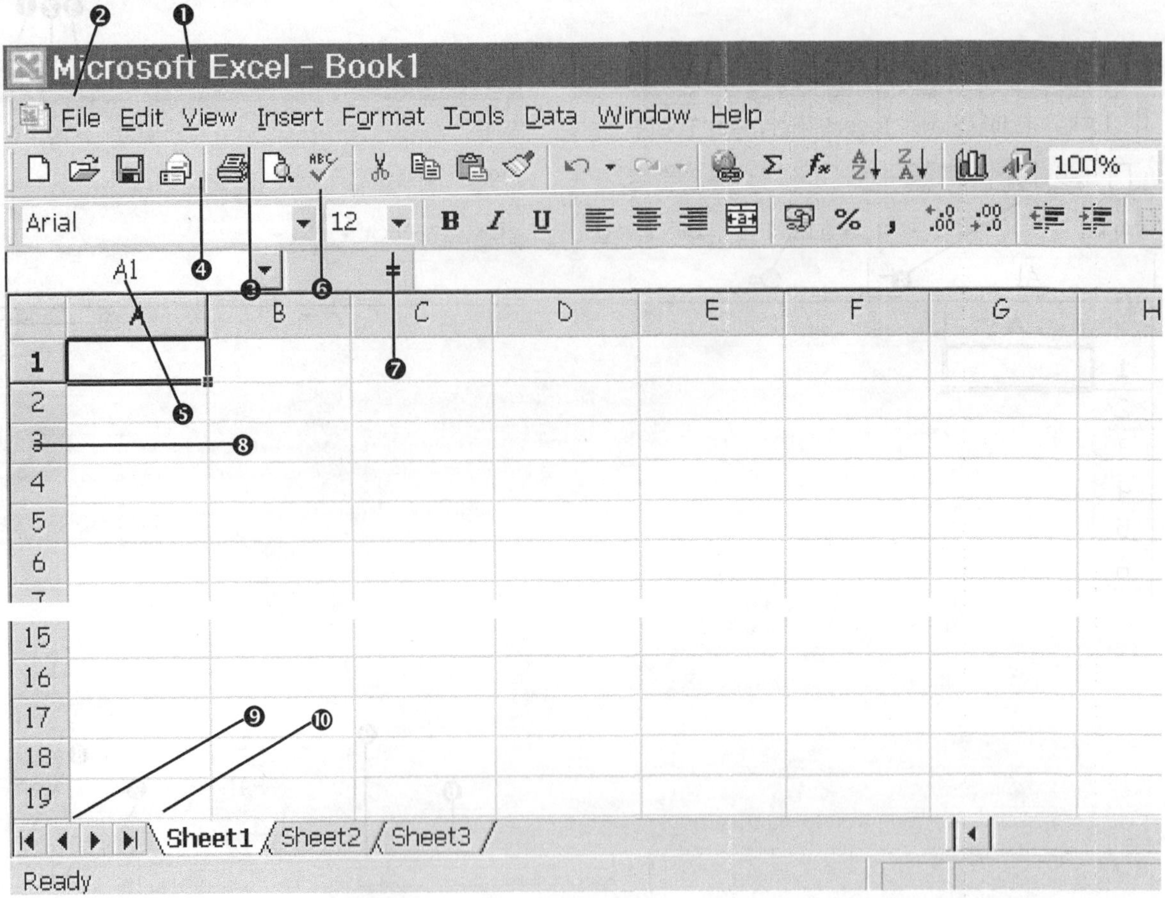

6	Horizontal button	Button for moving the screen horizontally
7	Office assistant	Click it to get the help
8	Horizontal bar	Horizontal scrollbar
9	Vertical button	For moving the screen vertically
10	Vertical bar	Vertical scrollbar

5.2.2 Creating a Worksheet in Excel for Windows

We have learnt quite a number of commands and naturally would like to use them in a worksheet. So let us create a worksheet and use these commands side-by-side to see how they work out.

Supposing we have the financial highlights of a company as given on the next page:
As you can see that there are quite a number of fields which have to be calculated. This will act as a good exercise for you to do.

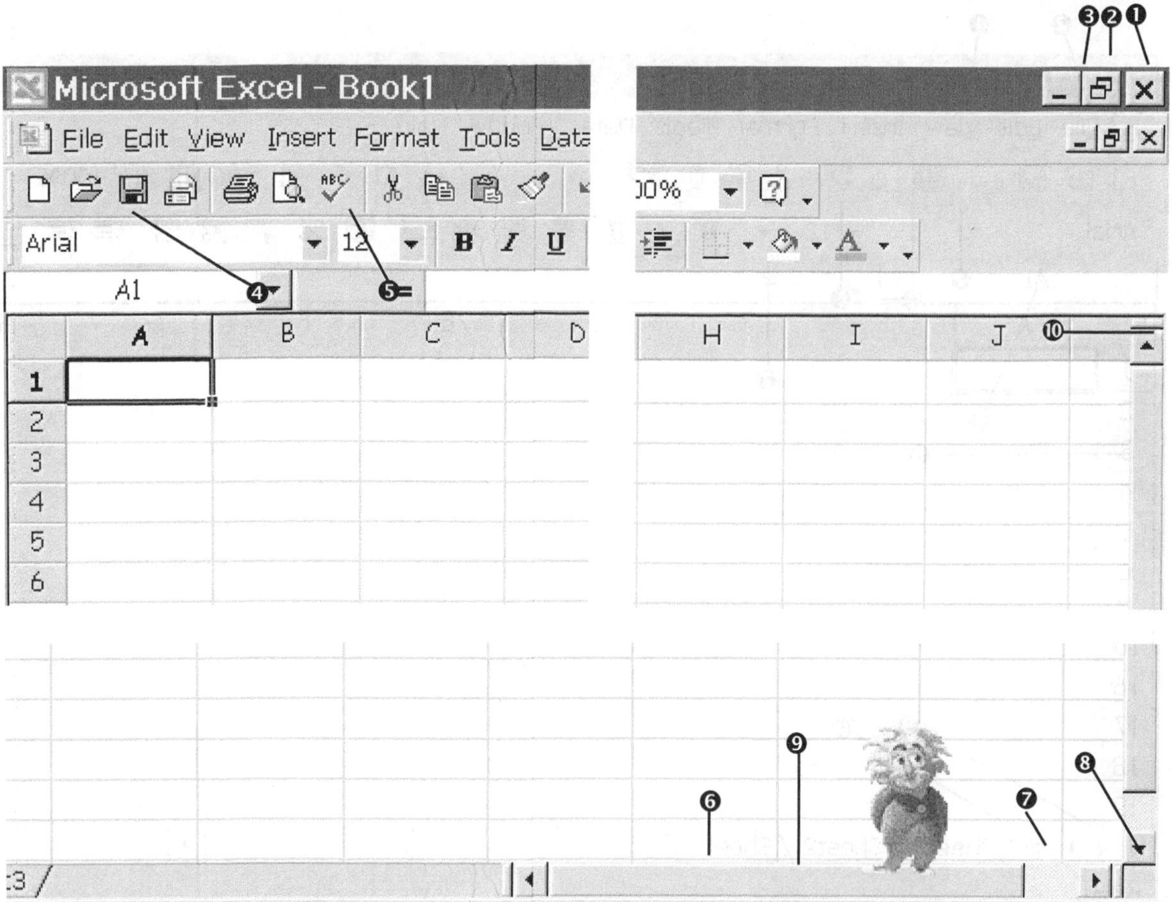

Year	Total Income (A)	Interest Paid (B)	Profit (C)	Tax (D)	Profit After Tax (E)
1992	4,500	To be	To be	To be	To be
1993	5,500	Calculated	Calculated	Calculated	Calculated
1994	7,000	as 15%	as Income	as 12% of	as Profit
1995	8,000	of the	minus	the Profit	minus Tax
1996	9,000	Total	Interest		(C) - (D)
1997	12,000	Income	(A) - (B)		
1998	15,000				
1999	20,000				

Let us start from the very beginning, i.e., start the software Microsoft Excel. You will end up with a blank worksheet, ready for you to take action, with the first cell **A1**, totally at your command to do something, as shown in the figure below.

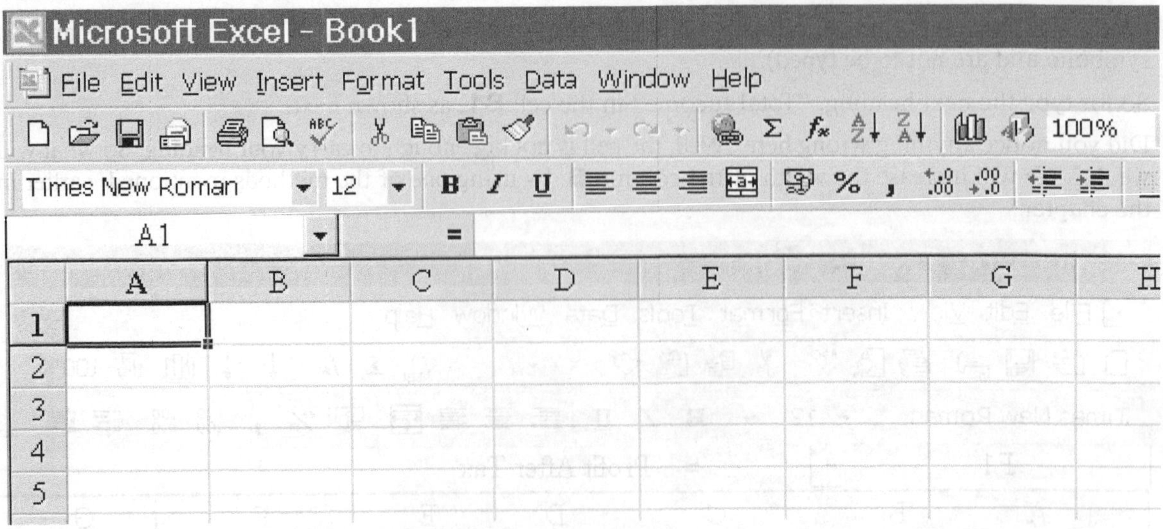

So what we have to do here. We have to type "Year". So just type the word Year and press **Enter**. You will see the word being shown in the formula bar too. This will also take you to the cell **A2**. But, for typing the next heading, you have to go to the cell **B1**. So use the arrow keys right and up to reach **B1**.

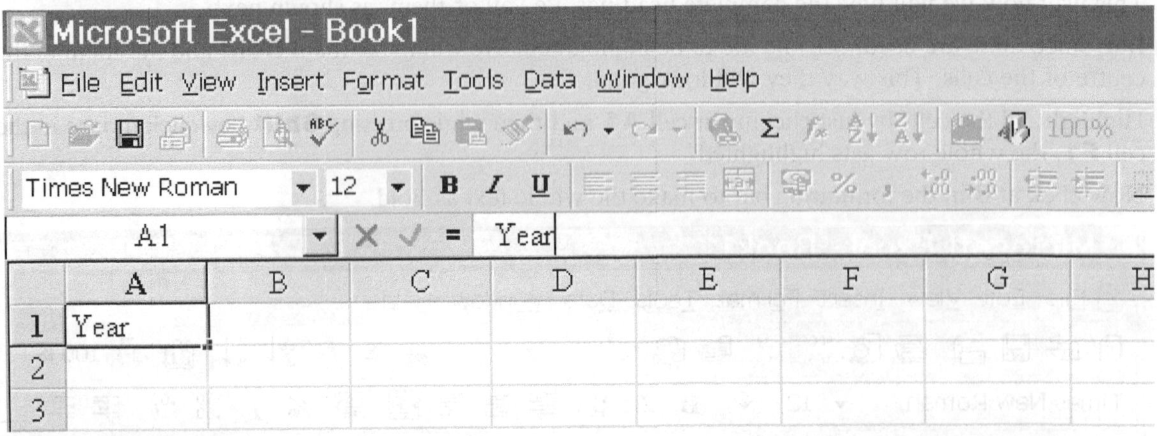

Next we have to type "Total Income". (Please note that for the sake of convenience I have shown this

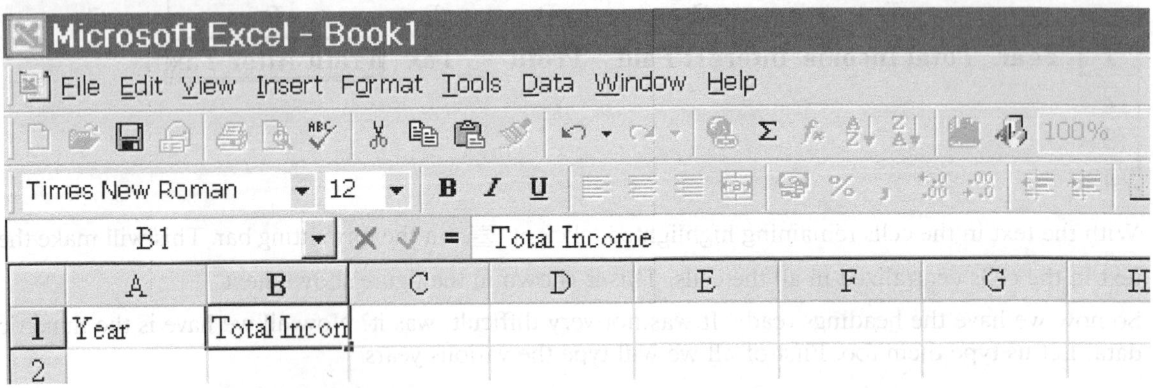

heading in 2 lines, but, if permitted we will type it in one line. Also (A), (B), etc., in the table are just symbolic and are not to be typed).

So for type the next heading, "Total Income" in the cell **B1**, as shown next.

Did you notice anything wrong here? Well, the cell is not big enough to carry your heading. So what will we do? We will increase the width of the column **B**, by using one of the methods mentioned earlier in the chapter.

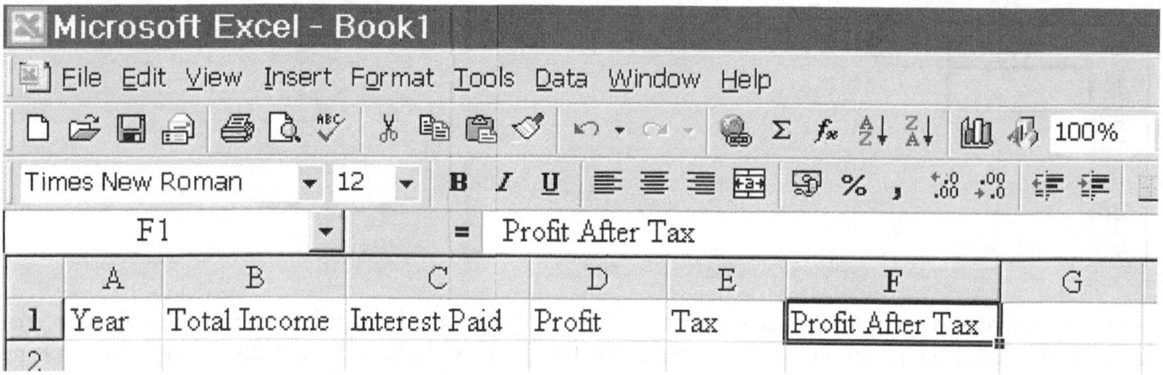

This way now we will type the complete headings, i.e., all of them, as shown next.

But, since these are headings, and are to be highlighted. We will make them **Bold** and put them in the centre of the cells. This way they will look good.

Highlight all the cells by just clicking at cell **A1** and then while pressing **Shift** key click mouse in the cell **F1**, the whole row gets highlighted.

Now click at B in the formatting bar to make the whole text as Bold.

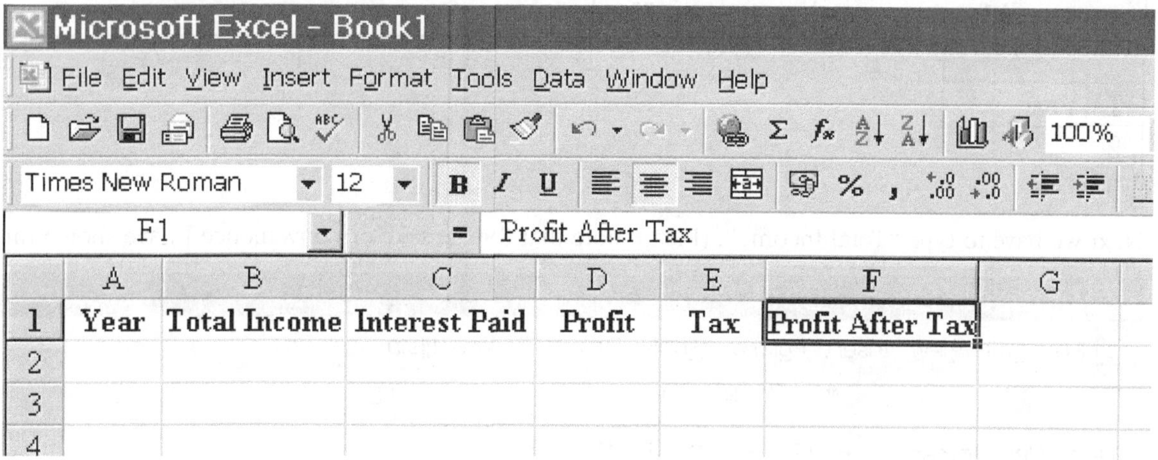

With the text in the cells remaining highlighted, click at  in the formatting bar. This will make the text in the cells centralized in all the cells. This is shown in the figure shown next.

So now we have the headings ready. It was not very difficult, was it? Now all we have is the numeric data. Let us type them too. First of all we will type the various years.

By using the arrow keys, reach the cell **A2**. This is here that we have to type the first year, i.e., **1992**. Type it and press **Enter** to see the data getting aligned to the right. Remember, Excel aligns the numeric data to the right as a default. By pressing **Enter** you must have reached **A3** and this is where you wanted to be for typing the next year, i.e., **1993**.

So now type one year and press **Enter** to reach the next cell for typing the next year, till you reach the last year, i.e., **1999**. At this stage your worksheet will look like the one shown on the next page.

Next step is also easy. You have to just type the numbers in the cells **B2** to **B9**. All these figures are available with you. Just type one figure and press **Enter** to reach the next cell and so on till you reach the last cell in the column. After doing this your worksheet will look like the one shown next on the next page.

It would not be a bad idea to save this worksheet at this stage. For god forbid, if something happens, like

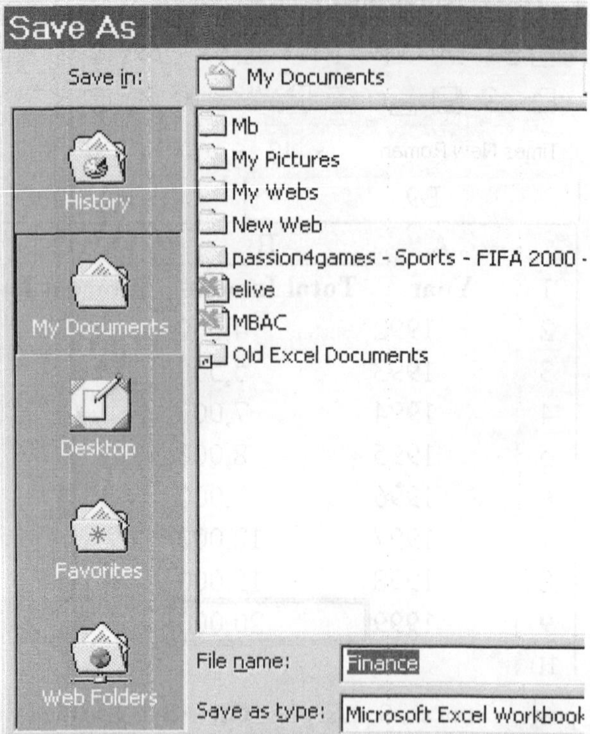

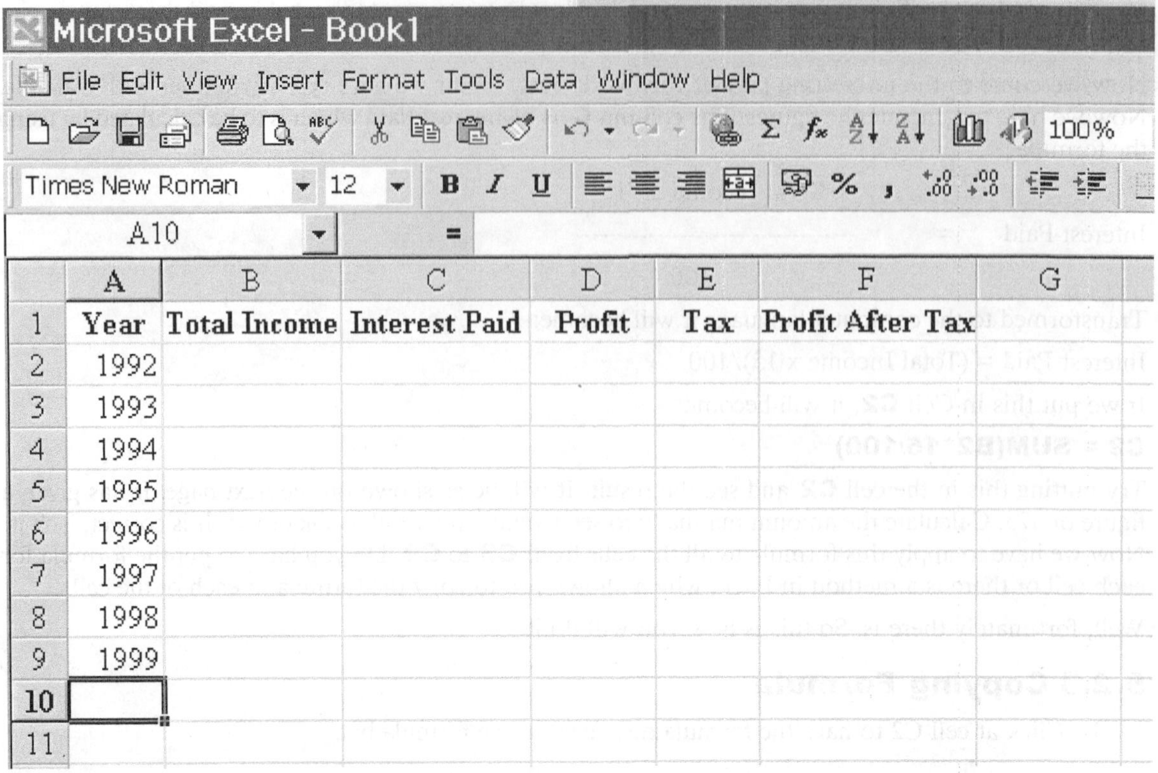

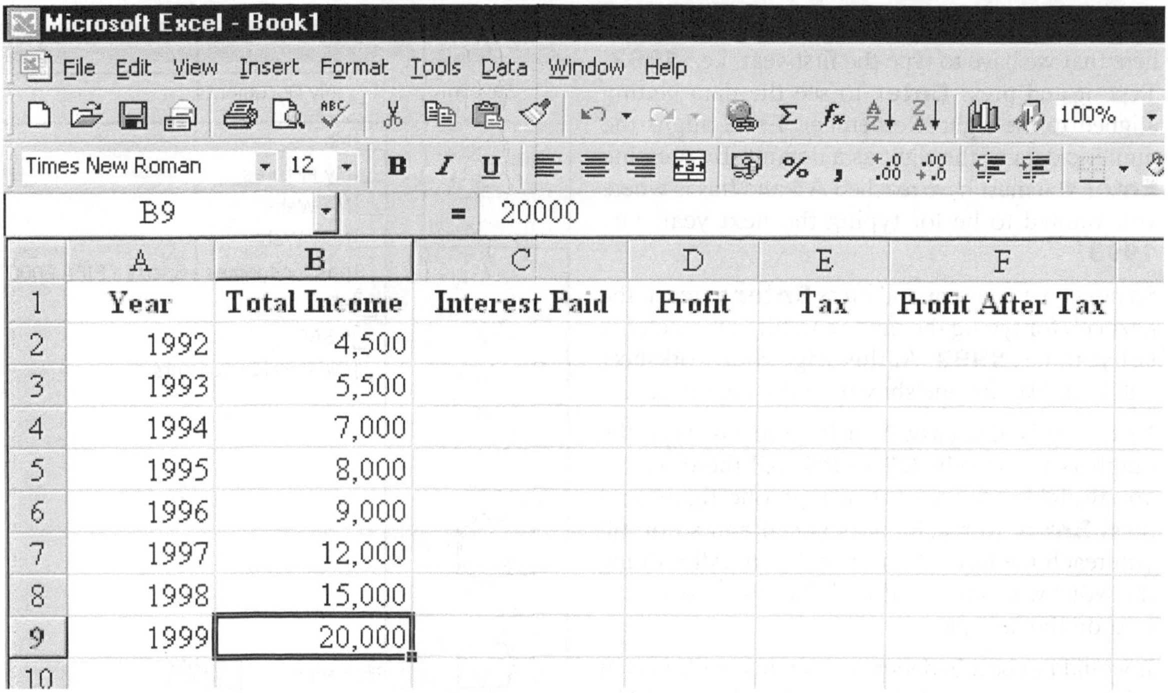

	A	B	C	D	E	F
1	Year	Total Income	Interest Paid	Profit	Tax	Profit After Tax
2	1992	4,500				
3	1993	5,500				
4	1994	7,000				
5	1995	8,000				
6	1996	9,000				
7	1997	12,000				
8	1998	15,000				
9	1999	20,000				
10						

power cut or so. So just press **Ctrl+S** to give the save command, as you would give in any other software. Now all you have to do it to give it a name and decide where you want to save this worksheet. Let us give the name **Finance** to it.

Now we come to the interesting part of this worksheet. So far we have typed whatever was available. Now we have to generate the figures. The column **C** is of Interest Paid which is to be calculated by using the formula.

$$\text{Interest Paid} = \frac{\text{Total Income} \times 15}{100}$$

Transformed to the computer language it will become:

Interest Paid = (Total Income x 15)/100

If we put this in Cell **C2**, it will become:

C2 = SUM(B2*15/100)

Try putting this in the cell **C2** and see the result. It will be as shown on the next page. It has given a figure of 675. Calculate the amount manually to see whether the result is Ok or not. It is correct, isn't it? Now we have to apply this formula to all the cells from **C3** to **C9**. Do you have to put the formula for each cell or there is a method in Excel which allows you to copy the formula in each of the cell.

Well, fortunately there is. So this is how you will do it.

5.2.3 Copying Formula

1. Click at cell C2 to have the formula displayed in the formula bar.

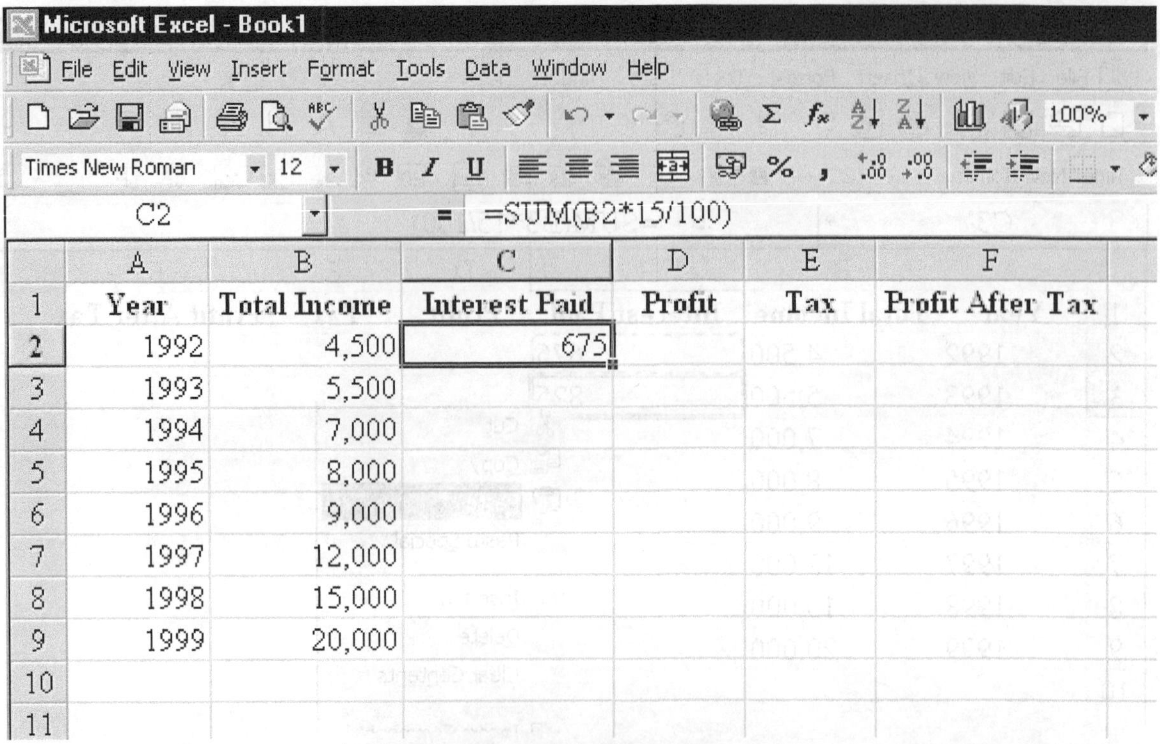

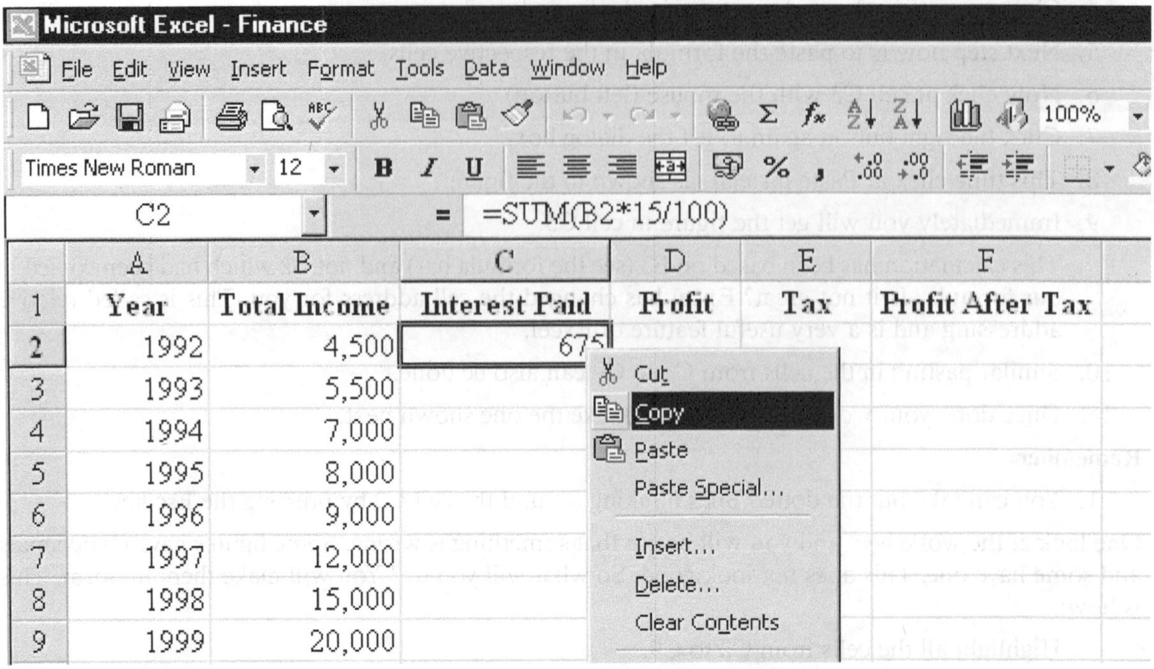

2. Now with your mouse having clicked at cell C2, press the right button of the mouse.
3. You will get a dialog box, as shown below, which has various commands at your disposal.

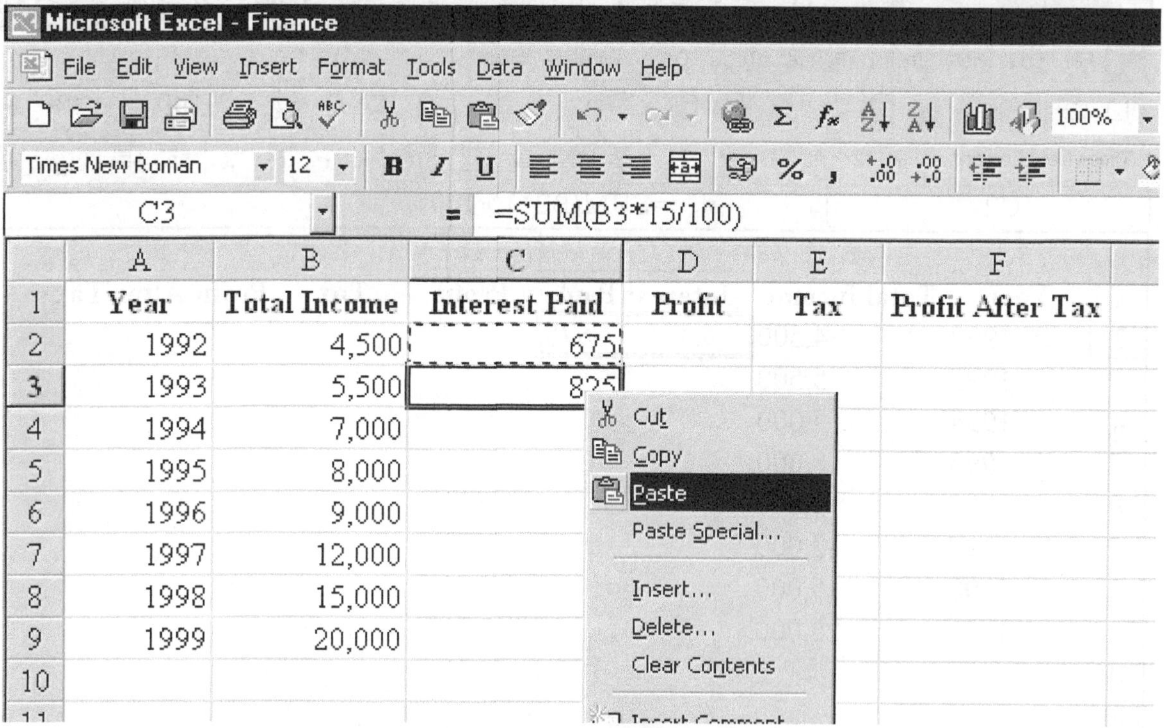

4. Choose copy, as shown here, to copy the formula.
5. Next step now is to paste the formula in the respective cells.
6. Now click at cell C3 with the mouse (left button).
7. Click the right button again to get the dialog box.
8. This time click at Paste instead, as shown in the figure.
9. Immediately you will get the figure in cell C3.

   This calculation has been based on B3 (see the formula bar) and not B2 which had been copied in our formula. Is it not great? Excel has changed the cell address for you. This is called relative addressing and is a very useful feature of Excel.
10. Similar pasting in the cells from C4 to C9 can also be done.
11. Once done your worksheet should look like the one shown next.

Remember

1. You can take out the dotted lines blinking around the cell C2 by pressing the Esc key.

One look at the worksheet and you will notice that something is wrong. Some figures have no decimals and some have one. This does not look good. So what will you do? You will make them uniform. This is how:

1. Highlight all the cells from C2 to C9.
2. From the Format menu, call the command Cells, which gives rise to a dialog box, as shown on the next page.

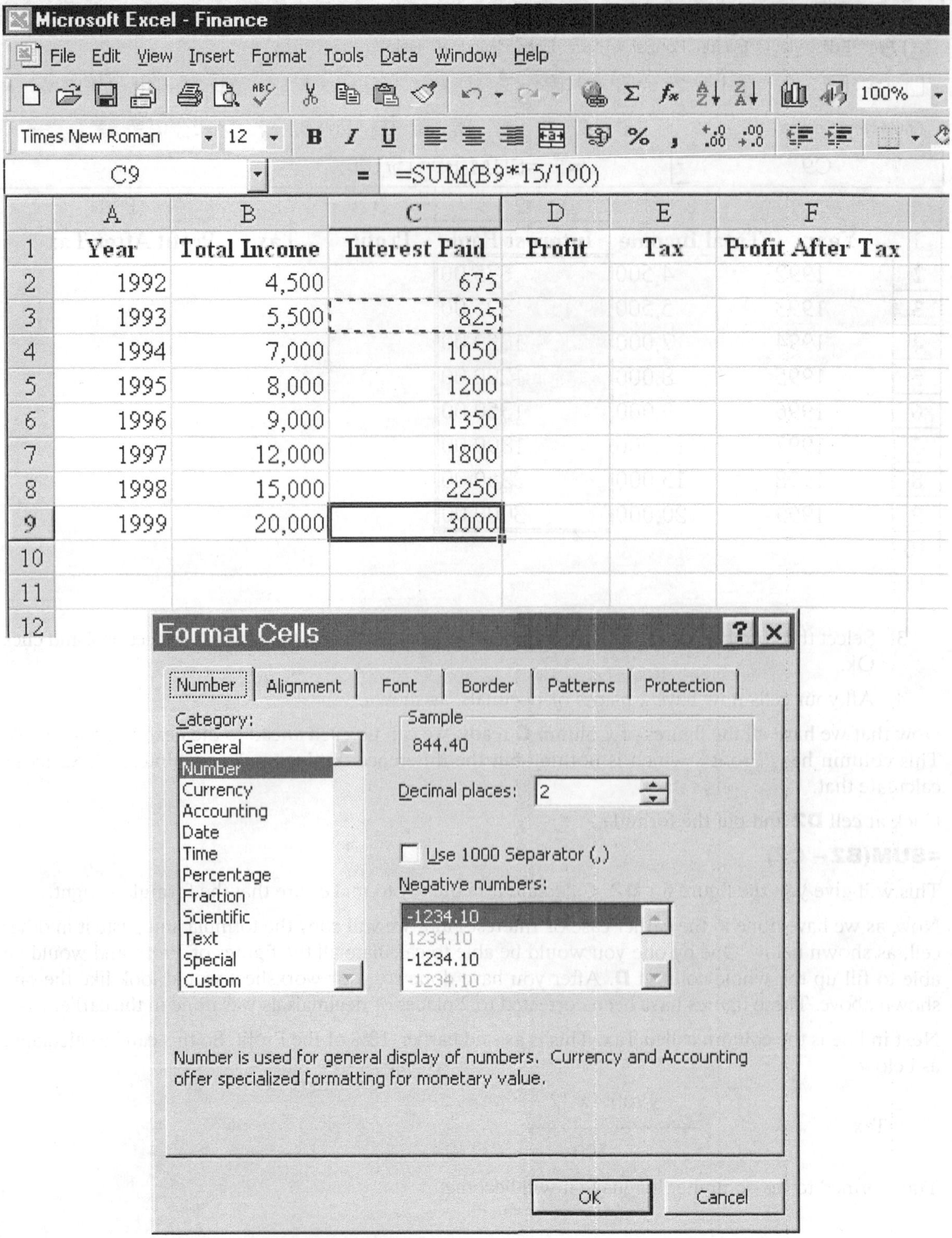
Microsoft Excel - Finance
File Edit View Insert Format Tools Data Window Help
100%
Times New Roman 12
C9 = =SUM(B9*15/100)
A B C D E F
1 Year Total Income Interest Paid Profit Tax Profit After Tax
2 1992 4,500 675
3 1993 5,500 825
4 1994 7,000 1050
5 1995 8,000 1200
6 1996 9,000 1350
7 1997 12,000 1800
8 1998 15,000 2250
9 1999 20,000 3000
10
11
12
Format Cells
Number Alignment Font Border Patterns Protection
Category:
General
Number
Currency
Accounting
Date
Time
Percentage
Fraction
Scientific
Text
Special
Custom
Sample
844.40
Decimal places: 2
Use 1000 Separator (,)
Negative numbers:
-1234.10
1234.10
-1234.10
-1234.10
Number is used for general display of numbers. Currency and Accounting offer specialized formatting for monetary value.
OK
Cancel

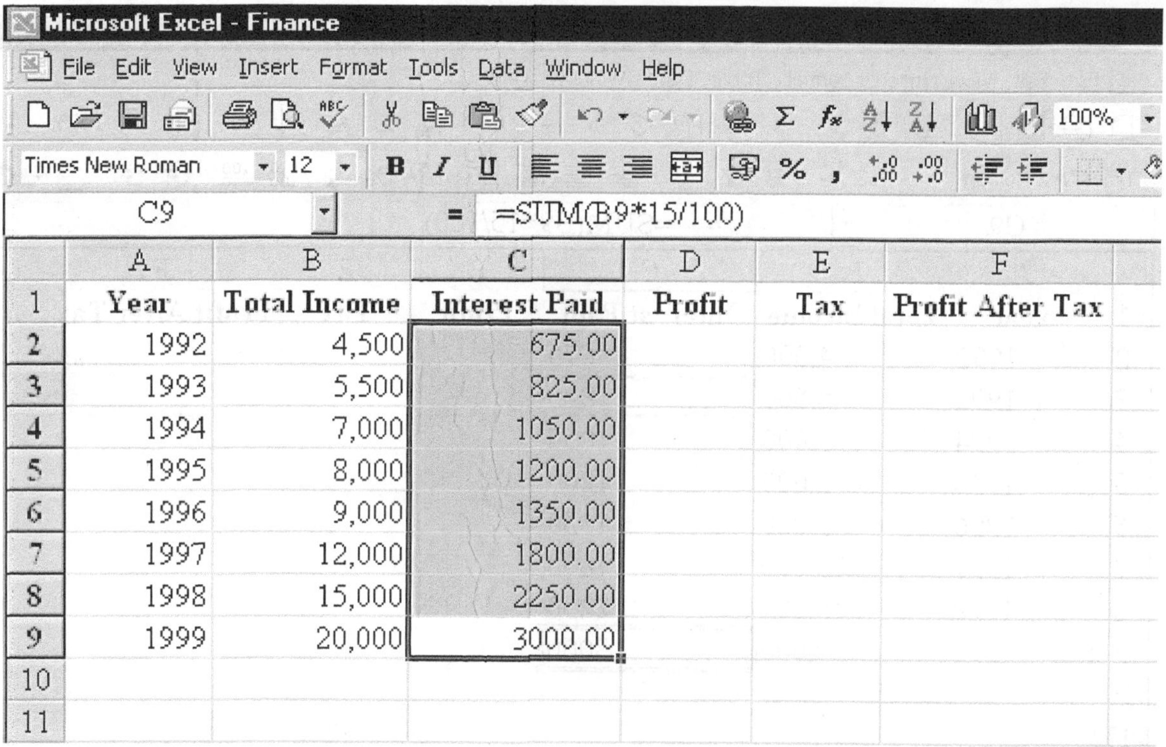

	A	B	C	D	E	F
1	Year	Total Income	Interest Paid	Profit	Tax	Profit After Tax
2	1992	4,500	675.00			
3	1993	5,500	825.00			
4	1994	7,000	1050.00			
5	1995	8,000	1200.00			
6	1996	9,000	1350.00			
7	1997	12,000	1800.00			
8	1998	15,000	2250.00			
9	1999	20,000	3000.00			
10						
11						

3. Select the Number panel and then number Category and select the Decimal places as 2 and click Ok.
4. All your cells now have 2 places of decimals, as shown.

Now that we have all the figures of Column **C** ready, we can proceed ahead to the next column, i.e., **D**. This column has "Profit", which is nothing but the difference of "Income" and "Interest". So let us calculate that.

Click at cell **D2** and put the formula

=SUM(B2 – C2)

This will give you the figure for **D2**. Calculate it manually to make sure that the formula is right.

Now, as we have done in the earlier case of Interest Paid, we will copy the formula and paste it in other cell, as shown below. One by one you would be able to calculate all the figures of Profit and would be able to fill up the whole column **D**. After you have done so, your worksheet would look like the one shown above. These figures have been corrected to 2 places of decimals as was done in the earlier case.

Next in line is the column called Tax. This is as said earlier, 12% of the Profit. So this can be calculated as below:

$$\text{Tax} = \frac{\text{Profit} \times 12}{100}$$

Transformed to the computer language it will become:

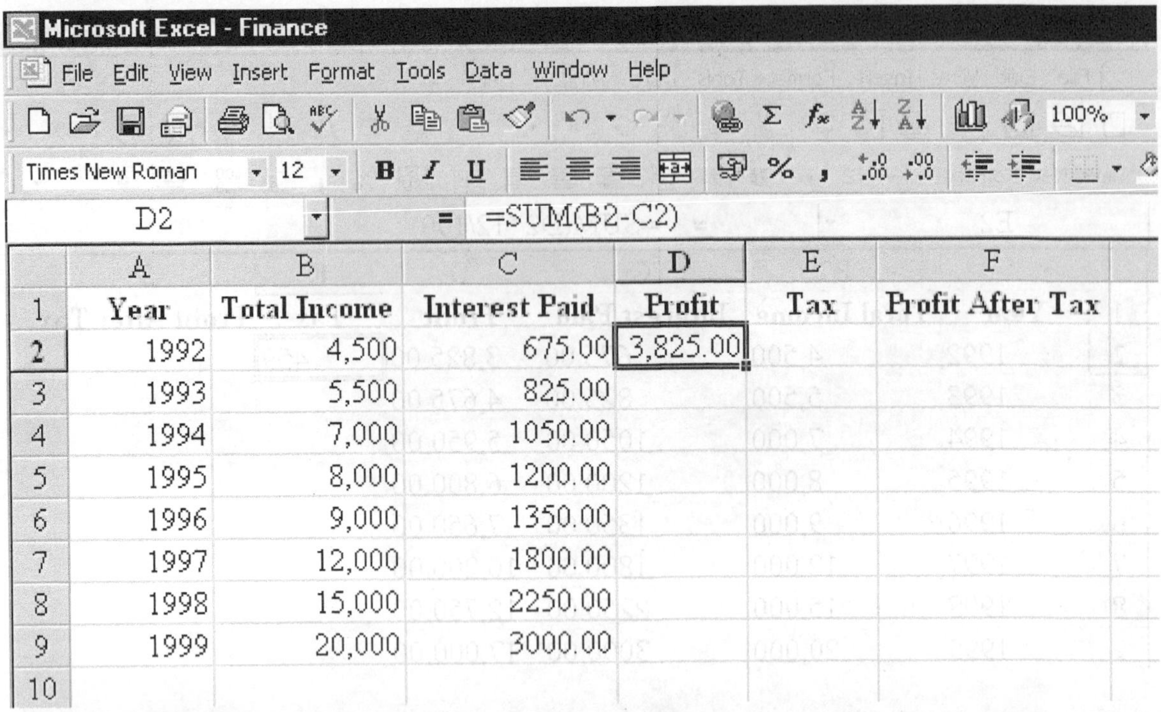
Microsoft Excel - Finance
File Edit View Insert Format Tools Data Window Help
100%
Times New Roman 12
D2 = =SUM(B2-C2)
A B C D E F
1 Year Total Income Interest Paid Profit Tax Profit After Tax
2 1992 4,500 675.00 3,825.00
3 1993 5,500 825.00
4 1994 7,000 1050.00
5 1995 8,000 1200.00
6 1996 9,000 1350.00
7 1997 12,000 1800.00
8 1998 15,000 2250.00
9 1999 20,000 3000.00
10

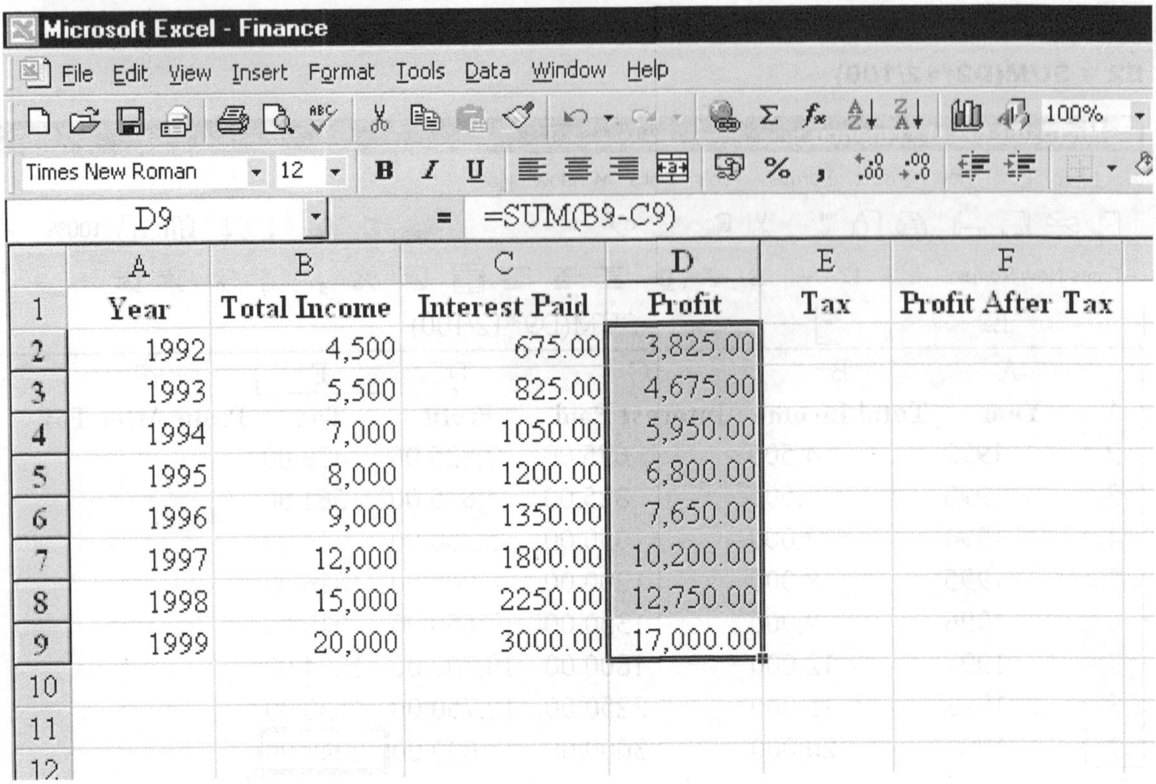
Microsoft Excel - Finance
File Edit View Insert Format Tools Data Window Help
100%
Times New Roman 12
D9 = =SUM(B9-C9)
A B C D E F
1 Year Total Income Interest Paid Profit Tax Profit After Tax
2 1992 4,500 675.00 3,825.00
3 1993 5,500 825.00 4,675.00
4 1994 7,000 1050.00 5,950.00
5 1995 8,000 1200.00 6,800.00
6 1996 9,000 1350.00 7,650.00
7 1997 12,000 1800.00 10,200.00
8 1998 15,000 2250.00 12,750.00
9 1999 20,000 3000.00 17,000.00
10
11
12

Microsoft Excel - Finance

E2 = =SUM(D2*12/100)

	A	B	C	D	E	F
1	Year	Total Income	Interest Paid	Profit	Tax	Profit After Tax
2	1992	4,500	675.00	3,825.00	459	
3	1993	5,500	825.00	4,675.00		
4	1994	7,000	1050.00	5,950.00		
5	1995	8,000	1200.00	6,800.00		
6	1996	9,000	1350.00	7,650.00		
7	1997	12,000	1800.00	10,200.00		
8	1998	15,000	2250.00	12,750.00		
9	1999	20,000	3000.00	17,000.00		

Tax= (Profit x 12)/100

If we put this in Cell **E2**, it will become:

E2 = SUM(D2*12/100)

Microsoft Excel - Finance

E9 = =SUM(D9*12/100)

	A	B	C	D	E	F
1	Year	Total Income	Interest Paid	Profit	Tax	Profit After Tax
2	1992	4,500	675.00	3,825.00	459.00	
3	1993	5,500	825.00	4,675.00	561.00	
4	1994	7,000	1050.00	5,950.00	714.00	
5	1995	8,000	1200.00	6,800.00	816.00	
6	1996	9,000	1350.00	7,650.00	918.00	
7	1997	12,000	1800.00	10,200.00	1224.00	
8	1998	15,000	2250.00	12,750.00	1530.00	
9	1999	20,000	3000.00	17,000.00	2040.00	

Let us apply this formula in **E2** and see what happens. It gives you the result as 459. Copying this formula to the other cells, i.e., from **E3** to **E9**, you can fill up the whole column and make the worksheet look like the one shown on the next page.

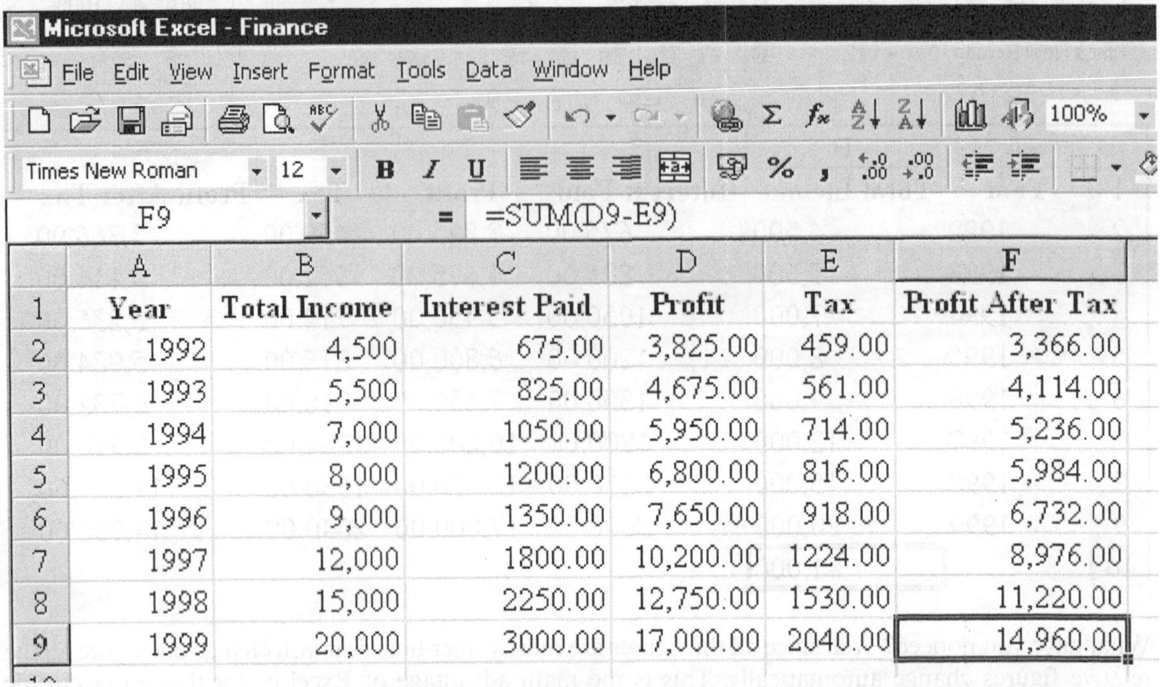

	A	B	C	D	E	F
1	Year	Total Income	Interest Paid	Profit	Tax	Profit After Tax
2	1992	4,500	675.00	3,825.00	459.00	3,366.00
3	1993	5,500	825.00	4,675.00	561.00	4,114.00
4	1994	7,000	1050.00	5,950.00	714.00	5,236.00
5	1995	8,000	1200.00	6,800.00	816.00	5,984.00
6	1996	9,000	1350.00	7,650.00	918.00	6,732.00
7	1997	12,000	1800.00	10,200.00	1224.00	8,976.00
8	1998	15,000	2250.00	12,750.00	1530.00	11,220.00
9	1999	20,000	3000.00	17,000.00	2040.00	14,960.00

The last column in this case is the "Profit After Tax", which can be calculated after subtracting "Tax" from the "Profit". This calculation I am not showing here, since I assume that you should be able to do this easily. However, your resultant worksheet should look like the one shown next.

You think the worksheet is complete. No. You still have to do the column totals without which the whole worksheet looks incomplete.

For this follow the following steps.

1. Click at cell B10 to get the total of figures from B2 to B9.
2. Now click at Σ symbol in the Standard toolbar.
3. It will search for the numeric cells above and put the formula for the same and highlight the cells it has selected.
4. It will wait for your Ok in the form of Enter to put the result.
5. Press Enter to get the total in the cell B10, as shown on the next page.

Similarly all the other columns can be summed up showing the result as shown below.

Now you can say that your worksheet is complete. But, supposing we want to make any change. This is done delibrately to show you the main advantage of Excel software.

Supposing, we change the figure of the year 1996 from 9,000 to 9,200, which we can assume that it was wrongly given to us or was a typing mistake. It is shown on next page. Try changing this figure in the cell **B6** and see the resultant effect.

Microsoft Excel - Finance

B10 = =SUM(B2:B9)

	A	B	C	D	E	F
1	Year	Total Income	Interest Paid	Profit	Tax	Profit After Tax
2	1992	4,500	675.00	3,825.00	459.00	3,366.00
3	1993	5,500	825.00	4,675.00	561.00	4,114.00
4	1994	7,000	1050.00	5,950.00	714.00	5,236.00
5	1995	8,000	1200.00	6,800.00	816.00	5,984.00
6	1996	9,000	1350.00	7,650.00	918.00	6,732.00
7	1997	12,000	1800.00	10,200.00	1224.00	8,976.00
8	1998	15,000	2250.00	12,750.00	1530.00	11,220.00
9	1999	20,000	3000.00	17,000.00	2040.00	14,960.00
10		81,000				

What have you noticed? Well since all the figures are mostly inter-linked, if you change one figure all the relative figures change automatically. This is the main advantage of Excel or for that an electronic spreadsheet.

Now if you apply this to the accounting department and assume that these figures relate to actual working of the finance department. Try changing the figures of one voucher and the poor accountant would have to sit probably the whole night to recalculate all the totals in the Balance Sheet. But, now with this kind of spreadsheet, this can be done in a flash.

Coming back to our worksheet. There are 3 things more to be done. Firstly, we will decorate it using the options available under the **AutoFormat** command. Then we will see a preview of our worksheet and then print it on our printer.

For decorating with the AutoFormat. Call the command from the Format menu, after highlighting the cells which you want to include in this AutoFormat and you will see the dialog box, which was shown earlier. As you can see, there are various options available under this. Ranging from Simple, Classic, Accounting to 3-D ones. For our worksheet we are going to choose the one called Classic 2.

Just click at this and it would be applied. I am quite sure you would be interested to know the result of this. See the worksheet shown above for the result. I am quite sure that you are impressed with your work. You can make it look more impressive using the features of Borders, Patterns, etc.

Now that you have to print it on your printer to see the final result. But, before that we would like to see its **Preview**. This command is part of the **Print** command which is available under the **File** menu.

There are various other options in the print dialog box, shown on the next page, alongwith the print preview of the worksheet.

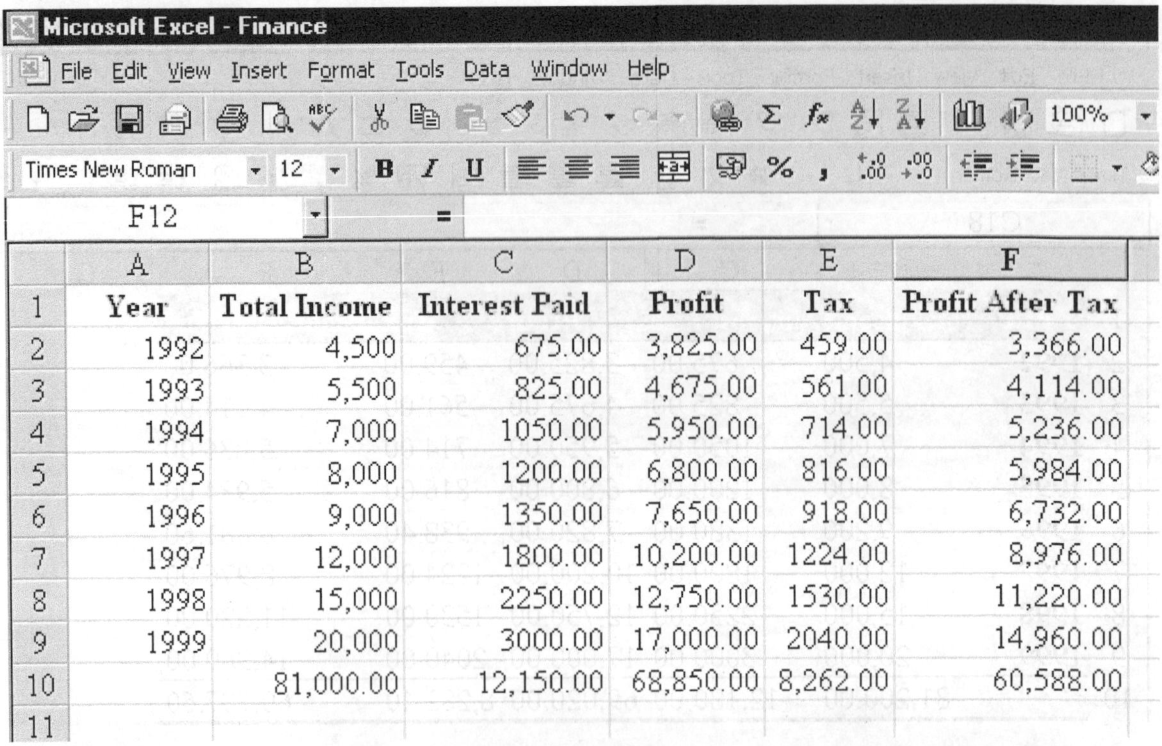

Microsoft Excel - Finance

F12 =

	A	B	C	D	E	F
1	Year	Total Income	Interest Paid	Profit	Tax	Profit After Tax
2	1992	4,500	675.00	3,825.00	459.00	3,366.00
3	1993	5,500	825.00	4,675.00	561.00	4,114.00
4	1994	7,000	1050.00	5,950.00	714.00	5,236.00
5	1995	8,000	1200.00	6,800.00	816.00	5,984.00
6	1996	9,000	1350.00	7,650.00	918.00	6,732.00
7	1997	12,000	1800.00	10,200.00	1224.00	8,976.00
8	1998	15,000	2250.00	12,750.00	1530.00	11,220.00
9	1999	20,000	3000.00	17,000.00	2040.00	14,960.00
10		81,000.00	12,150.00	68,850.00	8,262.00	60,588.00
11						

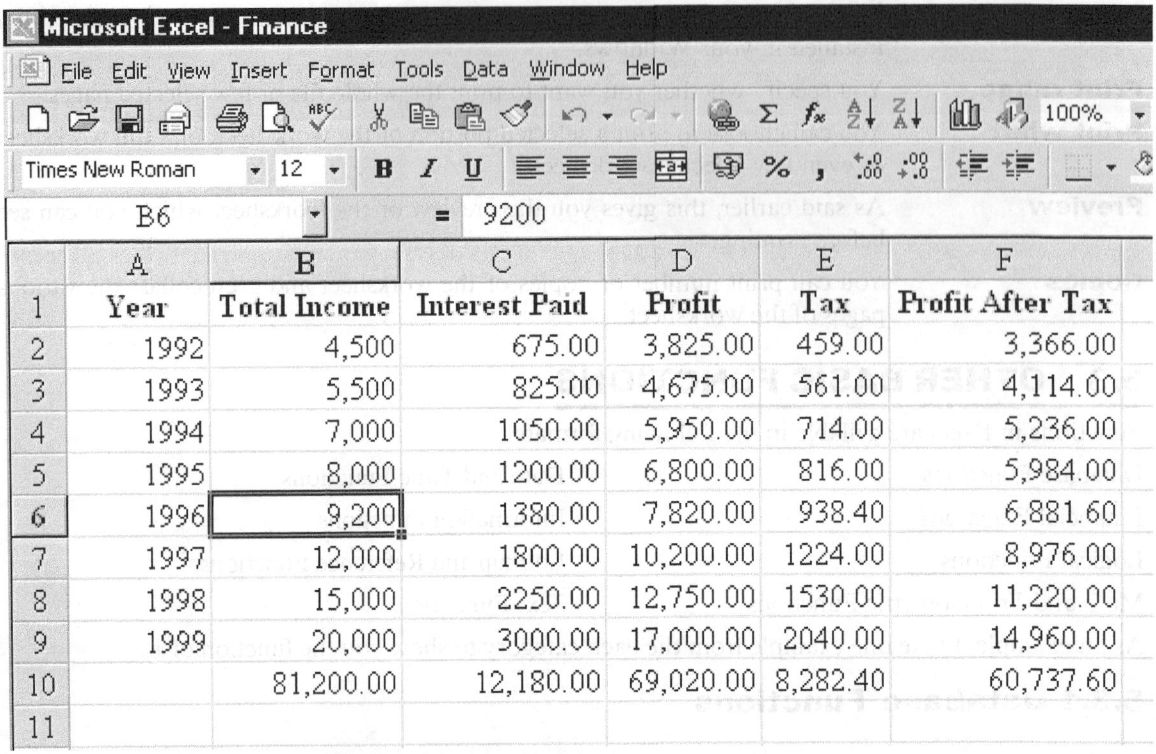

Microsoft Excel - Finance

B6 = 9200

	A	B	C	D	E	F
1	Year	Total Income	Interest Paid	Profit	Tax	Profit After Tax
2	1992	4,500	675.00	3,825.00	459.00	3,366.00
3	1993	5,500	825.00	4,675.00	561.00	4,114.00
4	1994	7,000	1050.00	5,950.00	714.00	5,236.00
5	1995	8,000	1200.00	6,800.00	816.00	5,984.00
6	1996	9,200	1380.00	7,820.00	938.40	6,881.60
7	1997	12,000	1800.00	10,200.00	1224.00	8,976.00
8	1998	15,000	2250.00	12,750.00	1530.00	11,220.00
9	1999	20,000	3000.00	17,000.00	2040.00	14,960.00
10		81,200.00	12,180.00	69,020.00	8,282.40	60,737.60
11						

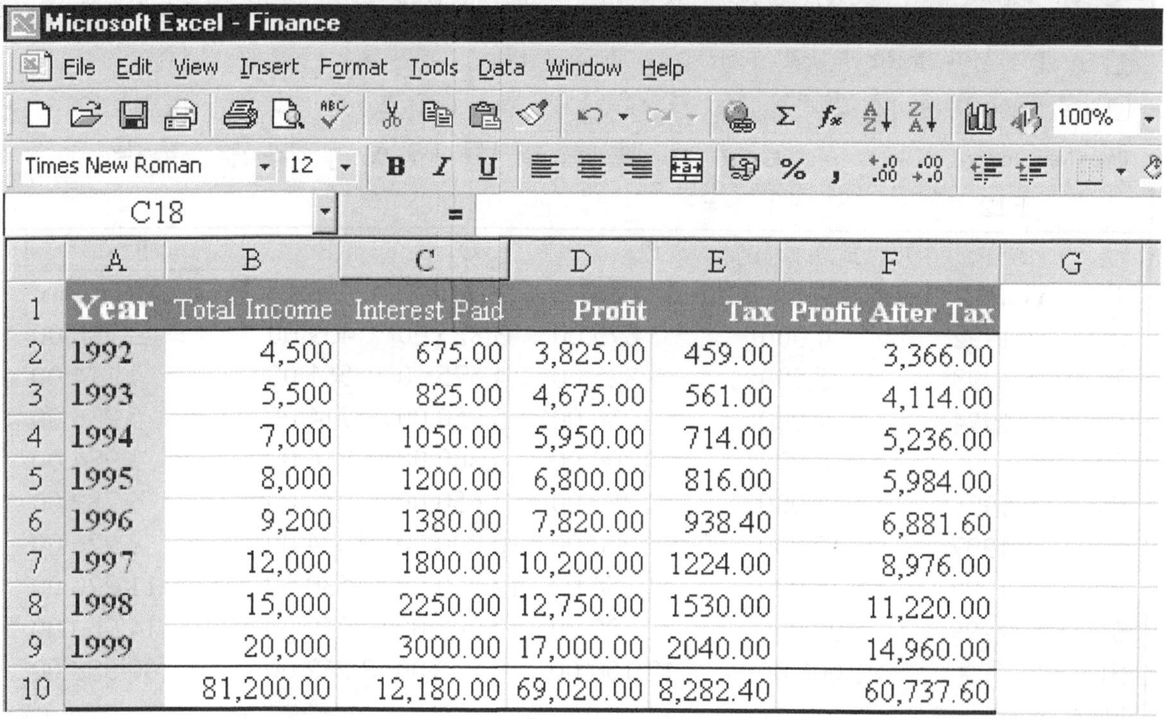

	A	B	C	D	E	F	G
1	Year	Total Income	Interest Paid	Profit	Tax	Profit After Tax	
2	1992	4,500	675.00	3,825.00	459.00	3,366.00	
3	1993	5,500	825.00	4,675.00	561.00	4,114.00	
4	1994	7,000	1050.00	5,950.00	714.00	5,236.00	
5	1995	8,000	1200.00	6,800.00	816.00	5,984.00	
6	1996	9,200	1380.00	7,820.00	938.40	6,881.60	
7	1997	12,000	1800.00	10,200.00	1224.00	8,976.00	
8	1998	15,000	2250.00	12,750.00	1530.00	11,220.00	
9	1999	20,000	3000.00	17,000.00	2040.00	14,960.00	
10		81,200.00	12,180.00	69,020.00	8,282.40	60,737.60	

Printer You have to specify the various options of your printer. It is usually the printer installed in your Windows.

Print range You specify whether you want to print the whole file or few selected pages.

Print what You can choose to print a selected portion of the worksheet, or a full worksheet or even few selected worksheet.

Preview As said earlier, this gives you the preview of the worksheet which you can see before printing.

Copies You can print number of copies of the worksheet and even collate the various pages of the worksheet.

5.3 OTHER BASIC FUNCTIONS

Functions in Excel are avilable in the following formats:

Database Functions	Date and Time Functions
Financial Functions	Information Functions
Logical Functions	Lookup and Reference Functions
Math and Trigonometric Functions	Text Functions

As an example, I take one example from the each category to show you the function of it.

5.3.1 Database Functions

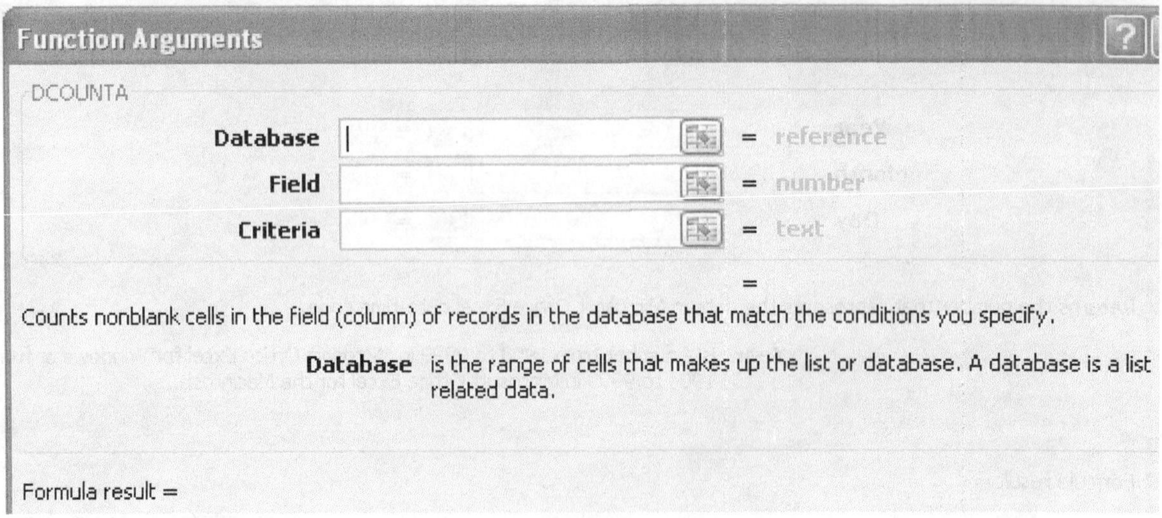

Function DCOUNTA

Syntax **=DCOUNTA(Database, Field, Criteria)**

Description Counts non blank cells in a particular field of records that match specified criteria in a database.

5.3.2 Date and Time Functions

Function DATE

Description Returns the sequential serial number that represents a particular date. If the cell format was General before the function was entered, the result is formatted as a date.

Syntax **=DATE(Year, March, Day)**

Year: The year argument can be one to four digits. Microsoft Excel interprets the year argument according to the date system you are using. By default, Excel for Windows uses the 1900 date system; Excel for the Macintosh uses the 1904 date system.

For the 1900 date system

- If year is between 0 (zero) and 1899 (inclusive), Excel adds that value to 1900 to calculate the year. For example, DATE(108,1,2) returns January 2, 2008 (1900+108).
- If year is between 1900 and 9999 (inclusive), Excel uses that value as the year. For example, DATE(2008,1,2) returns January 2, 2008.
- If year is less than 0 or is 10000 or greater, Excel returns the #NUM! error value.

For the 1904 date system

- If year is between 4 and 1899 (inclusive), Excel adds that value to 1900 to calculate the year. For example, DATE(108,1,2) returns January 2, 2008 (1900+108).
- If year is between 1904 and 9999 (inclusive), Excel uses that value as the year. For example, DATE(2008,1,2) returns January 2, 2008.
- If year is less than 4 or is 10000 or greater or if year is between 1900 and 1903 (inclusive), Excel returns the #NUM! error value.

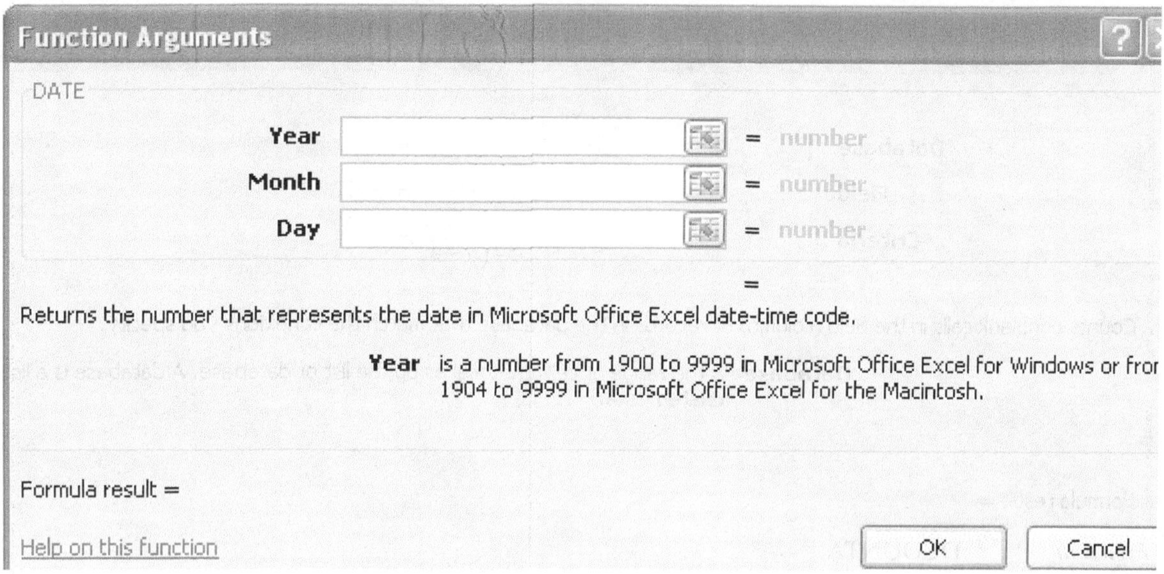

Month is a positive or negative integer representing the month of the year from 1 to 12 (January to December).

- If month is greater than 12, month adds that number of months to the first month in the year specified. For example, DATE(2008,14,2) returns the serial number representing February 2, 2009.
- If month is less than 1, month subtracts that number of months plus 1 from the first month in the year specified. For example, DATE(2008,-3,2) returns the serial number representing September 2, 2007.

Day is a positive or negative integer representing the day of the month from 1 to 31.

- If day is greater than the number of days in the month specified, day adds that number of days to the first day in the month. For example, DATE(2008,1,35) returns the serial number representing February 4, 2008.
- If day is less than 1, day subtracts that number of days plus one from the first day in the month. For example, DATE(2008,1,-15) returns the serial number representing December 16, 2007.

5.3.3 Financial Functions

Function DB

Syntax **=DB(Cost, Salvage, Life, Period, Month)**

where the terms are:

Cost A numeric value that indicates the total amount paid to acquire the asset.

Life An integer value that indicates the number of periods that the asset will be depreciated over.

Period An integer value that indicates the period that you want to calculate the depreciation for, such as 2 for the second year's depreciation amount.

Month An optional value that indicates the number of months in the first year of depreciation.

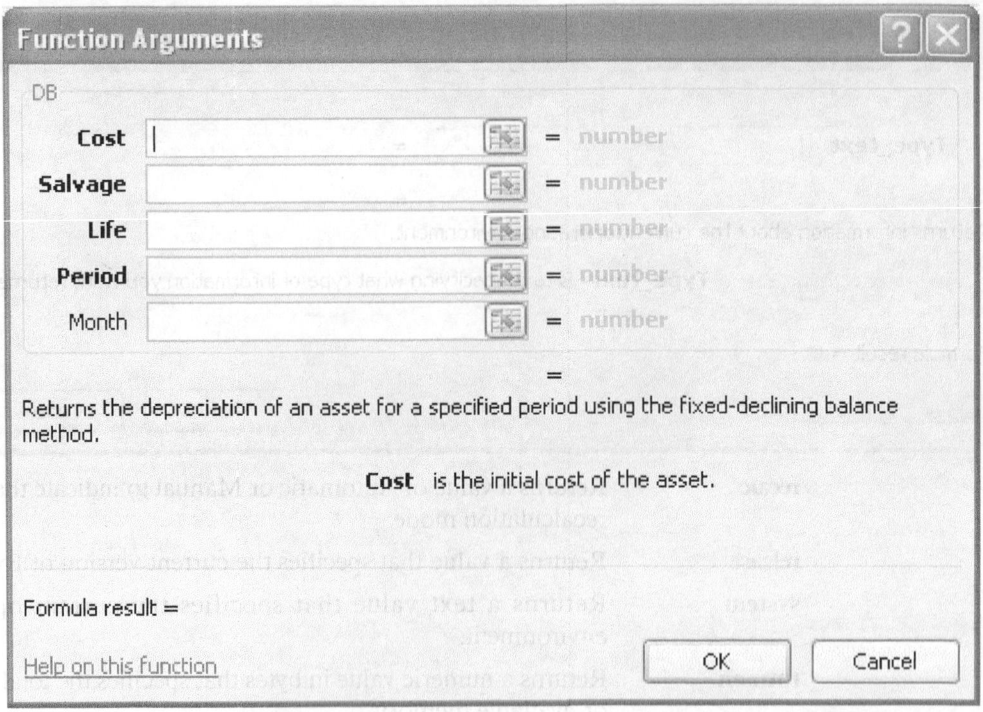

Description Returns the depreciation of an asset for a specified period using the fixed-declining balance method.

5.3.4 Information Functions

Function INFO

Syntax **=INFO(Type_Text)**

where the terms are:

Info_Type	This required argument specifies one of the following text values that indicates the type of information that should be returned about the operating system.
directory	Returns the path of the current directory or folder.
memavail	Returns a numeric value that indicates the amount of memory available in bytes.
memused	Returns a numeric value that indicates the amount of memory currently being used.
numfile	Returns an integer value that specifies the number of active worksheets.
origin	Returns a reference to the top-left visible cell based upon he current scrolling position.
osversion	Returns a text value that identifies the current operating system version.

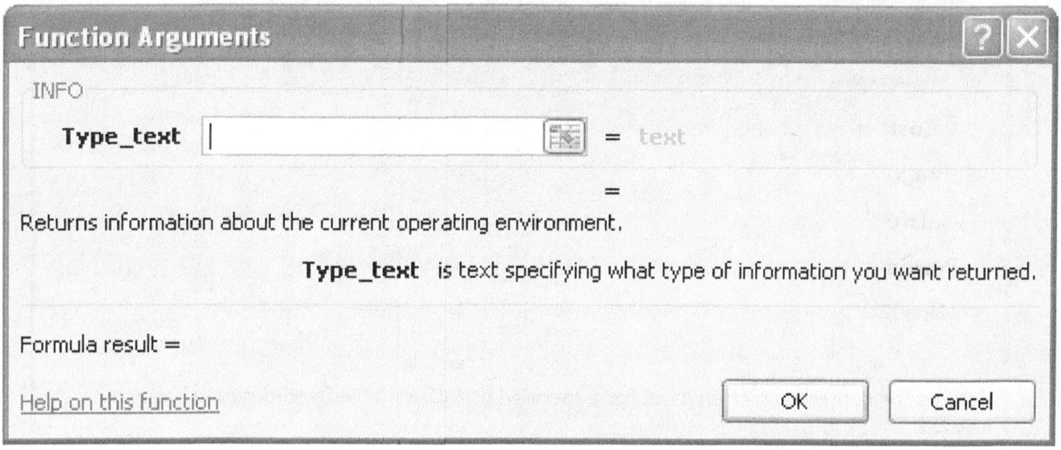

recalc	Returns a value of Automatic or Manual to indicate the current recalculation mode.
release	Returns a value that specifies the current version of Excel.
system	Returns a text value that specifies the current operating environment.
totmen	Returns a numeric value in bytes that specifies the total amount of available memory.

Description Returns information about the current operating environment.

5.3.5 Logical Functions

Function IF

Syntax **=IF(Logical_Test, Value_If_True, Value_If_False)**

Description Specifies a logical test to perform.

Logical_test is any value or expression that can be evaluated to TRUE or FALSE. For example, A10=100 is a logical expression; if the value in cell A10 is equal to 100, the expression evaluates to TRUE. Otherwise, the expression evaluates to FALSE. This argument can use any comparison calculation operator.

Value_if_true is the value that is returned if logical_test is TRUE. For example, if this argument is the text string "Within budget" and the logical_test argument evaluates to TRUE, then the IF function displays the text "Within budget". If logical_test is TRUE and value_if_true is blank, this argument returns 0 (zero). To display the word TRUE, use the logical value TRUE for this argument. Value_if_true can be another formula.

Value_if_false is the value that is returned if logical_test is FALSE. For example, if this argument is the text string "Over budget" and the logical_test argument evaluates to FALSE, then the IF function displays the text "Over budget". If logical_test is FALSE and value_if_false is omitted, (that is, after value_if_true, there is no comma), then the logical value FALSE is returned. If logical_test is FALSE and value_if_false is blank (that is, after value_if_true, there is a comma followed by the closing parenthesis), then the value 0 (zero) is returned. Value_if_false can be another formula.

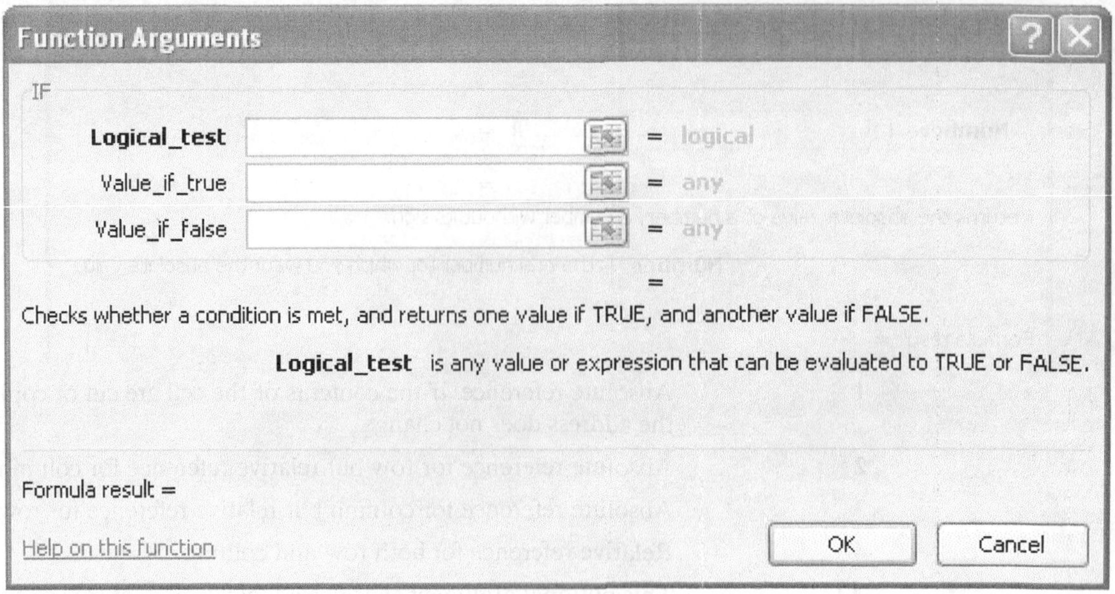

5.3.6 Lookup and Reference Functions

Function ADDRESS

Syntax **=ADDRESS(Row_Num, Column_Num, Abs_Num, Sheet_Text)**

where the terms are:

Abs_Num This optional argument specifies an integer value of 1, 2, 3, or 4 indicating the type of cell reference to return.

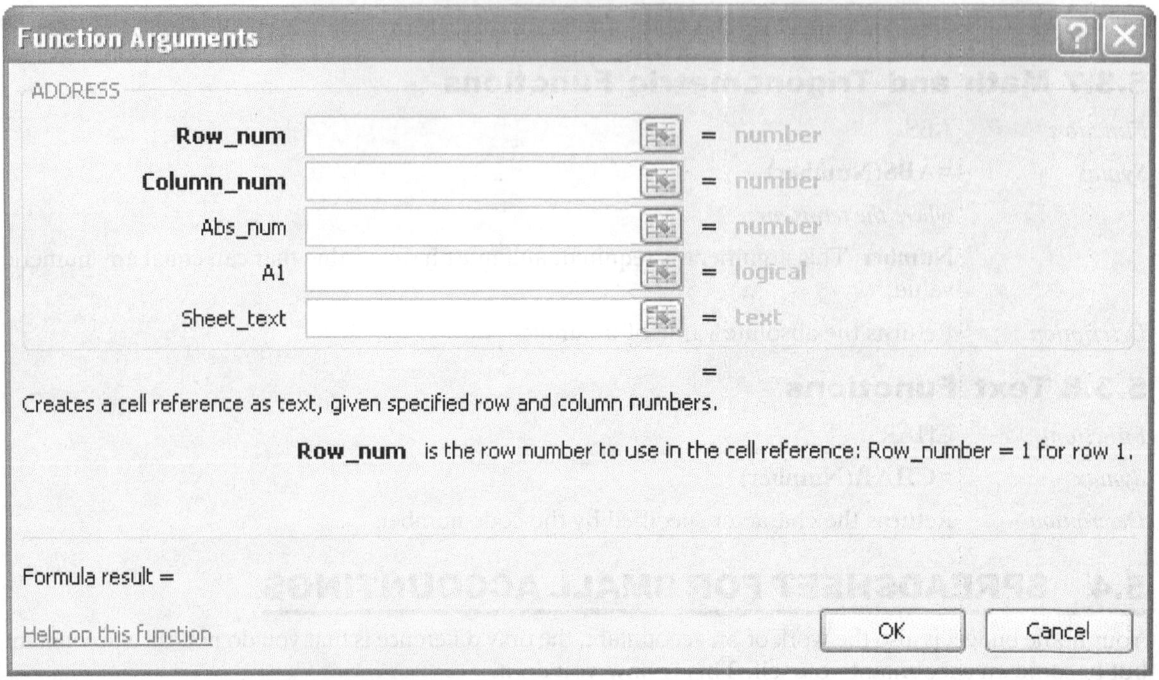

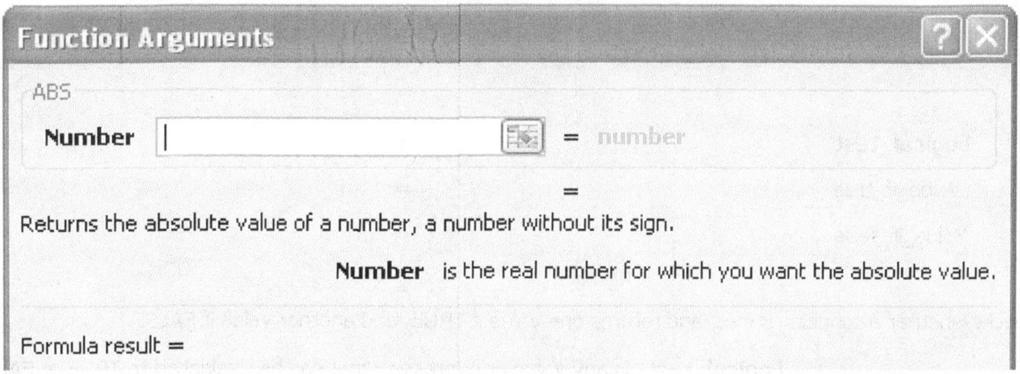

1	Absolute reference. If the contents of the cell are cut or copied the address does not change.
2	Absolute reference for row but relative reference for column.
3	Absolute reference for column but relative reference for row.
4	Relative reference for both row and column.
A1	This optional argument specifies a logical value of true or false that indicates the style used to represent the cell address.
Sheet_Text	This optional argument is used to specify the name of a sheet that you want to reference.

Description Returns the number of areas in a reference.

Row_num is the row number to use in the cell reference.

Column_num is the column number to use in the cell reference.

Abs_num specifies the type of reference to return.

5.3.7 Math and Trigonometric Functions

Function ABS

Syntax **=ABS(Number)**

where the terms are:

Number This argument is required, and must have a value that can equal any numeric value.

Description Returns the absolute value of a number.

5.3.8 Text Functions

Function CHAR

Syntax **=CHAR(Number)**

Description Returns the character specified by the code number.

5.4 SPREADSHEET FOR SMALL ACCOUNTINGS

Your home budget is also the work of an accountant, the only difference is that you do not call a accountant but become an accountant yourself. This is how you do it.

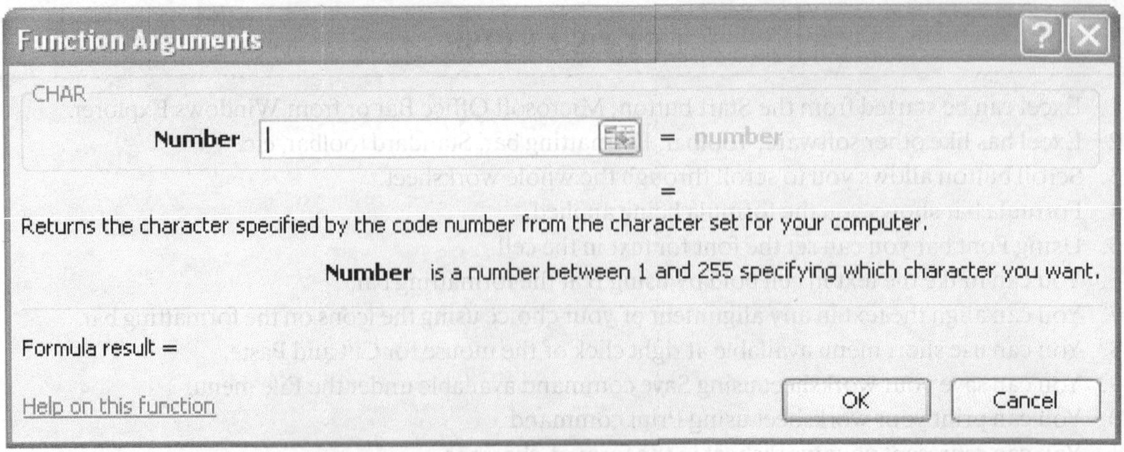

1. Click at New.
2. From the Templates, choose the Personal Monthly Budget.
3. A spreadsheet for the same comes on the screen.
4. Enter the data which you want to change.
5. You total accounts for month are ready.

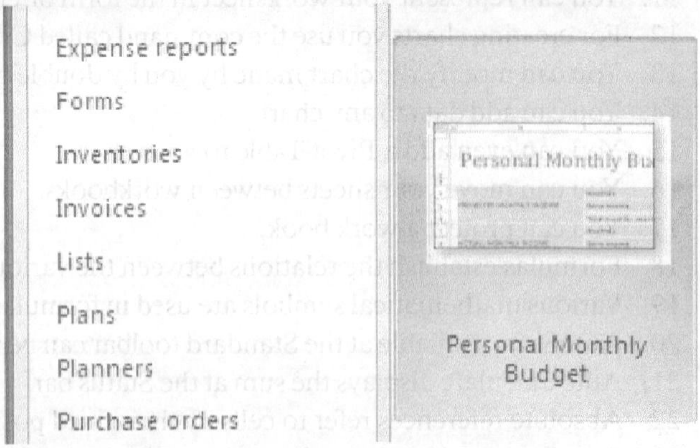

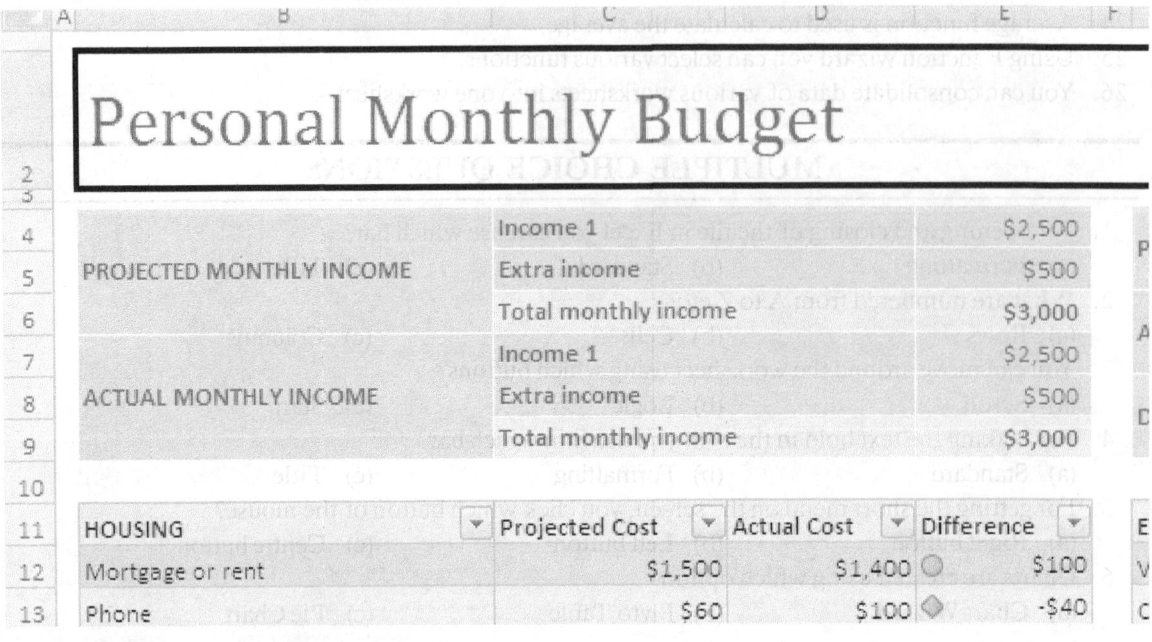

LET US REVISE

1. Excel can be started from the Start button, Microsoft Office Bar or from Windows Explorer.
2. Excel has like other software, Toolbar, Formatting bar, Standard toolbar, etc.
3. Scroll button allows you to scroll through the whole worksheet.
4. Formula bar shows you the formula being applied.
5. Using Font bar you can set the font for text in the cell.
6. You can make the text in cell bold by using B at the formatting bar.
7. You can align the text in any alignment of your choice using the icons on the formatting bar.
8. You can use short menu available at right click of the mouse for Cut and Paste.
9. You can save your worksheet using Save command available under the File menu.
10. You can print your worksheet using Print command.
11. You can represent your worksheet in the form of chart too.
12. For creating charts you use the command called Chart Wizard.
13. You can modify the chart made by you by double clicking the chart.
14. You can add data to any chart.
15. You can even add a Pivot Table to your chart.
16. You can move your sheets between workbooks.
17. You can protect a work book.
18. Formulas establish the relations between the various cells.
19. Various mathematical symbols are used in formulas.
20. AutoSum, available at the Standard toolbar can be used to calculate the sum instantenously.
21. AutoCalculate displays the sum at the Status bar.
22. Absolute references refer to cells by their fixed position in the worksheet.
23. Sum function is commonly used for all calculations.
24. Average function is used to calculate the average.
25. Using Function wizard you can select various functions.
26. You can consolidate data of various worksheets into one worksheet.

MULTIPLE CHOICE QUESTIONS

1. For opening and closing of the file in Excel you can use which bar?
   (a) Formatting (b) Standard (c) Title
2. What are numbered from A to Z etc?
   (a) Rows (b) Cells (c) Columns
3. You can move around the worksheet using which buttons?
   (a) Scroll (b) Logic (c) Start
4. For making the text bold in the cell, you use B in which bar?
   (a) Standard (b) Formatting (c) Title
5. For getting the short menu on the screen, you click which button of the mouse?
   (a) Right button (b) Left button (c) Centre button
6. Charts are created using which option.
   (a) Chart Wizard (b) Pivto Table (c) Pie Chart

7. For editing the chart, you ____________ the chart itself.
   (a) Click (b) Delete (c) Double click
8. In Excel a formula starts with ___________.
   (a) = sign (b) + sign (c) - sign
9. In Excel worksheets are given _____ extension.
   (a) .xls (b) .doc (c) .bmp
10. In Microsoft Excel, you use _______ for calcualtions.
    (a) Formula (b) Row (c) Cell
11. Formula which can be used directly from the Standard toolbar is
    (a) AutoSum (b) Auto (c) Sum
12. The result of AutoCalculate is shown at ___ bar.
    (a) Standard (b) Formatting (c) Status
13. Sum function needs to have ______ before it.
    (a) + (b) – (c) =
14. To access to any formula in Microsoft Excel, you need to go through _____
    (a) Function Wizard (b) File (c) Formula
15. Anything that is typed in a worksheet appears:
    (a) in both the active cell and the formula bar
    (b) in the active cell only
    (c) none of the above
16. The formatting toolbar
    (a) is placed just below the Standard toolbar
    (b) is used to apply common formats
    (c) both of above
17. The combination of the column letter and row number for a cell in an Excel worksheet is called a
    (a) cell identification number (b) cell reference (c) cell identity
18. In Excel the simplest way to move data from one location to another is
    (a) by menu commands (b) by mouse (c) by drag and drop method
19. Using borders you
    (a) can add lines above, below or to either side of a cell
    (b) can add a single line or multiple lines, along one side of a cell or around it.
    (c) both a and b above
20. Cell address B$6 in a formula means it is a
    (a) relative cell reference (b) absolute cell reference (c) mixed cell reference
21. A function in Excel
    (a) is a ready made formula (b) is a shortcut formula (c) both of above

TRUE/FALSE QUESTIONS

1. Microsoft Excel is a spreadsheet program.
2. Using Formatting toolbar you can format the data.
3. There is only one worksheet in a spreadsheet.
4. Formula is displayed in the formula bar.

5. You cannot have fonts applied to the data.
6. You cannot align the data in a cell.
7. For cut and paste you can use the shortcut menu available at right click of the mouse.
8. A worksheet cannot be given a name.
9. Before printing you cannot see a preview of the worksheet.
10. You cannot represent your worksheet data in the form of a chart.
11. Chart Wizard is used for creating the chart.
12. Once created a chart cannot be modified.
13. You cannot add a Pivot Table to your chart.
14. You cannot move your data in between the various sheets of the workbook.
15. A password protection can be made of the worksheet.
16. A formula can estabish relation between cells.
17. All mathematical symbols can be used in the formula.
18. AutoSum is used for calculating sum.
19. AutoCalculate displays the sum at Formatting toolbar.
20. Absolute references refer to cells by their fixed position in the worksheet.
21. Average function would calculate the average.
22. You cannot consolidate data of various worksheets.
23. Function Wizard cannot be used for various functions.
24. Data and Time functions would give you the various options of data and time.
25. Text functions would give you the various options of text.
26. A formula can have a mixed reference of the cells.
27. A border cannot be added around the data in the worksheet.

MATCHING COLUMNS

Match the matter in Column A with the matter in Column B.

Column A	Column B
A. Formating toolbar	1. Sheets in a workbook
B. Functions	2. A selection of cells
C. Standard toolbar	3. Beginning of a formula
D. Cols	4. Right click of the mouse
E. Rows	5. A combination of column letter and row number of a cell
F. Worksheets	6. Used for performing standard operations
G. Active cell	7. Refers to an absolute location of a specific cell
H. Range of cells	8. Mathematical function
I. =	9. Monthly instalment calculator
J. Short cut menu	10. Used for formatting data in cells
K. Cell reference	11. Ready made formula
L. Absolute reference	12. Horizontal row
M. TRUNC()	13. Vertical columns
N. PMT()	14. A selected cell

FILL IN THE BLANKS WITH APPROPRIATE WORDS

a. Chart	b. .xls	c. An active cell	d. AVERAGE
e. Scroll	f. Cell	g. =	h. Columns
i. Sheets	j. Chart Wizard	k. Right button	l. Standard

1. Cross section of a row and column is called ______.
2. In Excel a formula starts with ______ sign.
3. For opening and closing of the file in Excel you can use the ________ bar
4. In Excel worksheets are given ______ extension
5. Charts are created using ________..
6. The function ________ is used for calculating average.
7. You can move around the worksheet using ________ buttons.
8. For editing the chart, you double click _______.
9. In Excel ______ are numbered from A to Z.
10. For getting the short menu on the screen, you click ______ of the mouse.
11. A selected cell in Excel is called _______.
12. A workbook can have a number of ________.

DESCRIPTIVE TYPE QUESTIONS

1. Describe various methods of starting Excel.
2. Describe the various components of the Excel worksheet window.
3. Describe the method of copying formula.
4. Describe the process of saving a worksheet.
5. Describe how would you insert a chart in the worksheet.
6. Describe the working of the Chart Wizard.
7. Describe the process of modifying chart.
8. How would you add data to the chart?
9. Describe the process of creating a Pivot Table.
10. How would you audit a worksheet? Explain.
11. Describe the process of inserting a comment in the worksheet.
12. Describe how the logical functions work in worksheet.
13. Describe how would you put Headers and Footers in a worksheet.
14. How would you merge two worksheets?
15. Describe the method of putting Outlines to worksheets.
16. How would you put labels on your rows and columns of the worksheet?
17. How would you protect your worksheet?
18. How would you name a range of cells?
19. Describe the various type of references.
20. Describe the command Goal Seek.
21. Describe the process of naming sheets.
22. How would you create a style?
23. How would you copy entries between workbooks?

24. Write down the steps to protect the workbook.
25. Which mathematical symbols are used in Microsoft Excel formulas?
26. Which type of errors you get while using formulas?
27. How would you use AutoSum?
28. Describe the process of using AutoCalculate.
29. Describe Absolute and Mixed References.
30. How is the Sum function used?
31. How would you use the AVERAGE function?
32. What is Function Wizard?

ANSWERS TO OBJECTIVE QUESTIONS

Multiple Choice Questions

1. b	2. c	3. a	4. b
5. a	6. a	7. c	8. a
9. a	10 a	11. a	12. c
13. c	14. a	15. a	16. c
17. b	18. c	19. c	20. b
21. c			

True False Questions

1. T	2. T	3. F	4. T
5. F	6. F	7. T	8. F
9. T	10. F	11. T	12. F
13. F	14. F	15. T	16. T
17. T	18. T	19. F	20. T
21. T	22. F	23. F	24. T
25. T	26. T	27. F	

Matching Columns

A. 10	B. 11	C. 6	D. 13
E. 12	F. 1	G. 14	H. 2
I. 3	J. 4	K. 5	L. 7
M. 8	N. 9	Q. 14	R. 2

Fill in the Blanks with Appropriate Words

1. f	2. g	3. l	4. b
5. j	6. d	7. e	8. a
9. h	10. k	11. c	12. i

Chapter 6 Computer Communication and Internet

6.1 BASIC OF COMPUTER NETWORKS

It is not that the Personal Computers are for personal use only. They can be used for sharing of information too with others having similar type of equipments. Logically it sometimes is more feasible to have a number of PCs than having a bigger computer which can give the same throughput as the number of PCs. But, overall it becomes a expensive proposition and sometimes is not feasible, specially for individuals and small businesses or small companies.

Another problem arises for those who are physically placed at a distance. They would need to send messages and receive messages, or use the same data at, or share program at, many different locations. One answer to this problem is to keep separate data files at each location, but this approach is very costly and potentially a dangerous solution. It is very expensive to maintain these redundant files of data and difficult to ensure the continuing accuracy of data at any one location. The solution of both, the need for more power and the ability to receive, send messages and share data, are found in data communication technology.

6.1.1 LAN

A network covering a small geographic area, like a home, office, or building. Current LANs are most likely to be based on Ethernet technology. The defining characteristics of LANs, in contrast to WANs (wide area networks), include their much higher data transfer rates, smaller geographic range, and lack of a need for leased telecommunication lines.

A local area network (LAN) is two or more computers directly linked within a small well-defined area such as a room, building, or group of closely placed buildings. A LAN may be made up of only microcomputers or any combination of microcomputers and large systems.

A LAN usually consists of the following:

1. Two or more computers
2. Peripheral devices such as printers and hard-disk drives
3. Software to control the operation of the computers or other devices connected to the LAN
4. Special cables, usually coaxial or fibre optic, to connect the computers and other devices
5. A plug-in board to handle the data transmissions.

Some computers require that all the computers be of a certain brand, while others allow a variety of brands to be connected. The number of computers in a LAN varies from smaller LANs that typically connect 2 to 25 computers, to large LANs that can connect as many as 10,000 computers.

The length of the cable connecting a computer to a LAN also varies depending on the LAN. Most LANs allow cables of about 1,000 feet, but some allow cables of several miles to be used. The data transfer speeds range from several thousand bits per second to around 10 million bits per second.

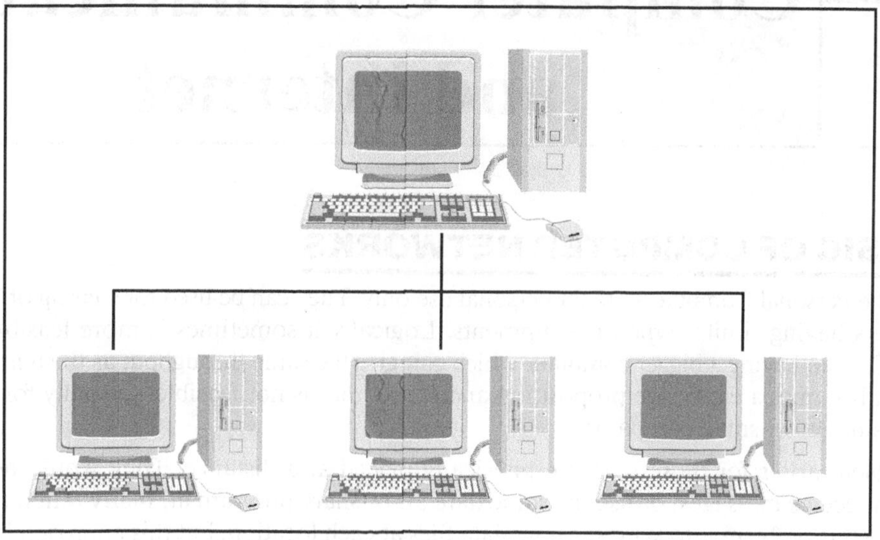

Some programs allow the user of more than one operating system; others allow only one. On some LANs file access is limited to one user at a time; on others, more than one user can access a file simultaneously.

6.1.1.1 Hardware for LAN

The following are the major hardware components/devices for establishing LAN:

1. Transmission Channel
2. Network Interface Unit or NIU
3. Servers
4. Workstations.

6.1.1.2 Server and Workstations

One of the major benefits of implementation of LAN is sharing expensive resources such as storage devices, printers, etc. This is achieved through providing servers on the LAN. It is dedicated computer that controls one or more resources. This contains both hardware and software interface for LAN. Three major categories of services used in LANs are:

1. File Server
2. Printer Server
3. Modem Server.

In networking, file server is used to share storage for files. Besides providing storage space for files in a LAN environment, it is used for taking periodical backup, and also to provide gateway to other servers with and between LANs. Similarly printer server is used to handle printing works of all workstations connected in the network. In LAN environment also modem is required to get connected to other network or simply to use a telephone. A modem server is used to share this expensive resource by all connected workstations in a network ring.

6.1.1.3 Software for LAN

LAN operating system is required to operate on the LAN system. It has basically two aspects:

1. Server Software
2. Workstation Software.

LAN operating system facilitates :

1. Sharing of expensive resources, e.g., printer, storage space, etc.
2. Security for data
3. Connection to other network.

There are various types of LAN operating system. Some popular LAN operating systems are :

— Novel Netware
— Ethernet
— Corvus
— ArcNet
— LAN Server
— Omni Net
— PC Net
— IBM PC LAN
— Etherlink Plus, etc.

6.1.1.4 Features of Local Area Networks

- Typically connects computer in a single building or campus.
- Developed in 1970s.
- Medium : optical fibres, coaxial cables, twisted pair, wireless.
- Low latency (except in high traffic periods).
- High speed networks (0.2 to 100 Mb/sec).
- Speeds adequate for most distributed systems
- Problems : Multi media based applications
- Typically buses or rings.

6.1.1.5 Advantages of Local Area Networks

- It allows sharing of expensive resources.
- High speed data transfer.
- More applications can be used.
- Increases productivity.

6.1.1.6 Disadvantages of Local Area Networks

- High cost.
- Required high memory.
- More manpower and resources needed to maintain.
- User loses control.

- Difficult to keep confidential.
- Data loss due to high memory requirements

6.1.2 WAN

A WAN is a data communications network that covers a relatively broad geographic area and that often uses transmission facilities provided by common carriers, such as telephone companies. WAN technologies generally function at the lower three layers of the OSI reference model: the physical layer, the data link layer, and the network layer. A wide area network is two or more computers that are geographically dispersed, linked by communication facilities such as telephone system or microwave relays. This type of network is usually limited to use by large corporations and government agencies because of the high cost involved in building and maintaining them. The main difference between a WAN and LAN is that LAN is under the complete control of the owner, whereas the WAN needs the involvement of another authority like telecom department. LANs are successful and capable of handling very high data transfer rates at low cost because of the small area covered. Besides LANs have a lower error rate than WANs.

6.1.2.1 Hardware Requirements for WAN

There are mainly 4 hardware devices which are required to establish linkage between geographically separated computers. These are:

1. Bridges
2. Routers
3. Gateways
4. X.25 Standard Interface.

These are explained below.

Bridges: These are used to connect two LANs that use the identical protocols over a wide area. The bridge acts as an address filter which picks up packets from one LAN that are intended for a destination on another LAN and passes these packets on the network. The amount of processing required at the bridge is minimal because all the devices use the same protocols. In case the distance between two LANs is very large then the user is required to employ two identical bridges at either end of the communication link.

Routers: It is a special type of device that can be used to connect networks that may not be similar. Such type of devices provide connectivity between two LANs and two WANs over large geographical distances. These devices operate at the Network Layer of the OSI model. These devices participate in a routing protocol to access the network topology, and on the basis of this information routers compute the best route from a sender to the receiver.

Gateways: These are used to connect two dissimilar LANs. The terms Gateways and Routers are used interchangeably, though there is discriminating difference between the two. A router operates at the network layer whereas a gateway operates on the application layer of the OSI model. A gateway is required to convert data packets from one protocol format to another before forwarding it, as it connects two dissimilar networks.

X.25 Standard Interface: X.25 is a protocol for interfacing to a Public Packet Switched Network. It is not a protocol used for implementing a network. Two systems that support X.25 can't necessarily be connected back-to-back. They can only be connected through a DCE in a Public Packet Switched. International Telegraph and Telephone Consultative Committee (ITTCC) developed X.25 as the standard interface between the Data Terminal Equipment (DTE) and Data Circuit Terminating Equipment

(DCTE). This recommendation has been widely accepted as the industry standard for public packet switched networks.

6.1.2.2 Types of Wide Area Networks

There are mainly two types of WAN:

Public Networks: These are those networks which are installed and run by the telecommunication authorities and are made available to any organization or individual who go for their subscription.

Private Networks: The basic technique used in all forms of private WAN is to use private circuits to link the locations to be served by the network. Between these fixed points the owner of the network has complete freedom to use the circuits in any way they want. They can use the circuits to carry large quantities of data or for high speed transmissions. Private wide area networks can be built using whatever standard technology is available.

6.1.2.3 Features of Wide Area Networks

- Developed in 1960s.
- Generally covers large distances (states, countries, continents).
- Medium : communication circuits connected by routers.
- Routers forwards packets from one to another following a route from the sender to the receiver. Store-and-Forward
- Hosts are typically connected (or close to) the routers.
- Typical latencies : 100ms - 500ms.
- Problems with delays if using satellites.
- Typical speed : 20 - 2000 Kbits/s.
- Not (yet) suitable for distributed computing.
- New standards are changing the landscape.

6.2 INTERNET

Before you understand what Internet is, you must understand what networking is. It is a method of connecting two or more computers, either by means of connecting them or through wireless. Now come to Internet. It is a network consisting of millions of machines. Millions of machines are networked together to share the data and information. Data you require may be scattered across the globe updated and kept consistent by the owner of the data and you can retrieve it when needed via Internet.

Now with the onward march of technology it is possible to keep a program that work with the data along with the data that it works on and calls upon both when needed, a sort of 'just in time' software that you call upon when you need and discard when no longer required.

You no longer need to locally store and maintain the data and programmes. Internet is not just one network. It is a co-ordinated union of networks. Computer users on the Internet anywhere in the world, very much like a telephone user can communicate with user anywhere in the world. So internet is also called Internet works. Internet is also the common language of different or computers dissimilar in hardware and software to communicate with each other, via a standard protocol (protocol is a set of rules and regulations for computers to communicate via networks).

Sitting on a PC at home one can trip round the globe in minutes, one can get any kind of information one

needs. Internet is a large source of enjoyable, important and up to data information, which can be accessed and shared by millions of users across the world. Every information on the internet is there because some person or group of people, somewhere in the world, had an idea, developed it and then most important, made it available to the entire world using Internet. It has become a major part of business.

6.2.1 Concept of Internet

All computers and other equipments that are given network are basically connected to each other with the help of cables. The messages travel across the network with the help of networking protocols. The protocols used over the Internet provide addresses for the computers attached to the physical network. In this way, different types of networks communicate with each other using the same protocol. To interpret the information being transmitted it is essential that the right software and hardware be in place.

The commonly used protocols are:

Internet Protocols (IP)

Transmission Control Protocol (TCP)

Together they are called as TCP/IP protocol. It offers a simple naming and addressing scheme, whereby resources on the Internet can be easily located.

6.2.2 Application of Internet

One can use Internet for many different purposes like as discussed below:

1. Sending and receiving E-mails (it is an instantaneous way of sending and receiving messages, called electronic mail) round the world at minimal price.
2. Finding information on any topic or can be used as educational tool. One can find information on infinite number of topics ranging from how to make a cake to how to write a program for a computer. To visit a bookstore on the Internet can be done on the Internet sitting at home PC.
3. One can participate in discussions on wide range of topics from recreational activities to scientific researches via a utility called Usenet news group.
4. It is also used to send data in the form of files from one computer to other with the facility called FTP (File Transfer Protocol). There are sites offering information on paid basis but on the other hand there are many sites, which provide information free of cost. These are called anonymous FTP sites. The biggest advantage of FTP is one doesn't have to wait for days to receive some information after ordering with FTP files as it will be available in minutes after ordering.
5. One can use it for research purpose. With every major university connected to Internet one can be sure to find information that helps in research projects.
6. It is also a form of education. Using Internet is a great learning experience. One will learn things from the content one is reading and will also be more proficient at navigating computer tools, forming searches for information. Writing and typing skills also improve.
7. One can enjoy reading jokes, stories, articles, play games with other users on Internet, join with chess matches and one can enjoy Internet relay chat to talk to different people round the world.
8. One can login on to other network as if one is a member of that network. This is done through a utility called Telnet. This is only possible if one gets permission to log on to that network.
9. To search some topics on the Internet one can use gopher.

10. Archive is a search utility that searchs on the Internet based on file names or partial file names.
11. One can make profits on the Internet. Internet can be an effective medium for business communications. Services such as gopher and World Wide Web (WWW) are the best ways to distribute information about your product or service. E-mail is a great medium to communicate with contacts and customers in business.
12. To find a particular world on the Internet in text documents one can use the utility WIAS (Wide Area Information System).
13. One can have a live talk with persons all round the world and can hold meetings as if sitting just by there side by video conferencing of multimedia conferencing.

6.3 SERVICE ON INTERNET

To understand how the information is transferred through the Internet, we will have to study more about the Internet technology. After all it is very strange that it allows you share information not in the form of written words but also allows you to have the information in the vocal form.

Remember what I had said earlier, about Packet Switching. This packet switching technology is still used to transfer the data. Digital data made up of a series of 0s (OFFs) and 1s (ONs) are grouped in unique sequences. Each sequences of 0s (OFFs) and 1s (ONs) have a particular meaning, which is translated by the computers to enable you to view the matter on your computer's screen. To understand it more clearly, do remember that computers do not understand languages in the manner in which we speak and write. Instead, they understand languages based on electrical impulses that go 'ON' and 'OFF'. Speaking scientifically, such a system is called the Binary System in which specific combinations of 'ON' and 'OFF" are used.

Thus, a message, sent by you through the Internet, first gets converted (translated) by your computer in to a digital format, made up of a series of ONs (1s) and OFFs (0s) that are grouped in specific and unique sequences. Each sequence of 1s and 0s has a particular meaning. At the final receiving point, these sequences are reconverted (re-translated) by your friend's computer so that your friend can read your message on his computer's screen.

It is not that the Internet is used only for sending and receiving information. It has its commercial aspect too. Internet today offers a number of standardized services to all its users. In fact, it is like a multipurpose tool to communicate with one another, collect information and enhance your knowledge about the subjects that you like, conduct research, play games, invest in shares or just look around (usually called browsing) in search of recipes or even jokes or the latest technological developments. The description that follows will acquaint you with some of the well-known ways in which Internet is used worldwide.

6.3.1 Information Retrieval

One of the most commonly used services on the Net comprises retrieval of information about various topics that interest you. This retrieval (getting) of information is made possible through the World Wide Web (popularly called WWW or W3).

6.3.2 Internet and E-mail

The Internet facility used to the maximum is e-mail. It involves writing messages on a computer and transmitting them to another computer so that the addressee can read them, thus saving paper, time, energy and cost. In fact, it can be said that e-mail is the essence of all communications on the Internet. Practically, everyone with Internet access does have an e-mail account.

6.3.3 Newsgroups (Usenet)

The Internet provides you a major avenue to communicate with large groups. Popularly, referred to as 'Newsgroups', this service is technically called Usenet and comprises a distributed bulletin board system. The information (news) shared by Usenet groups can be 'unmoderated' (unedited) or 'moderated' (edited.).

6.3.4 Accessing People

Internet would help you in locating your long lost friend, who was probably lost in school or college. That person must have an e-mail account. Rest is easy. For this purpose, you can visit a commonly used site such as whowhere (use your search engine to locate it by typing http://whowhere.lycos.com). Now, to find the e-Mail address, type the name of the person in the name field. Thereafter, type the e-mail server domain name (like hotmail.com) in the domain field. Once you click the Go Get It button, the result will be displayed on your computer's screen. You will also find that the on-screen display serves as a link, wherefrom, you can get the person's e-mail address.

6.3.5 Telnet

It is a text-based Internet service that connects you to a remote host (server). Using a special protocol known as the Network Terminal Protocol, it enables you to log onto another computer on the Internet and use its resources as if they existed on your own machine. To use this service, you need to provide your valid login and user password.

6.3.6 Chat

Everybody likes to chat. Even if it on the Internet. You can in fact chat with totally unknown people. Technically known as Internet Relay Chat (IRC), it is multi-user and multi-channel chatting net that allows users to communicate in real time. Remember! Chatting through IRC is in the written form, i.e., while communicating with some one, you type your message and the receiver responds (types back) with his/her comments. In short, it is a form of instant talking, almost like a telephone conversation but in a written form. Residing on many systems on the Net, it is a software, which provides access to a series of interactive services. By availing these services, one can chat or play on-line games with people on the Internet.

6.3.7 FTP (File Transfer Protocol)

It connotes an Internet service that transfers files from one computer to another. It is a common procedure to download and upload files over the Internet. With FTP you can login to another Internet site and transfer (meaning send or receive) files. FTP works on the client/server principle. A client program enables the user to interact with a server in order to access information and services on the server computer.

6.3.8 Anonymous FTP

Some sites have public file archives that you can access by using FTP with the account name 'anonymous' and your e-Mail address as the password. This type of access is called anonymous FTP.

6.3.9 E-commerce

e-commerce means doing business online. It refers to any manner of conducting business on line by an individual/organization. As part of e-commerce, large organizations also send data from the Internet to conduct research and plan their marketing strategies globally. With credit cards becoming more popular along with computerized banking services, payment for services through Internet is becoming very easy.

6.3.10 Employment Generation

Job placement agencies and employers have started to increasingly use the Internet as a source of recruitment by advertising on the Net to fill up vacancies. Side by side, people seeking job or better employment opportunities also use the Internet.

6.3.11 Medicare

Doctors now increasingly use the Internet to know the latest treatment techniques to benefit their patients. Hospitals sometimes use video conferencing to provide on-line guidance for conducting complicated operations.

6.3.12 Shopping Online

Some department stores offer their products, both new and old to Internet users to payment, which is usually made in advance through a credit card. While in the case of software, developers often post the software they have written – a process similar to posting a message. You can also download and use these programs free of cost and give a feedback to the programmer about its usefulness.

6.3.13 Entertainment

Internet now gives you unlimited opportunities to watch latest films, TV programs and listen to music. You can download your favorite movies and music from different sources.

6.3.14 World Wide Web (WWW)

The World Wide Web is a collection of million of files stored in thousand of computers (called Web server) all over world. Using WWW a user can download files, listen to sounds, view video files and jump to other documents or Net sites by using hypertext links.

6.3.15 Educational Opportunities

Suppose you wish to study in America after passing the Senior Secondary examination. Just surf the Web and you will find that almost every university in the U.S. maintains a web site. Each of these sites provides extensive information, ranging from courses available to credit prices, course fees, etc., details of programs leading to various degrees and career planning services

Lastly I can say that with the help of computer and Internet, you can see the World on your desktop itself. And that too anytime of the day.

6.4 WWW AND WEB-SITES

A global hypertext system that uses the Internet as its transport mechanism is called World Wide Web. In a hypertext system, you navigate by clicking hyperlinks, which display another document (which also contains hyperlinks). What makes the Web such an exciting and useful medium is that the next document you see could be housed on a computer next door-or halfway around the world. The Web makes the Internet easy to use.

Created in 1989 at the European Laboratory for Particle Physics (CERN), a research institute in Switzerland, the Web relies upon the HyperTExt Transport Protocol (HTTP), an Internet standard that specifies how an application can locate and acquire resources (such as document, sound or graphic) stored on another computer on the Internet. HTTP provides transparent, easy-to-use access to Web documents, FTP (File transfer Protocol) file archives, Gopher menus, and even UseNet newsgroups, users of Web

navigation software, called Web browsers, simply click on an underlined word or phrase, and HTTP takes care of locating and downloading the desired documents. Most Web documents are created using the HyperText markup language (HTML), a markup language that is easy to learn and will soon be supplanted by automated tools. Incorporating hypermedia (graphics, sound, animations, and video), the Web has become the ideal medium for publishing information on the Internet.

A key 1995 agreement on security protocols ensures that Web will quickly become an important commercial medium, in which consumers can browse on-line catalog uses and place orders without worrying about anyone intercepting the supplied credit card information.

6.4.1 Basic Features

Before we go any further in WWW we must learn more about the basics of it. We had earlier learned what Home page, Web page, Hypertext Hyperlinks, etc., mean. Now we will learn what all comes into play when a web page is opened. The following information is not sequential.

1. Information System
2. Graphical Navigation
3. Platform
4. Distribution
5. Accessing Information
6. Interactiveness

Let us read about them in details.

6.4.1.1 Information System

As we all know that Internet is full of information. It is upto you to explore it. This information is available in the form of a book. As you can jump from one page to another, the Web also allows you to skip from one page to another using the Hyperlink. Once this information is there on the screen, you can copy, move or transfer it to your hard disk for later reading.

6.4.1.2 Graphical Navigation

The best part of Web is that it can display both text and graphics with equal ease. What's more there are sites which have sound and video too. So much so that they can be called truly multimedia applications.

6.4.1.3 Platform

The World Wide Web is not limited to any one kind of machine, or developed by any one company. The Web is entirely cross-platform. It can be displayed on any computer hardware using any operating system.

6.4.1.4 Distribution

When you run the Internet and access any site, everything works in RAM. There is no hard disk space involved. The information is totally distributive and can be distributed anywhere even to the hard disk, only if the need be.

6.4.1.5 Dynamic

A web site goes through various changes at various instances. So everytime you load the site, you get the latest site on your screen. You need not go to buy any new software or hardware for that purpose. The web site developer would probably not come and tell you when the site is updated. So while getting the data from the site make sure that you are getting the latest data.

6.4.1.6 Accessing Information

As mentioned earlier, Internet is full of information. You can get the information from the net using any of the method, maybe FTP, Usenet, Telnet or even e-mail. Although the most popular way of getting the information is by using the software called browsers and the famous ones are Microsoft Internet Explorer and Netscape Navigator. Web browsers can also read files from other Internet services and you can create links to information on those systems just as you would create links to information on Web pages.

6.4.1.7 Interactiveness

This means that web sites are not just one way information. There are sites which ask for information from you, the users too. This information is mostly taken in the form of Form. This way the web site developers not only get the information but also are able to access and compile the information in any form.

6.5 ELECTRONIC MAILS

The Internet facility used maximum is e-mail. It involves writing messages on a computer and transmitting them to another computer so that the addressee can read them, thus saving paper, time, energy and cost. In fact, it can be said that e-mail is the essence of all communications on the Internet. Practically, everyone with Internet access does have an e-mail account.

6.6 COMMUNICATION ON INTERNET

Internet is a very big source of communication. Now, you can by sitting on your PC communicate with another person sitting on PC at any place in the World. This happens with the help of telephone lines, modem, wireless hi-fi systems, and other means of communications.

6.6.1 Newsgroups (Usenet)

The Internet provides you a major avenue to communicate with large groups. Popularly, referred to as 'Newsgroups', this service is technically called Usenet and comprises a distributed bulletin board system. The information (news) shared by Usenet groups can be 'unmoderated' (unedited) or 'moderated' (edited.).

6.6.2 Chat

Everybody likes to chat. Even if it on the Internet. You can in fact chat with totally unknown people. Technically known as Internet Relay Chat (IRC), it is multi-user and multi-channel chatting net that allows users to communicate in real time. Remember! Chatting through IRC is in the written form, i.e., while communicating with some one, you type your message and the receiver responds (types back) with his/her comments. In short, it is a form of instant talking, almost like a telephone conversation but in a written form. Residing on many systems on the Net, it is a software, which provides access to a series of interactive services. By availing these services, one can chat or play on-line games with people on the Internet.

6.7 BASIC INTERNET TERMINOLOGY

Before you start using (browsing/surfing) the Web, it is necessary for you to understand the following terms and their meanings specially in connection with the Internet:

Home page: It is the first page that you would see on the Website. Also known as the Welcome page. It is from here that you would start the navigation of various other pages of the site.

Hypertext and Hyperlinks: Information on the Web is made available in the form of Hypertext. It is a method of presenting information wherein some portion is highlighted. When this highlighted portion is selected, it displays more information on the topic/s that you choose.

The highlighted items selected by you are technically called Hyperlinks. In fact, they allow you to navigate from one Web document to another on the same computer or on a different computer in your own city, country or anywhere else in the world.

Internet Information Server: It is a group of Internet servers including the additional capabilities of Windows NT and Windows 2000.

Internet Protocol: It is responsible for the addressing and sending data from one computer to another computer.

Internet Service Provider: It is one gateway to the Internet. As mentioned earlier, you need this service to connect to Internet from your computer.

Multimedia: At the heart of the Web is the ability to display multimedia information, such as images, audio, video, animation, and other multimedia data types.

Transmission Control Protocol: It uses a set of rules to exchange messages with other Internet points at the information packet level.

Web Browser: It is a software application that resides on your PC and can display text, images, and multimedia data found on different Web pages. It allows you to specify a Web page, navigate using links, and bookmark your favourite Web pages, the commonly used Web browsers are Internet Explorer and Netscape Navigator.

Web Server: A Web server refers to a location (computer) on the Internet that contains information in the form of Web pages. Technically speaking, a Web Server means a computer on the Internet having the capability to run software. A page stored on a Web server can be accessed by Web users. It may also be mentioned here that Internet Service Providers (ISPs) normally offer space on their Web servers on which their registered users can publish their Web pages free of charge.

Web Site: A Web site comprises of a collection of Web pages that may be maintained and updated by an organization like a Government or University department, a business house, a research institution etc. even a single individual can also create and maintain his/her own Web site to promote certain ideas. The information on a Web site is stored in the form of a series of files that may be stored on one or more computers. Do remember that the material on a Web site is stored in Hypertext.

Web Page: A Web page refers to a document on the Web. Web pages can be used to display written text, show pictures, play music/sound effects and run video. Do also remember that you need to use Hyper Text Markup Language (HTML) to create Web pages.

LET US REVISE

1. When more than two computers are connected to each other and share information, resources and remote systems then this is called Networking.
2. PAN is used for communication among the personal devices (intrapersonal communication), or for connecting to a higher level network and Internet. The reach of a PAN is typically a few meters.
3. A network covering a small geographic area, like a home, office, or building is called Local Area Network.
4. WAN technologies generally function at the lower three layers of the OSI reference model: the physical layer, the data link layer, and the network layer.
5. If connected to the Internet, the intranet or extranet is normally protected from being accessed from the Internet without proper authorization
6. The length of the cable connecting a computer to a LAN also varies depending on the LAN.
7. One of the major benefits of implementation of LAN is sharing expensive resources such as storage devices, printers, etc.
8. Three major categories of services used in LANs are: File Server; Printer Server and Modem Server.
9. Some popular LAN operating systems are : Novel Netware; Ethernet; Corvus; ArcNet LAN; Server Omni Net; PC Net; IBM PC LAN and Etherlink Plus, etc.
10. Features of LAN are: Typically connects computer in a single building or campus; Developed in 1970s; Medium : optical fibres, coaxial cables, twisted pair, wireless; Low latency (except in high traffic periods); High speed networks (0.2 to 100 Mb/sec); Speeds adequate for most distributed systems; Problems : Multi media based applications; Typically buses or rings and Ethernet, Token Ring.
11. Internet is network of networks.
12. Nobody controls Internet.
13. NSFnet is the backbone of communication service for the Internet.
14. Intranet is a private network within a company or an organization.
15. A message, sent by through Internet, first gets converted by your computer into a digital format, made up of a series of ONs (1s) and OFFs (0s).
16. For connecting to Internet, you need a computer system with a software like Microsoft Internet Explorer or Netscape Navigator loaded into it; A telephone line. A modem (modular-demodulator); a connection provided by Internet Service Provider (ISP).
17. Home page is the first page that you would see on the Website.

MULTIPLE CHOICE QUESTIONS

1. Internet is network of :
   (a) Networks (b) Humans (c) Workers
2. Initially Internet was used for:
   (a) Medicine (b) Military Intelligence (c) Communications
3. What is not needed for running Internet:
   (a) Modem (b) Telephone Line (c) Printer

4. Using Internet you can chat with other users :
   (a) Yes (b) No
5. A browser allows you to search and log :
   (a) web sites (b) hard disk (c) modem
6. LAN is :
   (a) Local Area Network (b) Local Around Network (c) Love Area Network.
7. WAN is :
   (a) Windows Area Network (b) Wide Area Network (c) Well Area Network
8. e-mail is part of the Internet usage:
   (a) Yes (b) No
9. e-commerce is another name for doing ______ on Internet.
   (a) logging (b) business (c) research.

TRUE/FALSE QUESTIONS

1. A network covering a small geographic area, like a home, office, or building is called Local Area Network.
2. If connected to the Internet, the intranet or extranet is not protected from being accessed from the Internet without proper authorization.
3. A network bridge connects multiple network segments at the data link layer (layer 2) of the OSI model.
4. Routers are the networking device that forwards data packets along networks by using headers and forwarding tables to determine the best path to forward the packets.
5. Closely related to the concept of a model is that of an architecture.
6. Nobody controls Internet.
7. Internet can be used for various purposes.

MATCHING COLUMNS

Match the matter in Column A with the matter in Column B.

Column A	Column B
A. LAN	1. Personal Area Network
B. WAN	2. Client Computer
C. MAN	3. Wiring Connector
D. CAN	4. Local Computer
E. PAN	5. Stores and Sends Information
F. Node	6. Local Area Network
G. Host	7. Arrangement of Networking
H. HUB	8. Wide Area Network
I. Router	9. Campus Area Network
J. Topology	10. Metropolitan Area Network

FILL IN THE BLANKS WITH APPROPRIATE WORDS

a. Internet Service Provider	b. Hypertext	c. Intranet
d. Web	e. Home page	f. network of networks
g. Internet	h. Web pages	i. Internet Protocol

1. Internet is ____________________.
2. ________ is a private network within a company or an organization.
3. __________ is the first page that you would see on the Website.
4. Information on the Web is made available in the form of ____________.
5. ___________ is responsible for the addressing and sending data from one computer to another computer.
6. ________________ is one gateway to the Internet.
7. A Web site comprises of a collection of ________.
8. A Web page refers to a document on the ______.
9. ________ can be used for various purposes.

DESCRIPTIVE TYPE QUESTIONS

1. What is Internet?
2. How was Internet developed?
3. What all you need for running Internet?
4. What is a computer network?
5. Define the various types of networks.
6. Which are the various hardware components required for networking?
7. Describe the various models of network computing.
8. What is Local Area Networks?
9. Describe Wide Area Networks.
10. Describe the various network services.
11. Write short notes on the following:

Information Retrieval	Internet and e-mail
Newsgroups (Usenet)	Accessing People
Telnet	Chat
FTP (File Transfer Protocol)	Anonymous FTP
e-commerce	Employment Generation
Medicare	Shopping Online
Entertainment	World Wide Web (WWW)
Educational Opportunities on the Net	

ANSWERS TO OBJECTIVE QUESTIONS

Multiple Choice Questions

1. a	2. b	3. c	4. a
5. b	6. a	7. b	8. a
9. b			

True False Questions

1. T	2. F	3. T	4. T
5. T	6. T	7. T	

Matching Columns

A. 6	B. 8	C. 10	D. 9
E. 1	F. 2	G.. 4	H. 3
I. 5	J. 7		

Fill in the Blanks with Appropriate Words

1. f	2. c	3. e	4. b
5. i	6. a	7. h	8. d
9. g			

Chapter 7

WWW and Web Browsers

7.1 WEB BROWSING SOFTWARE

In broad terms it is the software which allows you to view the web sites. It is a multi-function software package which allows you to access, download, and display multimedia documents. Before we go any further, let us see what the basic features of a Web browser are.

7.1.1 Basic Features of Web Browsers

In all probability a web connection would have the following:

1. Client computer
2. Host computer
3. Internet Service Provider (ISP)
4. Communication network

Let us see what these are:

Client Computer: This is the base computer from where you access the Internet. This computer as expected would have modem, a telephone line attached to it and a software to browser the Internet, such as Internet Explorer or Netscape Navigator.

Host Computer: This is the computer which holds all the Web pages. They have giga bytes of hard-disk storage, considerable Random Access Memory (RAM) and a high speed processor. It runs special Web server software that reads requests sent from various client computers. The host computer also retrieves and sends an appropriate information to the client.

Internet Service Provider (ISP): It is the agency which acts as a media for providing the Internet access.

Communication Network: The message from client computer is converted to signals and transferred through telephone lines. These then reach the host computer. So to reach the signals fast you have to have very fast network. In India this is done by VSNL. In fact, ISP has a stack of modems that accepts multiple incoming calls simultaneously. Your connection is complete when it reaches the host computer.

7.1.2 Internet Explorer

The first page that you see on the screen of the browser on the screen is the home page of that browser. So in case of Netscape Navigator you will see Netcentre while in the case of Internet Explorer you would see msn.com. These software can be launched as you would launch any other software in a Windows environment. This can be done from the Start button, its icon on the desktop or even from Quick Launcher on the Taskbar. Once launched you would see their initial page on the screen. Here I am showing the opening page of Internet Explorer.

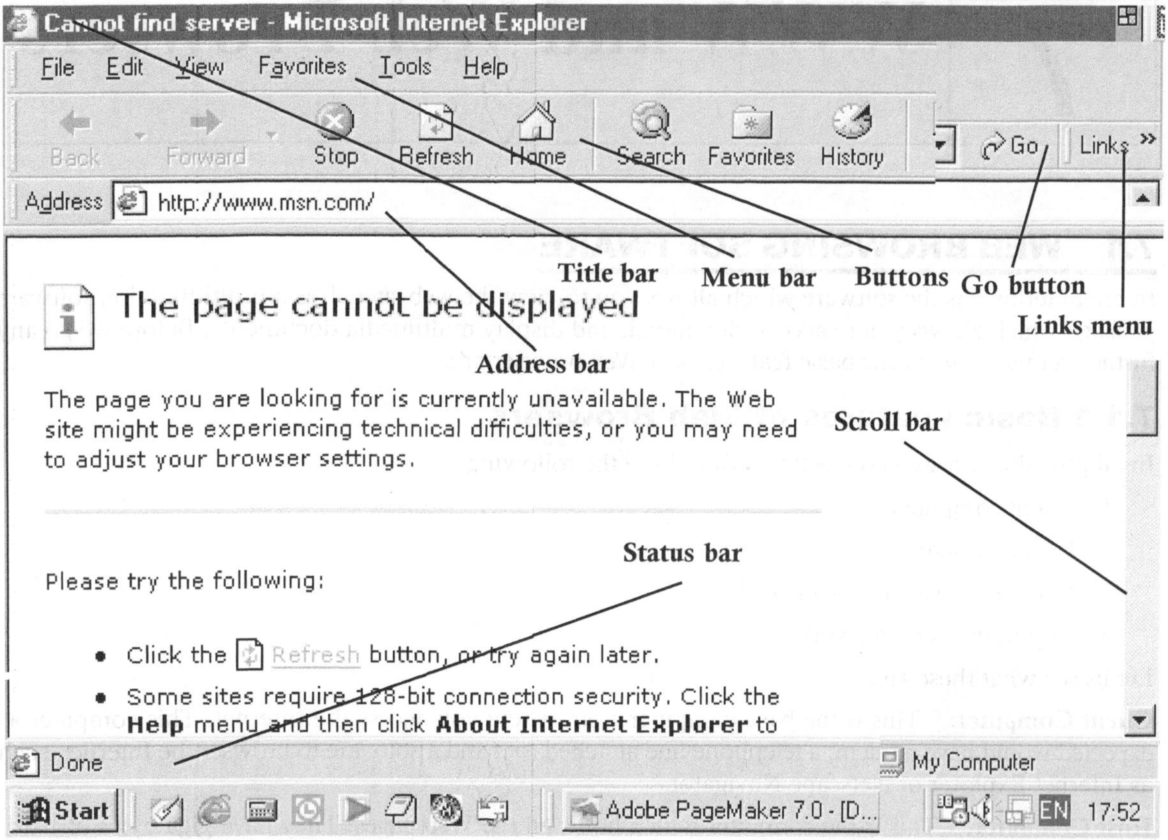

7.1.2.1 Working of Internet Explorer

As you would see from the Internet Explorer screen, there are various bars, having various buttons. Let us see what all them mean.

Title Bar	It displays the title of the current Web page.
Menu Bar	It gives access to all the features of the Explorer.
Buttons	The Internet toolbar contains some graphically styled buttons. They provide convenient shortcuts that enable you to navigate through the Web.
Link Menu	This menu selects several links to Microsoft related sites.
Go Button	After typing the URL, click on this button to display the Web page.
Scroll Bars	These bars help to move or scroll the screen up or down.
Status Bar	This bar displays information relating to the activity that is being currently carried out.
Address Bar	The URLs of various Web sites are typed on this bar.

7.1.2.2 Toolbar Buttons

As you can see there are various buttons on the toolbar of Internet Explorer. Let me explain what each one of them stands for.

Back	It displays a page in the list of previously viewed pages.
Forward	It displays a page in the list next to viewed pages.
Stop	It stops downloading the current page.
Refresh	It downloads the current page again, ensuring that the latest version of the Web page is displayed.
Home	It displays the home page.
Search	It displays or hides the Search Explorer bar, which provieds access to Internet search engines.
Favorites	It displays or hides the Favorites Explorer bar, which provides access to your favorite sites.
History	It displays or hides the History Explorer bar, that provides access to sites you may have visited recently.

Full Screen	It switches to or from full screen view, which provides maximum viewing space for Internet Explorer's document area.
Mail	It launches your mail or newsreader program, by default Outlook Express, and lets you send links and pages to others via e-mail.
Print	It prints the current page, if your printer is online.

7.1.2.3 Getting to a Web Site

As mentioned earlier, you can start the browser by one of the 3 methods mentioned. Now to go to the site, you have to type the name of the site complete with all the dots. You must ensure that you have made the connection to the net via your modem and telephone line, before pressing the Go button.

If the address of the site to be visited is not known, enter keyword/s in the Search Box and click the Search button on the toolbar and follow the instructions that appear on the screen. You can also use the Search Engines like Yahoo, AltaVista, Google, HotBot. Enter the keywords in the Search Box and click Search or Go.

In the following case the required address was typed to get the website.

You can similarly type the name and press Go to get the required website.

7.1.2.4 Working with Favorites

As you can see there is a button called Favourite on the toolbar. This helps you in working with your favourite websites. These favourites can be obtained from the Start button too. The ones here are provided by the Microsoft but you can always add and delete from them.

Adding an item to Favorites: The Add To Favorites command allows you to create a favorite page listing for the page you are currently viewing. Do the following to add.

1. Click the Favorites menu and choose Add to Favorites. Or click Add to Favorites on the Favorites Explorer bar. The Add Favorite dialog box appears.

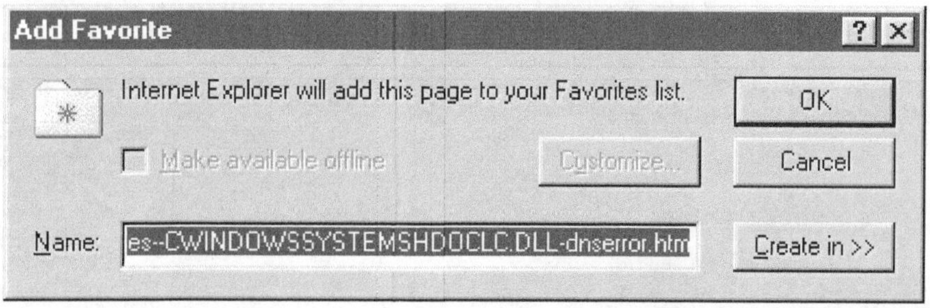

2. In the Name text box, make changes you want to the name of the page.
3. In the Create In box select the location of the favorite page.
4. Click the Ok button. This creates a favorite page listing for the current page.

Using Search Button: The search button here is an easy access to various search engines. To use the search feature, use the Search button. To use the search feature do this.

1. To choose a search engine click the customize button in the window.
2. Choose the desired category for your search.

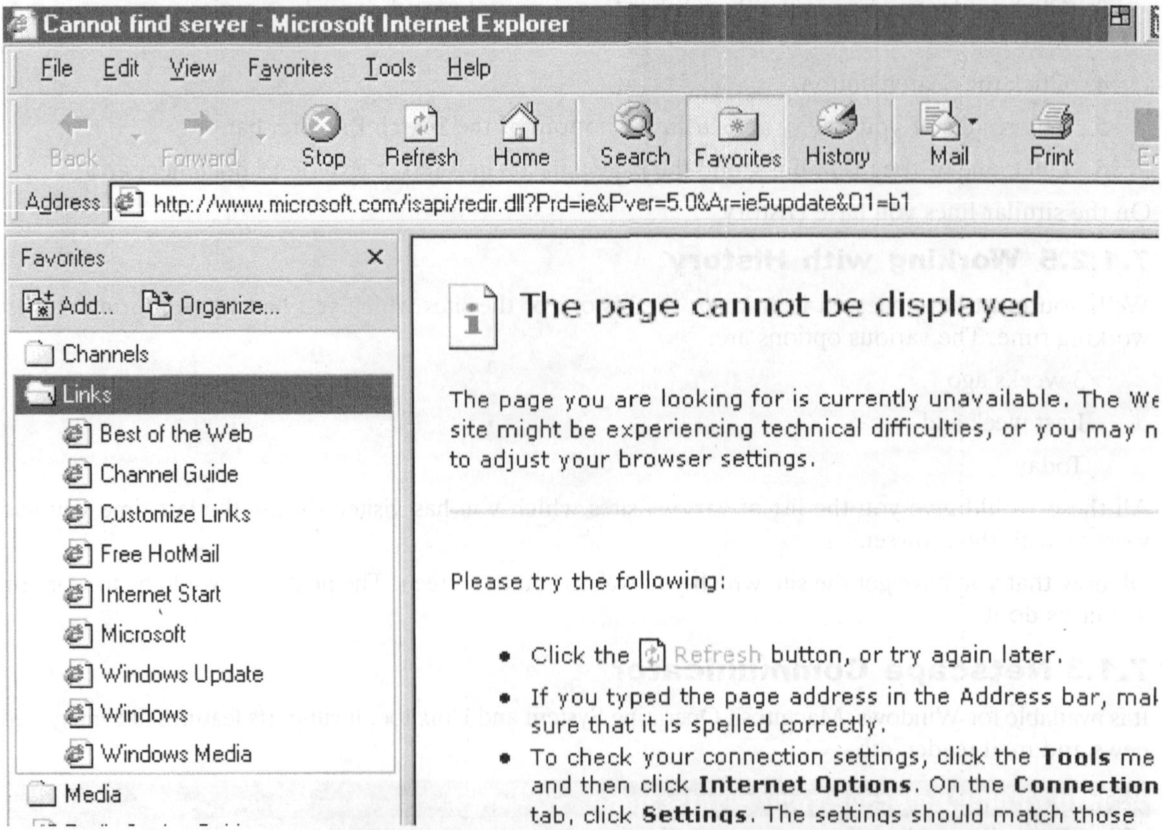
Cannot find server - Microsoft Internet Explorer
File Edit View Favorites Tools Help
Back Forward Stop Refresh Home Search Favorites History Mail Print
Address http://www.microsoft.com/isapi/redir.dll?Prd=ie&Pver=5.0&Ar=ie5update&01=b1
Favorites
Add... Organize...
Channels
Links
Best of the Web
Channel Guide
Customize Links
Free HotMail
Internet Start
Microsoft
Windows Update
Windows
Windows Media
Media
The page cannot be displayed
The page you are looking for is currently unavailable. The We
site might be experiencing technical difficulties, or you may n
to adjust your browser settings.
Please try the following:
Click the Refresh button, or try again later.
If you typed the page address in the Address bar, mal
sure that it is spelled correctly.
To check your connection settings, click the Tools me
and then click Internet Options. On the Connection
tab, click Settings. The settings should match those

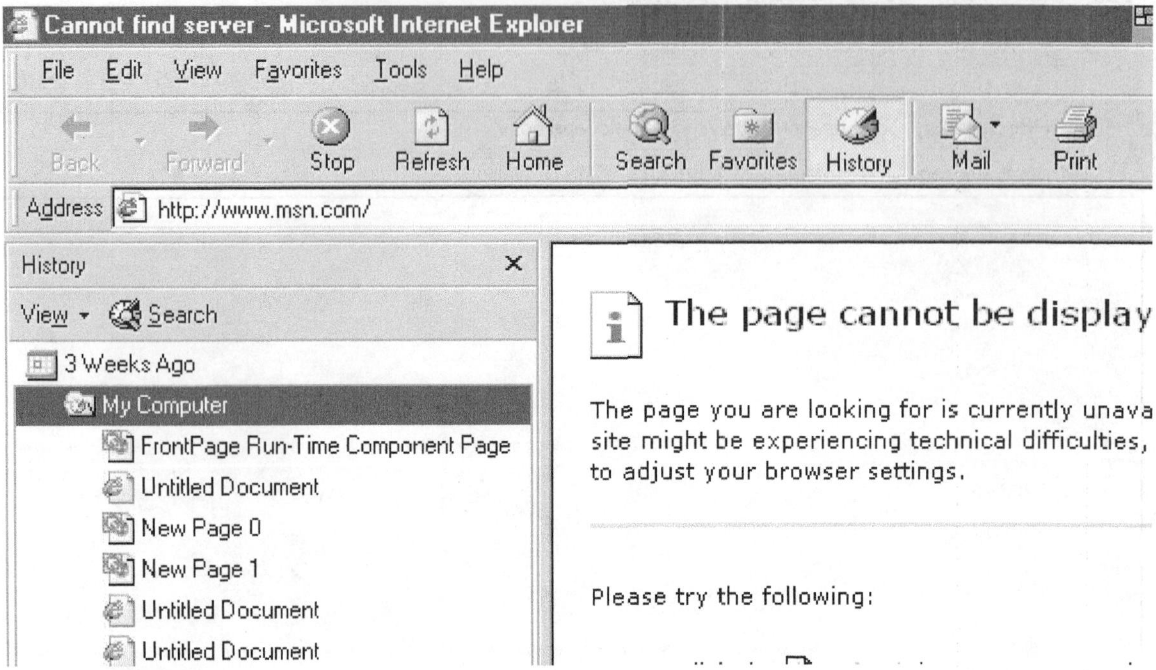
Cannot find server - Microsoft Internet Explorer
File Edit View Favorites Tools Help
Back Forward Stop Refresh Home Search Favorites History Mail Print
Address http://www.msn.com/
History
View Search
3 Weeks Ago
My Computer
FrontPage Run-Time Component Page
Untitled Document
New Page 0
New Page 1
Untitled Document
Untitled Document
The page cannot be display
The page you are looking for is currently unava
site might be experiencing technical difficulties,
to adjust your browser settings.
Please try the following:

3. Click in the text box in the Search Explorer bar, and type the words or topics you are trying to find.
4. Click the Search button.
5. The results of your query appear in the bottom of the Search Explorer bar.
6. Click one of the result links, and the page appears in Internet Explorer's document area.

On the similar lines you have History.

7.1.2.5 Working with History

Well, you must have guessed it. It keeps the history of the sites which you had visited during the last working time. The various options are:

3 weeks ago

Last week and

Today

All these would give you the list of various sites which you has visited during the last time you had worked with the browser.

Ok now that you have got the site which you wanted on the screen. The next step would be to work on it. Let us do it.

7.1.3 Netscape Communicator

It is available for Windows, Macintosh Operating System and Unix too. It supports features like integrated news and mail reader, etc.

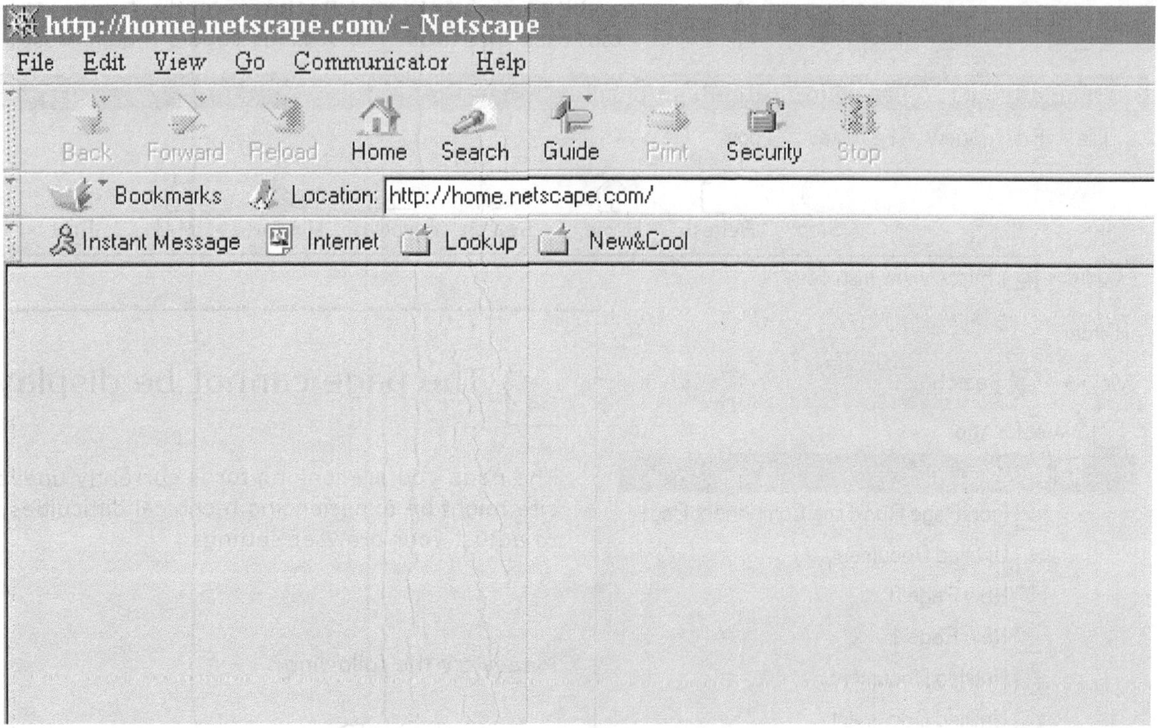

7.2 SURFING THE INTERNET

To upload a web site a host computer and server software is needed. This manages the communications protocols and the related software required to create a Web site on the Internet. The host machine usually uses Unix. There are different types of servers available.

A web server mostly performs the following jobs:

1. The server software includes configuration files and utilities to secure and manage the Web site in a variety of ways.
2. It passes requests to run CGI (Common Gateway Interface) scripts to the CGI applications. These scripts run external mini-programs, such as a database lookup or interactive forms processing.

7.2.1 Giving the URL address

A URL describes the location and a method of accessing a resource on the Internet. For example, the URL http://www.adobe.com describe the name of the site of the company called Adobe Corporation. The term URL is also used to describe the address system used on the Web.

Each URL is unique, identifying a particular point on the Internet. It consists of a string that supplies the Internet address of a resource on the WWW along with the protocol by which the resource is accessed. The most common URL is 'http' which gives the Internet address of a World Wide Web page. Some other URL types are 'gopher' which give the Internet address of a Gopher directory, and 'ftp' which gives the address of a FTP resource. All Web sites have URLs. One could say a URL is what a telephone number is to a telephone or a street address is to a house.

7.2.2 Search

So far we have learned about the various search engines. Let us know in brief know how these search engines work. As was mentioned in the case of various search engines above, each one of them uses either the directories, spiders and even the robots for searches. A spider strips away many other markup features so that it simply sees the pure HTML source. Search sites are basically of the following two types:

7.2.2.1 Search Directories

They contain a list of websites organized hierarchically into categories and sub-categories. These are created manually.

7.2.2.2 Search Engines

It continuously sends out the so called spiders which start on a homepage of a server and pursue all links stepwise.

When you open a search engine, it asks you what to search. If it is to be case sensitive, make sure that you are using the right case. Click Ok to begin the search and the result is shown in the form of URLs leading to the pages you need.

They are programs that locate needed information in a database, but especially an Internet accessible search service that enables you to search for information on the Internet. To use a search engine, you type one or more key words; the result is a list of documents or files that contain one or more of these words in their titles, descriptions, or text. The databases of most Internet search engines contain World Wide Web (WWW) documents; some also contain items found in Gopher menus and File Transfer Protocol (FTP) file archives.

Compiling the database requires an automated search routine called a spider, forms filled out by Web authors, or a search of other databases of Internet documents. The effectiveness of search engine can be measured in terms of Indexing and Term specificity. Since the Internet is a vast collection of information, it is difficult to find specific information you actually need. Therefore, search engines are more than a boom.

7.2.3 Moving around in a web-site

To move around the web site in a server, you can use the following keyboard shortcuts.

Enter	It activates the selected link
Shift + F10	It displays the context menu for the current link
Tab	It selects the next link
Ctrl + Tab	Cycled between frames
Shift + Tab	It selects the previous link
Alt + right arrow	It moves to the next page
Alt + left arrow	It returns to the previous page
F5	It refreshes display of the current page
Esc	It stops display of the current page
Ctrl + N	It opens a new window
Ctrl + O	It opens a document
Ctrl + P	It prints the current page
Ctrl + S	It saves the current page as a file

7.2.4 Printing or Saving portion of Web Pages

Following are some of the things which can be performed on the web pages.

7.2.4.1 Copying Data

For this follow the following steps:

1. Open the site from where you have to copy the data.
2. Select the data to be copied
3. Click the Edit menu
4. Click at Copy.
5. Minimize the software.
6. Open the software/document where you want to paste.
7. Paste the required data.

7.2.4.2 Saving Pictures from a Web Page

1. Open the site which has the required picture.
2. Right-click on the picture to be saved.
3. Choose the Save As option to save the picture.

4. Your picture would be saved on the clipboard and you can paste it in any other software/document.

7.2.4.3 Saving a Page or Picture without opening

1. Right-click the link for the item to be saved.
2. Choose the Save Target As option to save the picture.
3. Your picture would be saved on the clipboard and you can paste it any other software/document.

7.2.4.4 Making pages available for Off-line viewing

1. On the Favorites menu, click Add to Favorites.
2. Select the Make available off-line Check Box.
3. Your selected page would be available for the off-line viewing.

7.2.4.5 Downloading Files/Folders from Internet

The Internet allows you to download a fantastic variety of files/programs. You can access the needed material by using an Internet Browser. For this purpose, point to a link that is connected to a file on a Web site. You will find downloading to be easier from Web sites that are in your time zone. At night, you may often find the sites to be less busy and therefore, more easily accessible.

7.2.4.6 Printing a web Page

The various print options available to you are:

1. Printing all documents linked to the current page.
2. Printing a list of links contained on the current page.

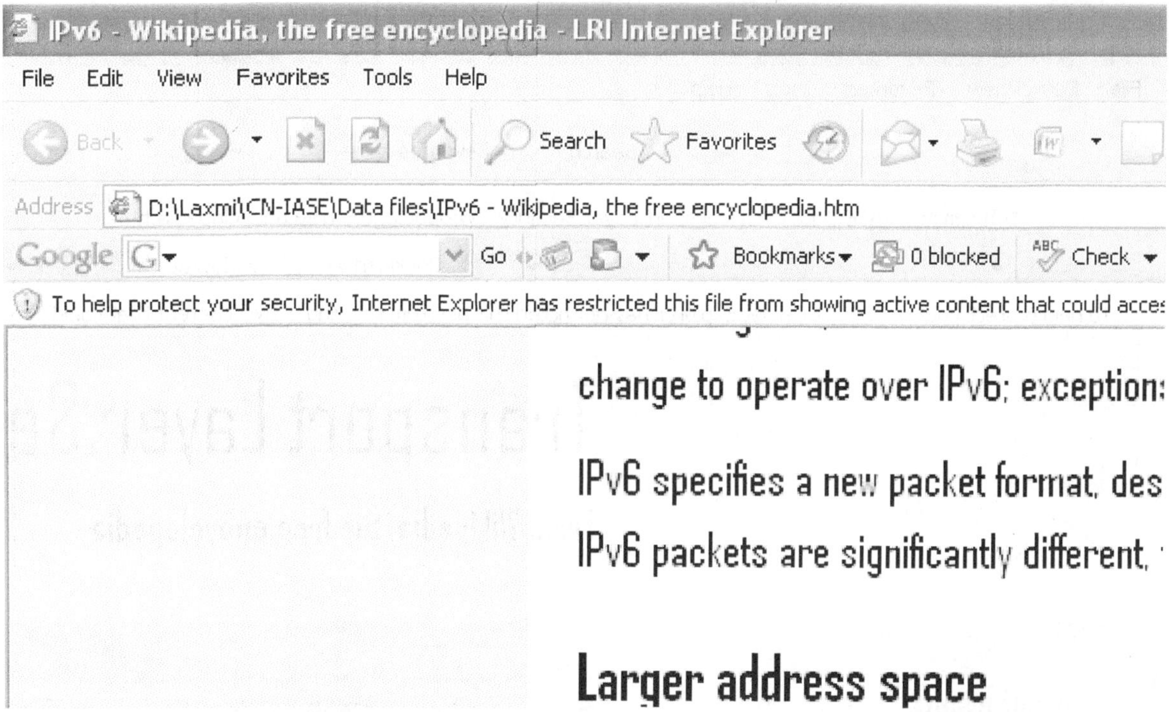

3. Printing selected portions of a page that has been constructed using frames. This option is available only if the current page has frames.

To print a Web page using the options, do the following:

1. Click at the File menu, and choose Print.
2. The print dialog box, as shown above, appears.
3. Select the printer, the pages and number of copies you want.
4. Click Ok to start printing.

7.2.4.7 Options of the Print dialog box

Option	Description
As laid out on screen	It prints the entire page as it appears on the screen
Only the selected frame	It prints one selected frame. This option requires you to select a few words in the area you want to print, prior to printing
All frames individually	It prints each frame on a separate page
Print All Linked documents	This option generates a printout of every document linked to the current page
Print Table of Links	This option produces a short printout listing all the URLs mentioned in the document

7.3 CHATTING ON INTERNET

Everybody loves chatting, specially girls. So how can Internet be far behind. It also allows you to chat with other unknown parties. As in the case of browsers, here also there are software which allow you to

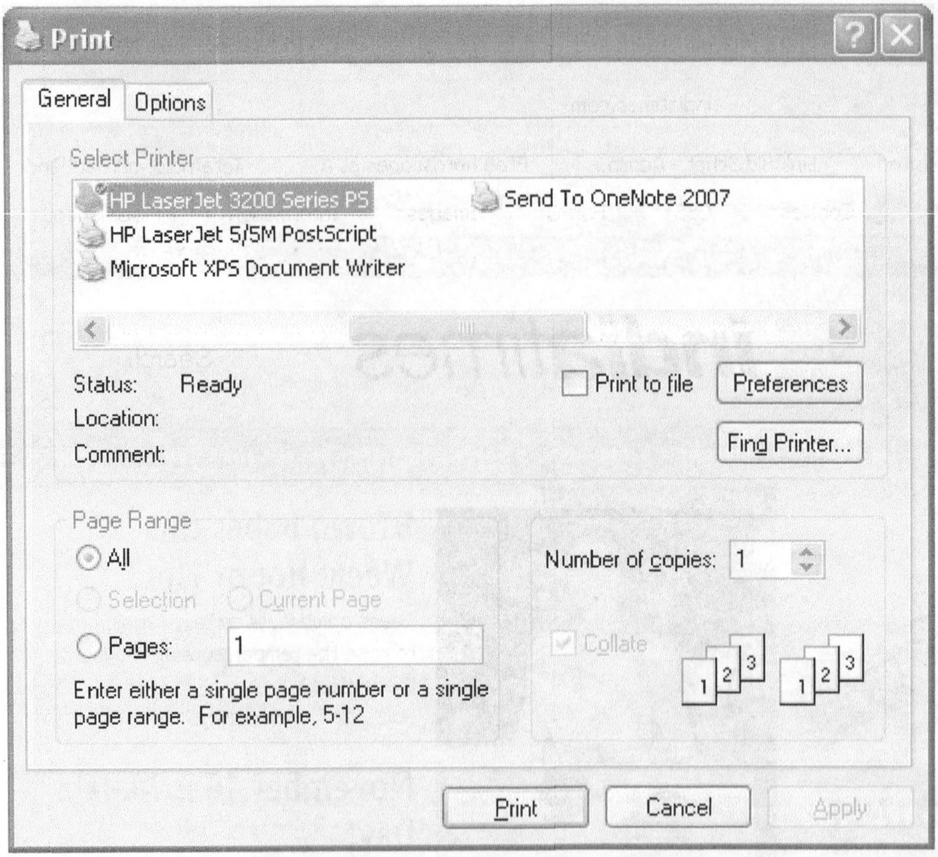

chat. Well, the popular among them is Yahoo! again. There are others too like, lycos.com, sifty.com, 123india.com, etc. To chat at yahoo.com you have to follow the following procedure:

1. Log on the site yahoo! and then click at Chat button.
2. The Yahoo chat page opens. When you chat for the first time you have to get registered at yahoo.
3. Click at sign up button to register.
4. The terms and conditions page opens, click at I Accept button to accept the conditions.
5. Sign on Yahoo!ID page. Fill in the details and click submit button. Once you get your Yahoo!ID, you can sign in and chat.
6. Now it will log you on its chat server and you select the chat room you want to join and you can now chat with other users. Names of other users, who are currently chatting, are displayed in a list box.
7. Type the message you want to submit and click submit button.
8. On some servers, you need to click at Send button to send your message.
9. On most chat sites, you can also change rooms by clicking at Room link. Room basically referes to a group of approachable chat users. One can chat with all other users in the same chat room. To chat with users in other chat rooms, one needs to change the rooms.

Firefox
Tata Indicom Broadband
Indiatimes: India News, Business, Movies...
www.indiatimes.com
Most Visited
Link Bid Script - Admin...
Free horoscopes at A...
TataIndicomBroadband
Disable
Cookies
CSS
Forms
Images
Information
Miscellaneous
Outline
infibeam.com
Aam Aadmi Offer
Enter
promo-code
MANGOPEOPLE
get 10% or upto
Rs 2000
cash back
in your
infibeam wallet
Shop Now
indiatimes
beta
Search
HOME
NEWS
ENTERTAINMENT
LIFESTYLE
TECHNOLOGY
BTown Babes this Week: Hot or Not?
These bombshells certainly know how to raise the temperatures! Who looks the hottest?
Bollywood - 7 hours ago
November 10 is Malala Day!
A tribute to Malala Yousufzai, the 15-year-old Pakistani girl who was shot in the head by the Taliban.
Asia - 7 hours ago
NEWS
Times of India
Economic Times
Navbharat Times
Maharashtra Times
Vijaya Karnataka
Ei Samay
e-Paper
OUR SITES
BoxTV
NEWS »
It Happens Only in India!
IndiaTimes - 7 hours ago
RSS better prepared for elections than Cong: Cong MP
Govt to Probe Communal Tension in UP
460 Places on Terror Watchlist
EC Bans 'Vajpayee Bags' in Himachal
ENTERTAINMENT »
WAGs

10. On chat servers, rooms are defined on the basis of shared interests like parenting, teenagers, ITpeople, society, Life and style, etc.

7.3.1 Working of IRC

When you send your message on Internet chat, your message is sent from your server to other servers where people on your channel are logged on. The message gets transferred from server to server. Each server sends you message to the client software of the people connected to the channel at each server. People can read and respond to your message at their computers.

7.3.1.1 Chat Software

There are various types of software available for chatting. Each one of them serves different purposes.

7.3.1.2 Internet Relay Chat

For this you need software like mIRC or Ircle.

7.3.1.3 Web-based Chat

For this you need web browser such as Netscape or Internet Explorer.

7.3.1.4 America Online Program

For this you need to have ICQ, AOL Instant Messager or other program.

7.3.1.5 Online conferencing

For this you need to have a conferencing program.

7.3.2 Basic Commands of IRC

Command	*Description*
/flush	It discards remaining output for the current command
/help	It displays a list of all IRC commands
/help command	It displays help information about the specified command
/help newuser	It displays information for new users
/join channel	It lets you join the specified channel
/list	It lists information about all channels
/list channel	It lists information about a specific channel
mode * + pi	It makes the current channel completely private
/msg.text	It sends a message to the last person who sent a message to you
/nick	It displays your own nickname
/nick nickname	It allows you to change your current nickname
/query	It stops sending private messages
/set novice off	It allows more advanced options, such as joining multiple channels
/who channel	It shows who is on the specified channel
/who *	It shows who is joined to the current channel

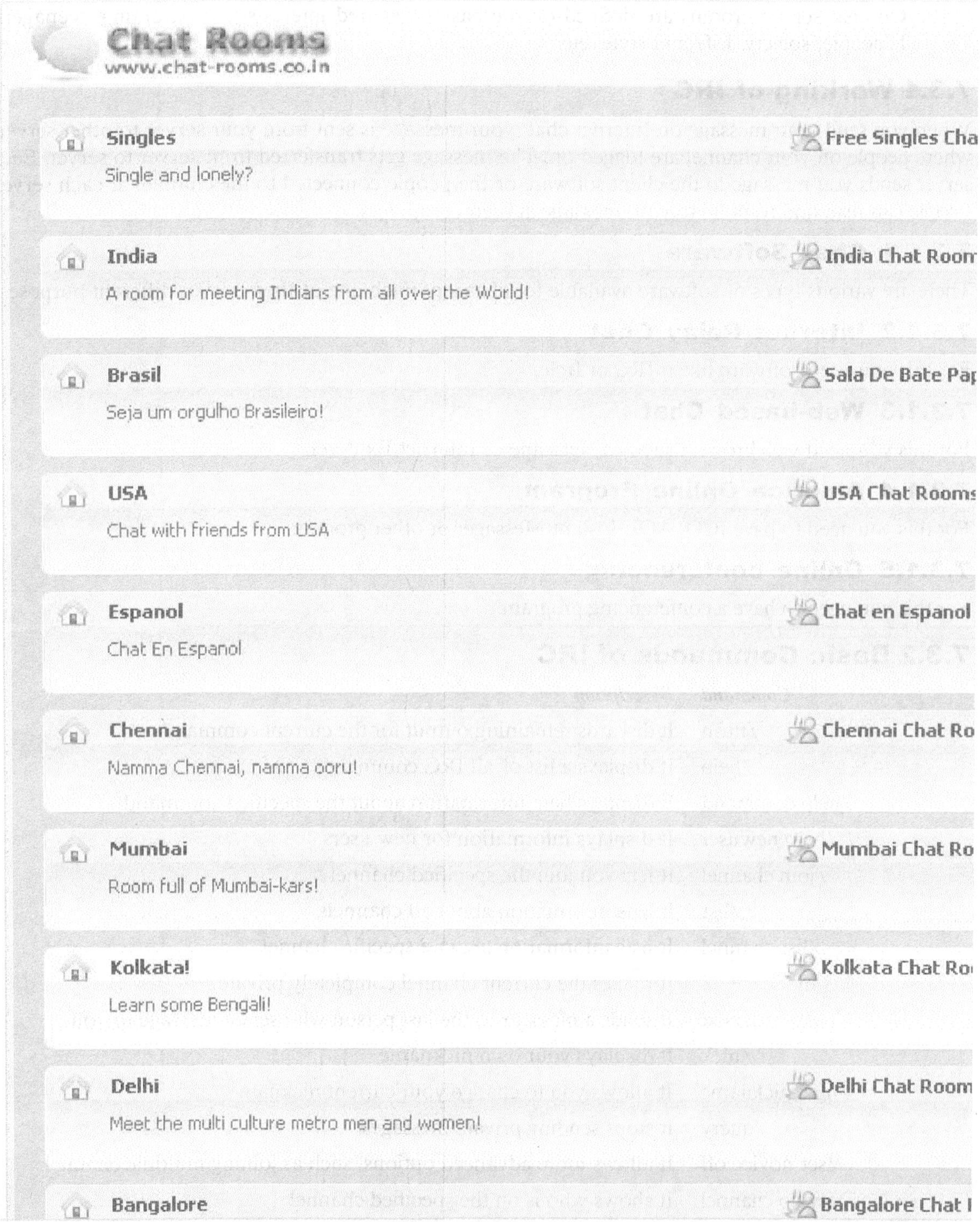
Chat Rooms
www.chat-rooms.co.in
Singles
Single and lonely?
Free Singles Cha
India
A room for meeting Indians from all over the World!
India Chat Room
Brasil
Seja um orgulho Brasileiro!
Sala De Bate Pap
USA
Chat with friends from USA
USA Chat Rooms
Espanol
Chat En Espanol
Chat en Espanol
Chennai
Namma Chennai, namma ooru!
Chennai Chat Ro
Mumbai
Room full of Mumbai-kars!
Mumbai Chat Ro
Kolkata!
Learn some Bengali!
Kolkata Chat Ro
Delhi
Meet the multi culture metro men and women!
Delhi Chat Room
Bangalore
Bangalore Chat

/who is nickname	It displays complete information about the person nickname
/whois*	It displays all information about everyone.

7.3.3 Chat Servers

These servers like Internet servers are there to give you information about the users. Each server has its own number of users. It has a host name, the name of the host that it accesses.

7.3.4 Smileys

Chatting allows you to show your face expressions in the form of smileys. Since while chatting you are not face to face, these smileys are the best way of conveying the message. Some of these are used in e-mails too. The complete list of them have been given in the e-mail section. You can in fact, divide the smileys into various categories, for example, the following one:

1. Basic Smileys
2. Emotional Smileys
3. Mega Smileys
4. Midget Smileys
5. Usenet Smileys
6. Widely used Smileys

LET US REVISE

1. Browser is the software which allows you to view the web sites.
2. Client computer is the base computer from where you access the Internet.
3. Host computer is the computer which holds all the Web pages.
4. ISP is the agency which provides the Internet access.
5. Common browsers are Microsoft Internet Explorer and Netscape Navigator.
6. There are various bars and buttons on the opening screen of the Explorer.
7. There are buttons on the toolbar to do various things.
8. Favorites helps you in working with your favourite websites.
9. Search button helps you in accessing various search engines.
10. History shows you the sites which you had visited during the last working time.
11. You can copy data from a web page.
12. You can download a web page into your hard disk.
13. You can also print the web page.
14. Internet allows you to chat with unknown users of Internet.
15. Popular software for chatting is Yahoo!
16. Chat servers are used for passing message from one place to another.
17. Each chat server has a name.
18. Smileys are the best way of conveying the message.

MULTIPLE CHOICE QUESTIONS

1. Browser is :
   (a) Hardware (b) Software (c) Computer
2. Search button helps you in accessing :
   (a) Search engines (b) Hard Disk (c) Directories
3. History shows the sites visited, Today, Last Week and :
   (a) 1 week ago (b) 2 week ago (c) 3 week ago
4. You cannot copy an image from the web site :
   (a) Yes (b) No
5. You can print a web page on the screen:
   (a) Yes (b) No
6. In India, the main networking service provider is :
   (a) BSNL (b) VSNL (c) MTNL

TRUE/FALSE QUESTIONS

1. Client computer is the base computer from where you access the Internet.
2. ISP is the agency which provides the Internet access.
3. There are various bars and buttons on the opening screen of the Explorer.
4. Favorites does not help you in working with your favourite websites.
5. History shows you the sites which you had visited during the last working time.
6. You cannot download a web page into your hard disk.
7. Internet allows you to chat with unknown users of Internet.
8. Chat servers are not used for passing message from one place to another.
9. Smileys are the best way of conveying the message.

MATCHING COLUMNS

Match the matter in Column A with the matter in Column B.

Column A	Column B
A. HTTP	1. To get information from users
B. Yahoo!	2. Web Browser
C. FTP	3. Place where the incoming messages are kept
D. Icons	4. Graphic representation of emotions
E. Forms	5. Search Engine
F. Lynx	6. Network of Networks
G. Inbox	7. Place where the outgoing messages are kept

H. Similey
I. Outbox
J. Internet

8. Hyper Text Transfer Protocol
9. Graphic representation of software
10. File Transfter Protocol

FILL IN THE BLANKS WITH APPROPRIATE WORDS

a. Yahoo! b. Telnet c. Local d. URL
e. VT-100 f. HTTP g. Search engines h. spiders

1. ________ is used as the communication protocol to transport hypertext documents over the Internet.
2. A __________ describes the location and a method of accessing a resource on the Internet.
3. __________ are used to search for different information on the net.
4. ________ is a popular search engine.
5. Search is done using ________.
6. ________ is the Internet service that allows you to log in to a remote Internet computer.
7. In telnet terminology, your computer is called the ________ computer.
8. To use Telnet, you turn a Telnet client program, which connects you to a remote Internet host and then emulates a ________ terminal.

DESCRIPTIVE TYPE QUESTIONS

1. What is a browser?
2. Define the various items on the Internet Explorer screen.
3. Describe the various buttons on Toolbar.
4. What are Favorites?
5. What is Search button used for?
6. Write short notes on the following:
   Client Computer Host Computer
   Internet Service Provider
7. What is Chat?
8. Describe the processing of registering for Internet Chat.
9. Describe the various types of smileys.

ANSWERS TO OBJECTIVE QUESTIONS

Multiple Choice Questions

1. b 2. c 3. c 4. b
5. a 6. b

True False Questions

1. T	2. T	3. T	4. F
5. T	6. F	7. T	8. F
9. T			

Matching Columns

A. 8	B. 5	C. 10	D. 9
E. 1	F. 2	G. 3	H. 4
I. 7	J. 6		

Fill in the Blanks with Appropriate Words

1. f	2. d	3. g	4. a
5. h	6. b	7. c	8. e

Chapter 8 Communication and Collaboration

8.1 INTRODUCTION

It is not that the Personal Computers are for personal use only. They can be used for sharing of information too with others having similar type of equipments. Logically it sometimes is feasible to have a number of PCs then having a bigger computer which can give the same thoughput as the number of PCs. But, overall it becomes an expensive proposition and sometimes is not fisible, specially for individuals and small businesses or small companies.

Another problem arises for those who are physically placed at a distance. They would need to send messages and receive messages, or use the same data at, or share program at, many different locations. One answer to this problem is to keep separate data files at each location, but this approach is very costly and potentially a dangerous solution. It is very expensive to maintain these redundant files of data and difficult to ensure the continuing accuracy of data at any one location. The solution of both, the need for more power and the ability to receive, send messages and share data, are found in data communication technology.

8.1.1 Communicating Data

When you send data from one location to another using any electronic means, it is called Data communication. Linking one computer to another permits the power and resources of that computer to be tapped. It also makes possible the updating and sharing of data at different location. Computers that are located in the same room office building, can communicate data through a direct cable link. For example, in a multiuser system, a single processing unit is linked by several dumb terminals through direct cables. Since multi-user systems link inexpensive terminals instead of the more expensive personal computers used with other systems, multi-user systems provide cost savings for small companies purchasing a complete system or adding users to a system currently in operation. In general, multi-user systems are most appropriate for companies requiring a shared data base for extensive data input and output. Computer located far away from the processor use a special form of data communication – telecommunication or telegraph. For example, teller and point-of-sale terminals are spotted in locations away from computers: airlines, car-rentals, railway reservation systems and hotel reservation systems have thousands of terminals located many miles from the processors. In these cases, the process of using communication facilities such as the telephone system and microwave relays to send data between computers is a form of data communication, sometimes referred to as telecommunication, or tele-processing.

Dr. George Stibitz was the first to link computer and computing devices and send data way back in 1940. He used telegraph lines to send data files from Dartmouth College in New Hampshire, USA to a Bell Laboratories calculator in New York City, USA. An early large-scale business application was the Sabre passenger reservation system, developed in late 1950s and early 1960s by American Airlines. Hundreds of terminals were linked to the central processing unit. Communication usage has grown steadily since then.

Now-a-days minis and larger machines are in constant communication with outlying terminals. With available attachments, computers can use telecommunications channels to link up with information

retrieval services, banks and electronic bulletin boards. An electronic-mail message can be sent from one place to another and an answer can be returned by electronic mail as soon as it is received. This service eliminates the hassle of continually trying to return a call, or long mail delays.

8.1.1.1 Data Transmission Techniques

Telephone lines are used for sending human voice. They were never planned to send Data. So to send data through telephone lines you have to convert the data into the format which can be read by telephone lines. These are called analog signals. For data communication between computers to take place over a telephone line, the digital pulses of the data to be transmitted must be converted to an analog signal before they are transmitted.

After its journey over the telephone lines, the analog signal must be re-converted to digital pulses so that it can be used by the receiving computer. The process of converting digital pulses to an analog signal is called modulation. And the process of re-converting an analog signal to digital pulses is called demodulation. The device that accomplishes modulation-demodulation process is called a modem.

There are 3 basic types of modems used in microcomputers.

8.1.1.2 Acoustic Coupler Modem

This is used to provide the necessary interface. The acoustic coupler is attached to a portable terminal and a standard telephone handset fits into rubber cups located on the coupler. The acoustic coupler modem sends data through the mouthpiece and receives data through the earpiece of the handset. The digital pulses produced by the terminal are converted into audible tones that are picked up by the handset receiver. The signals from these tones are then sent to the processor location where another modem converts them back to digital pulses.

8.1.1.3 External Direct-Connect Modem

It is external to the computer and connects directly to computer via RS-232 serial interface cable and to the telephone line via a modular phone jack. An external direct-connect modem may be equipped with microprocessors, storage chips and specialized communication chips. Such intelligent modem is programmed to automatically perform dialing, disconnecting functions, check the operating status using status lights and speakers, self test to verify the modem's ability to correctly transmit data, respond to commands from a communication program and change the speed at which data are transmitted.

8.1.1.4 Internal Direct-Connect Modem

It has all the needed communication circuitry on a plug-in board that fits into one of the expansion slots inside the computer. Internal direct connect modem also links directly to the telephone line via a modular phone jack.

These modems have many of the same special features as the external direct connect modems.

8.1.2 Communcation Channels

It is actually the media through which data is transmitted from one place to another. There are 3 types of communication channels.

8.1.3 Wire Cable

These are the most popular and widely used channels to transmit data from one location to another. This is so because it is cheaper and easier to use. Wire cable includes telegraph lines, telephone lines and coaxial cables. An advantage of wire cable is that the technology used to transmit data over wire cables

is standardized, thus reducing the compatibility problems. A disadvantage of wire cable is that it is subject to electrical interference making it less reliable than other types of communication channels. Another disadvantage is that wire cable must transmit data in analog form. Therefore, digital data must be converted to an analog signal before they reach the wire cable. This conversion not only needs special hardware, i.e., modem but also slows down the transmission of digital data. Various items used are:

8.1.3.1 Telephone Lines

Telephone lines may be used to transmit computer data using the modems. The lines themselves may be either leased or switched.

8.1.3.2 Leased Lines

A leased line is a telephone line that is leased for the express purpose of maintaining a communication channel between two computers. The line is not shared with any other users and is available at all times for data communication between the computers. A leased line is similar to a telephone connection that is always open. Both computers are always listening for a signal to start the communication. Leased lines are used in computer networks where computers or terminals in the network must be in constant contact with one another. For example, leased lines are used in a network employing point-of-sale terminals, as the terminals must be in constant contact with the main computer. Leased lines are often conditioned to limit the level of noise on the line. Conditioned leased lines are usually necessary to carry on high speed data communication. Security requirements often require that leased lines be shielded from outside interference and unauthorized snooping.

8.2 INTRODUCTION TO E-MAIL

Since the facility of e-Mail has been provided by Internet, people have more or less stopped using the post. It has been in fact, named as Snail mail, or the mail which moves at the snail speed. Whereas electronic mail is fast and moves over from one computer to another electronically at an amazing speed. Most of the Internet users are very happy with this facility. In fact, you can send not only the text, but pictures and graphics too. Most of the offices are sending their mail through computers. No more fussy papers or carbons. In fact, there is no need to file them too. All is stored in computers and can be accessed whenever needed. All you need is to open an e-mail account and start mailing your letters even if you do not have a computer. You can send the mail using your account number from any Cyber cafe too.

So to work with e-mail you must have an account of your own. For this, as already mentioned in the earlier chapter, each popular search engine allows you to open an e-mail account. Here, in our case, I am using the account opening process of Hotmail.com.

8.2.1 Opening of E-mail account

The following are the popular sites which allow you to open an e-mail account:

Yahoo	http://www.mail.yahoo.com
Hotmail	http://www.hotmail.com
Rediff	http://www.deiff.com
Mailcity	http://www.mailcity.com

Besides these most of your ISPs would allow you to open an account. Please remember that these e-mail services are all free and the sites do not charge any amount for using the same.

8.3 STRUCTURE OF AN E-MAIL

Like a formal letter e-mail also is divided into various sections. In a good business letter, you would have, date, the name and address of the person to whom the letter is addressed, salutation, text matter, sender's name, etc. Most of these you would find here too but with some difference. Lets see what an e-mail is supposed to have.

Headers: It is very important that your header must be loud and clear for it can be seen and read from a distance too.

To: The To: field contains the e-mail address of the person to whom you are sending the e-mail. If you are sending e-mail to someone in your own domain, you do not need to include @ domain.

From: In most of the cases, you would not be typing this, since it would be taken from the system. It in fact includes your e-mail address.

Subject: The Subject: field should contain a very short description (20-30 characters) of what your message is about. This field can also be called Subject of the Message: or simply message. It is not compulsary to have a subject.

Cc: You can send the copy of the same e-mail to another person. For this you have to mention the e-mail address of the second receipt. The software would take care that the same message is sent to the second recepient too.

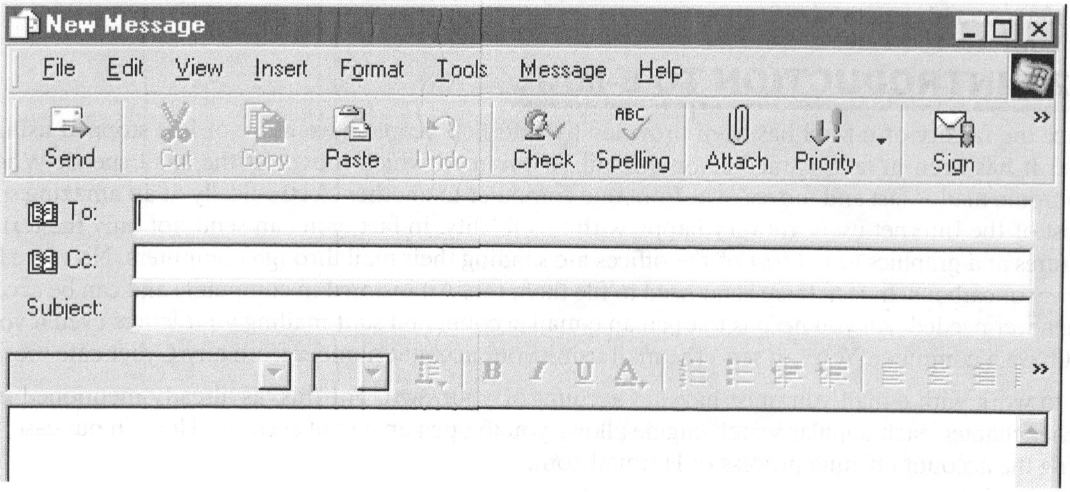

Bcc: It is the short form of Blind Carbon Copy, which gives you a way of copying and transmitting an e-Mail message to another person, without the first person (the main addressee), knowing about it.

Attachments: Using this option you can attach a file created in other software along with this e-mail. In most of the cases while applying for a job, the letter is typed in the e-mail text and the bio-data which is mostly in some word processing mode, attached to it.

Date: Date and time are usually taken from the system. You need not type it.

Body: The body of an e-Mail message is simply the text that you want to send to the other person.

8.4 ATTACHMENTS

You can attach files to your message, and you also attach or include as text the items in your Outlook folders.

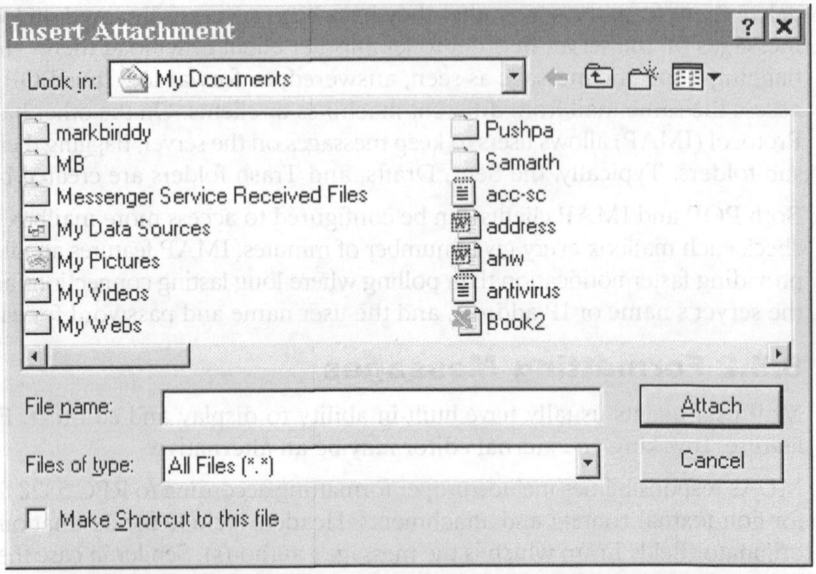

8.4.1 Attaching a File

1. From the Insert menu, choose Attachment or Picture whichever the case maybe.

   Or

   Click the Insert File button on the Standard toolbar.
2. In the Insert File dialog box, select the file you want to attach and click Insert.

The file icon appears at the bottom of the message. The recipient can view the attachment by double-clicking its icon.

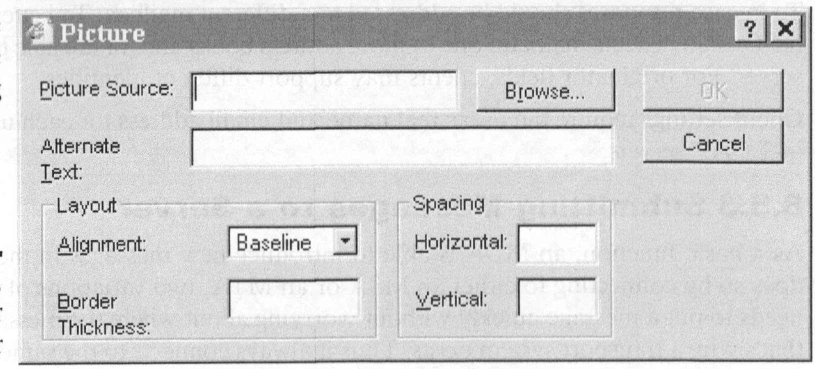

8.5 E-MAIL CLIENTS

An email client, email reader, or more formally mail user agent (MUA), is a computer program used to manage email.

Specifically, the term email client may refer to any agent acting as a client toward an email server, regardless of it being a mail user agent, a relaying server, or a human typing on a terminal. In addition, a web application providing message management, composition, and reception functionality is sometimes considered an email client.

8.5.1 Retrieving Messages from a Mailbox

Like most client programs, an MUA is only active when a user runs it. Messages arrive on the Mail Transfer Agent (MTA) server. Unless the MUA has access to the server's disk, messages are stored on a remote server and the MUA has to request them on behalf of the user. In the first case, shared disk, a user logs on a server and runs an MUA on that machine. The MUA reads messages from a conventionally formatted storage, typically mbox, within the user's HOME directory. The MTA uses a suitable mail delivery agent (MDA) to add messages to that storage, possibly in concurrence with the MUA. This is the default setting on many Unix systems. Webmail applications running on the relevant server can also benefit from direct disk access to the mail storage.

For personal computing, and whenever messages are stored on a remote system, a mail user agent connects to a remote mailbox to retrieve messages. Access to remote mailboxes comes in two flavors. On the one hand, the Post Office Protocol (POP) allows the client to download messages one at a time and only delete them from the server after they have been successfully saved on local storage. It is possible to leave messages on the server in order to let another client download them. However, there is no provision for flagging a specific message as seen, answered, or forwarded, thus POP is not convenient for users who access the same mail from different machines or clients. On the other hand, the Internet Message Access Protocol (IMAP) allows users to keep messages on the server, flagging them as appropriate. IMAP provides sub-folders. Typically, the Sent, Drafts, and Trash folders are created by default.

Both POP and IMAP clients can be configured to access more mailboxes at the same time, as well as to check each mailbox every given number of minutes. IMAP features an idle extension for real time updates, providing faster notification than polling where long lasting connections are feasible. Client settings require the server's name or IP address, and the user name and password for each remote incoming mailbox.

8.5.2 Formatting Messages

Mail user agents usually have built-in ability to display and edit text. Editing HTML text is a popular feature. Invoking an external editor may be an alternative.

MUAs responsibilities include proper formatting according to RFC 5322 for headers and body, and MIME for non-textual content and attachments. Headers include the destination fields, To, Cc, and Bcc, and the originator fields From which is the message's author(s), Sender in case there are more authors, and Reply-To in case responses should be addressed to a different mailbox. To better assist the user with destination fields, many clients maintain one or more address books and/or are able to connect to an LDAP directory server. For originator fields, clients may support different identities.

Client settings require the user's real name and email address for each user's identity, and possibly a list of LDAP servers.

8.5.3 Submitting Messages to a Server

As a basic function, an MUA is able to introduce new messages in the transport system. Typically, it does so by connecting to either an MSA or an MTA, two variations of the SMTP protocol. The client needs to put a message quickly without worrying about where the message eventually will be delivered: that's why a transport system exists. Thus it always connects to the same preferred server, however, how does that server know that it should accept and relay submissions from that client? There are two ways. The older method recognizes the client's IP address, e.g. because the client is on the same machine and uses internal address 127.0.0.1, or because the client's IP address is controlled by the same internet service provider that provides both internet access and mail services. The newer method, since the SMTP protocol has an authentication extension, is to authenticate. The latter method eases modularity and nomadic computing.

Client settings require the name or IP address of the preferred outgoing mail server, the port number (25 for MTA, 587 for MSA), and the user name and password for the authentication, if any. There is a non-standard port 465 for SSL encrypted SMTP sessions, that many clients and servers support for backward compatibility. Transport Layer Security encryption can be configured for the standard ports, if both the client and the server support it.

8.6 NETSCAPE MAIL CLIENTS

Like Microsoft even Netscape has also got its own mail software called Netscape Messenger. It supports

full-featured mail options. It looks like the Microsoft Internet Mail. With the help of Netscape messenger you can receive your e-mail and news very easily and quickly. Netscape messenger has a full feature of sending a mail to more than one person at a time.

8.6.1 Steps to send an E-mail using Netscape Messenger

- Click on the Mail icon on the loweer right corner of the Netscape Messenger Window or Choose Windows and then Netscape Mail.
- Netscape asks for your mail password. Type the password in the Password Entry Dialog box and then click OK button.
- Netscape display, the Netscape Mail window. Click on the To Mail toolbar button to display the Messenger Composition window.
- Type the recipient's mail address in the MailTo: text box.
- If you want to send copies of this message to more than one person then type the appropriate addresses in the Cc: text box.
- Type the subject for the message in the Subject: text box.
- Type the body of the message and then click Send button.

8.7 OUTLOOK EXPRESS

Outlook Express is an e-mail/news client that is included with Internet Explorer versions 4.0 through 6.0. As such, it is also bundled with several versions of Microsoft Windows, from Windows 98 to Windows XP, and is available for Windows 95 and Mac OS 9. In Windows Vista, Outlook Express was superseded by Windows Mail, then again by Windows Live Mail as separate software in Windows 7. Microsoft Entourage, sold as part of Microsoft Office for Macintosh, has replaced the Macintosh version.

Outlook Express is a different application from Microsoft Office Outlook. The two programs do not share a common codebase, but do share a common architectural philosophy. The similar names lead many people to incorrectly conclude that Outlook Express is a stripped-down version of Microsoft Office Outlook. Outlook Express uses the Windows Address Book to store contact information and integrates tightly with it. On Windows XP, it also integrates with Windows Messenger.

Microsoft Internet Mail and News was a freeware e-mail and news client and ancestor of Outlook Express. Version 1.0 was released in 1996 following the Internet Explorer 3 release. This add-on precedes the Internet Mail profile for Microsoft Exchange 4.0 bundled in Windows 95. Version 2.0 was released at the end of 1996. In 1997 the program was changed and renamed as Outlook Express and bundled with Internet Explorer 4. The executable file for Outlook Express, msimn.exe, is a holdover from the Internet Mail and News era. Internet Mail and News handled only plain text and rich text (RTF) e-mail, lacking HTML e-mail.

At one point, in a later beta version of Outlook Express 5, Outlook Express contained a sophisticated and adaptive spam filtering system; however this feature was removed shortly before launch. It was speculated on various websites and newsgroups at that time, that the feature was not stable enough for the mass market. Nearly two years later, a similar system, using a similar method of adaptive filtering, appeared as a feature of Microsoft Office Outlook.

Internet Explorer 5 required Outlook Express 5 to save Web Archive files.

Outlook Express 6 SP3 is the latest version which is part of Windows XP SP3. Extended support for Windows XP SP3, which covers security hotfixes, will end in 2014.

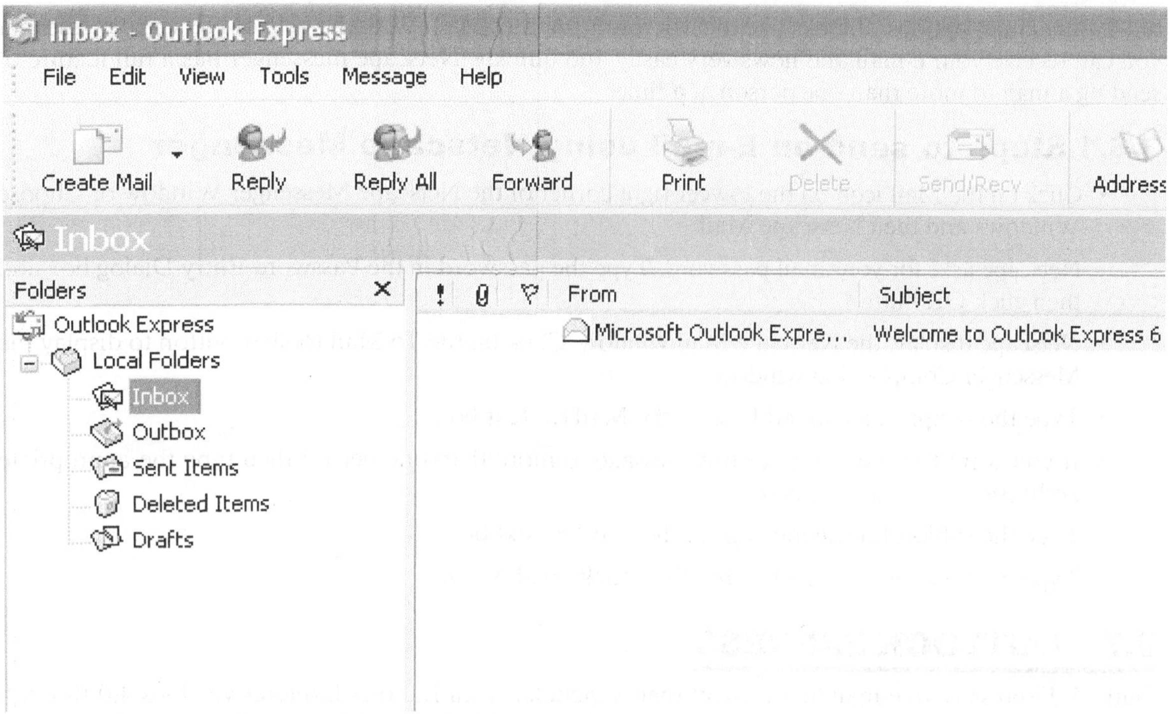

In October 2005, Microsoft announced that Windows Vista would exclusively include a new application named Windows Mail, based on large parts of Outlook Express source code. Microsoft was also concurrently developing Windows Live Mail Desktop (later renamed to Windows Live Mail), a mail client for its Hotmail service. Windows Live Mail was released in November 2007. In the future, support for Outlook Express and Windows Mail will be discontinued in favour of Windows Live Mail.

8.8 WEB BASED E-MAIL

Each E-mail service - whether it is an online service, commercial e-mail service, has its own way to handle mail. Most of the E-mail services use the Internet as their gateway (describe the path how messages are passed from one service to another service). Internet connects the computers around the world so that people could share information from e-mail service to someone's system, the message will travel across the Internet to reach its destination. We have given only the addressing of the message properly so that the Internet knows where to deliver the message. Here is some web based free E-mail account such as HotMetal and rediffmail.com, that offer web based e-mail access.

You can send mail in several ways while working with Internet. Following are the commands which are related to E-mail button on the Internet Explorer's toolbar.

- **Read Mail:** Opens Outlook Express and displays the content of your Inbox.
- **New Message:** Creates a new Outlook Express Mail Message.
- **Send a Link:** Create a link to attach files with e-mail message.
- **Read News:** Opens Outlook Express News for reading news.

8.9 E-MAIL ENCRYPTION

With no encryption, much like for postcards, email activity is plainly visible by any occasional eavesdropper. Email encryption enables to safeguard privacy by encrypting the mail sessions, the body of the message, or both. Without it, anyone (examples: the government (warrantless wiretapping, great firewall of China), fellow wireless network users such as at an Internet cafe or other public network, whether the network is open or not) with network access and the right tools can monitor email and obtain login passwords.

All relevant email protocols have an option to encrypt the whole session. Remarkably, those options prevent a user's name and password from being sniffed, therefore they are recommended for nomadic users and whenever the internet access provider is not trusted. On sending mail, users can only control encryption at the hop from a client to its configured outgoing mail server. At any further hop, messages may be transmitted with or without encryption, depending solely on the general configuration of the transmitting server and the capabilities of the receiving one.

Encrypted mail sessions deliver messages in their original format, i.e. plain text or encrypted body, on a user's local mailbox and on the destination server's. The latter server is operated by an email hosting service provider, possibly a different entity than the internet access provider currently at hand.

8.9.1 Encryption of the Message Body

There are two models for managing cryptographic keys. S/MIME employs a model based on a trusted certificate authority (CA) that signs users' public keys. OpenPGP employs a somewhat more flexible web of trust mechanism that allows users to sign one another's public keys. OpenPGP is also more flexible in the format of the messages, in that it still supports plain message encryption and signing as they used to work before MIME standardization.

In both cases, only the message body is encrypted. Headers, including originator, recipients, and subject, remain in plain text....

8.9.2 Standards

While popular protocols for retrieving mail include POP3 and IMAP4, sending mail is usually done using the SMTP protocol.

Another important standard supported by most email clients is MIME, which is used to send binary file email attachments. Attachments are files that are not part of the email proper, but are sent with the email. Most email clients use an X-Mailer header to identify the software used to send the message. According to RFC 2076, this is a common but non-standard header.

protocol	*use*	*plain text or encrypt sessions*	*plain text sessions only*	*encrypt sessions only*
POP3	**incoming mail**	**110**		**995**
IMAP4	**incoming mail**	**143**		**993**
SMTP	**outgoing mail**	**25**		**465**
MSA	**outgoing mail**	**587**		
HTTP	**webmail**		**80**	**443**

RFC 4409, Message Submission for Mail, details the role of the Mail submission agent.

RFC 5068, Email Submission Operations: Access and Accountability Requirements, provides a survey of the concepts of MTA, MSA, MDA, and MUA. It mentions that "Access Providers MUST NOT block users from accessing the external Internet using the SUBMISSION port 587" and that "MUAs SHOULD use the SUBMISSION port for message submission."

8.9.3 Port Numbers

E-mail servers and client use the following TCP port numbers by default, unless configured for specialized installations.

Note that while webmail obeys the earlier HTTP disposition of having separate ports for encrypt and plain text sessions, mail protocols use the STARTTLS technique, thereby allowing encryption to start on an already established TCP connection. RFC 2595 discourages the use of the previously established ports 993 and 995.

8.10 ADDRESS BOOK

Windows Address Book is a component of Microsoft Windows that lets users keep a single list of contacts that can be shared by multiple programs. It is most commonly used by Outlook Express. It was introduced with Internet Explorer 3 in 1996 and improved in subsequent versions. The Windows Address Book API can query LDAP servers or read/write data to a local .wab file. In Windows Vista, Windows Address Book was replaced with Windows Contacts.

The Windows Address Book is an application that has a local database and user interface for finding and editing information about people, making it possible to query network directory servers using Lightweight Directory Access Protocol. Other applications can also use the WAB. Microsoft Office Outlook uses its own PST store for email messages. However, it can import contacts from the .WAB format. Microsoft Exchange uses .PAB file for personal address book.

8.10.1 Features

- Can store comprehensive contact information in tabs including personal and business information
- Integrates with Outlook Express.
- Programmable API to work with other applications. Applications can also extend functionality such as adding more tabs and fields to store additional custom information, or customizing the toolbar.
- Can store contacts inside contact groups and folders.
- Can selectively send email to contacts only in plain text for additional security.
- Can export and import cards to and from vCard 2.1 and CSV formats. Can also import from LDIF and other formats.
- Search for entries in the contact database, arrange contacts by first name or last name.
- Automatically add contacts from received email.
- Prints contact lists as memo, business card or phone list styles.

8.11 SIGNATURE FILE

You can have Outlook add a signature, a special tag line, to each message you send.

8.11.1 Creating Default Signature

1. From the Tools menu, choose Options.
2. On the Signature tab of the Options dialog box, click at New.
3. In the Create New Signature dialog box, enter a name for the new signature and click Next.
4. In the Edit Signature dialog box, type the signature that will appear at the end of your message if this signature is selected.
5. You can make this signature as the default signature to appear at all messages sent by you.
6. Click Ok.

8.12 OPENING OF E-MAIL ACCOUNT

The following are the popular sites which allow you to open an e-mail account:

Yahoo	http://www.mail.yahoo.com
Hotmail	http://www.hotmail.com
Rediff	http://www.rediff.com
Mailcity	http://www.mailcity.com

Besides these most of your ISPs would allow you to open an account. Please remember that these e-mail services are all free and the sites do not charge any amount for using the same.

The following dialog boxes would show you how to create your own e-mail account with hotmail.

8.13 E-MAIL ORGANIZATION

With reference to the e-mail program named Outlook Express, the messages in the software can be roughly organized in the following folders:

Inbox	For all incoming messages
Outbox	For all messages queued for sending
Sent Items	For all messages previously sent
Deleted items	For all messages marked for deletion
Drafts	For all messages which are pending completion

All these can be seen in the figure on the next page.

Before we start reading and sending the e-mails, we must understand few e-mail terms which are quite useful in reading and sending messages.

8.13.1 Using Abbreviations

An abbreviation would save both time and space. It is important that the abbreviations used by you are understood equally well by the receiver of your e-Mail. So I give here a list of abbrevations which have by now become the universally accepted abbrevations around the world.

Full Word/Term/Phrase	*Abbreviation*
By The Way	BTW

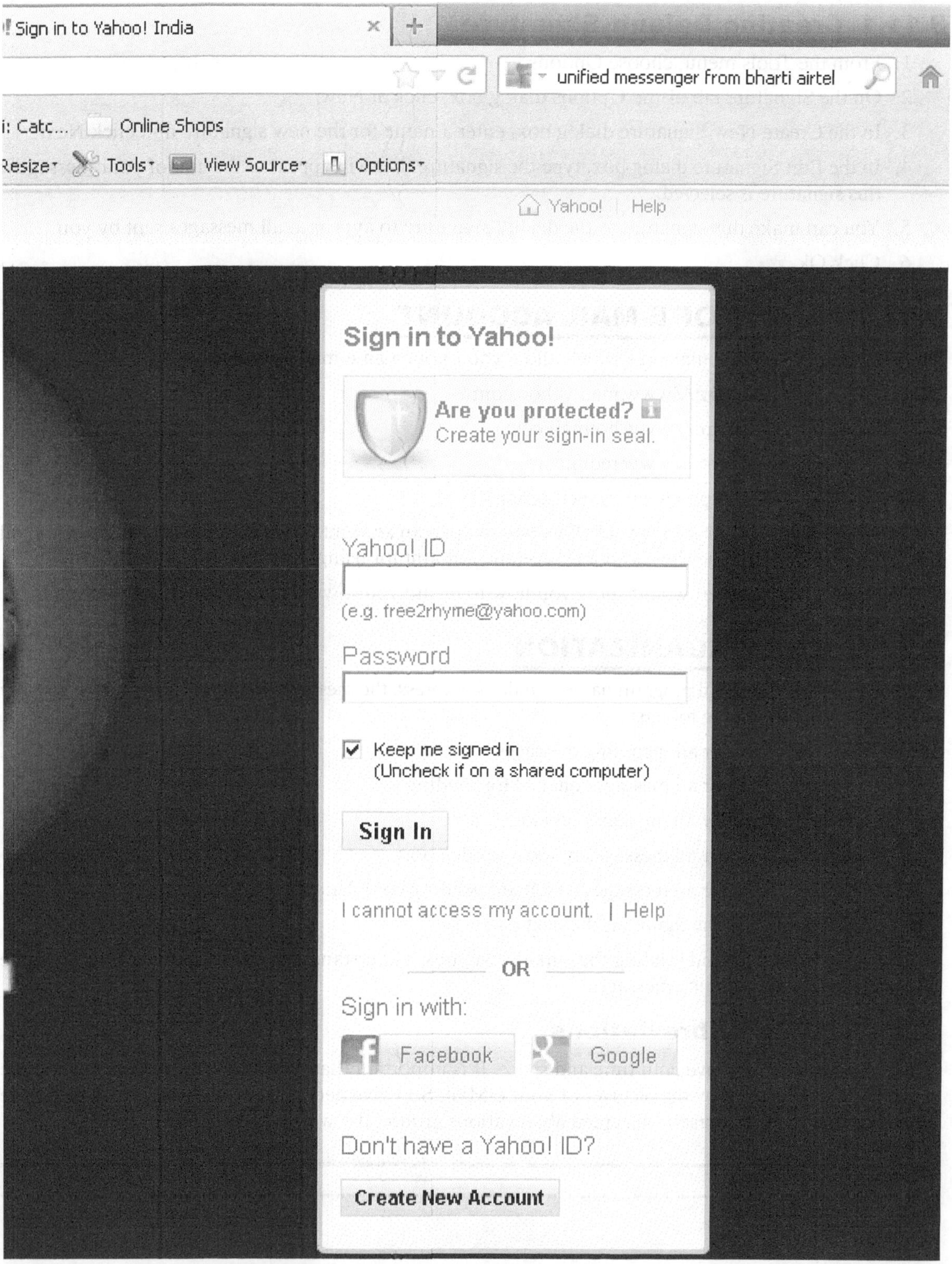
Sign in to Yahoo! India
unified messenger from bharti airtel
Online Shops
Tools
View Source
Options
Yahoo! | Help
Sign in to Yahoo!
Are you protected?
Create your sign-in seal.
Yahoo! ID
(e.g. free2rhyme@yahoo.com)
Password
Keep me signed in
(Uncheck if on a shared computer)
Sign In
I cannot access my account. | Help
OR
Sign in with:
Facebook
Google
Don't have a Yahoo! ID?
Create New Account

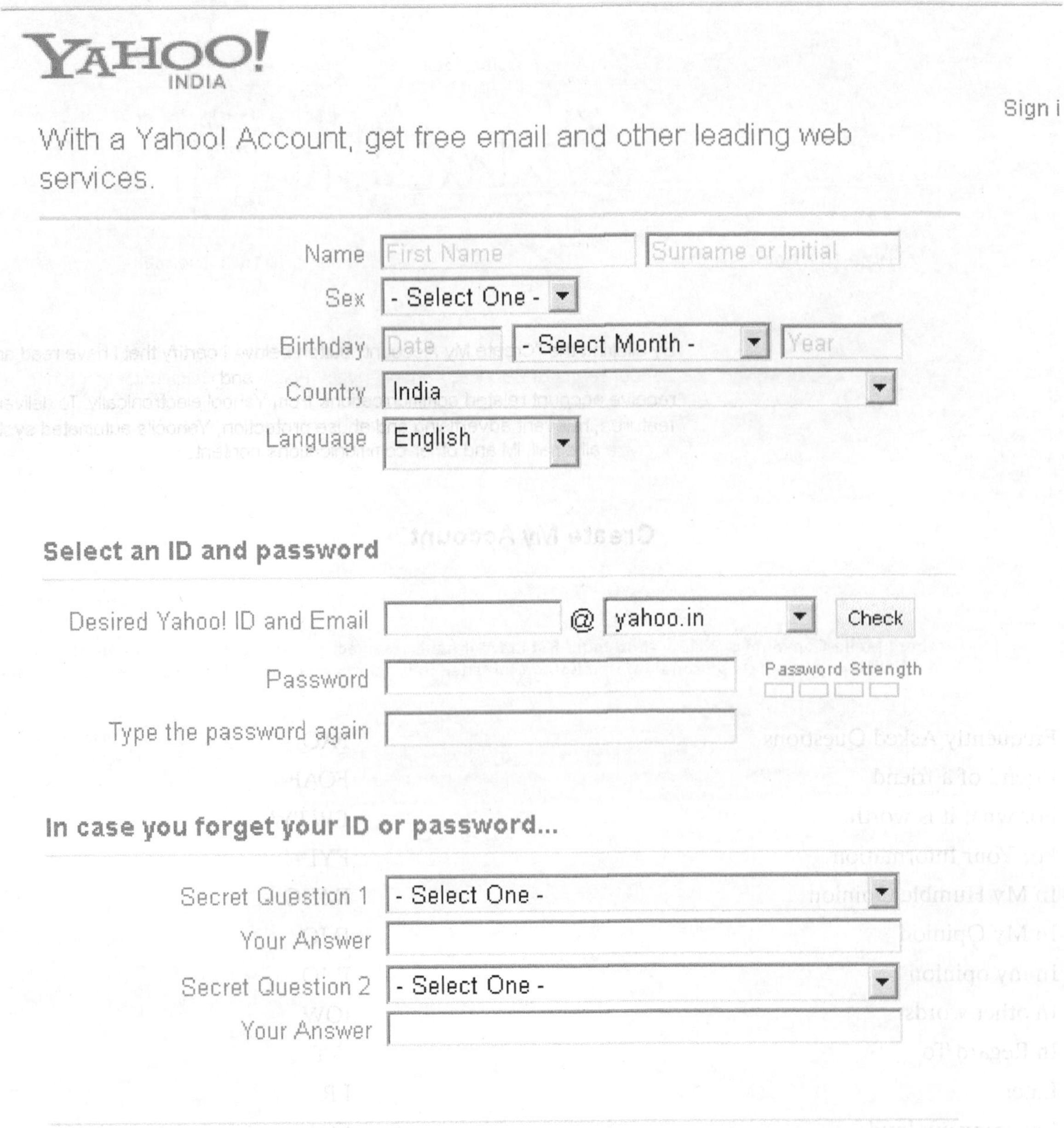

Sign i

With a Yahoo! Account, get free email and other leading web services.

Name [First Name] [Surname or Initial]

Sex [- Select One -]

Birthday [Date] [- Select Month -] [Year]

Country [India]

Language [English]

Select an ID and password

Desired Yahoo! ID and Email [ ] @ [yahoo.in] [Check]

Password [ ] Password Strength

Type the password again [ ]

In case you forget your ID or password...

Secret Question 1 [- Select One -]

Your Answer [ ]

Secret Question 2 [- Select One -]

Your Answer [ ]

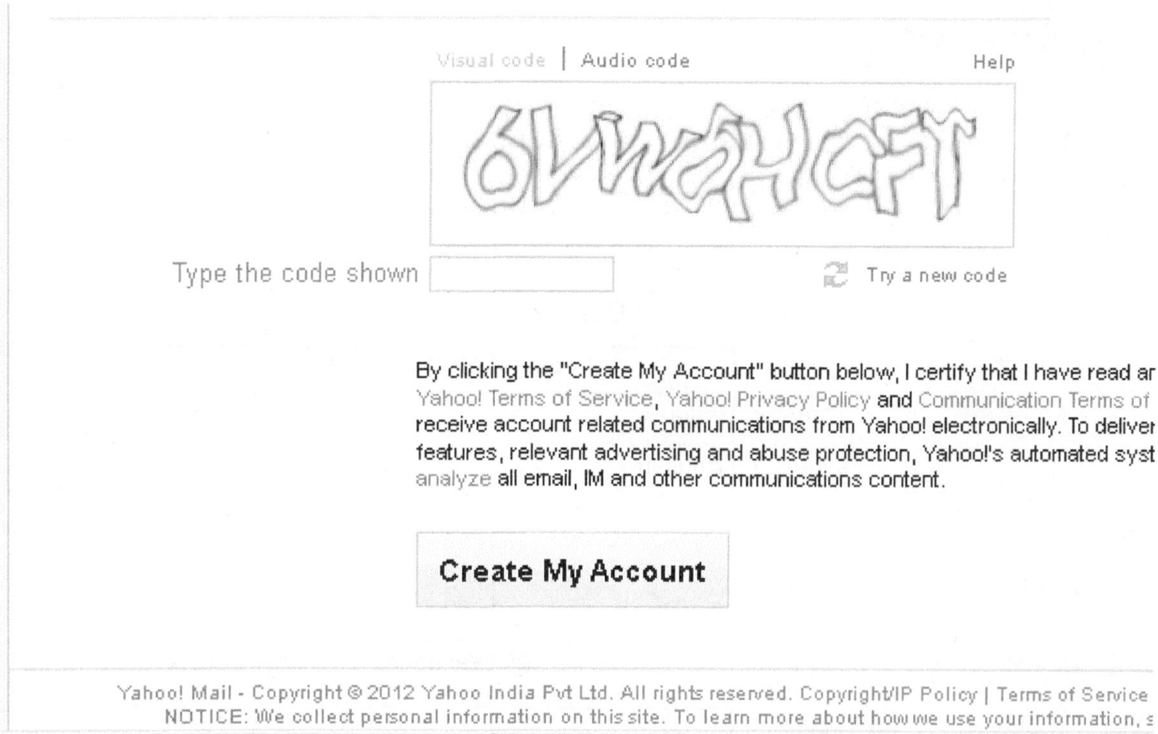

Frequently Asked Questions	FAQ
Friend of a friend	FOAF
For what it is worth	FWTW
For Your Information	FYI
In My Humble Opinion	IMHO
In My Opinion	IMO
In my opinion	IMO
In other words	IOW
In Regard To	IRT
Later	LR
Laughing out loud	LOL
Member of the appropriate sex	MOTAS
Member of the opposite sex	MOTOS
On The Other Hand	OTOH
Refer to/Regarding	RE:
Rolling on the floor and laughing	ROFTAL
Significant other	SO

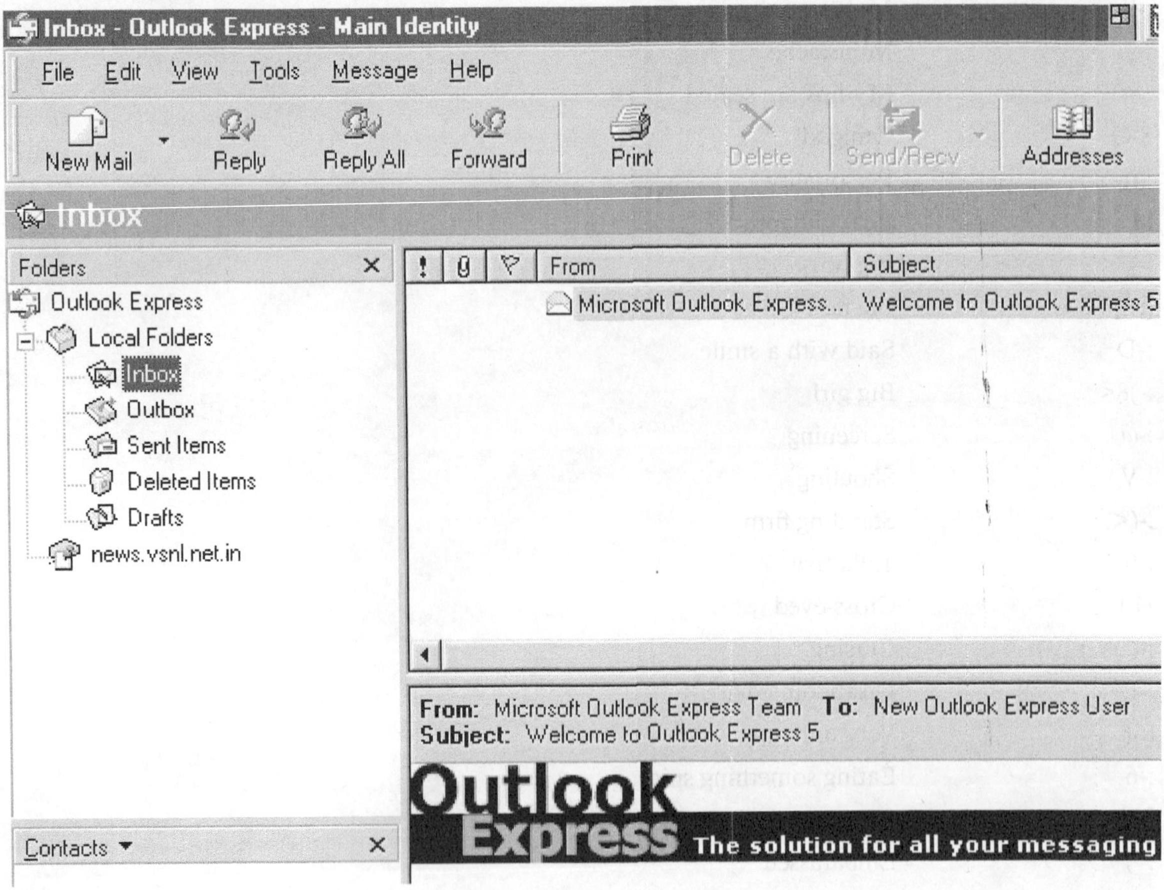

You	U
With respect to	WRT

8.13.2 Using Smileys

There are lots of ways that you can convey your messages across. Not, only in terms of abbreviations but in terms of small similies too. These are also like abbreviations are finding their way into most of the computers around the world. A smiley is a sequence of characters on your computer's keyboard. For example, the colon represents the eyes, the dash represents the nose and the right parenthesis represents the mouth.

Given below is a list of the most common smileys.

Emotions	*Meaning*
8:-)	Little girl
X-(	Mad
&-L	Makes me cry
:-(*)	Makes me sick

:-S	Makes no sense
:-{	Moustache
:-#	My lips are sealed
8-O	Omigod!
:^)	Personality
:-C	Real unhappy
:-)^<	Big boy
(:-)	Big face
:-D	Said with a smile
:-)8<	Big girl
:-@	Screening
:-V	Shouting
:-(<	Standing firm
:-0	Talkative
H-)	Cross-eyed
:-@!	Cursing
:-E	Disappointed
(:-(	Very unhappy
:-6	Eating something spicy
]-I	Wearing sunglasses
:”)	Embarassed
‘-)	Winking
L-O	Yawning

As you become proficient in e-Mailing, you will be able to learn many more of these fascinating emoticons, which exist in thousands.

8.14 WORKING WITH MESSAGES

The first thing that you would do on opening the software would be to receive the messages. For this you will have to click on Send/Receive button.

You can also set Outlook to automatically check for messages at regular intervals, or you can have Outlook check for message whenever you want.

1. Click the Send/Receive button on the Standard toolbar, as shown next.
2. The Internet connection will be made depending upon the type of connection you have. Its progress will be shown to you in the dialog box in the lower right corner of the window.
3. When messages arrive, Outlook asks you whether you want to start reading them. Click Yes in the Microsoft Outlook dialog box to starting reading messages, or click No to read them later.

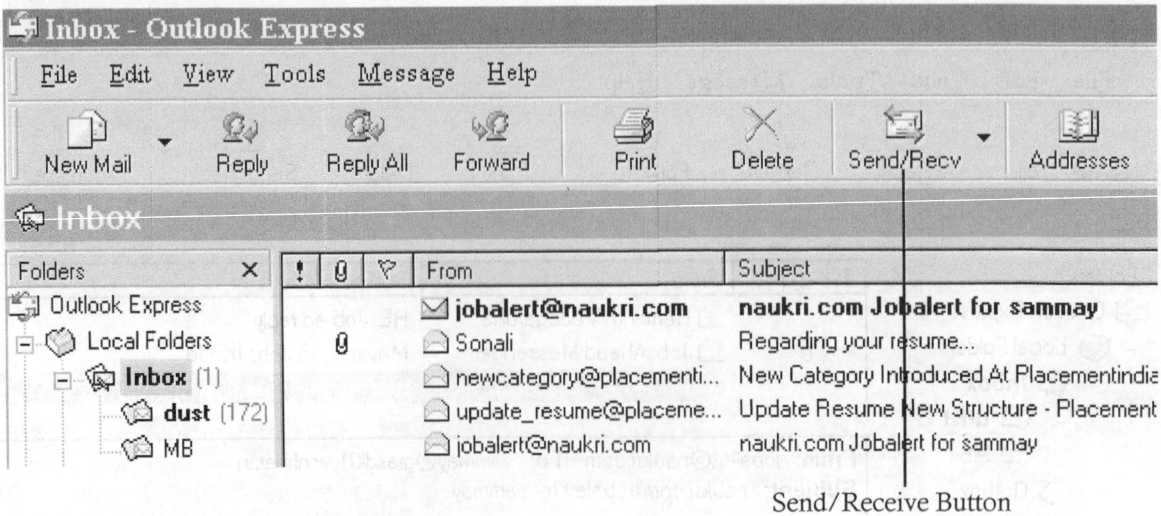

8.15 READING A MESSAGE

Once the messages have been received in the Inbox, they will be appended to the other ones, i.e., in the last. The last few messages are always new. There are various type of messages which are there in the mailbox.

The messages in the Inbox can have the following symbols attached to them.

- Unread message
- High importance message
- Low importance message
- Message that has been read
- Message with attachment
- Message that has been forwarded
- Message that has been replied to
- Meeting for which response is requested
- Follow-up flag

All these have a symbol attached to them.

8.15.1 Reading the Message

1. Double-click a message in the Inbox list.

   Or

   Select the message to open and press Ctrl + O

   Or

   Select the message to open and from the File menu, choose Open. Then choose Selected Items from the submenu.

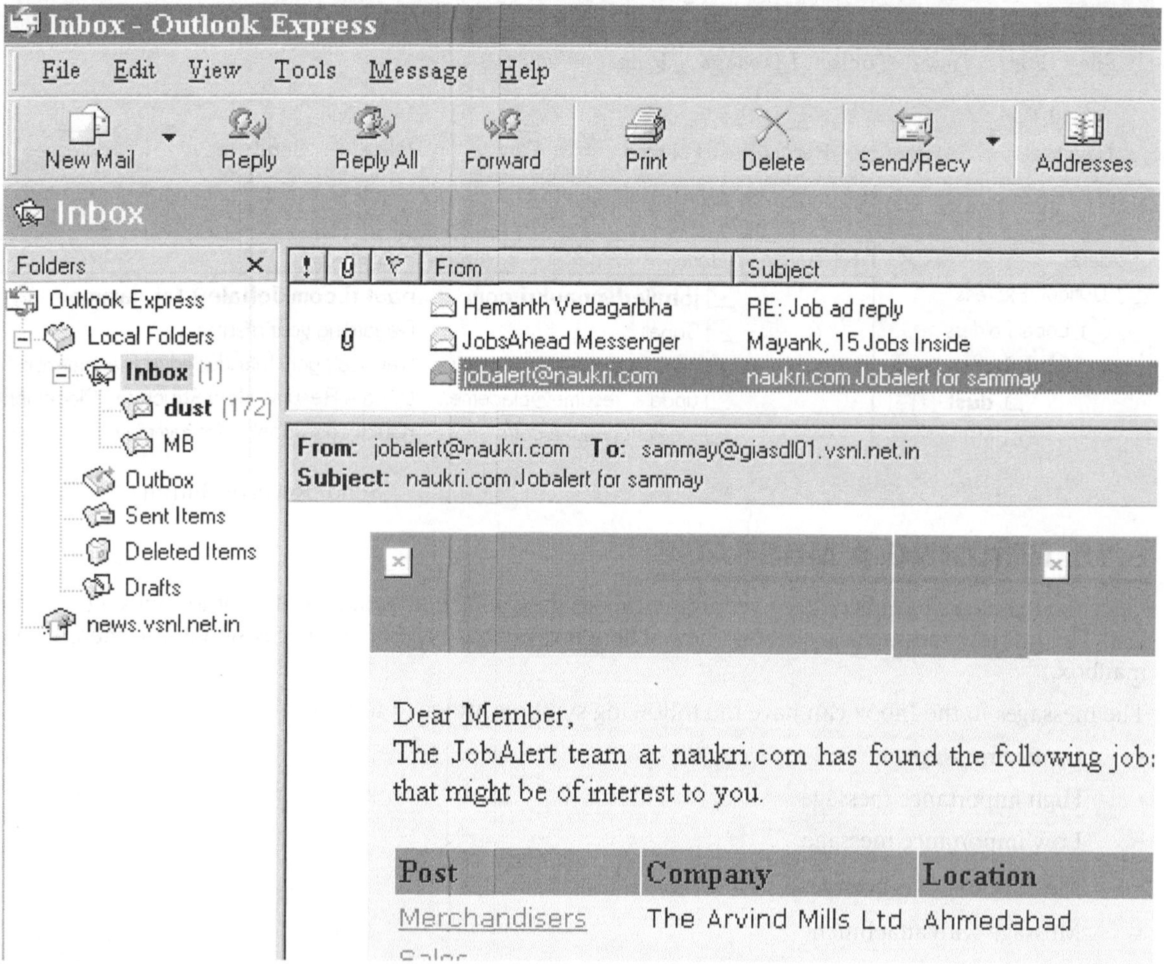

Each message opens in a separate window.

8.15.2 Replying to a Message

Once read, a message can either be replied or trashed.

8.15.2.1 To reply to a message

1. With a message selected in the Inbox window or with the message open, click the Reply button on the Standard toolbar. The reply has the sender in the To box and the original subject in the Subject box preceded by RE.
2. In the text area, type your reply. The reply appears above the original message.

8.15.2.2 Replying in a Phased Manner

You can reply in phases. You can type half a reply now, save it and then complete it later. In this case, since the reply is half baked, it is stored in drafts folder.

For this do the following:

1. Click Save on the Standard toolbar.

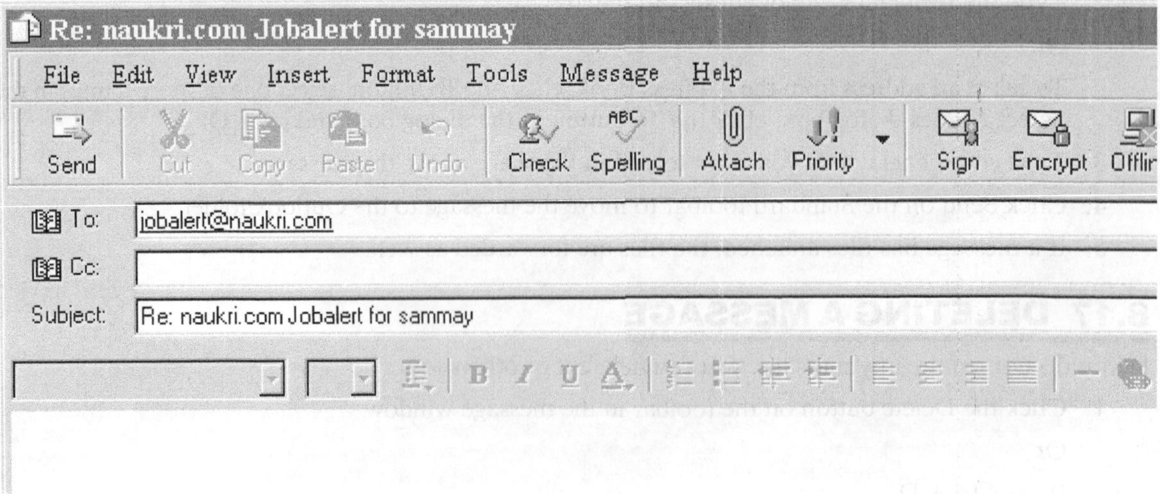

Or

From the File menu, choose Save.

2. Close the window.
3. Outlook places the reply in the Drafts folder. You can open it there to continue working on it.
4. To reply to all of them, click the Reply to All button on the Standard toolbar.
5. You can still edit a message that is waiting in the Outbox. Just double-click the message, make your changes, and then click Send again.

8.16 FORWARDING A MESSAGE

The message received from A can be sent to B by using Forward option. You can also add your own comments to it before sending it.

1. With a message selected in the Inbox window or with the message open, click the Forward button on the Standard toolbar.

   The new message shows the original subject in the Subject box preceded by FW, as shown here.

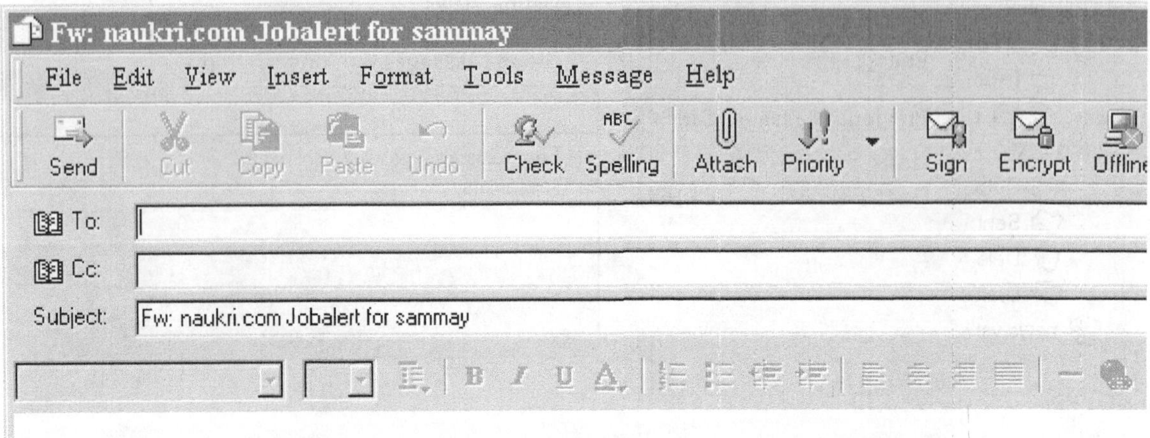

2. Type the recipient's e-mail address in the To box.

   Or

   To select an address from the Address Book, click the To button, select one or more names in the Select Names dialog box, click the To button in the dialog box, and click Ok.
3. Type comments which you want to add in the space above the message.
4. Click Send on the Standard toolbar to move the message to the Outlook folder.
5. If a message has files attached, the files are forwarded as well.

8.17 DELETING A MESSAGE

If you do not require any message, you can delete it or others too.

1. Click the Delete button on the toolbar in the message window.

   Or

   Press Ctrl + D

The message is moved to the Deleted Items folder.

8.18 CHANGING VIEW

Outlook lets you view the contents of a message folder in a number of ways.

1. From the View menu, choose Current View, and then choose a view from the submenu.
2. The view of the current folder is changed.

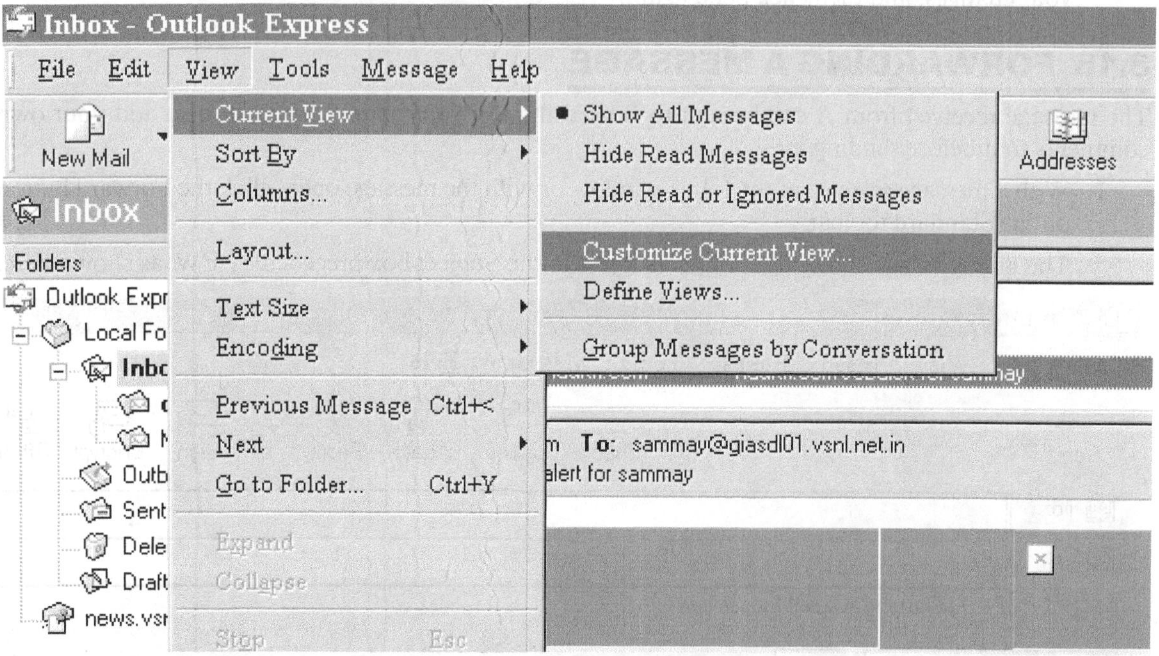

LET US REVISE

1. When you send e-mail to someone on the Internet, that message has to travel through a series of networks before it reaches the recipient.
2. There are a few message formats that have evolved into de facto standards and most messaging products include support for them.
3. Simple Mail Transfer Protocol (SMTP) is an Internet standard for electronic mail (e-mail) transmission across Internet Protocol (IP) networks.
4. In computing, the Post Office Protocol (POP) is an application-layer Internet standard protocol used by local e-mail clients to retrieve e-mail from a remote server over a TCP/IP connection.
5. The Internet Message Access Protocol (IMAP) is one of the two most prevalent Internet standard protocols for e-mail retrieval, the other being the Post Office Protocol (POP).
6. Multipurpose Internet Mail Extensions (MIME) is an Internet standard that extends the format of e-mail to support.
7. Like a formal letter e-mail also is divided into various sections. In a good business letter, you would have, date, the name and address of the person to whom the letter is addressed, salutation, text matter, sender's name, etc.
8. You can attach files to your message, and you also attach or include as text the items in your Outlook folders.
9. An email client, email reader, or more formally mail user agent (MUA), is a computer program used to manage email.
10. Like most client programs, an MUA is only active when a user runs it. Messages arrive on the Mail Transfer Agent (MTA) server.
11. Like Microsoft even Netscape has also got its own mail software called Netscape Messenger.
12. Each E-mail service - whether it is an online service, commercial e-mail service, has its own way to handle mail.
13. Windows Address Book is a component of Microsoft Windows that lets users keep a single list of contacts that can be shared by multiple programs.
14. e-mail is an important use of Internet.
15. All Internet Service Providers allow you to open an e-mail account.
16. In Outlook Express, Inbox is used for incoming messages..
17. Outbox is used for sending messages.
18. Sent items stores all messages previously sent.
19. Deleted items has the messages which are marked for deletion.
20. Drafts has all the half completed messages.
21. To cut down the time of writing a message, lots of abbrevations are used.
22. You can even use smileys in your message.
23. Various parts of the e-mail text are: Headers, To, From, Subject, Cc, Bcc, Attachments, Date and Body.
24. Using Send/Receive button on the standard toolbar, you can send and receive mail.
25. Various type of messages are: Unread message, High importance message, Low importance message, Message that has been read, Message with attachment, Message that has been forwarded, Message that has been replied to, Meeting for which response is requested and Follow-up flag.

26. For reading the message you can use Ctrl + O.
27. You can click the RE button for replying to a message.
28. By using FW you can forward a message.
29. You can delete a message by Ctrl+D.
30. You can create your own stationery for sending message.
31. You can create and put your own signature in messages.
32. You can attach a file to your message.
33. You can even attach a picture to your message.

MULTIPLE CHOICE QUESTIONS

1. Commonly used program for e-mail is:
   (a) Outlook Express (b) Internet Explorer (c) Microsoft Windows
2. Your half finished messages are stored in:
   (a) Inbox (b) Outbox (c) Drafts
3. MTA is:
   (a) Mail Transfer Agent (b) My Transfer Agent (c) Mail Travel Agent
4. MIME is :
   (a) Multipurpose Internet Mail External
   (b) Multipurpose Internet Mail Extensions
   (c) Multipurpose Indian Mail Extensions
5. IMAP is :
   (a) Internet Message Access Product
   (b) Indian Message Access Protocol
   (c) Internet Message Access Protocol
6. Commonly used program for e-mail is:
   (a) Outlook Express (b) Internet Explorer (c) Microsoft Windows
7. Your sent messages are stored in:
   (a) Inbox (b) Drafts (c) Outbox
8. For sending and receiving messages you click at:
   (a) Send/Receive button (b) Send button (c) Receive button
9. For replying you use which button :
   (a) REPLY (b) SEND (c) RE
10. For deleting a message you use Ctrl + :
    (a) D (b) Del (c) Esc

TRUE/FALSE QUESTIONS

1. There are a few message formats that have evolved into de facto standards and most messaging products include support for them.

2. In computing, the Post Office Protocol (POP) is an application-layer Internet standard protocol used by local e-mail clients to retrieve e-mail from a remote server over a TCP/IP connection.
3. Multipurpose Internet Mail Extensions (MIME) is an Internet standard that extends the format of e-mail to support.
4. You cannot attach files to your message, and you also attach or include as text the items in your Outlook folders.
5. Like Microsoft even Netscape has also got its own mail software called Netscape Messenger.
6. Each E-mail service - whether it is an online service, commercial e-mail service, has its own way to handle mail.
7. You cannot have Outlook add a signature, a special tag line, to each message you send.

MATCHING COLUMNS

Match the matter in Column A with the matter in Column B.

Column A	Column B
A. SMTP	1. Internet Message Access Protocol
B. POP	2. Multipurpose Internet Mail Extensions
C. IMAP	3. Carbon copy
D. MIME	4. Blind Carbon Copy
E. Bcc	5. Simple Mail Transfer Protocol
F. Cc	6. Point to Point Protocol

FILL IN THE BLANKS WITH APPROPRIATE WORDS

a. Multipurpose Internet Mail Extensions (MIME)
b. Internet Message Access Protocol (IMAP)
c. attach
d. Mail User Agent (MUA)
e. Mail Transfer Agent (MTA)
f. Simple Mail Transfer Protocol (SMTP)
g. Point to Point Protocol

1. ______________________ is an Internet standard for electronic mail (e-mail) transmission across Internet Protocol (IP) networks.
2. In computing, the __________________ is an application-layer Internet standard protocol used by local e-mail clients to retrieve e-mail from a remote server over a TCP/IP connection.
3. The ______________________ is one of the two most prevalent Internet standard protocols for e-mail retrieval, the other being the Post Office Protocol (POP).
4. _________________ is an Internet standard that extends the format of e-mail to support.
5. You can __________ files to your message, and you also attach or include as text the items in your Outlook folders.
6. An email client, email reader, or more formally ____________, is a computer program used to manage email.
7. Like most client programs, an MUA is only active when a user runs it. Messages arrive on the _________________ server.

DESCRIPTIVE TYPE QUESTIONS

1. What are E-mail Networks and Servers?
2. Define the various E-mail Protocols.
3. What goes in the sturucture of an e-mail?
4. Describe the process of attaching a file to an e-mail.
5. What do you understand by E-mail clients?
6. Write a short note on Outlook Express.
7. What do you understand by Web based E-mail?
8. How is Email Encryption done?
9. What do you understand by Address Book?
10. How would you attach signatures to the E-mail?
11. What is e-mail?
12. How would you create your own e-mail account?
13. Which are the different folders in Outlook Express?
14. Which type of messages you have in Outlook Express?
15. Describe the process of replying to a message.
16. How would you forward a message?
17. How would you create your own stationery?
18. How would you create your own signature?
19. Describe the process of attaching a file to your message.

ANSWERS TO OBJECTIVE QUESTIONS

Multiple Choice Questions

1. a	2. c	3. a	4. b
5. c	6. b	7. c	8. a
9. c	10. a		

True False Questions

1. T	2. T	3. T	4. F
5. T	6. F	7. F	

Matching Columns

A. 5	B. 6	C. 1	D. 2
E. 4	F. 3		

Fill in the Blanks with Appropriate Words

1. f	2. g	3. a	4. b
5. c	6. d	7. e	

Chapter 9

Making Small Presentations

9.1 CREATING A PRESENTATION

There are three methods of creating a presentation. They are given here.

9.1.1 Creating a Presentation using Wizard

The Wizard would create for you a complete presentation, just add few graphics and text here and there, your presentation is complete. To create a presentation using AutoContent, do the following:

1. Select New from the File menu.
2. Select AutoContent from the General Panel or Click at From AutoContent Wizard in the Task Pane, as shown above.

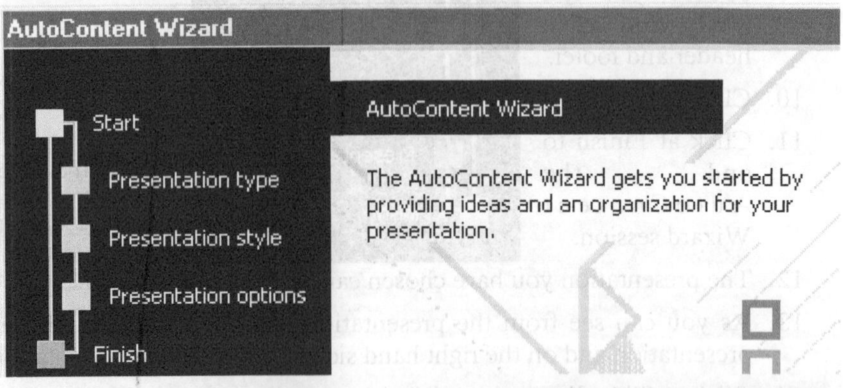

3. The first screen of the AutoContent Wizard appears on the screen.
4. Click Next
5. The next screen of the Wizard allows you to choose a type of presentation you want. I have chosen here the Selling a Product or Service from the Sales/Marketing heading.

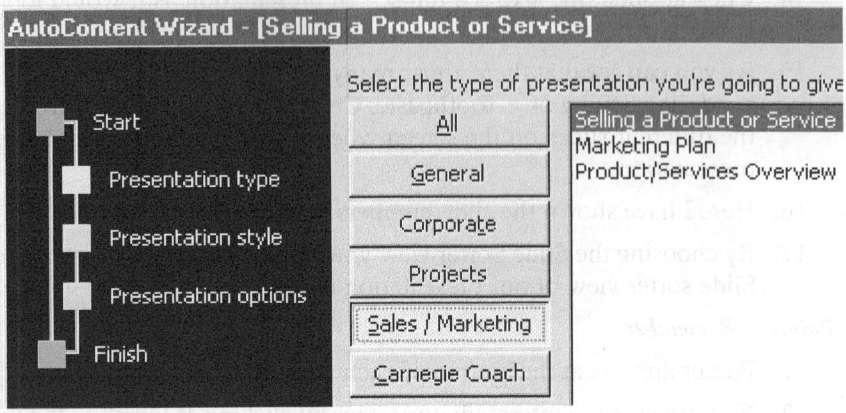

6. Click Next.
7. The next screen allows you to select the type of output you want. I have selected here the On-screen presentation.

   Various other options are also there which are shown here on the screen.
8. Click Next.

9. The next screen asks you to give title of the presentation and the text you want to appear on the footer page. I have put them as Selling of Toothpaste and New Toothpaste in the market. I have also chosen for the Date and Slide number to be displayed. Of course, you can have your own header and footer.

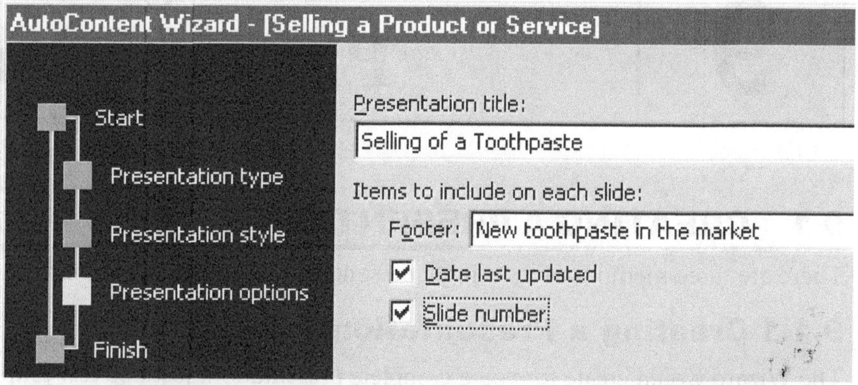

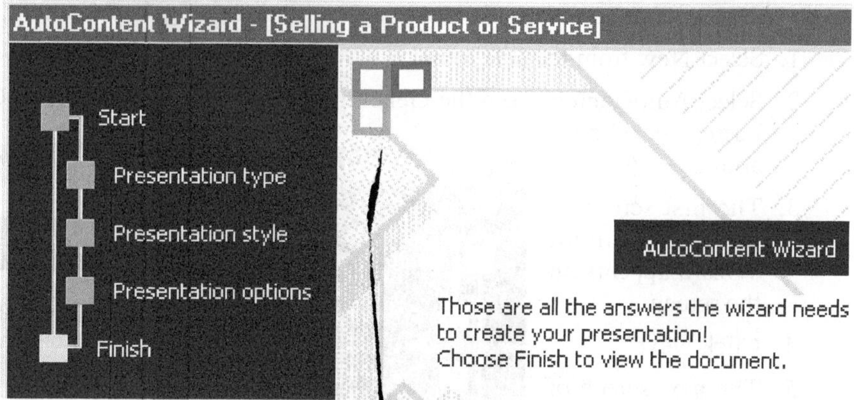

10. Click Next.
11. Click at Finish to end the AutoContent Wizard session.
12. The presentation you have chosen can be seen on the screen.
13. As you can see from the presentation, the left hand side of the screen contains text of the presentation and on the right hand side you can see the presentation.
14. Click at Slide Show to see full screen presentation as it would look on the screen. Press Esc to come back.
15. As you can see that there are as many as 8 slides in this presentation, each representing different head, like Selling of a Toothpaste, Customer requirements, Meeting the needs, etc. You can see the different slides on the screen when you move the vertical bar on the right hand side of the presentation.
16. Here I have shown the slide numbers 4 and 7.
17. By choosing the Slide Sorter view you can see all the slides on the screen but in very small form. Slide sorter view of our presentation is also shown.

Points to Remember

1. Footer appears at the bottom of each page on the presentation.
2. You can skip the intermediatory steps by clicking at Finish in the first dialog box of the Wizard.
3. Each presentation is given a look which is preset. You can change this according to your liking.
4. Two level of text is given on the left hand side of the presentation. The one with the serial number is the heading of the slide. The second level of text is the text which appears as the part of the presentation.
5. You can change this text about which you will read later.

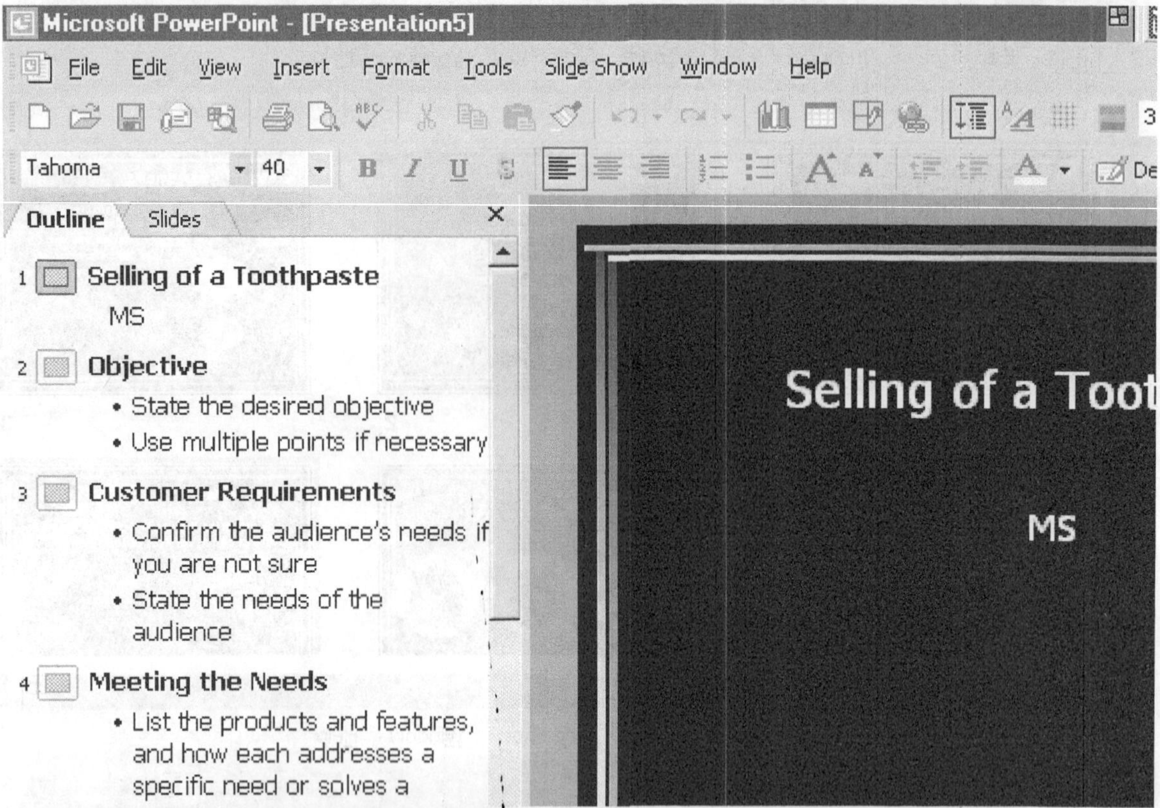
Microsoft PowerPoint - [Presentation5]
File Edit View Insert Format Tools Slide Show Window Help
Tahoma 40
Outline Slides
1 Selling of a Toothpaste
MS
2 Objective
• State the desired objective
• Use multiple points if necessary
3 Customer Requirements
• Confirm the audience's needs if you are not sure
• State the needs of the audience
4 Meeting the Needs
• List the products and features, and how each addresses a specific need or solves a
MS

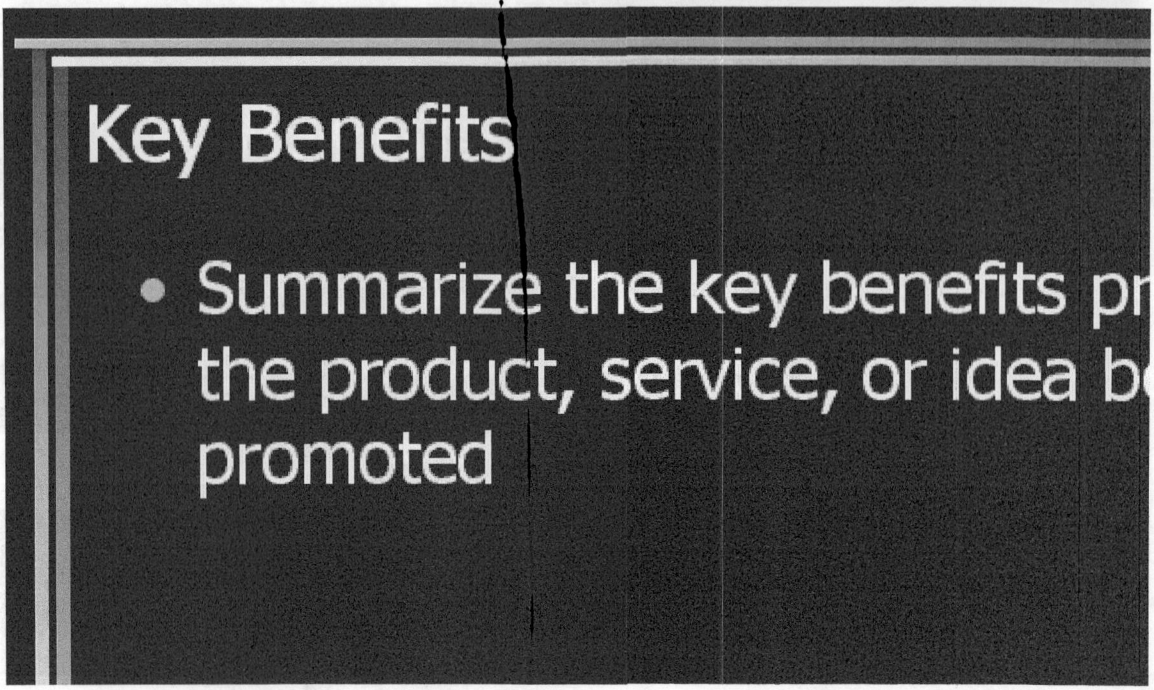
Key Benefits
• Summarize the key benefits pr
the product, service, or idea b
promoted

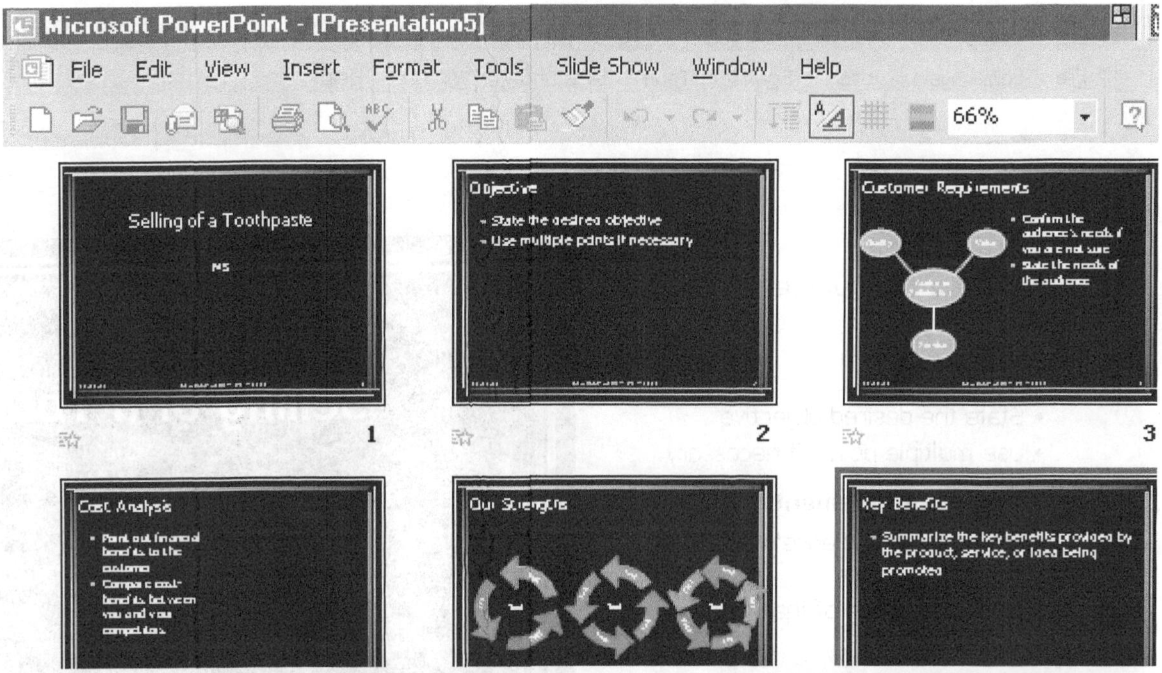
Microsoft PowerPoint - [Presentation5]
File Edit View Insert Format Tools Slide Show Window Help
66%
Selling of a Toothpaste
MS
1
Objective
State the desired objective
Use multiple points if necessary
2
Customer Requirements
Confirm the audience's needs if you are not sure
State the needs of the audience
3
Cost Analysis
Our Strengths
Key Benefits
Summarize the key benefits provided by the product, service, or idea being promoted

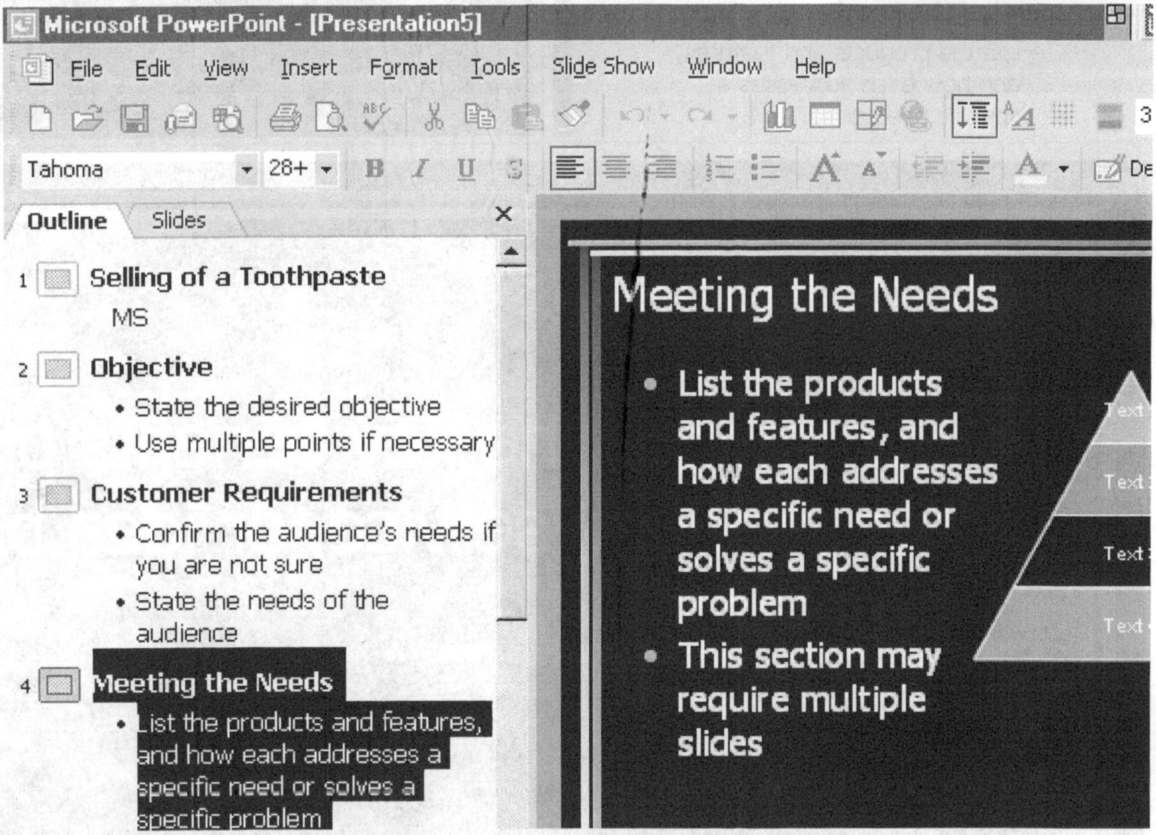
Microsoft PowerPoint - [Presentation5]
File Edit View Insert Format Tools Slide Show Window Help
Tahoma
28+
Outline
Slides
1 Selling of a Toothpaste
MS
2 Objective
State the desired objective
Use multiple points if necessary
3 Customer Requirements
Confirm the audience's needs if you are not sure
State the needs of the audience
4 Meeting the Needs
List the products and features, and how each addresses a specific need or solves a specific problem
Meeting the Needs
List the products and features, and how each addresses a specific need or solves a specific problem
This section may require multiple slides

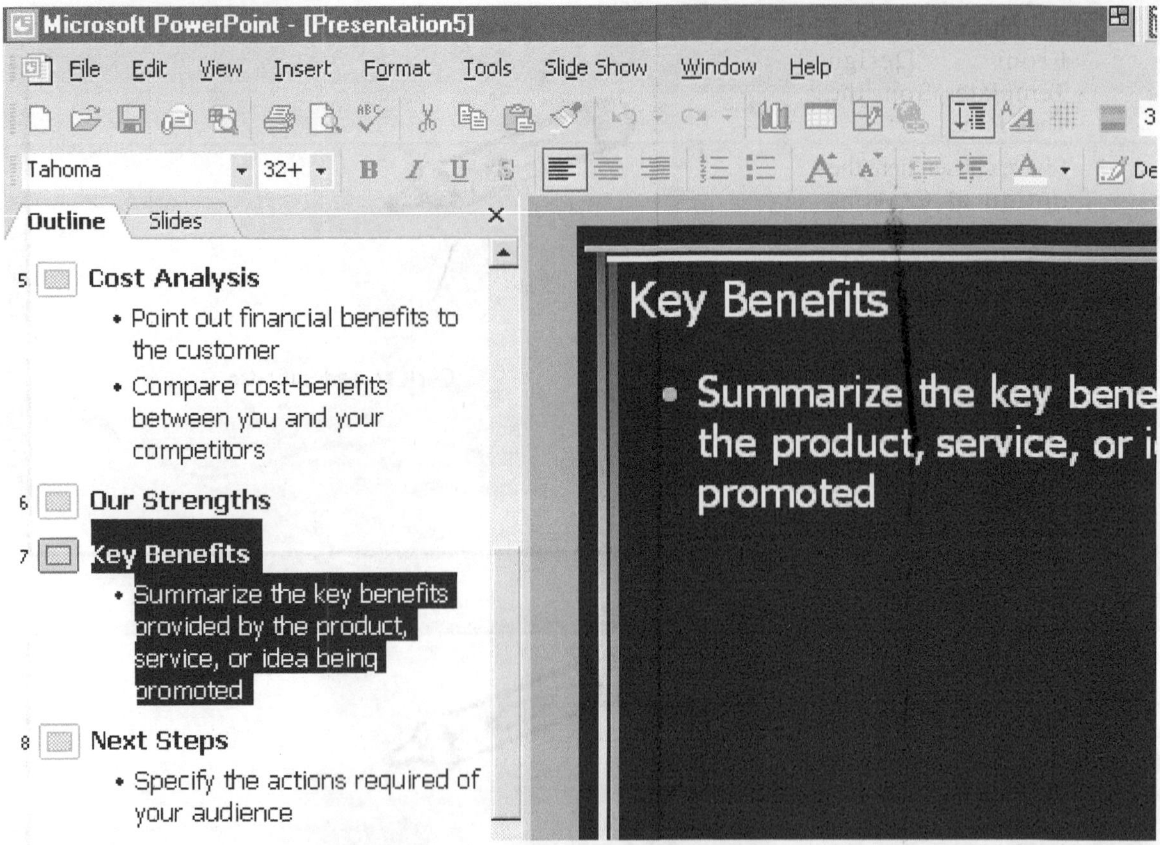

9.1.2 Creating Presentation from Template

As I had mentioned earlier that the software has available presentations, these are called Templates. These can be used for creating your own presentation. Templates can provide either the graphic design and color scheme of a presentation (design template) or suggest content and structure, using a set of slides whose text you can edit.

1. Select New from the File menu.
2. Select Design Templates option on the New Presentation

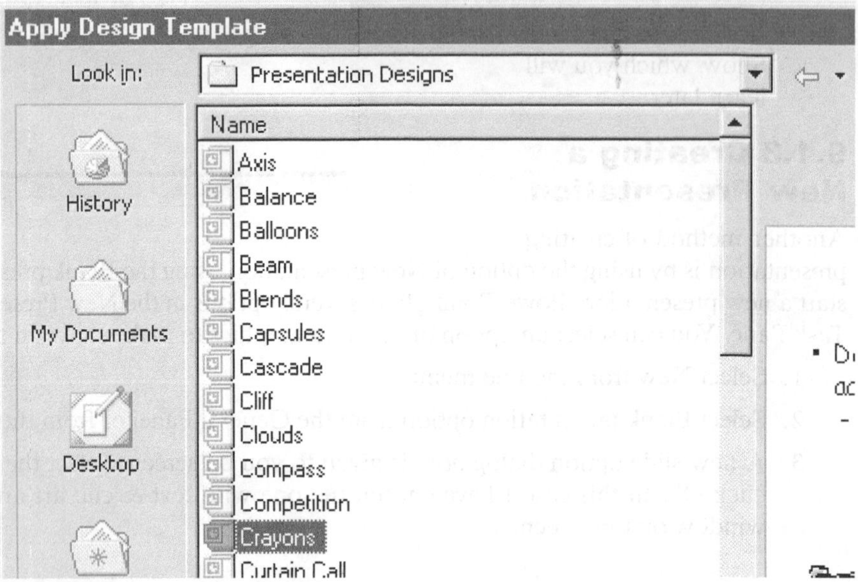

dialog box or select From Design Templates from the Task Pane.

3. I have chosen here the option of Crayons from the various options available under Presentation Templates.
4. You would be given a choice to choose the type of slide. Here you can type the title of your choice and then add the subtitle of your choice.
5. I have typed some text as shown.
6. From Insert menu, click at New Slide.
7. A new blank slide will appear.
8. This way you can keep adding slides and make your own presentation.
9. You can see its Slide Show, which you will learn later.

9.1.3 Creating a New Presentation

Another method of creating presentation is by using the option of New presentation using the Blank presentation option. When you start a new presentation, PowerPoint offers several options in the New Presentation dialog box or in the Task Pane. You can select an option of text and graphics to make show on the screen.

1. Select New from the File menu.
2. Select Blank presentation option from the General Panel or from the Task Pane.
3. A new slide option dialog box, is given to you on screen. Select the type of slide you want and click Ok. In this case I have chosen the one with text & clip art and it is shown on the small window on the screen.

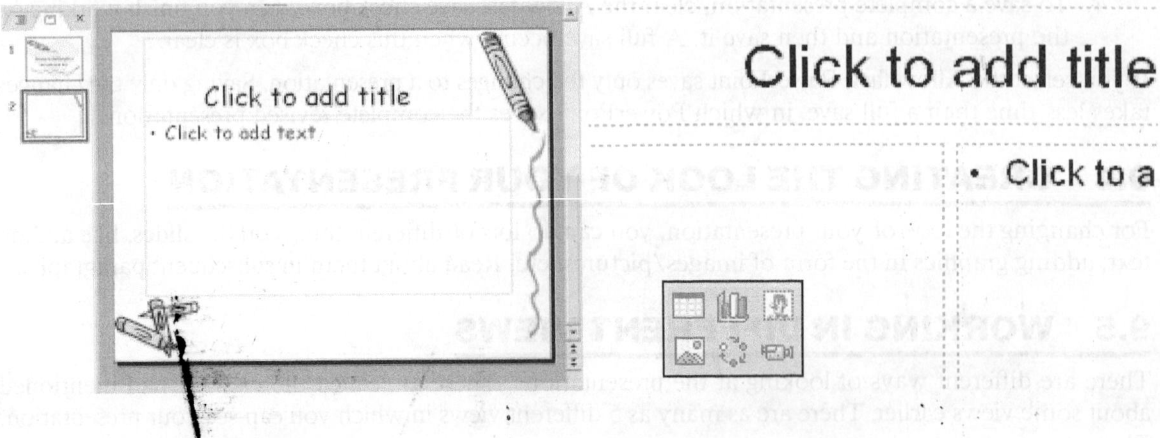

4. Add the text for the title.
5. In the second box type the text which you want to type.
6. The graphic icon allows you to add graphics of various types, i.e., Table, Chart, Clip Art, Picture, Diagram and Media Clip.
7. I have chosen to add a Picture here and have chosen the picture of Capitol Hill.
8. See how it looks when inserted in the slide on the next page.
9. On the other hand you can choose a different option of text, graphics and even the type of slide too.

9.2 OPENING A PRESENTATION

An existing presentation can be opened by using the Open command from the File menu. The dialog box shows the existing presentation files, select the one which you want to open and press Enter. The presentation would come on the screen and can be worked upon using the various available commands.

9.3 SAVING A PRESENTATION

You can save the presentation you are working on by choosing Save Options from File menu or by clicking the Save button on the Standard toolbar. If you are Saving the presentation for the first time, Save As dialog box appears where you have to enter the file name.

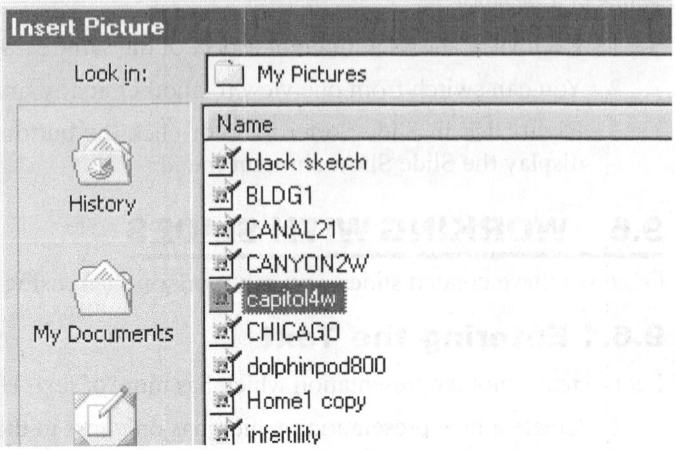

Speed up Saving a Presentation

1. On the Tools menu, click at Options to get the options dialog box.
2. Click on the Save panel.
3. To Save only the changes to a presentation, select the Allow fast saves check box and then continue to Save as you work on the presentation.

4. To save a complete presentation, clear the Allow fast save check box when you finish working on the presentation and then save it. A full save occurs when this check box is clear.

If you select the Allow fast, PowerPoint saves only the changes to a presentation. Saving only the changes takes less time than a full save, in which PowerPoint saves the complete revised presentation.

9.4 CREATING THE LOOK OF YOUR PRESENTATION

For changing the look of your presentation, you can do lots of different things on the slides, like adding text, adding graphics in the form of images/pictures, etc. Read about them in subsequent paragraphs.

9.5 WORKING IN DIFFERENT VIEWS

There are different ways of looking at the presentations. These are called the views. I had mentioned about some views earlier. There are as many as 5 different views in which you can see your presentation. They are:

9.5.1 Outline view

It displays only the text of the presentation in the outline form, allowing you to work easily with the content.

9.5.2 Normal view

It displays 3 panes that show the outline, the slide, and an area in which you can enter speaker's notes.

9.5.3 Slide Sorter view

It displays thumbnail views of your slides so that you can reorganize the slides and change the overall look of the presentation. In this view you can also add and edit the transition effects for the slide show.

9.5.4 Slide Show view

It displays the presentation one slide at a time in sequence as an automatic slide show.

9.5.5 Notes Page view

It is available only from the view menu, lets you enter and edit speaker's notes for the presenter.

Points to Remember

1. Each view shows a different aspect of the same presentation.
2. You can switch from one view to another at any time.
3. Right-click in Slide Sorter view or click the button at lower left corner of the current slide to display the Slide Show shortcut menu.

9.6 WORKING WITH SLIDES

Once you have created slides, you can work on them using the various commands given here.

9.6.1 Entering the Text

Let us create another presentation which has more of text. Here, we will add the text as per the following:

1. Create a new presentation which has only text in the slide.

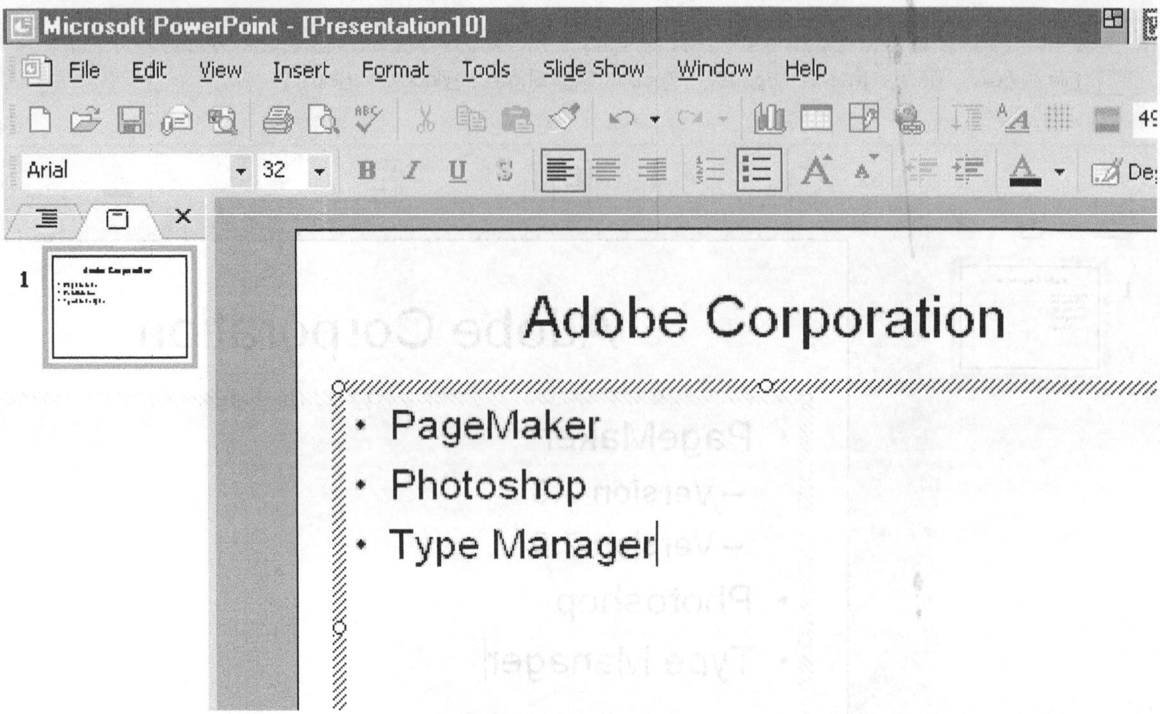

2. Type the name Adobe Corporation in the title bar.
3. In the next box, type the name of the famous software of the company called PageMaker.
4. Pressing enter would lead you to another sub heading.
5. Type here the next heading, Photoshop.
6. Similarly press enter and type Type Manager.
7. At this stage your presentation would look like the one shown on the next page.
8. Now we come to adding text in between the main headings, i.e., sub-headings.
9. Place your cursor at the end of the first heading, i.e., after PageMaker and press Enter. A new heading with 2 will appear. Just press Tab to get the bulleted text format. Type here the first line of your tabbed matter, which is Version 6.5.
10. Press enter again to get the new line and type version 7.0.
11. At this stage your presentation will look like, the one shown on the next page.
12. You can thus type the date in the steps required by you.
13. Next obvious step would be change the data, read on.

9.6.2 Changing Display

You can hide the text of the bulleted text or the sub-heading and let only the headings remain visible. For this do the following:

1. Highlight the text you want to hide.

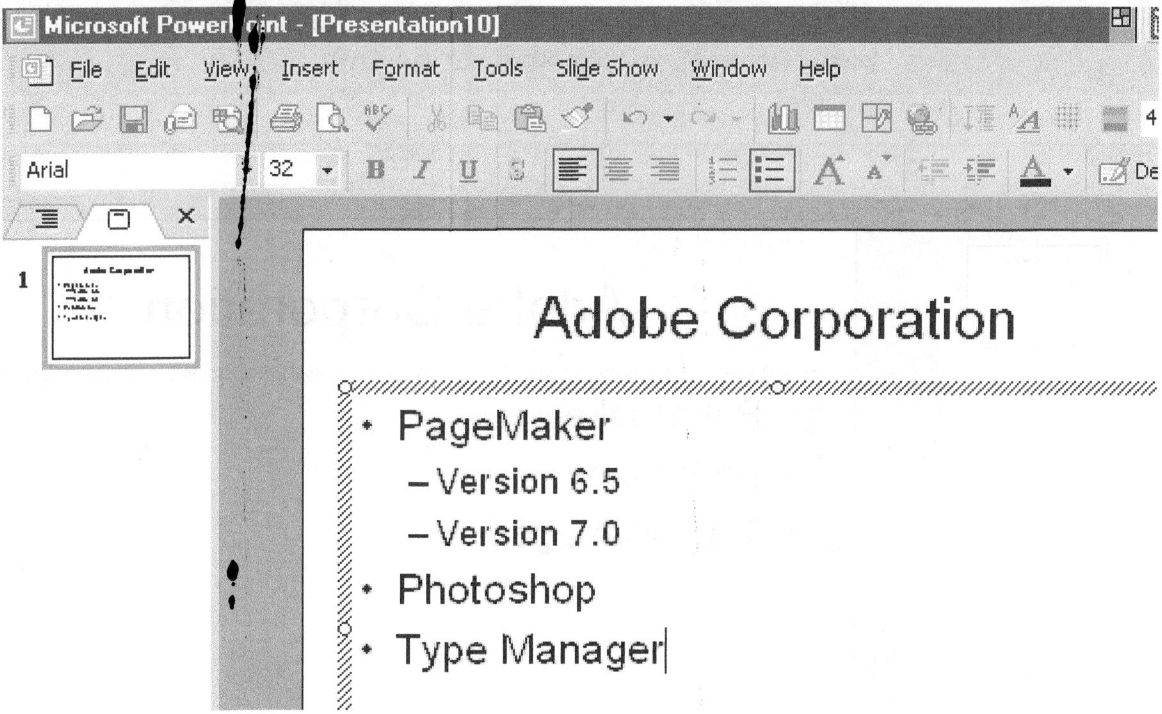

2. With text highlighted, click at right mouse button to get another submenu.
3. Select Collapse from here.
4. The text will be hidden and only the heading will remain in view, as shown on next to next page.
5. The heading which has text hidden underneath it is indicated by the text being shown as underlined.
6. When you press the Expand button after highlighting the heading which has text underneath it, the text will be expanded.

9.6.3 Moving the Text

You can move up or down a particular heading for reorganizing. For this do the following:

1. Highlight the text you want to move.
2. With text highlighted drag the text up or down.
3. Leave the mouse button at the place where you feel like placing the text.
4. The text will be moved there.

9.6.4 Changing the Colour

The colour schemes are always used to suit the atmosphere. So it depends where the presentation is going to be. Depending upon that the colour of the presentations are selected.

9.6.4.1 To Change the Colours

1. Select Background from Format menu.

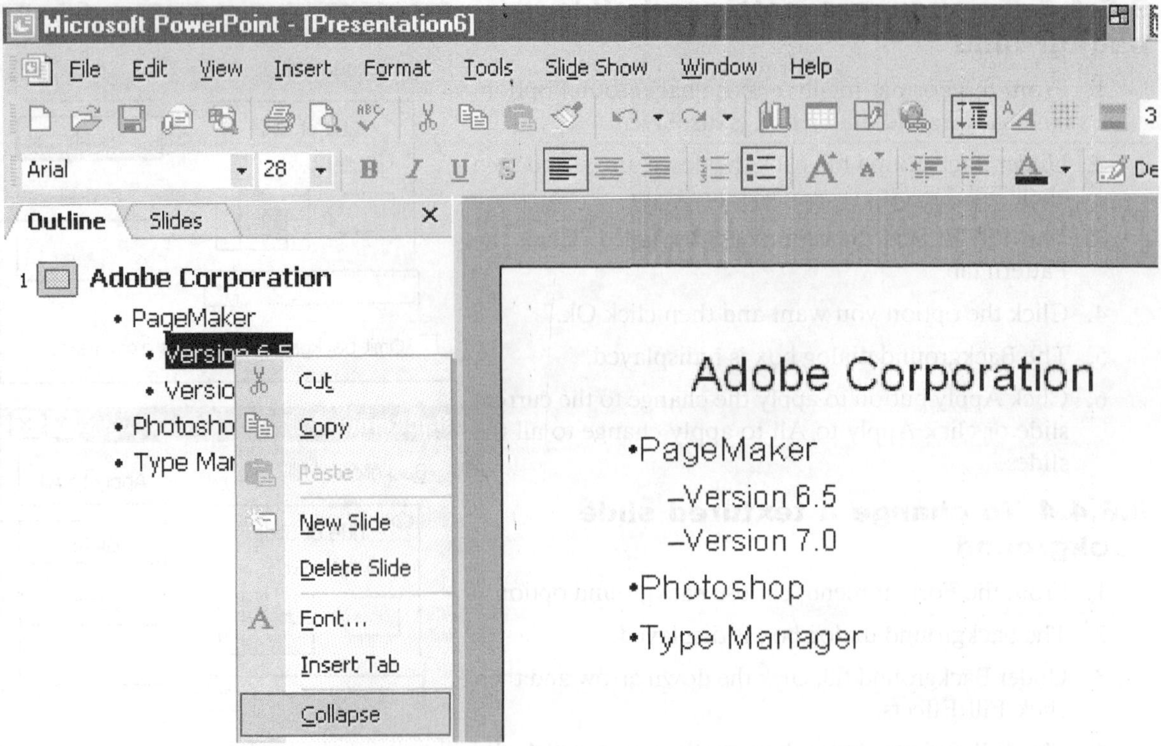

Or

Right click outside the placeholder areas in Slide or Normal view and choose slide colour scheme from the shortcut menu

2. Background dialog box appears, as shown here.
3. Under Background fill, click the down arrow.
4. To change to a colour in the colour scheme, click one of the eight colours below Automatic.
5. To change to a colour which is not there, click at More colours.
6. Click the colour you want on the standard tab or click the custom tab to mix your own colour and then click Ok.
7. Click Apply button to apply the changed colour to the current slide or click Apply to All, to apply the change to all slides in the presentation.

9.6.4.2 Working with Shaded Background

1. From the Format menu, choose background option. The background dialog box is displayed.
2. Under Background fill, click the down arrow and then click Fill Effects.
3. The Fill Effects dialog box is displayed. Click the Gradient tab.
4. Click the options you want and then click Ok.
5. The Background dialog box is redisplayed.
6. Click Apply button to apply the change to the Current slide or click Apply to All to apply change to all the slides.

9.6.4.3 To change a patterned slide background

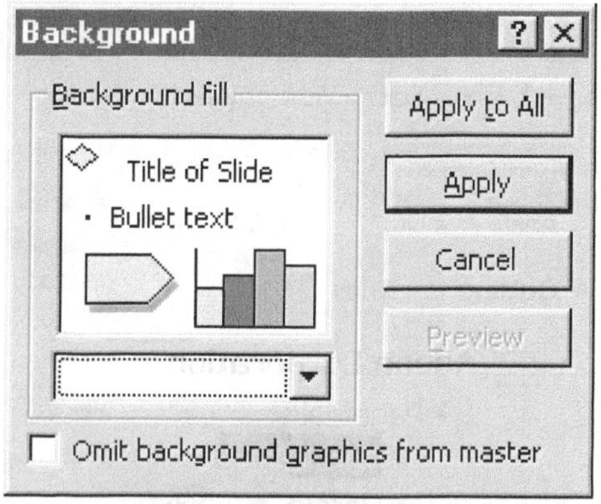

1. From the Format menu, choose background option. The background dialog box is displayed.
2. Under Background fill, click the down arrow and then click Fill Effects.
3. The Fill Effects dialog box is displayed. Click the Pattern tab.
4. Click the option you want and then click Ok.
5. The Background dialog box is redisplayed.
6. Click Apply button to apply the change to the current slide or click Apply to All to apply change to all the slides.

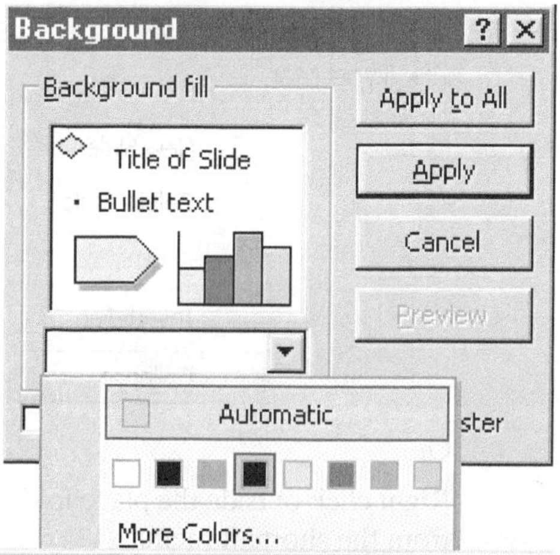

9.6.4.4 To change a textured slide background

1. From the Format menu, choose background option.
2. The background dialog box is displayed.
3. Under Background fill, click the down arrow and then click Fill Effects.
4. The Fill Effects dialog box is displayed. Click the Texture tab.
5. Click the texture you want and then click Ok.
6. The Background dialog box is redisplayed.
7. Click Apply button to apply the change to the current slide or click Apply to All to apply change to all the slides.

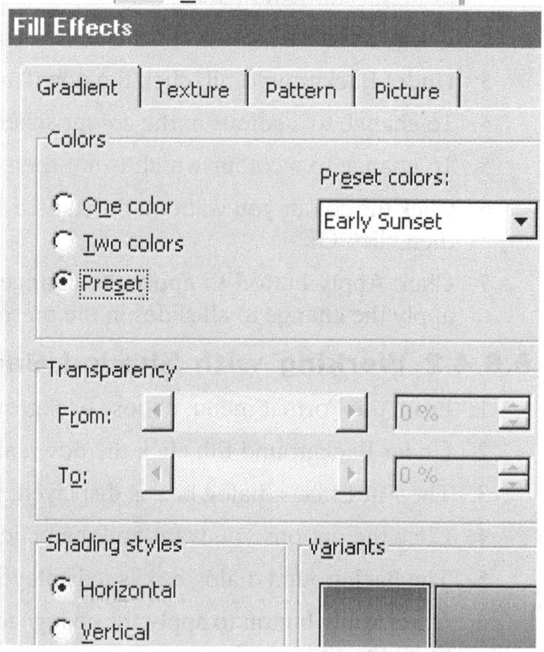

9.6.4.5 To change a slide background picture

1. From the Format menu, choose background option.
2. The background dialog box is displayed.
3. Under Background fill, click the down arrow and then click Fill Effects.
4. The Fill Effects dialog box is displayed. Click the Picture tab.
5. Click the Select Picture and find the folder that contains the picture you want. Double click the file name and then click Ok.
6. The Background dialog box is redisplayed.

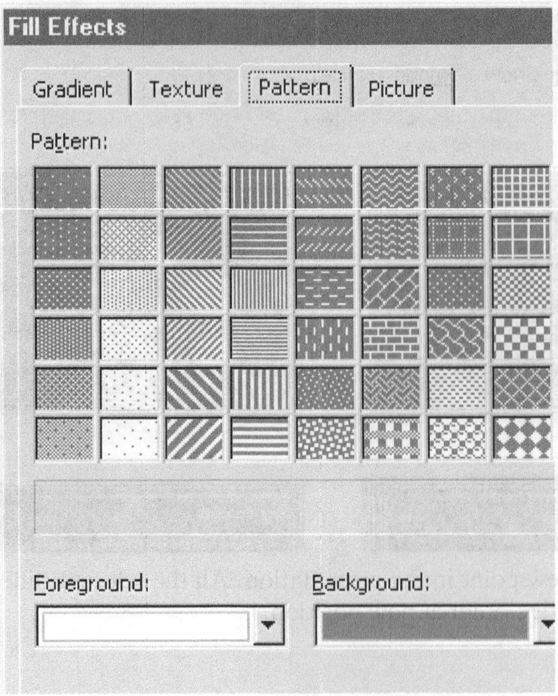

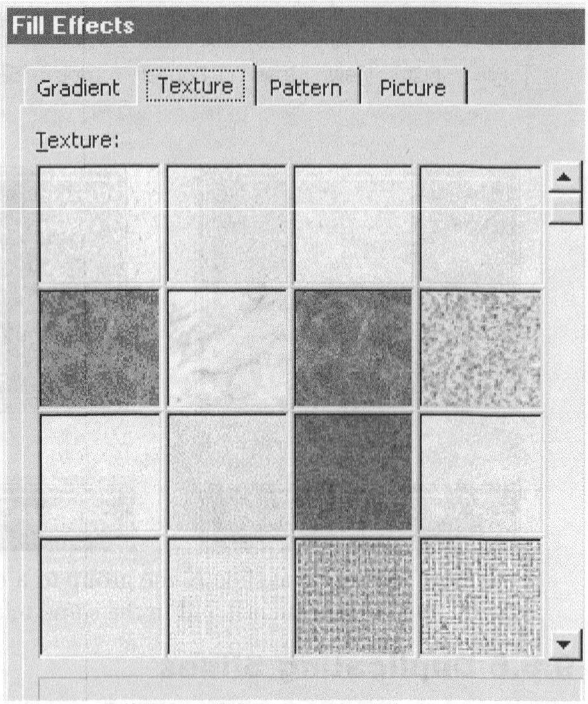

7. Click Apply button to apply the change to the current slide or click Apply to All to apply change to all the slides.

9.6.5 Reordering Slides

As you see from the view, each slide is numbered. These numbers belong to their order of display. This order can be changed at any point of time in the presentation.

9.6.5.1 To Change the Order of the Slides

1. Click with the mouse the slide whose position you want to change.
2. Pressing the mouse button drag the slide to a new position.
3. A vertical line appears to indicate where the slide will drop when you release the mouse button. In the figure on the next page, the slide 6 is being moved to a between position number 3 and 4.
4. Releasing the mouse button will drop the slide at the right place.
5. In the figure on the next page (bottom), you will see that the slide 6 has been placed between the number 3 and 4. The numbering of all the slides has been changed subsequently.

Points to Remember

1. You can select several slides to move by drawing a selection box around the group of slides and then dragging the group to the new position.
2. You can also select several slides by holding down the Shift key and selecting the first and last slides in the series.
3. To gather slides from different parts of a presentation, hold down the Ctrl key as you click each

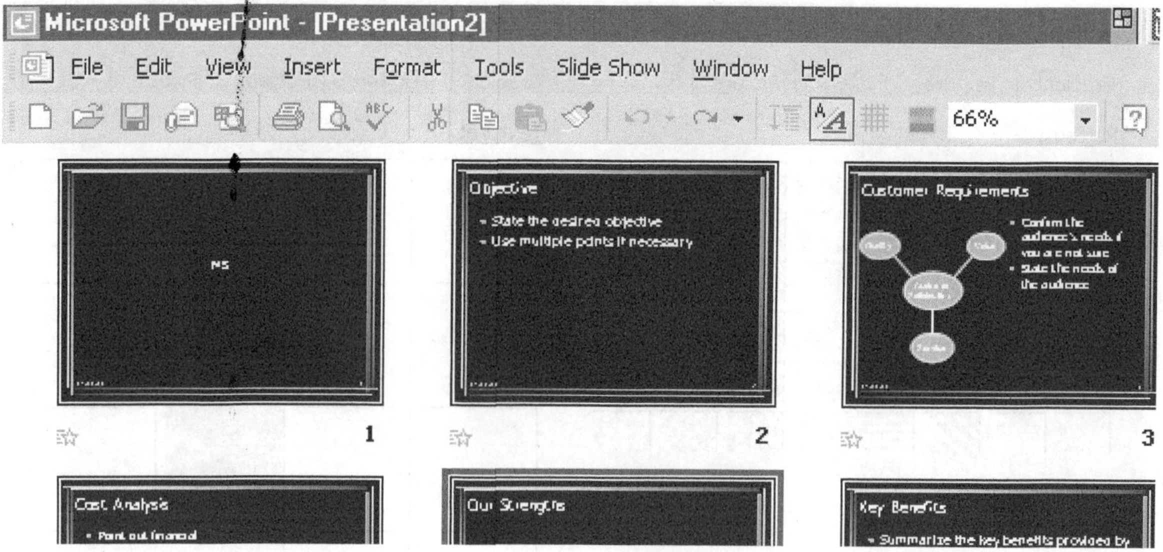

slide. Drag any one slide in the group to a new point in the presentation. All the selected slides will appear in sequence and in the same relative order at new position.

9.6.6 Duplicating Slides

You can duplicate selected slides in Slide Sorter view and see the effect on the flow of slides immediately.

To Duplicate a slide or slides:

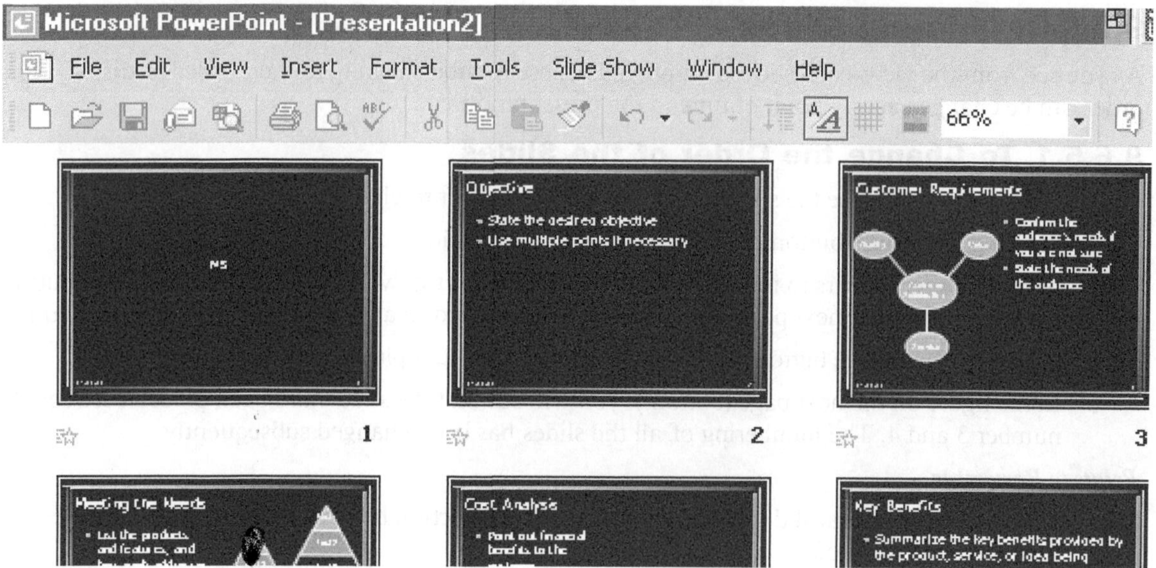

1. Select the slide or slides you want to duplicate.
2. Select Slide number 2 .
3. Press Ctrl + D or click at Duplicate in the Edit menu to duplicate the slide.

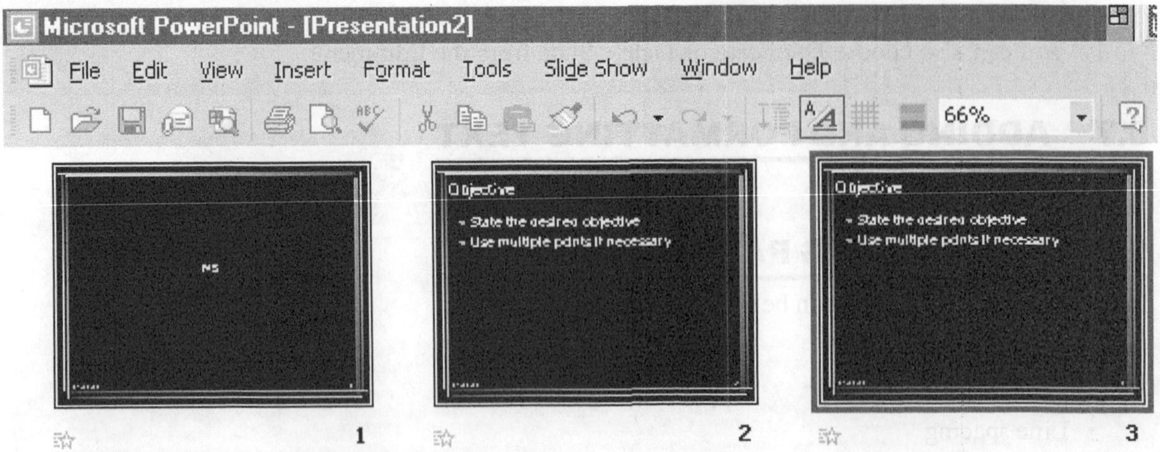

4. See the result next.
5. Slide 2 has been duplicated as Slide number 3.

9.6.7 Deleting Slides

You can delete the selected slides in Slide Sorter view and see that the numbering of other slides change immediately.

To delete a slide or slides:

1. Select the slide or slides you want to delete.
2. Supposing we want to delete these new 3 numbered slides.
3. Press Del or Ctrl + X to delete the slides.
4. See the result of the deletion on the next page.
5. Notice the line after the slide number 2 indicating that the slides have been deleted from here.

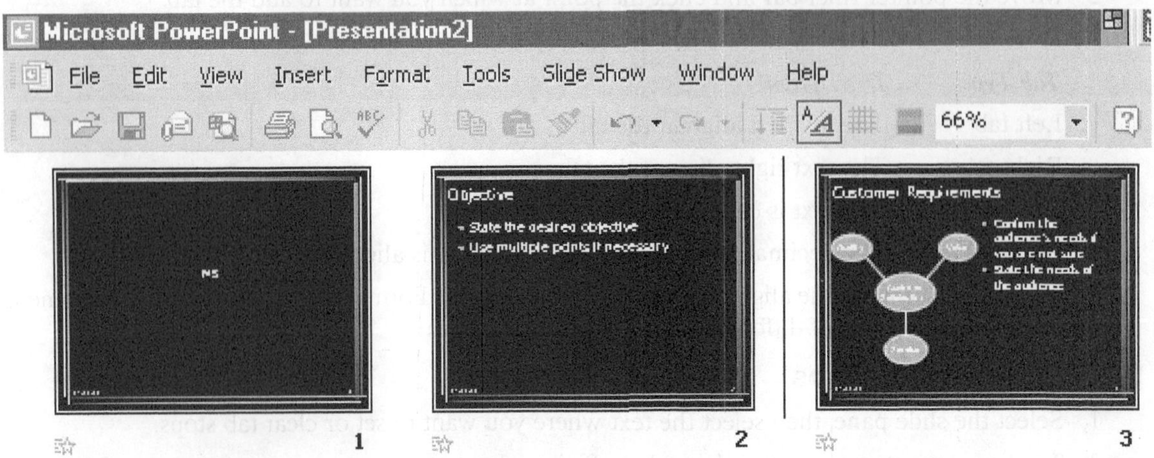

Remember

1. You can also choose Duplicate or Delete Slide from the Edit menu.

9.7 ADDING AND FORMATTING TEXT

See under working with Slides.

9.8 FORMATTING PARAGRAPHS

In PowerPoint a paragraph can be formatted for the following:

- Alignment
- Tab and Indents
- Line spacing
- Space before and after the paragraph

Let us see how each one of them is used.

9.8.1 Alignment

We all know about the alignment. We also know that there are 4 main alignments like Left, Right, Centre and Justify. PowerPoint supports all of them. As you would do in any of the word processing software, here also you just highlight the text of the para and click at Alignment in the Format menu.

9.8.2 Tabs and Indents

You would usually set tabs for making the text in the tabular manner. The tab is a small marker and tells the text where you want to stop. PowerPoint gives you the option of choosing four different tab stops: left, right, center and decimal tabs. In PowerPoint tabs are set in the following manner.

1. Choose the type of tab you want by clicking in the tab selection box at the left of the horizontal ruler until the tab type appears.
2. Move the pointer ruler bar and click the point at which you want to add the tab.

   Different types of tab types

Tab Type	*Description*
Left tab	The text left align at the tab
Right tab	The text right align at the tab
Center tab	The text is center align at the tab
Decimal tab	The decimal point where the numbering is aligned

   You can also change the alignment of text by opening the Format menu and choosing Alignment. A small pop-up box of different alignment choices appears.

9.8.2.1 Clearing Tabs

1. Select the slide pane, then select the text where you want to set or clear tab stops.
2. To clear a tab stop, drag the tab marker off the ruler.

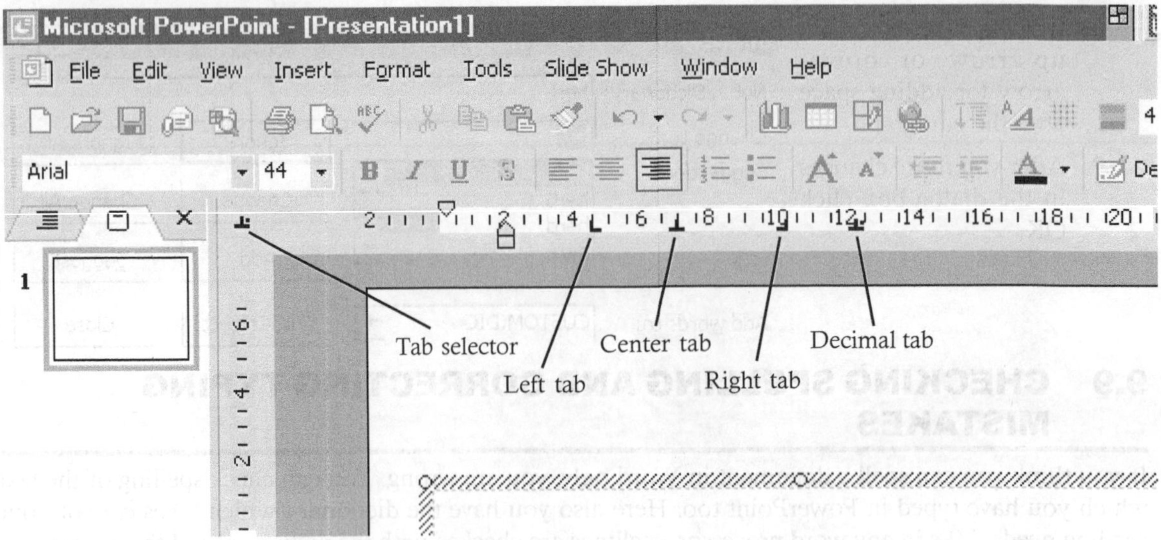

9.8.2.2 Setting Paragraph Indents

1. In this slide pane, select the text you want to set an indentation for.
2. If the ruler is not displayed, click View menu and choose Ruler.
3. To set the indent for the first line of a paragraph, drag the upper indent marker.
4. To set the left indent for other lines in a paragraph, drag the lower indent marker. The rectangular part of the lower indent marker also moves with it.
5. To maintain the relationship between the first line and the rest of the paragraph, move both markers by dragging the rectangular part of the lower market.

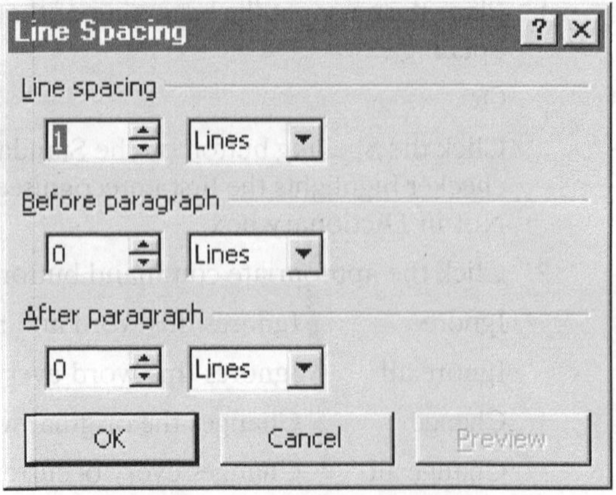

9.8.3 Line spacing

You may not need this for setting the line space but PowerPoint provides you with the option of changing the line space, in case it is required. For this do the following:

1. In the Slide pane, click anywhere in the paragraph you want to add space between lines.
2. Click the Format menu and choose Line Spacing. The Line Spacing dialog box appears as shown here.
3. In the Line spacing section, click up-arrow or down-arrow to increase or decrease the number of lines you want separating text lines.
4. In the Before Paragraph area, you do the same thing.
5. In the Slide pane, click anywhere in the paragraph if you want to add space after.

6. In the spinner box, click up-arrow or down-arrow for adding space after the paragraph.
7. After you make changes in the dialog box click OK.

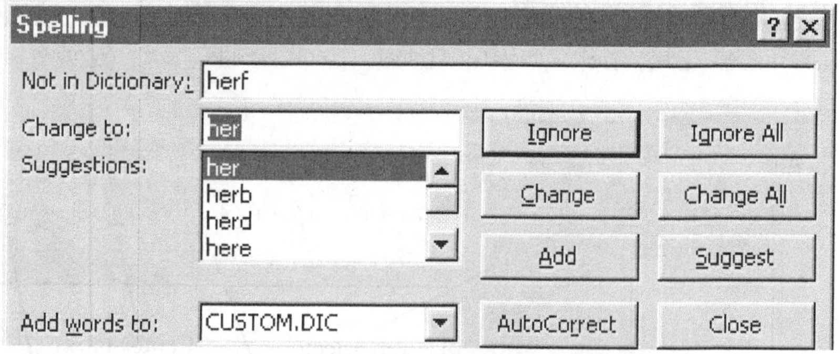

9.9 CHECKING SPELLING AND CORRECTING TYPING MISTAKES

If you think you can spell a document in Word only, you are wrong. You can check spelling of the text which you have typed in PowerPoint too. Here also you have the dictionary which takes care of your spelling needs. Like in any word processor, spellings are checked with the dictionary and the wrong ones are pointed out.

The spelling checker moves through your presentation one slide at a time and then checks the Notes Pages (if any) before closing the Spelling dialog box. You can stop using the spelling checker at any time by clicking the Close button in the Spelling dialog box.

1. Place the cursor at the beginning of the text in the first slide and click Tools menu and then choose Spelling...

   Or

   Click the Spelling button on the Standard toolbar to display the Spelling dialog box. The spelling checker highlights the first unrecognised word in the presentation file and displays the word in the Not in Dictionary box.
2. Click the appropriate command button, from the following lists:

Ignore	Ignores this word and moves on
Ignore all	Ignores this word every time you find it.
Change	Changes the original word by replacing it with the word in the Change to: box.
Change all	Changes every occurrence of this word to the word in the Change to: box.
Add	Adds this word to the dictionary so the speller does not stop here any more.
Suggest	Searches the dictionary and displays possible replacement words (you choose the one that is correct).

3. The spelling checker takes the indicated action and then highlights the next unrecognized word.
4. Repeat step 2 until the spelling checker displays a message saying that the entire presentation has been checked.
5. Click OK.

9.9.1 Using AutoCorrect

This is another feature which is there in the Word processing. It takes care of all your typing mistakes if

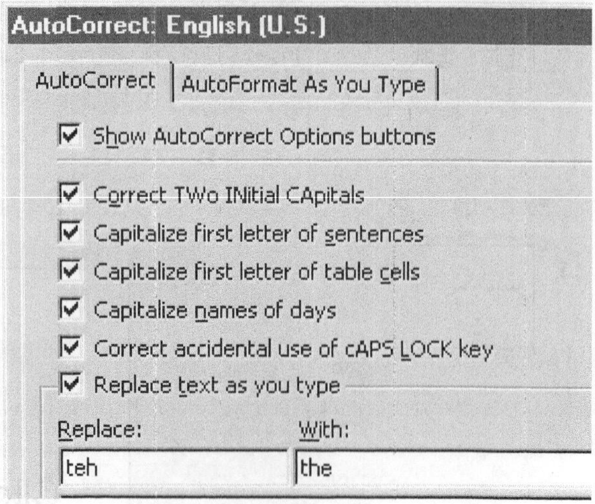

it knows them in advance. For example, as shown here, if you have the bad habit of typing teh instead of the, then say that to the computer and it will take of this error every time it occurs. So Autocorrect will take care of all your commonly made errors.

I suggest you just sit with the dialog box and go through it and then add the most common mistakes you make.

For this do the following:

1. Click Tools menu and choose AutoCorrect… the AutoCorrect dialog box appears.
2. In the Replace: text box, enter the characters or words you want to type in order to have AutoCorrect, change them to a word or a phrase.
3. In the With: text box, enter the word or phrase you want to appear after you enter the word.
4. Configure the way AutoCorrect works by selecting and deselecting the options.
5. To delete any desired character, select the characters in the Replace: box and click delete.
6. Click OK when you have finished configuring the dialog box.

9.10 MAKING NOTES, PAGES AND HANDOUTS

There are three important tools for your presentation. These tools are:

9.10.1 Notes Pages

These pages are like the script for your presentation. In this script you have an image of slides along with the words you want to deliver for the specific slide.

9.10.2 Handouts

These printed pages are the hard copies of the presentation slides which you can distribute to your audience.

9.10.3 Master

These are control elements of a slide like the title master which controls appearance of the title on all the slides.

9.10.4 Using Notes Pages

Notes Pages act like a cheat sheet for your presentation. You would write the text you want to read without letting the audience know that you are reading during the course of a presentation for each slide.

9.10.4.1 Creating Notes

PowerPoint offers two ways for preparing Notes Pages. These notes can be prepared while working on slides or after you have finished with all the slides.

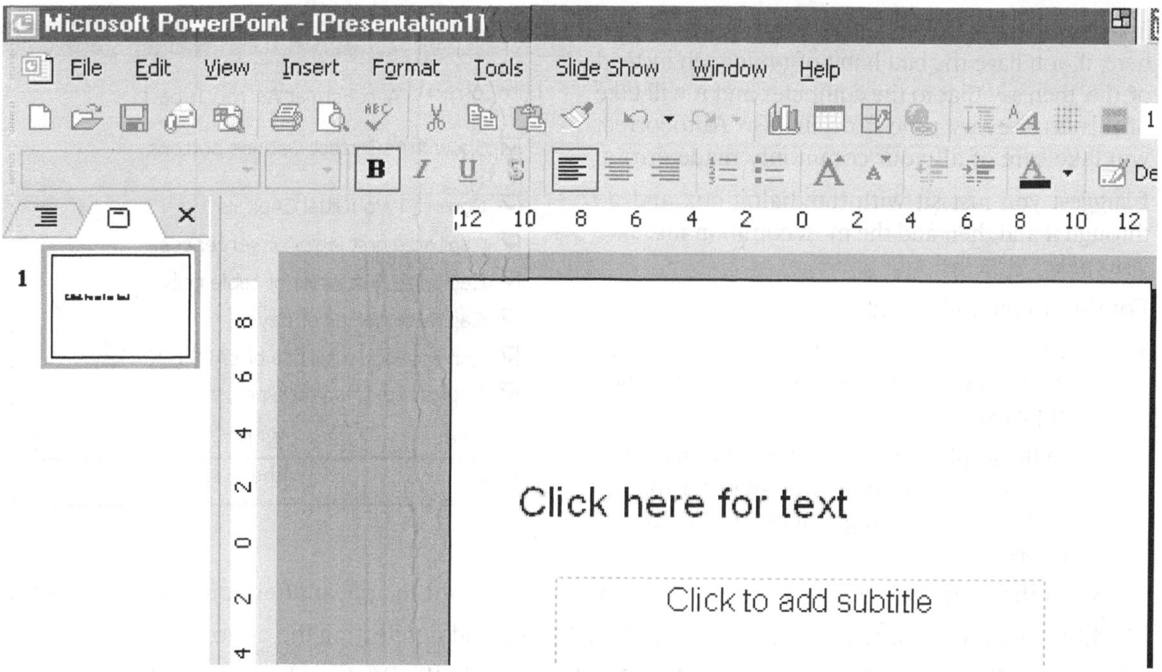

To create notes using Notes Pages, do this:

1. Click the View menu and choose Notes Pages.
2. In the Notes Page View, you see the entire Notes page as it will print. There is a picture of the slide at the top and a text place holder at the bottom. Click the place holder to begin entering the text for your Note.

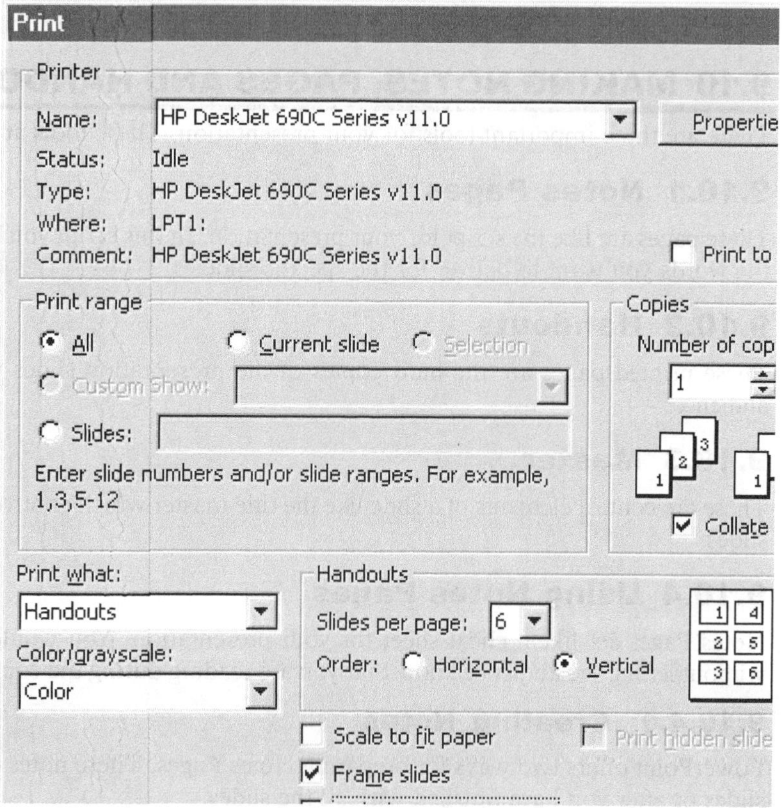

9.10.5 Printing Handouts

You can print your entire presentation in the form of handouts. These handouts are used to distribute among the audience in advance. You can also print specific slides, notes pages or outline pages.

For this do the following:

1. Open the presentation you want to print.
2. Click the File menu and Print. The Print dialog box appears.
3. In the Print what: box, click the item you want to print.
4. If you select Handouts, you can then select a number of slides per page and whether the order should be horizontal or vertical,
5. Select any other options you want to apply.
6. After applying the option in the handouts section, click OK.

9.10.6 Handouts Master

The Handouts Master can be used to modify your Handout format. For this do the following:

1. Click the View menu, highlight Master and choose Handout Master. The Handout Master appears.
2. In the Handout Master view, you can select the two slides per page, three slides per page or the six slides per page formats by clicking on the Handout Master toolbar as shown.

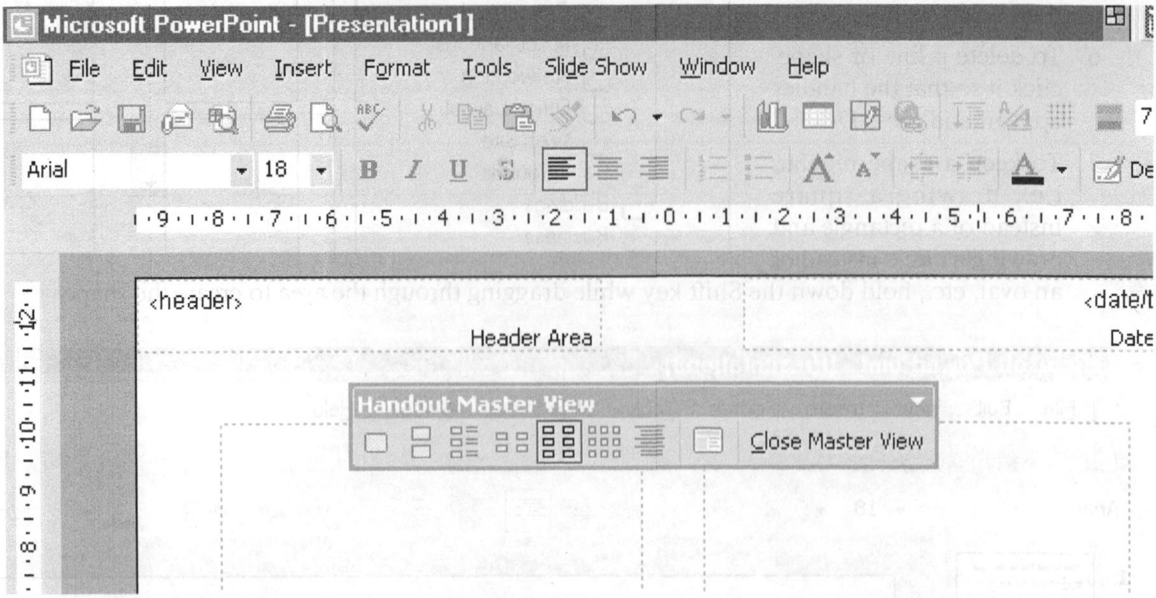

3. To apply any changes to the Handout Master, just follow the procedure as for the Notes master.
4. Save the presentation file to save any changes you make to the Handout Master.
5. You cannot change the position of the slide images on the Handout Master.
6. There is no notes text placeholder on the Handout Master.

9.11 DRAWING AND WORKING WITH OBJECTS

You can add pictures, graphics, etc., in the slides of the presentation. You can even add these as backgrounds too.

9.11.1 Drawing Shapes and Lines

Using the drawing tools available with PowerPoint you can draw the various figures like squares, circles, etc.

1. In Slide view, click one of the drawing tools or menus on the drawing toolbar.
2. Drag with the mouse pointer to create the shape.
3. Click the shape and choose Colours and Lines from the Format menu.
4. In the Colours and Lines dialog box, choose a fill colour, line colour, and line style. Click Ok.
5. To type text inside the shape, click the shape and then begin typing.
6. To delete a line or shape, click it so that the handles appear, and press Del.
7. To keep a shape regular, i.e., drawing a square instead of a rectangle and drawing a circle instead of an oval, etc., hold down the Shift key while dragging through the area to create the shape.

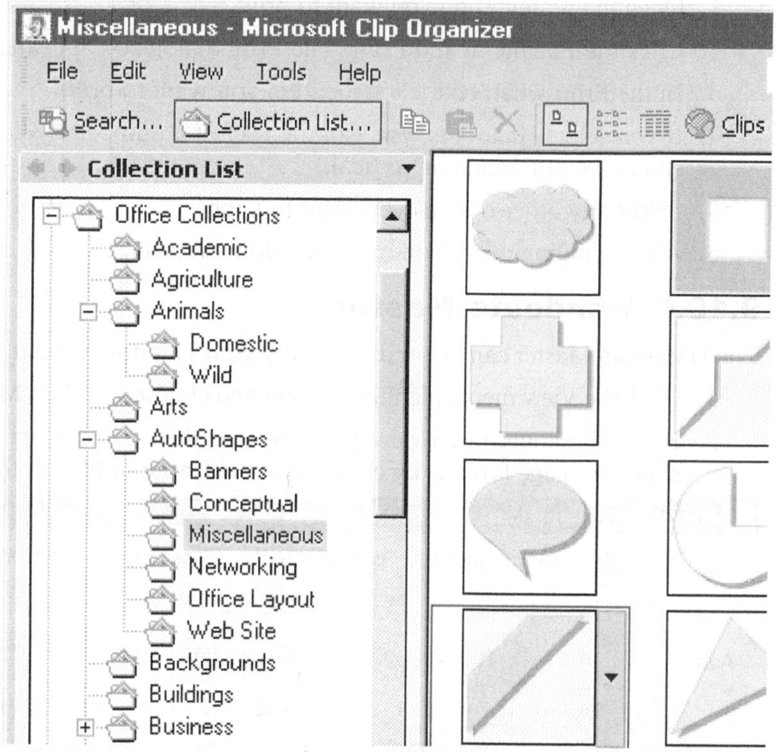

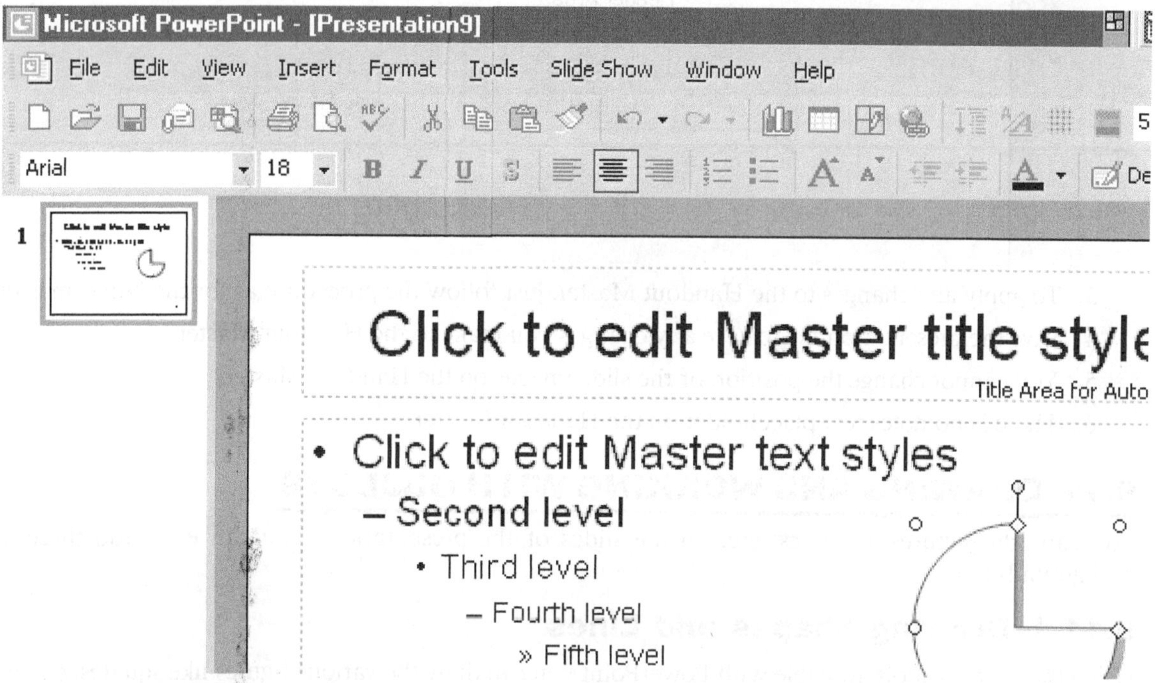

9.11.2 Adding Text Box

Supposing on a slide you want to add some text in the form of some message or an afterthought. You can always do so by adding a text block on the slide.

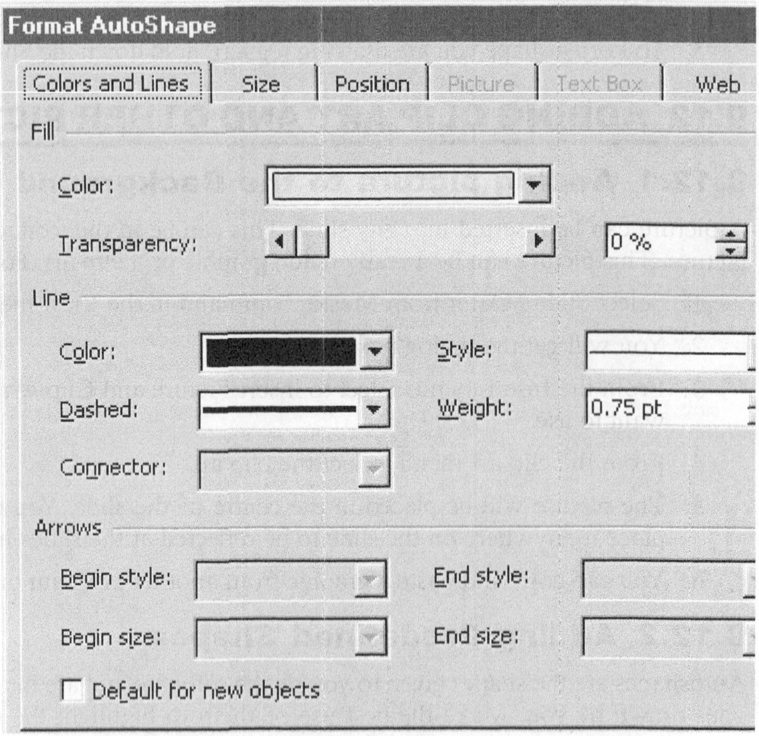

1. Select Text Box from the Insert menu.
2. Click in the slide where you want the text box to appear.
3. Type the text. The box expands to surround the text. Press Enter to create a new line of text within the box.
4. For precise control over the parameters of the text box (fill and line colour, word wrapping, internal margins, position, and so on), double-click one of the sides of the object to format the object.
5. In the Format Text Box dialog box, select the formatting you want.
6. Click Ok.

Remember

1. Change the location of the text box by clicking one of the sides (not at a handle) and dragging the box to the new location.
2. You can also add text to any other shape by clicking in the shape and typing.

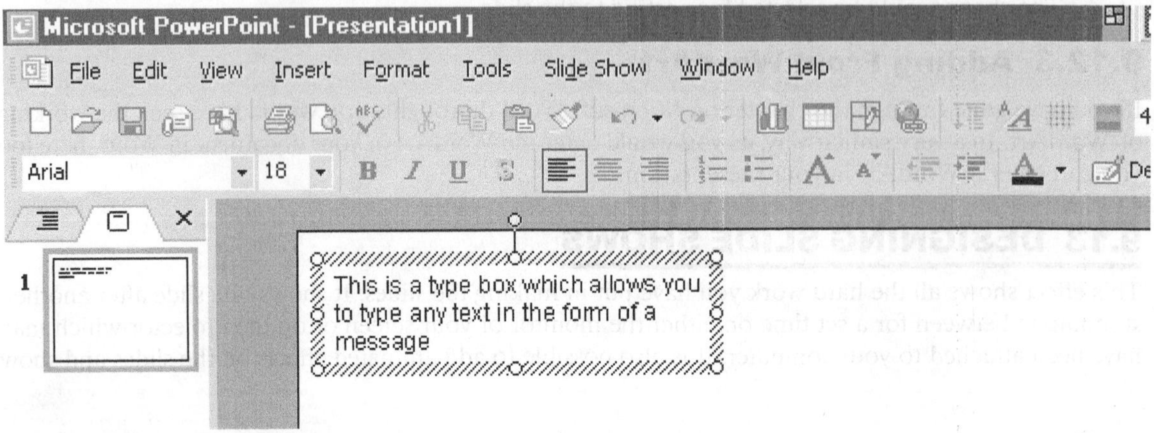

3. After you have entered the text, you can change the shape of the text box by dragging the side handles.
4. To delete a text box, click one of the sides so that the insertion point inside disappears and press Del.
5. To keep a shape you are drawing regular, hold down the Shift key as your drag to draw the shape.

9.12 ADDING CLIP ART AND OTHER PICTURES

9.12.1 Adding picture to the Background

A picture can be inserted into any slide. This can be in the form of a logo of a company or any other picture. This picture can be a ready made graphic or a clip art. For this do the following:

1. Select Slide Master from Master command in the View menu.
2. You will get the dialog box.
3. From the Insert menu, select to insert Picture and Clip Art or any other picture which you may want to use.
4. From the clip art menu, select the clip art.
5. The picture will be placed in the centre of the slide. You can increase or decrease its size and place it anywhere on the slide to be reflected at the slides in the presentation.
6. You can copy and paste a graphic from another program onto the slide master.

9.12.2 Adding Predefined Shapes

Autoshapes are the shapes given to you by the software and are much more better looking than the usual ones drawn by you. Make the best use of them to highlight the text or that matter anything in your presentation.

1. AutoShapes button is available on the drawing toolbar.
2. Clicking on it will lead to the various other options on the menu, as shown on the next page. It has Lines, Connectors, Basic Shapes, Block Arrows, Flowchart, Stars and Banners, Callouts, and Action Buttons. More AutoShapes will lead you to more shapes.
3. Select one of the menu and then the shape.
4. The shape would be selected for pasting to the slide.

9.12.3 Adding From WordArt

If you have gone through the chapter on Microsoft Word thoroughly you would have seen the working of WordArt. In a very similar way, as you would enter the WordArt in your document in Word, here too you can enter a WordArt in your presentation.

9.13 DESIGNING SLIDE SHOWS

This effect shows all the hard work you have put in making the slides. It shows one slide after another, stopping in between for a set time on either the monitor of your screen or on the projector which may have been attached to your computer. It is also possible to add animated effects on the slides and show

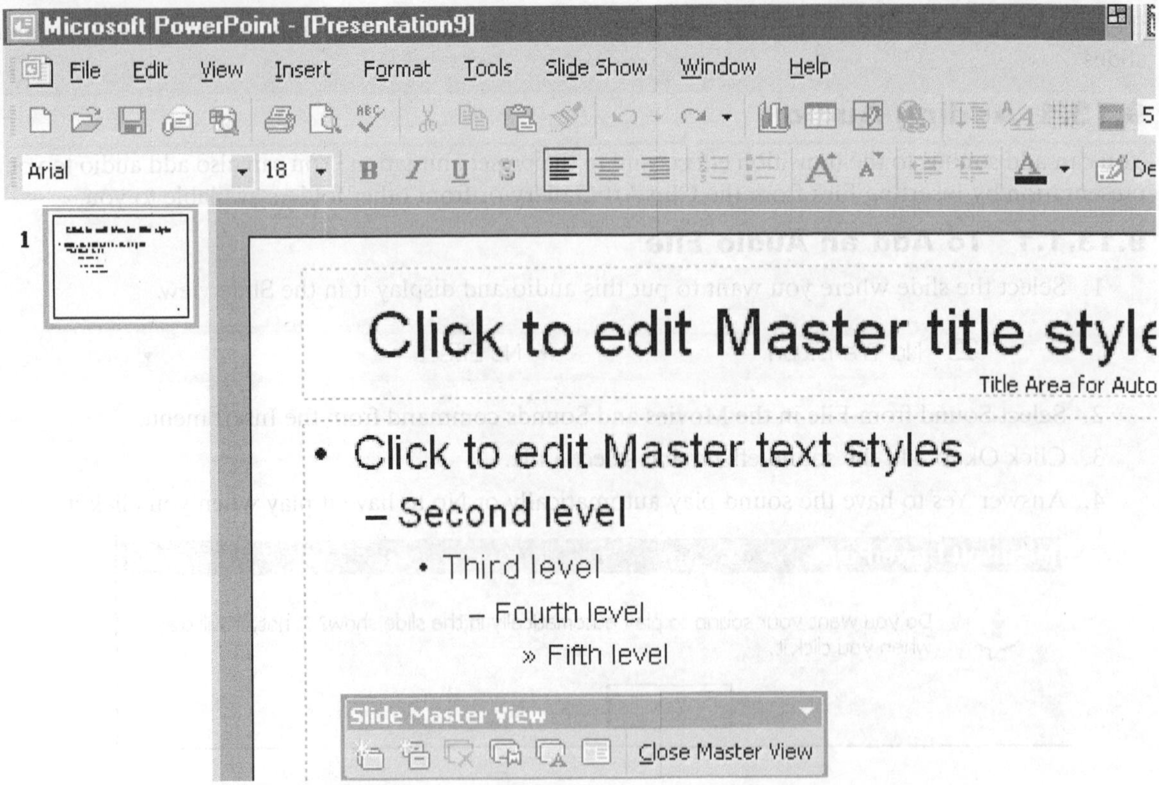
Microsoft PowerPoint - [Presentation9]
File Edit View Insert Format Tools Slide Show Window Help
Arial 18
Click to edit Master title style
Title Area for Auto
Click to edit Master text styles
– Second level
Third level
– Fourth level
» Fifth level
Slide Master View
Close Master View

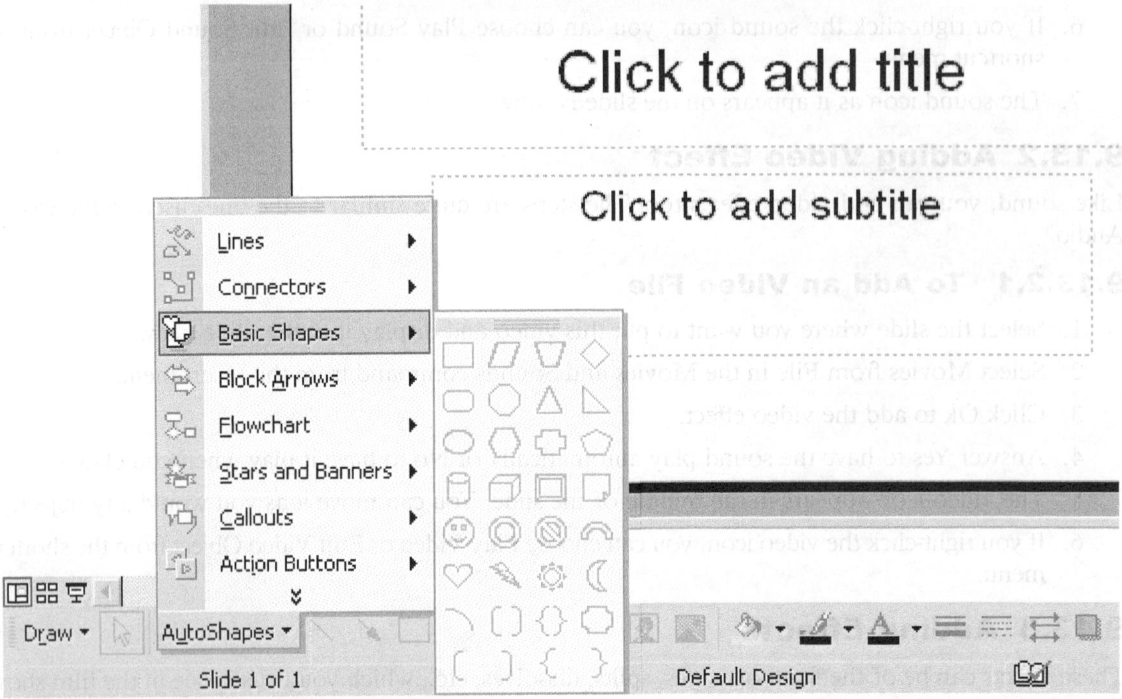
Click to add title
Click to add subtitle
Lines
Connectors
Basic Shapes
Block Arrows
Flowchart
Stars and Banners
Callouts
Action Buttons
Draw
AutoShapes
Slide 1 of 1
Default Design

them in a sophisticated manner. It is also possible to add audio, video, narration, music, etc., to your slides.

9.13.1 Adding Audio

You can add sounds to the transition effects and to the preset animation. You can also add audio to your presentation by inserting files from the Clip Art Gallery or from other folders available to you.

9.13.1.1 To Add an Audio File

1. Select the slide where you want to put this audio and display it in the Slide view.

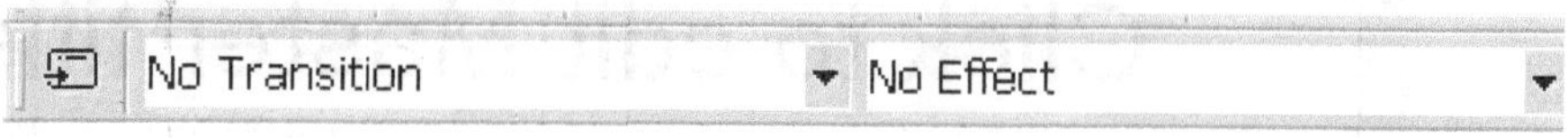

2. Select Sound from File in the Movies and Sounds command from the Insert menu.
3. Click Ok to add the sound effect, and select a file.
4. Answer Yes to have the sound play automatically or No to have it play when you click it.

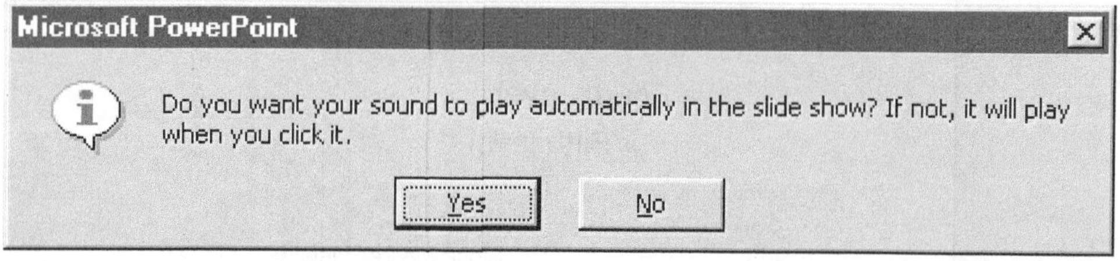

5. The sound icon appears in the middle of the slide. You can move it as you would any object.
6. If you right-click the sound icon, you can choose Play Sound or Edit Sound Object from the shortcut menu.
7. The sound icon as it appears on the slide is shown next.

9.13.2 Adding Video Effect

Like sound, you can add video effects too. The steps are quite similar to the ones used in the case of Audio.

9.13.2.1 To Add an Video File

1. Select the slide where you want to put this video and display it in the Slide view.
2. Select Movies from File in the Movies and Sounds command from the Insert menu.
3. Click Ok to add the video effect.
4. Answer Yes to have the sound play automatically or No to have it play when you click it.
5. The video icon appears in the middle of the slide. You can move it as you would any object.
6. If you right-click the video icon, you can choose Play Video or Edit Video Object from the shortcut menu.

9.13.3 Adding Effects

These effects can be of the form of wipes, splits, dissolves, etc., which you usually see in the film show. For this you have to work in the Slide Sorter view.

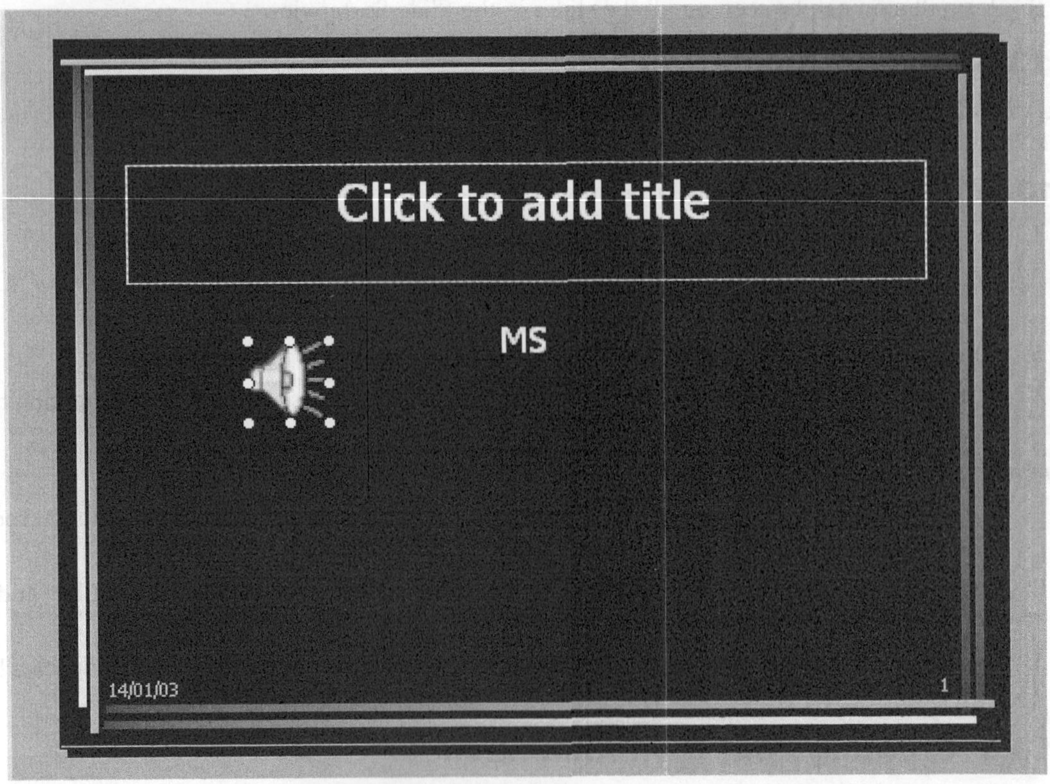

9.13.3.1 To Add a Transition View

1. Choose the slide on which you want to put this effect.
2. Click on the arrow next to the transition effect as shown on next page.
3. This will lead to the Slide Transition dialog box as shown on next page.
4. In this dialog box, choose a transition effect from the drop-down list, a speed (slow, medium, or fast) and the advance option (on mouse click or after a period of time).
5. Click Apply to All to apply this transition effect to all slides, or click Apply to apply it only to the selected slide.
6. To apply the same transition effect to multiple slides, hold down the Shift key while you click the slides and then choose a transition effect.

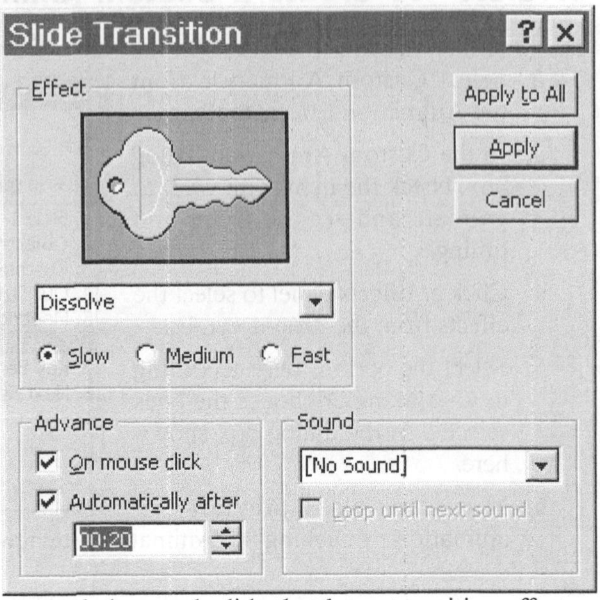

7. To preview the transition effect in Slide Sorter view, click the transition icon that appears below each slide that has a transition effect.

8. A small icon can be seen on all the slides in the Slide Sorter view.

9.13.4 Adding Animation

You can add animation to the slides which are going to be displayed. This helps in presenting a slide with special effects. You can choose from the various animations available.

9.13.4.1 To Select an Animation

1. In the Slide Sorter view click at the slide to which you want to add the animation effect.
2. Once it has been applied, you can see the small icon being put under the slide to show that this slide has an animation effect.
3. You can see the preview of this animation effect by clicking at the preview button.
4. If you want you can apply different effects on various slides and see the whole presentation having the different effects.

Remember

1. You can also apply effects using the buttons on the Animation Effects toolbar. Choose Toolbars from the View menu and then choose Animation Effects from the pop-out menu.
2. To apply the same present animation effect to multiple slides, hold down the Shift key and click the slides and then choose an effect.
3. To preview the animation effect in Slide Sorter view, click the animation icon that appears below each slide that has an animation effect.

9.13.5 Creating Your Own Animation

It is possible to have your own animation which can give you more control over the display of the presentation. This can be applied to both text and objects. These can be created only in Slide view.

9.13.5.1 To Create a Custom Animation

1. Select the slide where you want to put this animation and display it in the Slide view.
2. Select Custom Animation from the Animation Effects toolbar.
3. In the Custom Animation dialog box, check the items you want to animate and set the order and timing.
4. Click at Effects panel to select the effects from the drop-down list.
5. Select the options here according to your liking or choose the ones selected in the dialog box shown here.

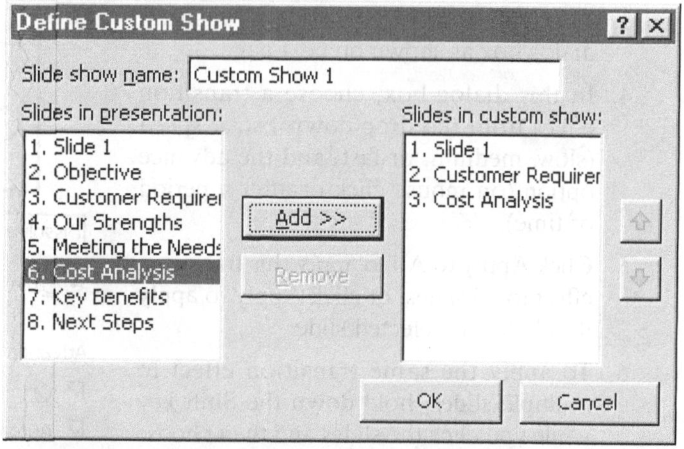

6. You can also preview an animation by clicking the Animation Preview button on the Animation Effects toolbar.

9.13.6 Adding Action Buttons

These buttons allow you to play sound, video at your choice when displaying the presentation.

9.13.6.1 To Add an Action Button

1. Select the slide to which you want to add this button. This can be done in any view except Slide Sorter view.
2. Select Action buttons from the Slide Show menu.
3. Select a button of your choice.
4. Position the button in your slide at any place of your liking.

5. On clicking the button PowerPoint will give rise to a new dialog box called Action settings.
6. Make the necessary settings and click Ok.
7. You action button is now properly placed in the slide.
8. You can add actions to other objects simply by selecting them and then choosing Action settings from the Slide Show menu.

9.14 RUNNNG AND CONTROLLING A SLIDE SHOW

Now comes the most important part of the software where you are going to setup the whole show of presentation to run without your help. You can choose to hide few slides for not displaying.

To Set Up the Slide Show:

1. From the Slide Show menu, choose Set Up Show.
2. In the dialog box, as shown on the next page, choose the type of show, which slides to show or hide, and the method to advance slides.
3. Click Ok.
4. Click the Projector Wizard button in the Set Up Show dialog box for help connecting your computer to a projector.

5. Choose Custom Shows from the Slide Show menu to add slides from this presentation to a custom show.
6. Even though a slide is hidden, you can display it by clicking a hyperlink or an action pointing to it.

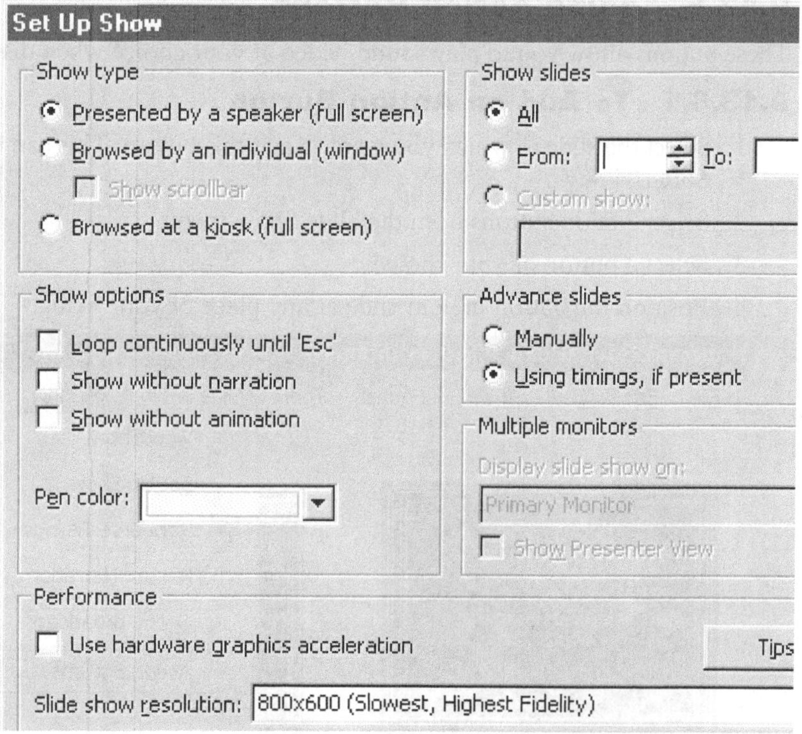

9.14.1 Rehearsing the Show

As we see the preview of the page before printing. PowerPoint also allows you to do the same. For this you have what is called the Rehearsing of the Show.

You can run the show from any view.

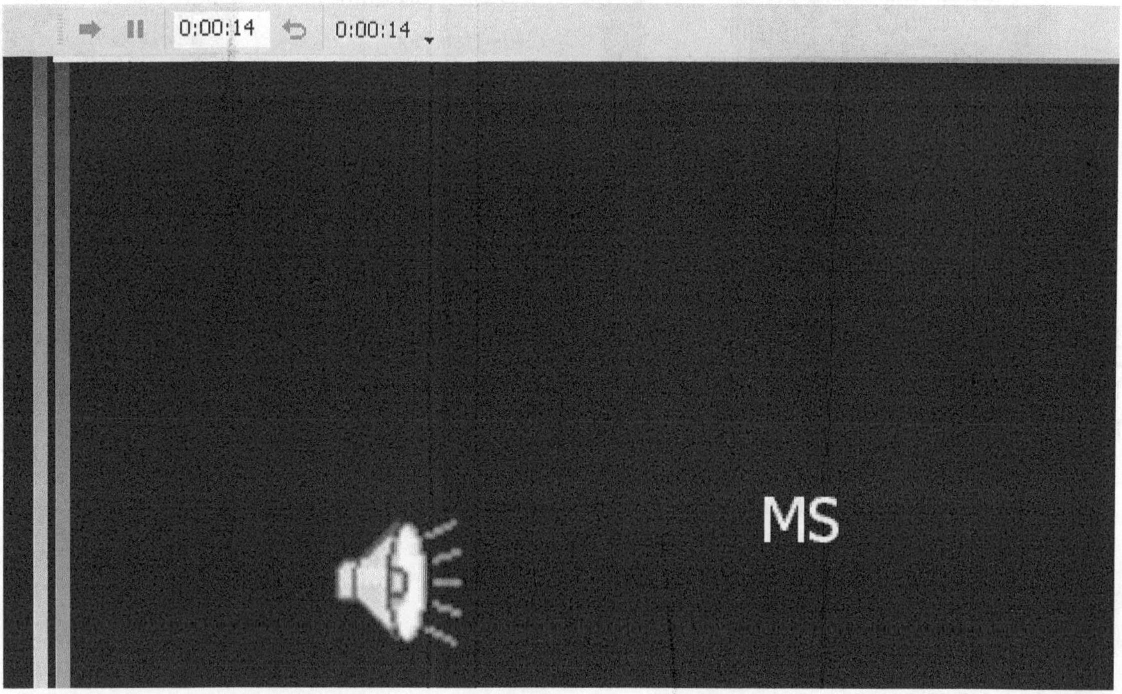

9.14.1.1 To Rehearse the Slide Show

1. From the Slide Show menu, choose Rehearse Timings.
2. You can click the Rehearse Timings button on the Slide Sorter toolbar too in the Slide Sorter view.
3. The show begins with the timer set at the top left hand corner of the screen, as shown on the previous page.
4. To use these timings, choose Use Slide Timings in the Set Up Show dialog box.
5. To advance through the slide show, click anywhere on the slide. You can also right-click anywhere and choose an action from the shortcut menu.

9.15 PRINTING PRESENTATIONS

Most presentations are designed to be presented in color, but slides and handouts are typically printed in black and white or shades of gray, also known as grayscale. When you print in grayscale, color images are printed in variations of gray tones between black and white.

When you print your slides, PowerPoint sets the colors in your presentation to match the selected printer's capabilities. You can size the slides to fit different paper sizes, including letter and ledger, or you can specify a custom size. In PowerPoint you can print other parts of a presentation, such as handouts, notes pages, or a presentation in Outline view.

9.15.1 Set the slide size and orientation for printing

1. To change your printing options, do the following:
2. On the Design tab, in the Page Setup group, click Page Setup.
3. In the Slides sized for list, click the size of paper on which you will be printing.

Notes:

- If you click Custom, type or select the measurements that you want in the Width and Height boxes.
- To print an overhead transparency, click Overhead.

To set the page orientation for the slides, under Orientation, under Slides, click Landscape or Portrait. All slides in a presentation must be set to one orientation.

9.15.2 Print the slides

1. Click Print in the File menu.
2. In the Page Setup group, in the Print What list, select Slides.
3. Click Options, point to Color/Grayscale, and then click one of the following:
   - Color If you print to a color printer, this option prints in color.
   - Grayscale This option prints images that contain variations of gray tones between black and white. Background fills are printed as white, so that the text will be more legible. (Sometimes grayscale appears the same as Pure Black and White.)
   - Pure Black and White This option prints the handout with no gray fills.
4. Click Print.

LET US REVISE

1. AutoContent Wizard creates presentation by asking you just few questions.
2. You can even create a presentation using the Templates given with the software.
3. You can create a presentation using the various optional slides given.
4. You can save your presentation.
5. Various views in PowerPoint are: Outline view, Normal view, Slide sorter view, Slide show view and Notes page view.
6. You can enter your text in the slides of your presentation.
7. Using Collapse you can change the view of the slides.
8. You can move the text up and down in the slide.
9. You can change colours of the slides.
10. You can have a patterend background of the slide.
11. A slide with textured background can also be created.
12. You can have picture in the background of a slide.
13. You can format text paragraphs for Alignment, Tabs, Indents and Line Spacing.
14. Like Word processing, you can check spelling of your text.
15. Using Autocorrect, you can preset corrections for your wrongly spelled words.
16. You can have charts in your presentations.
17. You can have various types of charts like bar charts, pie charts, etc.
18. You can change the various elements of the charts.
19. Organization charts are used to represent organizations.
20. You can have pictures in the background of slide.
21. You can draw various shapes to put in the presentation slides.
22. You can add a text box in your slide.
23. You can add text from Word Art in your presentation slide.
24. You can change the order of the slides.
25. You can duplicate a particular slide.
26. You can delete a slide.
27. You can make slide show to show all the slides one by one.
28. Audio clips can be added to the slides.
29. Video clips can also be added to the slides.
30. You can add actions in your slides.
31. Even animations can be added to the slides.
32. Notes Pages are used to have the text on the slides but it is not shown.
33. Handouts can be printed for all your slides.
34. You can create your own animation and add to the slide.

MULTIPLE CHOICE QUESTIONS

1. PowerPoint is used for:
   (a) Word processing (b) Spreadsheets (c) Presentations
2. Overhead projections can be created using PowerPoint:
   (a) Yes (b) No
3. AutoContent Wizard creates a
   (a) Document (b) Presentation (c) Spreadsheet
4. There is no need to use templates in PowerPoint:
   (a) True (b) False
5. You can view your presentation through various views :
   (a) Yes (b) No
6. You can move your text in the slide, up and down:
   (a) Yes (b) No
7. A slide with background picture can be created in PowerPoint:
   (a) Yes (b) No
8. You can even have textured patterns in the background of a slide:
   (a) Yes (b) No
9. You can add organization format in the form of a :
   (a) Table (b) Chart (c) Graphic
10. You can use a picture as a background for a slide:
    (a) Yes (b) No
11. Various alignments available for text formatting in PowerPoint are Left, Right, Center and :
    (a) Justify (b) Natural (c) Reverse
12. Various tabs available in PowerPoint are, Left, Right, Center and :
    (a) Comma (b) Decimal (c) Full stop
13. Optional command which allows you to preset your errors is called:
    (a) Autoset (b) Autoplay (c) Autocorrect
14. Notes pages have on them:
    (a) text (b) graphic (c) pictures
15. You can view all slides continuously by using:
    (a) Show (b) Slide show (c) Slides
16. You can set tabs using
    (a) Ruler (b) Scale (c) Footer

TRUE/FALSE QUESTIONS

1. PowerPoint helps in creating charts, graphs, slides, handouts, overheads, and various other formats of presentations which any office would require.
2. PowerPoint cannot be started from Start button.
3. AutoContent Wizard creates presentation by asking you just few questions.

4. There are no templates in PowerPoint.
5. You can create a presentation using the various optional slides given.
6. The presentations cannot be saved.
7. You can use different views to see various positions of the slides.
8. You can enter your text in the slides of your presentation.
9. Using Collapse you can change the view of the slides.
10. You cannot move the text of your slides.
11. You can change colours of the slides.
12. There is no provision for background colour of the slides.
13. A slide can have a textured background too.
14. You can have picture in the background of a slide.
15. You can format text of the slides like that of a paragraph in word processing.
16. There is no provision for spell checking of the text in PowerPoint.
17. Using Autocorrect, you can preset corrections for your wrongly spelled words.
18. You cannot have charts in your slides.
19. You can change the various elements of the charts.
20. Organization charts are used to represent organizations.
21. You can have pictures in the background of slide.
22. You cannot add a text box in your slide.
23. You can add text from Word Art in your presentation slide.
24. You cannot reorder all the slides.
25. You cannot duplicate a particular slide.
26. You cannot delete a slide.
27. It is not possible to see all the slides continuously.
28. Audio and video clips cannot be added to the slides.
29. Actions and animations can be added to the slides.
30. Notes Pages are used to have the text on the slides but it is not shown.
31. Handouts can be printed for all your slides.
32. You can create your own animation and add to the slide.

MATCHING COLUMNS

Match the matter in Column A with the matter in Column B.

Column A	Column B
A. AutoContent Wizard	1. Adding text box on the slide
B. Template	2. It can be changed
C. Oragnization chart	3. Changes the view
D. AutoCorrect	4. To check spelling of the text of the slides
E. Alignment	5. Ready made presentation
F. Background colour	6. Making a copy of the slide
G. Text box	7. Printed format of presentation slides

H. Notes Pages	8. A chart to represent an organization
I. Collapse	9. To give space between lines of the text
J. Slide Show	10. Aligning text of the slides
K. Spell checking	11. Can be inserted in the slides
L. Reordering slides	12. Self generating presentation
M. Duplicating slides	13. Can be set from the Ruler
N. Handouts	14. To run slides one by one
O. Line spacing	15. A utility to correct your wrong words
P. Drawing shapes	16. Pages to contain notes
Q. Tabs	17. Can be added to the slide
R. Customized animation	18. Changing the order of slides

FILL IN THE BLANKS WITH APPROPRIATE WORDS

a. Organization chart	b. Decimal	c. AutoCorrect	d. Video
e. Audio	f. Notes pages	g. AutoContent	h. Handouts
i. Ruler	j. Template	k. Collapse	l. Slide Show

1. A presentation can be created easily using __________ or __________.
2. You can run all the slides one by one using __________.
3. You can add clips of types ________ and ______ to the slides.
4. Besides Left, Right and Centre the other Tab in PowerPoint is ________.
5. A chart which is used to represent the various levels of office, etc., is called ___________.
6. For correcting the words which are often misspelled you use ________.
7. While presenting a presentation, the speaker looks at its _________.
8. Speech, etc., which is printed beforehand for distribution is called _________.
9. To change view of a presentation, you use the ________ command.
10. Tabs are set using _______.

DESCRIPTIVE TYPE QUESTIONS

1. Describe the process of creating a presentation using AutoContent Wizard.
2. Describe the method of creating a presentation using Templates.
3. How would you create a presentation using the various slide options?
4. Describe the various views of looking at presentations in PowerPoint.
5. Describe the process of entering text into slides.
6. What is the function of Collapse?
7. Describe the various type of backgrounds which you can have in your slides.
8. How would you change the alignment of the text of the slides?
9. How would you make sure that there is no misspelled word in your text.
10. How would you set the various options of AutoCorrect?
11. Describe the process of adding an audio clip to the slide.

12. How is a video clip added to the slide?
13. What is a Note Page?
14. What is a Handout?
15. How are actions and animations added to the slides?
16. How is a chart added to the slide?
17. Describc thc process of changing the chart style.
18. Describe the process of adding graphics, pictures, etc., in the slide.
19. What is an organization chart?
20. What is a text box?
21. How would you create a slide show?
22. Describe the use of reheasing the slide show.
23. Describe the process of duplicating the slides.
24. How would you change the background colour of a slide?
25. How would you insert text created from WordArt into a slide?
26. What happens when you delete a slide?

ANSWERS TO OBJECTIVE QUESTIONS

Multiple Choice Questions

1. c	2. a	3. b	4. b
5. a	6. a	7. a	8. a
9. b	10 a	11. a	12. b
13. c	14. a	15. b	16. a

True False Questions

1. T	2. F	3. T	4. F
5. T	6. F	7. T	8. T
9. T	10. F	11. T	12. F
13. T	14. T	15. T	16. F
17. T	18. F	19. T	20. T
21. T	22. F	23. T	24. F
25. F	26. F	27. F	28. F
29. T	30. T	31. T	32. T

Matching Columns

A. 12	B. 5	C. 8	D. 15
E. 10	F. 2	G. 1	H. 16
I. 3	J. 14	K. 4	L. 18
M. 6	N. 7	O. 9	P. 17
Q. 13	R. 11		

Fill in the Blanks with Appropriate Words

1. g, j	2. l	3. d, e	4. b
5. a	6. c	7. f	8. h
9. k	10. i		

Index